The Poetics of Grace

Christian Ethics as Theodicy

The Poetics of Grace

Christian Ethics as Theodicy

VOLUME 1, THE HOPE OF GOD'S CALLING

JEPH HOLLOWAY

CASCADE *Books* · Eugene, Oregon

THE POETICS OF GRACE: CHRISTIAN ETHICS AS THEODICY
Volume 1, The Hope of God's Calling

Cascade Books
An Imprint of Wipf and Stock Publishers
199 W. 8th Ave., Suite 3
Eugene, OR 97401

www.wipfandstock.com

ISBN 13: 978-1-62032-039-6

Cataloguing-in-Publication data:

Holloway, Joseph O.

The poetics of grace : Christian ethics as theodicy : volume 1, the hope of God's calling / Jeph Holloway.

xiv + 290 pp. ; 23 cm. Includes bibliographical references and index.

ISBN 13: 978-1-62032-039-6

1. Bible. N.T. Epistles of Paul—Criticism, interpretation, etc. 2. Christian ethics—Biblical teaching. 3. Theodicy. I. Title.

BT160 .H64 2013

Manufactured in the U.S.A.

For Joy

Contents

Preface

Some people think evangelical Christianity is in a lot of trouble. Writing "as a lifelong evangelical," David French describes what he calls "a moral collapse—and a corresponding collapse in positive influence" by evangelical Christianity in American culture.[1] He is not alone in his lament. David Fitch wonders about "the end of evangelicalism" and insists, "What cannot be denied . . . is the negative trajectory of both the influence and perception of evangelicals in North American culture as a whole."[2] I will not spend time detailing all the possible reasons for what Fitch describes as the "precipitous decline" of contemporary American evangelicalism, but will only register my agreement, acknowledge my own complicity, and offer the suggestion that the very designation of "evangelical" for what generally goes by that name in the United States hints at the problem.

I am persuaded that what so often counts for contemporary evangelical Christianity is anything but evangelical. "Evangelical," of course, derives from the New Testament term for "gospel," *euangelion*, and has to do with the dramatic assertion that God through Christ is at work reconciling the world to himself, overturning the false claims of any number of alternatives that purport to be the source of peace or order or truth. Whenever Christians believe that the path to peace or order or truth is any other than what we find "in the word of truth, the gospel [*euangelion*] of your salvation" (Eph 1:13), something has gone seriously wrong. The popular attachment of the word "evangelical" to voting blocks and party platforms of this or that sort testifies to a confusion concerning how God is at work in this world.

The notion that transformative evangelical witness would now achieve public character chiefly through what seems like any other

1. French, "Evangelicals' Collapsing Cultural Influence."
2. Fitch, *End of Evangelicalism?*, xii.

lobbying effort requires some explanation. The confusion likely has an understandable heritage. Stanley Hauerwas has observed, "We are told we live in a morally bankrupt age. People think what was at one time unthinkable; indeed they *do* what was once unthinkable."[3] For many Christians the times in which we live have occasioned a sense of loss and panic—loss due to the notion that we no longer enjoy the positions of influence and cultural leverage we think we once possessed, panic at what we consider the troubling consequences of such loss. It is not uncommon to hear from "evangelical" voices that it is high time for Christians to "take a stand" and to expend every effort to restore a nation that has drifted from a godly past into its present moral morass.

Christians are troubled, and with good reason. We properly recognize a profound sense of obligation to be agents of God's will for the good of God's creation. At the same time, we are perplexed at how we can best go about this in ways that are faithful and effective. A necessary question is what strategies and tactics God would have the Christian community employ towards ends of positive, transformative significance. *The Poetics of Grace* offers an exploration of such concerns through engagement with Paul's Letter to the Ephesians.[4] What follows is not a verse-by-verse commentary on Ephesians, neither is it a study of "ethics in Paul's Letter to the Ephesians." This is a work in the field of Christian ethics that seeks a serious encounter with Ephesians in order to pursue an "evangelical" approach to faithful, effective, and transformative impact in the world, out of the conviction that engagement with this letter points in directions of effective witness more consonant with the gospel than are often employed.

Attention to a few preliminary matters will prepare the way for what follows. First, the title of this book merits brief explanation. The word "poetics" is sometimes used in a literary setting to describe how texts become vehicles for reflecting the diverse aspects of human experience and their representation in such a fashion that provides for a sense of order and meaningful arrangement. In Scripture, the related term *poiesis* refers to God's work of creation or simply to something fashioned for a purpose. The title of this book plays a little with the terminology to suggest that

3. Hauerwas, *Peaceable Kingdom*, 2.

4. I will let others continue the debate concerning authorship of Ephesians. I appreciate the argument made by N. T. Wright that the theological framework that engendered suspicions about Pauline authorship no longer holds and that the issue is less settled than many assume. See his *Paul: In Fresh Perspective*, 18–19.

our engagement with the biblical text provides for a sense of order and meaningful arrangement of our lives, and in that engagement God is at work fashioning our lives in such a way as to reflect and fulfill the divine purpose. Thus, in Eph 2:10, Paul announces, "We are his workmanship [*poiema*], created in Christ Jesus for the purpose of good works, which God prepared beforehand, that we should walk in them." Paul has already indicated that this work of (new) creation is analogous to God's initial work of creation in that it is strictly an expression of God's grace (2:8–9). *The Poetics of Grace* seeks to describe how through the story of the gospel God invites our participation in God's own transformative work that creates life out of death (2:1–10) and peace out of enmity (2:11–22) in pursuit of God's ultimate intent to reconcile a fractured creation (1:9–10).

Another preliminary matter has to do with the apparently wide and diverse set of voices that are brought into dialogue with Ephesians. I intend to highlight the significance of what we find in Ephesians by way of conversation and contrast with alternative outlooks in both the history of philosophy and in various circles of Christian theology and ethics. The point of these conversations will become clearer through the course of this work. I simply want to offer here that what might seem to be a far-flung, indeed, sprawling discussion ranging from Plato and Aristotle to Nietzsche and Niebuhr is concerned with providing a number of different vantage points from which the distinctive contributions and challenges of Ephesians might be better viewed and appreciated. The discipline of Christian ethics demands, at any rate, acquaintance with those forces that figure large on our cultural landscape. We cannot rightly understand the world in which we live without critical engagement with the likes of Kant and Nietzsche. Above all, engagement with these other perspectives will make it clear what is at stake in whether or not we learn to "say and see" with the apostle in such a way that we are enabled to "walk worthy" of our calling in a manner that will truly redound "to the praise of the glory of his grace" (1:6).

Finally, this work will appear in two related volumes in a way that (to some degree) reflects the apparent shift in emphasis moving from Ephesians 1–3 to Ephesians 4–6. Both volumes will emphasize that a Christian ethic shaped by an encounter with Ephesians cannot focus strictly, or even mainly, on isolated moments of decision, asking in the face of some moral dilemma, "What should I do?" Rather, Christian ethics must provide a much more comprehensive embrace of all of life, our vision, our loyalties, our histories, and our hopes. In general, though, volume 1, *The Hope of God's Calling*, offers an account of the gospel that establishes such comprehensive claims on our lives. It would be wrong to construe the gospel in such a way (as some do Ephesians) that only subsequently and in a derivative fashion would we then talk about "ethics." Substantive matters of moral significance will still occupy us in the first volume, which primarily concerns itself with the implied narrative of Ephesians 1–3, a narrative celebrating how God is at work through Christ and the body of Christ to manifest God's purpose for all of creation. Volume 2, *The Worthy Walk*, though, will give attention to how Ephesians provides for the formation and moral shaping of our lives in such ways, as indicated in Ephesians 4–6, that we can truly serve in this world as agents of the divine purpose for all of creation. The more concentrated attention given to various ethical "issues" in each chapter (e.g., work and bioethics) serves to remind us that we simply cannot wait to have everything all sorted out before we get down to "practical matters." To talk about new life in Christ, for example, is obviously not merely an abstract concept, but a reality that makes demands on what counts as life and how we might properly honor it. To talk about an ecclesial ethic is finally inseparable from what God intends for the more immediate arena of family life. From some standpoints, it might make more sense to wait till a complete analysis of the "foundation" of Christian ethics is laid before we move on to "areas of application." The following chapters are structured to express the insistence that practice is embedded in knowing and knowing in practice.

The transition between Ephesians 1–3 and Ephesians 4–6 properly serves as a transition to the argument of this work: "Now to him who is able to do exceeding abundantly beyond all that we ask or think, according to the power that works within us, to him be the glory in the church and in Christ Jesus to all generations forever and ever. Amen" (3:20–21).

Acknowledgments

In Ephesians, Paul stresses the importance of truthful speech (see 1:13; 4:15, 25). Honesty here demands recognition of the debts incurred along the way—many assumed long before the writing of this book. Several churches have played various and important roles in shaping my life as a Christian, and in them my understanding of the Christian faith has been formed: Glenwood Hills Baptist Church in Lithonia, Georgia; First Baptist Church of Forrest Hills, Texas; Lois Baptist Church (down a dirt road in north central Texas); Western Hills Baptist Church in Fort Worth, Texas; First Baptist Church of Alton, Missouri; and Central Baptist Church in Marshall, Texas. There have been important people in these and other churches along the way who have been sources of encouragement and instruction to me and my family. I cannot always specify their contributions, but that I have been borne along the way by their support and love is undeniable.

There have been professors and colleagues over the last thirty years from whom and with whom I have learned immensely. Guy Greenfield and Bruce Corley played pivotal roles in my earliest serious engagements with the letters of Paul. Rodney Reeves, Randy Richards, and Warren Johnson are three New Testament scholars who have been colleagues, friends, and invaluable resources in an ongoing pursuit of greater acquaintance with the wisdom of the apostle. Bill Tillman was patient in introducing me to the wide world of theological ethics; he might regret having exposed me to the work of Stanley Hauerwas, but it is way too late to do anything about that. I certainly owe an immense debt to John Harris, Dean of the School of Christian Studies at East Texas Baptist University. He has saved me from myself on more than a few occasions and his unflagging spirit of enthusiasm is mostly encouraging.

Others have contributed to this work in ways that might not at first be so apparent. Doug Lockard, director of the ETBU Jazz Ensemble, as

Acknowledgments

well as the North Grove 6 have provided ways of maintaining some measure of equilibrium in my life, for which I will be forever grateful. Debra Summers, Administrative Assistant in the School of Christian Studies at ETBU, exhibits a constant wisdom and grace that helps everybody in our department look a whole lot better than we warrant. Jared Jaggers, graduate assistant for our department, has done invaluable work in the preparation of this manuscript for publication, and I greatly appreciate his help.

My sons, Joseph and James, kept after me for years to do the hard work of putting down in writing the things I say I believe. I love them both and am grateful for their high expectations. Above all, my wife, Joy, has been the steady source of encouragement, love, and patience without which I would simply be a wreck. To dedicate this book to her is an embarrassingly small expression of what she actually deserves.

Christian Ethics as Theodicy

W

e live in the world in light of the world we live in. Truman Burbank only slowly came to realize that truth. A television star from birth, Truman does not know that his life is the object of attention and devotion by millions of viewers, that all of his family, friends, and coworkers are paid actors, that his hometown of Seahaven Island Township is a giant soundstage, and that everyone but him is in on the secret. Only when he has reached his late twenties do things happen that seem strange to Truman and lead him to start doubting certainties he had lived with for so long. As the 1998 film *The Truman Show* starring Jim Carry moves to its climax, Truman seeks to escape from the "reality" so carefully constructed to keep him in the dark and ventures forth from the security and safety of Seahaven to face the unknowns of an unscripted world.

Any number of interpreters have seen in *The Truman Show* a revisiting of the story of Adam and Eve, and the parallels are certainly there.[1] Some have viewed the show's creator, Christof, as an image of a controlling, manipulating God and Truman as a type of Adam. But in this story, Adam is not expelled from the Garden; the "true man" walks out on God and seeks to establish his own identity without recourse to the illusions of faith. Truman becomes the symbol of a mature humanity that has learned to do without the false comforts of constricting beliefs. What might greet Truman as he leaves the set through a door in the side of the "sky" over Seahaven is uncertain: "Truman walks into the darkness. It doesn't matter what awaits him on the other side of that darkness—the point is that he decides to stand up and face the real world, as scary as it may be, like

1. E.g., Reinhartz, *Scripture on the Silver Screen*, 5–23.

an adult with a brain instead of cowering like a child in the supposed safety of Christof's—or God's—supposed benevolence."[2]

This interpretation of the film misses the mark. It might very well be the case that Christof is presented as an image of God. Christof, though, serves as a false image, a false god representing the hold on and power over our lives by those forces (including those who make movies) that want to make sure we do not challenge the accepted, tried-and-true explanations for "the way things are"—explanations that demand our compliance and devotion to what we are told will keep us safe and secure. *The Truman Show*, in other words, is an exercise in what might be called a *social theodicy*. It reveals how views of reality operate to help us make sense of a world in which there are genuine threats. A social theodicy functions to help us make sense of our world, but also tells us our place in that world and what way of life can help us best find order and security as we accept its "sacred canopy," a view of reality covering all aspects of life that promises structure and stability over against disorder and peril.[3]

In this sense, Truman faced a situation similar to our own. He was faced with the challenge of looking past the conventional, the "givens" of everyday life. He was confronted with the uncomfortable prospect that much, perhaps nearly all, that was familiar to him was distorted, false, and illusory. Christians have to be willing to examine what presentations of reality are offered to us by those powerful forces (including those who make the movies) that explain our world to us, our place in that world, and what way of life can help us best find order and security. We live in the world in light of the world we live in. A crucial issue for any effort at exploring the Christian way of life is whether or not we have an accurate understanding of the world that we live in. That means we need, in some way, to explore this issue of theodicy.

Augustine is widely viewed in circles of philosophical theology as one of the earliest proponents of what we might call a *philosophical theodicy*. These days philosophical arguments are constructed to argue that belief in God (*Theos*) can justly (*dikē*) be maintained even in a world of evil and suffering. In the aftermath of Alaric the First's sack of Rome (CE 410), it is said that Augustine was concerned to defend the Christian

2. Johanson, review of *The Truman Show*.

3. The phrase "sacred canopy" was coined by sociologist Peter Berger to describe a set of beliefs and convictions that finds institutional expression in a society, objectifying and legitimizing its fundamental view of reality. To challenge the socially defined reality is to risk being judged either evil or mad or both. See his *Sacred Canopy*, 39.

faith against those who argued that Rome's calamity was the result of an abandonment of the ancient Roman gods by an empire that had officially turned to Christianity. What had long been an issue of personal struggle and perplexity for Augustine now becomes a matter of the public defense of the Christian faith. How to defend, or justify, belief in the Christian understanding of God in the face of evil and suffering? A standard account of an Augustinian theodicy proposes that in his great work *The City of God* the North African bishop sought to defend belief in a good and all-powerful God who is the creator of all things by describing evil not as something that exists in and of itself, but as the privation or corruption of what is essentially good by the misuse of freedom by both spiritual and human creatures. John Hick, a proponent of this interpretation of Augustine, summarizes this understanding by saying that for Augustine, ". . . the whole creation is good, and evil can consist only in the corrupting of a good substance; it is the privation of some good which is proper to the world as God made it." How has this corruption come about? "Augustine attributes all evil, both moral [sin] and natural [earthquakes, disease, violent weather, etc.], directly or indirectly to the wrong choices of free rational beings."[4] Thus, any obstacle to belief in the goodness of God is countered by removing the responsibility of evil from God and placing it squarely on the shoulders of those who misuse the good gifts of God.

The challenges to this proposal are many and will not be entertained here. What will be offered is the assertion of Terrence W. Tilley that this interpretation of Augustine misreads the bishop's own intent and interests. Hick might have retrieved important Augustinian resources for a proper theological accounting of sin and evil (e.g., the notion of evil as the privation or corruption of good), but, Tilley insists, "Augustine did not write a theodicy."[5] Augustine was not concerned as a philosopher to provide "a 'solution' to the 'problem of evil'" so that objective inquirers could explore the feasibility of theistic belief. Such an enterprise only developed since the seventeenth century in the context of the Enlightenment period when the burden of proof shifted to those who would defend the existence of God. Augustine was not occupied with such a task. Rather, he was concerned as a pastor to instruct members of the faith community—the church—as to the nature of evil and God's redemptive response to it.[6]

4. Hick, *Evil and the God of Love*, 59.

5. Tilley, *Evils of Theodicy*, 115.

6. Ibid., 118–30.

Efforts at defending the justice of God and that belief in God is just, even in a world of evil and suffering, perhaps have some value.[7] Augustine's approach, however, likely reflects an intuition guided by deep acquaintance with Scripture. The concerns of theodicy, as the term is normally understood, are not really the focus of what Scripture has to say about matters of evil and suffering. What we find in the Bible about such matters is quite often very different. As Tilley says, "Theodicies [of the philosophical variety] do not respond to complaints or laments. They are not addressed to people who sin and suffer. They are addressed to abstract individual intellects who hear purely theoretical problems."[8] What Scripture has to say about evil and suffering is far more concrete and personal, even sometimes "hitting too close to home," than what might be found in many philosophical discussions of evil and suffering.

It is certainly the case that when we take note of the expressions of cruelty and suffering in the world around us, and even (in our more honest moments) admit perplexity about the fractures and failures in our own lives, we often wonder why a good and just God, the Creator of all things, allows such. Certainly there are passages of Scripture that offer specific rationales for this or that expression of evil and/or suffering.[9] In addition, these explanations vary given different instances of evil and suffering in varying situations.[10] The broader concern of canonical testimony, though, attends to a very different question.

7. Tilley, though, does identify several of the "evils of theodicy," among which is that the entire enterprise is dedicated to "showing how worldly evil is consistent with the reality of the god of providential theism"—a philosophical construct and not necessarily the God of Abraham, Isaac, and Jacob—or "demonstrating how evil can be shown to be coherent with and incorporated into an accepted theistic faith" (ibid., 226–27). The concern seems to be that such a neat arrangement renders it more likely that the convinced theodicist would acquiesce to the presence of evil as in some way finally fitting into God's good order of things.

8. Ibid., 229. See also Hauerwas, *Naming the Silences*; he argues there simply is no problem of evil, that is, in terms of how traditional theodicies address the issue. According to Hauerwas, theodicies done in the abstract mode of theory generally begin with "the pagan assumption that god or the gods are to be judged by how well it or they insure the successful outcome of human purposes" (56).

9. See Crenshaw, *Defending God*, for an extensive discussion of various explorations of the issues raised in the Hebrew Bible. For a much broader survey, see the essays in Laato and de Moor, *Theodicy in the World of the Bible*.

10. Laato and de Moor (*Theodicy*, xxix–liv) offer a sixfold typology embracing the variety of themes found in the monotheistic Jewish and Christian world of the Bible. They identify the following motifs: 1) retribution—God punishes those who violate the divine will (e.g., the Deuteronomistic History); 2) education—the innocent

WHAT IS GOD DOING ABOUT EVIL?

Alain Badiou gives to his work *Ethics* the subtitle *An Essay on the Understanding of Evil*. In so doing he makes explicit what is at least implicit in many studies of what is called "ethics"—that our contemplation of, deliberation on, and pursuit of the good life is intimately related to our often keen awareness that things are, or can go, terribly wrong. Standard topics for ethical discussion seem to rely on this sad truth. Economic issues demand exploration because we know that greed, on the one hand, and poverty, on the other, have a crushing impact on their victims. Bioethical issues, such as resource allocation or physician-assisted suicide, require analysis and recommendation because of the great capacity for power in the arenas of life and death to turn destructive. Political theory obtains its significance from the recognition that political power tempts its bearers to acts of oppression and corruption. It is not that good depends on evil for its existence.[11] Indeed, as Badiou says, "If evil exists, we must conceive it from the starting point of the good."[12] It seems to be the case, though, that because things can and do go terribly wrong, we must engage in the critical and reflective task of ethics.

For Christians, the belief that God is the good creator of a good creation compels us to ask about evil. Because of good, we have to think and talk about evil. Because of evil, however, we have to think and talk about the good—about what is good, what is the good life, and how it is we can participate in it.

Christian ethics will think and talk about good and evil within a certain frame of reference and will ask its own questions concerning the relationship between God, good, and evil. Certainly philosophical questions concerning the relationship between God, good, and evil have been discussed for centuries. The concerns of philosophy of religion are not of

---

sometimes suffer in order to gain a better understanding of life (e.g., the book of Lamentations); 3) eschatology—imbalances of suffering and good in this life will be resolved in the age to come (e.g., apocalyptic); 4) divine mystery—human beings will not always understand the meaning of suffering (e.g., Ecclesiastes); 5) communion—humans can draw closer to God through the experience of suffering (e.g., selected psalms and the experience of Job); and 6) determinism—suffering is the assignment of fate (e.g., Ecclesiastes?).

11. We have already seen that Augustine argues it is the other way around; that is, that evil is parasitic on the good as its loss or corruption. For a recent analysis of this Augustinian theme, see Mathewes, *Evil and the Augustinian Tradition*.

12. Badiou, *Ethics*, 60.

primary significance here, though. Christian ethics asks a different question than does philosophical theodicy—not whether it is just to believe in God in a world of evil and suffering, but rather what God is doing in such a world. What is God doing about evil? This is a question that begins from the standpoint of faith, and faith of a particular sort. The questions of philosophical theodicy hold faith itself in reserve. Faith is only proper if its questions can be answered to everyone's satisfaction. Only then, philosophers of religion suggest, do we take evil and suffering with the seriousness they deserve.

While the question of what God is doing about evil might not be the explicit starting point for many who have engaged in the discipline of Christian ethics, I do want to suggest it is the underlying question again and again in any of a number of different voices that have contributed to the exploration of moral vision and practice from a Christian standpoint. For example, Dietrich Bonhoeffer's *Ethics* offers the insistence that our very grappling with good and evil as the subject matter of "ethics" exhibits the fundamental problem of our estrangement from God—that we have been "torn . . . loose from life." Our "knowledge" of good and evil testifies to our disunion with God, whereby we are "estranged from God, other human beings, material things, and [ourselves]."[13] For Bonhoeffer, while "the knowledge of good and evil appears to be the goal of all ethical reflection," it must be the "first task of Christian ethics . . . to supersede that knowledge."[14]

Bonhoeffer's insistence might sound surprising. He simply draws, however, on the story of Adam and Eve and the serpent to remind us that the human quest to know for ourselves the difference between good and evil is but the constant repetition of "a falling away" from our origin, in which all knowing is only a knowing of God. "The knowledge of good and evil," says Bonhoeffer, "is thus disunion with God. Human beings can know about good and evil only in opposition to God."[15]

Bonhoeffer does not consider the enterprise that generally goes by the name "ethics" to exhibit the mature capacity on the part of humans to discern the good, the noble, and the true. "Instead, the [usurped] knowledge of good and evil means a complete inversion of their knowledge, which before had consisted solely in knowing God as their origin."[16] It

13. Bonhoeffer, *Ethics*, 302–3.
14. Ibid., 299.
15. Ibid., 300.
16. Ibid., 301.

is not that there are not those equipped with either sophisticated ethical arguments, on the one hand, or intense ethical passion, on the other. For Bonhoeffer, though, writing during the ominous days of the rise of Nazism, those capacities offer little in the face of the magnitude of evil at work in history. Those with the cool, calculating tools of reason, always wanting to weigh fairly all sides of the argument, suffer from a "defective vision" that leaves them "crushed between the colliding forces without having accomplished anything at all." Alternatively, those burning with ethical passion "believe they can face the power of evil with the purity of their will and their principles." These too fail to consider the serious nature of the challenge of evil and "like a bull that charges the red cape instead of the one holding it, [they] finally tire and suffer defeat."[17]

Whether it is the professional analyst or the passionate activist, for many the initial question of ethics has to do with, "What should I do?" Bonhoeffer, however, insists the standard questions that so often are the focus of a Christian ethic—"How can I be good?" and "How can I do something good?"—must be abandoned from the outset. "When the ethical problem presents itself essentially as the question of my own being good and doing good, the decision has already been made that the self and the world are the ultimate realities."[18] Such a beginning cannot serve well a Christian ethic. Bonhoeffer asserts, "The source of a Christian ethic is not the reality of one's self, nor the reality of the world, nor is it the reality of norms and values. It is the reality of God that is revealed in Jesus Christ."[19] For Bonhoeffer, Christian ethics is not first and foremost about what I should I do. It is rather about what God is doing.

But for many, of course, to approach Christian ethics this way is to invite trouble from the start. This trouble results from certain prevailing features of our modern and postmodern context that will resist this way of exploring the relationship between God and evil. On the one hand, one of the fundamental shifts to occur in the modern era has to do with this very issue of the relationship between God and evil. As we have seen, Terrence Tilley has complained that use of the term "theodicy" to describe the way in which premodern (prior to the seventeenth and eighteenth centuries) thinkers struggled with the relationship between God and evil is a mistake.[20] If we understand theodicy as the effort to justify belief in

17. Ibid., 78.
18. Ibid., 47–48.
19. Ibid., 49.
20. Tilley, *Evils of Theodicy*, 221–55.

God in light of issues of evil and suffering, Kenneth Surin trenchantly observes that "pre-seventeenth-century Christian thinkers were certainly not unaware of the conceptual difficulties that [tensions] generated; but, unlike their post-seventeenth-century counterparts, they did not regard these problems as constituting any sort of ground for jettisoning their faith."[21] M. Sarot has chronicled the differences between an outlook that would more likely represent a biblical view concerning God and evil from attitudes reflecting contemporary tendencies. Premodern inquiry took place *within* the context of faith and cast its suspicions about evil toward *humanity*, seeking *practical strategies* for maintaining *faithfulness* within the Christian community. Modernity is itself very much defined by a different set of concerns: abstract discussion *about* religious belief directs its suspicion *against God* and seeks *theoretical* justification for the existence of God in order to persuade *nonbelievers* of the intellectual viability of theistic belief.[22]

Christian ethics, though, will insist that to begin in faith, to begin with belief in the good God who is the good Creator of the good creation, is not to avoid the questions of evil and suffering, but is to raise them in a most intense and distinctive way. To ask, "What is God doing about evil?" is to begin with certain affirmations about God and ourselves. It is to affirm that the cruelties and sufferings that humanity inflicts and endures are themselves an "affront to God's character and purpose, which is for people to flourish in abundant life in companionship with him."[23] To ask, "What is God doing about evil?" is, in effect, to place the burden, not just where it belongs, but in the hands of the only One who can do anything about the situation that confronts us. First to ask, "What is God doing about evil?" is to admit to a situation that is larger than us; it is to recognize that we face challenges that require a response beyond what our own resources can manage. First to ask, "What is God doing about evil?" is to confess that we are in over our heads and need God's redemptive work to liberate us, that we might participate in God's purposes for creation.

On the other hand, as D. A. Carson writes, "The hardest thing to get across these days is the notion of sin. To talk about sin is to say that certain behavior and attitudes and beliefs are wrong, and that is the one thing postmodernism does not permit us to do."[24] There is a peculiar

21. See his *Theology and the Problem of Evil*, 9.

22. Sarot, "Theodicy and Modernity."

23. Wells, *God's Companions*, 8.

24. Carson, "Maintaining Scientific and Christian Truths," 113.

double-mindedness in our contemporary cultural context. First, there is a certain brand of moral relativism that insists that all moral judgments are either simply the expression of personal preference and/or are the effect of particular social conditions. In either case they do not actually refer to any objective moral truth. There are also, however, frequent appeals to a vision of rightness that appears to be violated when certain privileges are denied or certain indignities suffered. Special interest politics suffers from the dual threat of victimization, on the one hand, and the apparent moral indifference of the universe, on the other. The only recourse is strident protest and the use of intimidation to get one's way. If there is no moral truth, it is useless to argue for one's case, since all arguments are simply camouflage for self-interest. Substantive argument is then replaced by intimidation and the brute expression of power. How we have come to the state of affairs in our culture where one would loudly but incoherently insist, "I have the right to determine my own values!" will be explored below.

THE GRAND NARRATIVE

This study of Christian ethics will pursue the question of what God is doing about evil as a deliberate alternative to either the theoretical mode of modernity or the presumptions of a postmodern relativism. While the focus here is on matters that find expression in Ephesians, these matters also reflect something of a significant view increasingly held among biblical scholars concerning the grand narrative of Scripture as a whole as it relates to the mission of the church.

Michael W. Goheen has written concerning "the urgency of reading the Bible as one story."[25] While there are obstacles to this task, some inherent in the wide range of materials in the Bible and some in the postmodern resistance to the idea of "grand narrative" as such, "the church's reading of the Bible has usually presupposed its narrative unity, that is, that the whole of the Bible—or the Bible read as a whole—tells a coherent story."[26] According to New Testament scholar N. T. Wright, the coherent story, or narrative, of the Bible offers a particular response to what he calls "worldview questions"—those questions that reflect the ultimate concerns of human beings, embracing "all deep-level human perceptions

25. Goheen, "Urgency of Reading," 469–83. See also Bartholomew and Goheen, *The Drama of Scripture.*

26. Bauckham, "Reading Scripture as a Coherent Story," 38.

of reality."[27] Christian theology, according to Wright, understands Scripture to answer four such worldview questions. To the question, "Who are we?" Scripture responds by insisting that we are creatures made in God's image, given both special status and special responsibilities. In response to the question, "Where are we?" the Bible offers that we inhabit God's creation, which is good (not evil, as the Gnostics say) but not God (as pantheists believe). If we ask, "What is wrong?" the biblical narrative describes humanity as being in a state of rebellion against its creator, a state that implies a "cosmic dislocation between creator and the creation," placing the world "out of tune with its created intention." The fourth and final worldview question, "What is the solution?" consumes the major plotline of the Bible, which describes the Creator of all things as acting in past, present, and future "to deal with the weight of evil set up by human rebellion, and to bring his world to the end for which it was made, namely that it should resonate with his own presence and glory."[28]

In light of these worldview questions, Wright reads the overarching story of the Bible in terms of a grand narrative consisting of five acts: Act 1—God's good act of creation; Act 2—the Fall of human rebellion, which distorts and threatens all of creation; Act 3—the story of Israel, the descendents of Abraham in covenant relationship with Yahweh, the God of Israel and all of creation; Act 4—the story of Jesus, Israel's messiah and divine agent of the world's redemption; and Act 5—the story of the early church as bearer and inscriber of the New Testament message, along with the ongoing story of the church's creative fidelity to the biblical narrative as it reflects on, draws out, and implements "the significance of the first four Acts."[29] More recently, Bartholomew and Goheen have adopted Wright's outline of the biblical narrative but have rightly appended a sixth act that affirms and finalizes the redemptive act of God in Christ with the full realization of God's kingdom to come.[30] This understanding of a coherent biblical narrative, while certainly not possessing the status of universal scholarly consensus, itself generates and sustains the approach to Christian ethics presented here. The biblical narrative as outlined here might be understood as offering in all its complexity and with all its subplots an extensive answer to the question, what is God doing about evil?

27. Wright, *New Testament and the People of God*, 122–23.

28. Ibid., 132–33.

29. Ibid., 141–43.

30. Bartholomew and Goheen, *Drama of Scripture*, 26–27; for further critique of Wright's outline, see also Wells, *Improvisation*, 51–53.

Paul's Letter to the Ephesians provides an important frame of reference for many aspects of the understanding of Christian ethics presented here. One thing, though, will certainly be clear—Ephesians is quite concerned to address the issue of evil in a way that resonates and even encapsulates the overarching scriptural narrative. There are many ways in which Ephesians expresses its concern with what God is doing about evil. The last chapter certainly makes it explicit that the way of life depicted in Ephesians that is the appropriate and enabled response to God's work of redemption in Christ will be lived out in conflict with powerful forces that stand opposed to God's good will (6:10-18). It is as if Paul concludes his book by reminding his readers what is ultimately at stake.[31] Timothy Gombis has recently demonstrated, however, that the theme of divine warfare, of God's triumph in Christ over all competing powers, runs throughout the book. The calling and challenge described in the book of Ephesians has everything to do with how God has achieved that triumph through Christ (chapters 1-2), how Paul's imprisonment exemplifies that triumph (chapter 3), and how it is that God empowers the church to participate with God in that triumph and to do so in the particular ways described in chapters 4-6.[32] Ephesians fundamentally attends to the question of what God is doing about evil.

This question itself begs a prior question. What is the character of this evil? Theologians and philosophers have sometimes drawn a distinction between what might be called "natural evil" (earthquakes, famine, flood, tornadoes, disease, etc.) and "moral evil" (murder, theft, adultery, pride, envy, greed, etc.). Susan Nieman observes that the distinction is a modern one, and premodern voices like Paul or Augustine would have spoken only of an entire creation that has known privation or the loss of the original goodness of divine intent—whether that loss finds expression in "natural" threats or at the hands of human moral agents.[33] While Paul does indicate close connections between a suffering creation and the need for humanity's redemption in Romans 8, there is less overt discussion of such concerns in Ephesians (though Ephesians does demonstrate a most comprehensive view of God's redemptive intent; e.g., 1:9-10). And while what Paul has to say in Ephesians about the character of a broken and corrupted creation cannot be taken for the whole of a biblical

31. See Yoder Neufeld, *"Put on the Armour of God."*
32. Gombis, "Triumph of God in Christ."
33. Neiman, *Evil in Modern Thought*, 3-4.

theology on evil, what is said here is worth consideration, if for no other reason than to underscore the significance of the matter for what Paul has to say about God's work of redemption and how it relates to the moral vision encountered in Ephesians.

It should be stressed, though, that Paul's account of "the problem of evil" will not reflect some generalized account of "the human condition." Paul provides neither a philosophical anthropology nor a phenomenology of sin based on a neutral account subject to empirical investigation. His view of what God is doing about evil does not start from an understanding of the plight of evil that then seeks solace in some divine resolution. Paul does not anticipate a Ludwig Feuerbach, the nineteenth-century German philosopher who saw the Christian view of God as constructed out of humanity's failure to embody its own unrealized ideals. Paul's account of sin and evil in Ephesians is always given from the standpoint of grace and salvation in Christ. His description of those who were "*formerly*" dead in their trespasses and sins in 2:1–3 is given from the standpoint of those who are "*now*" alive in Christ (2:4–7). Those who "*now* in Christ Jesus . . . have been brought near by the blood of Christ" are called to "remember" that they were "*formerly* far off" (2:11–13). Paul's depiction of the walk of the Gentiles (4:17–19) is described as a "*former* manner of life" (4:22) and is known for what it is only in light of having "learned Christ," from the standpoint of "the truth as it is in Jesus" (4:20–21).[34]

The important point here is the one made by Stephen Long: "Sin is a derivative concept, secondary to our knowledge of God."[35] This is certainly so, at least as Christians understand things. While whatever we call evil will, as Badiou has told us, require some prior account of what we consider good, this will mean for Christians that our understanding of evil and sin will derive from our prior understanding of who God is and what God is up to as revealed in Jesus Christ. As Stanley Hauerwas insists, "We only learn what our sin is as we discover our true identity through locating the self in God's life as revealed to us through the life, death, and resurrection of Jesus Christ."[36] If Christian ethics is concerned to address matters of evil and sin, it will have to do so from the standpoint of God's redemptive work. Thus, for Christians, Christian ethics must be *Christian* ethics. And Christian ethics, as a *theological theodicy*, will

34. See Tachau, *"Einst" und "Jetz" im Neuen Testament*; for the use of the "once"/ "now" motif in Ephesians, see Holloway, *Peripateō*, 189, 211.

35. Long, *Goodness of God*, 44.

36. Hauerwas, *Peaceable Kingdom*, 31.

answer the question of what God is doing about evil in a most specific way: *God, through God's redemptive work, is creating a people whose lives, sustained in worship, bear witness to God's purpose for creation.*

This understanding of Christian ethics has several important features that are best accounted for in dialogue with, on the one hand, alternative proposals for describing the moral life and, on the other hand, significant themes found in Ephesians. Such a dialogue suggests that Christian ethics will have the following important characteristics.

1. *Theocentric*—Christian ethics begins with the question, "What is God doing about evil?" Paul's Letter to the Ephesians is bound by a twofold reference to God's grace and peace (1:2 and 6:23-24), announcing God's initiative and agenda. Out of the abundance of divine mercy and love, God is at work to achieve reconciliation for a fractured cosmos. Christian ethics will reflect the insistence of Ephesians that the life that God calls believers to exhibit in this world is the life made possible by God's grace for the purpose of God's peace.

2. *Redemptive*—Christian ethics highlights the redemptive work of God in Christ as the central feature of God's triumph over evil. This triumph over evil, announced in 1:19-23, is detailed in Ephesians 2, where Paul characterizes God's redemptive work though Christ in terms of new life in the one body of Christ. Christian ethics will reflect the insistence of Ephesians that the life that God calls believers to exhibit in this world is a life that frees them from destructive powers that threaten what God has intended for humanity from the beginning.

3. *Ecclesial*—Christian ethics considers the community of faith created by Jesus Christ to be the primary locus of God's redemptive activity in the world and essential to God's engagement in the conflict with evil. The creation of one, new humanity in Christ, the church, is a fundamental feature of Ephesians' message of the divine triumph over evil, as God employs the church's witness to the "powers" to demonstrate the power of the gospel to reconcile (3:9-10). Christian ethics will reflect the insistence of Ephesians that the life that God calls believers to exhibit in this world is one that bears witness to the divine intent to unite all things together in Christ.

4. *Narrative*—Christian ethics gives greater attention to matters of character and virtue that testify to the broad contours of the moral life as a

whole, seeing life as a coherent story, than to matters of individual and isolated moral judgments. Paul's moral admonitions in Ephesians are less concerned to answer the question, "What should I do?" than to present fairly general dimensions of Christian habits that qualify daily life in ways that reflect the character of God's engagement with the world. Christian ethics will encourage believers to "walk worthy" of their calling, to respond to God's invitation to join with God in the divine triumph over evil and express that triumph in the mundane tasks of speech, work, relationships, sex, money, and marriage. The concern is less of this or that instance of decision and more of the coherency of past, present, and future in the entirety of our lives.

5. *Liturgical*—This understanding of Christian ethics views worship as central to Christian moral witness and as that task that shapes all other commitments and tasks. Ephesians is filled with expressions of worship—doxology and petition, proclamation and thanksgiving—and Paul's vision for the moral life of believers does not begin with the explicit moral admonitions of Ephesians 4–6, but with the invitation to orient life toward God in praise given in the letter's opening doxology (1:3–14). Christian ethics understands that we live in the world in light of the world we live in and that worship is the means by which we perceive the world truly so that we might live in it faithfully.

6. *Eschatological*—Convinced that what God intended for creation from the beginning will find its realization in the new creation, this approach to Christian ethics finds content and courage for witness in that promise and hope. Eschatology is often thought to pertain only to those events and issues related to "the last things." Paul insists, however, that God's grace is the offer of new life that even now lives as witness to what God willed from the beginning (2:10). The ultimate intent of that will is revealed as the uniting together of all things in Christ (1:10), a reconciled heaven and earth that realizes God's peace. As an eschatological ethic, Christian ethics will explore ways in which the divine purpose for all of creation that will one day be realized can find concrete witness even when "the days are evil" and believers still await the "day of redemption."

These dimensions of a Christian ethic are dramatically on display in Paul's Letter to the Ephesians and offer a distinctive challenge for believers. The degree of that distinctiveness will be made clear as these various aspects of a Christian ethic are contrasted with alternative approaches to the moral life. The insistence in Ephesians on seeing Christian moral witness in the world as thoroughly bound up with the redemptive work of God in Christ, for example, is a direct contrast to any understanding of the moral life that draws a wedge between theology and ethics. A concern for the narrative character of Christian ethics differs in many ways from those approaches that focus strictly on matters of moral judgment and decision-making without regard to who it is that makes such judgments.

Each of the following chapters seeks to clarify the specific concerns highlighted in Ephesians by way of contrast with alternative strategies that have sometimes even become the preoccupation of many Christians. Each chapter will also stress that these concerns must find concrete expression in the commitments and practices of believers whose lives are shaped in a worship that celebrates the gospel. What might it mean, then, for Christians in the realm of work and money to live life on the basis of God's gifts of abundance rather than in the fear of scarcity? If God's work of redemption in Christ reveals what God intends for humanity, does that have any bearing on matters of *in vitro* fertilization or gene therapy? What difference does it make for how Christians practice marriage that they understand themselves first as members of God's household? If the gospel, the word of truth (1:13), effects transformation of people's whole lives, then how will that become manifest in matters of persistent traits and habits (of speech, for example)? If Ephesians invites believers to a worship that celebrates the triune God as the true source of the world's good, what significance does that have for demands for our allegiance to other entities such as the state? If God's purpose for creation is "to unite all things in Christ" (1:10), then how might that purpose shape the present witness of the church in matters where fracture and hostility are still so evident in our world?

The concern will be to give display to something of what Paul intends when he calls believers to "walk worthy" of their calling. Indeed, such concrete witness is necessary to what God is doing about evil. The argument of this book is precisely that our positive response to this challenge is essential to how God is at work in this world and that gravitation to other strategies is simply a failure to believe the gospel. Such alternatives, as attractive as they sometimes appear, are inadequate to the task and simply echo back to a broken world its own confusion. What is God doing about evil? God, through God's redemptive work, is creating a people whose lives, sustained in worship, bear witness to God's purpose for creation.

AN IMPORTANT QUALIFICATION

Before we explore further this understanding of Christian ethics, a candid admission is appropriate, and that is to the limits of this proposal. What follows reflects not only essential features of what we find in Paul's Letter to the Ephesians, but resonates with the broader testimony of the biblical witness as a whole. As such, what is here outlined serves to indicate the character and content of the necessary moral witness of the people of God in a world that awaits its redemption. But is this all of what God is doing about evil? Is an ecclesial ethic rooted in confession of Christ not by definition *sectarian*, focused on a minority segment of a wider population, and thus a drastic restriction on God's participation in creation? To say that the community of faith formed by common allegiance to Jesus Christ is the primary locus of God's redemptive activity in the world is not to say that it is the only way in which God is active for the sake of the new creation God intends to achieve. Sam Wells insists, "The church may be the principal way God works in the world, but it is by no means the only one."[37] To assume otherwise almost confuses the church with the kingdom of God—a temptation often enough pursued, but a temptation nonetheless. The church's essential role is as witness to the kingdom, but with the recognition that that witness will always be judged as partial and too often marred by the blemishes of pride and despair.

While that witness is essential and here understood as the primary arena in which the concerns of Christian ethics find expression, there still can and must be asserted a confidence that God is also providentially at work beyond the boundaries of explicit Christian confession and practice for the sake of the good of God's creation and the realization of God's will. This confidence both frees the church to pursue its more specific moral witness and encourages the church that, in spite of appearances to the contrary, God employs that witness to significant effect in this world. It frees the church for its more specific moral witness by removing from the church the burden of having to make sure that history comes out all right.[38] It encourages the church when the church recognizes that, because it does not have to manage the world, its moral witness need not be subject to prevailing measures of effectiveness.[39] It will be worthwhile

---

37. Wells, *Improvisation*, 39.

38. See Hauerwas, *Peaceable Kingdom*, 106.

39. Wells (*Improvisation*, 55) reminds us that Christians "are not called to be effective or successful, but to be faithful. . . . Christians can afford to fail, because they trust

to give some attention to the character of that wider providential work of God in creation and history, though, in order to illuminate the character and necessity of this more specific moral witness required of the church.

Language highlighting the providential work of God in Ephesians (e.g., 1:11) must be seen in tension with themes of redemption and parenesis that indicate that not everything is in accordance with God's will (5:10). In light of what we will read there, one cannot say, "Whatever is, is right." On the one hand, Paul encourages that close attention be given to daily conduct that expresses the character of the Christian community, "because the days are evil" (5:15–16). On the other hand, Paul encourages a way of life that corresponds to the ways of the Holy Spirit, whose present presence in the lives of believers is the assurance of the coming "day of redemption" (4:30). Paul's emphasis on God's work of redemption and his extensive instruction in the face of genuine moral challenges make it difficult to uphold a conventional view of providence that says, "Everything comes to pass as God wills it, and thus everything is just as it is meant to be."[40] Otherwise, Paul's language concerning an aggrieved Holy Spirit (4:30) or of divine wrath (5:6) is simply disingenuous.[41]

How should we think, then, of divine providence, and what difference does it make for a proper understanding of the task of Christian ethics? One expression of God's providential work as indicated in Scripture is in how God employs "the nations" in order to achieve some particular goal or purpose. A brief examination of this biblical theme as it pertains

---

in Christ's victory and God's ultimate sovereignty. Their faithful failures point all the more to their faith in their story and its author."

40. A conventional expression of the doctrine of divine providence as voiced and challenged by Wood, *Question of Providence*, 60. Joe Jones insists that God's providence is "not discernible simply by looking at how the world unfolds, at how the events of the world happen. We can determine little about the provident purposes of God in creating and governing the world simply by observing the course of events in the world. We do not know a God whose will and purpose are simply as such the unfolding of all events, for such a god would be 'fate.'" See his *Grammar of Christian Faith*, 262–63.

41. See Meadors, "'It Never Entered My Mind,'" 185–214. Meadors challenges the popular presentations of Wayne Grudem and John Piper, who want to affirm a view of divine sovereignty that ultimately makes God the primary agent for evil and sin. "Particularly awkward," says Meadors (190), "is the rationalization that God is the universal primary agent of the abominations that God himself despises." Most "difficult for theistic determinism," he argues (201–2), "are biblical passages that explicitly identify evil as incongruous with God's will and nature. . . . The Bible is very clear that God does not will sin or evil."

to significant events in the aftermath of September 11, 2001, will illuminate something of the relationship between the specific understanding of the task of Christian ethics as pursued here and the sense of God's broader providential work.

Interest in "the nations" is one example of a biblical emphasis on the wider providential work of God. Both testaments of Scripture clearly assert that history is the arena of divine activity and that the nations of the earth—and not just a covenant people with privileged access to divine mysteries—are also partners in achieving God's purpose. This theme is displayed in many ways in both testaments: from the genealogy of the nations in Genesis 10 to the triumphal assertions of the book of Revelation. Amos 9:7 makes clear the divine involvement in the history and migrations of peoples other than the nation of Israel, and Acts 2:23 insists that Roman responsibility for the death of Jesus serves to accomplish the larger purposes and work of God. These are specific illustrations of a widely employed motif in Scripture that the nations serve as "unwitting" partners of Yahweh, the God of Israel, in carrying out the purpose of God and in so doing testify to "the large horizon of Yahweh's governance."[42]

The ambiguity of this testimony, however, must be noted. In particular, the events of and surrounding the Babylonian destruction of Jerusalem and exile of many of its inhabitants (ca. 587 BCE) illustrate the difficulties in tracing the providential work of God in history. The books of Jeremiah and Habakkuk both give examples of the challenge of reading events in terms of God's governance and what particular conclusions might be drawn from such a reading. Even in the aftermath of exile, the Old Testament bears witness to alternative (though not necessarily competing) explanations of and responses to what God was doing in the events of destruction and captivity.[43] Without the advantage of hindsight it was far more difficult to determine the precise significance of the presence and threat of Babylonian power. The books of Jeremiah and Habakkuk display the challenge of tracing the hand of God while in the middle of things.

Prior to the final siege and destruction of Jerusalem, Zedekiah, king of Judah, had assembled a number of the kings of the surrounding kingdoms facing the same Babylonian threat (ca. 594 BCE). Evidently, as we

42. Brueggemann, *Theology of the Old Testament*, 492.

43. See Klein, *Israel in Exile*. Brueggemann (*Theology of the Old Testament*, 75) describes the exile as providing Israel "a moment of enormous literary generativity, when a variety of daring articulations of faith were undertaken."

can infer from Jeremiah 27, the plan was to join forces together in the hope that their combined strength could "break the yoke of Babylon" and rid the smaller ancient Near Eastern states of the oppressive presence of the Babylonian king, Nebuchadnezzar. No doubt to Zedekiah's embarrassment, though, the prophet Jeremiah appeared in public wearing bonds and an ox yoke on his neck, conveying the unpopular message that Nebuchadnezzar was Yahweh's instrument of justice and judgment and that resistance to Babylonian power would only bring disaster. As Thomas Overholt puts it, "The political domination of Palestine by Nebuchadnezzar is . . . interpreted by the prophet as being due to Yahweh's explicit plan, which no merely human decision to rise up in revolt can overcome."[44] A problem arose, however, when another voice, presenting itself in the full-throated authority of a prophet, offered an alternative and much more positive assessment of the situation (Jer 28:1–11). "Hananiah the son of Azzur, the prophet, who was from Gibeon" countered Jeremiah's dark message of judgment, indicated that the Babylonian situation was more or less manageable, and "took the yoke from the neck of the prophet Jeremiah and broke it" (v. 10). Hananiah then insisted on a significantly different rendering of God's activity in current events than did Jeremiah: "Thus says Yahweh, 'Even so will I break within two full years, the yoke of Nebuchadnezzar, king of Babylon from the neck of all the nations'" (v. 11).

The obvious discrepancy between these two prophetic readings of God's engagement in history was certainly a problem for those seeking prophetic authority for official policy. On the one hand, "to all outward appearances Hananiah was also a true Yahweh prophet," so that "here we have earnest men in opposition, prophecy against prophecy," with completely different assessments of the same situation.[45] On the other hand, the Deuteronomic principle for testing prophecy—whether or not a particular prophetic word comes to fulfillment (Deut 18:21–22)—was of no help, as the crisis of the moment called for an immediate response one way or the other. Further still, Jeremiah himself seems to have had difficulty in sorting out the options. Perhaps weary of the tone of his own burdensome message (and its troublesome consequences for him personally; see Jer 20:7–18), he had expressed sympathy for the more encouraging themes sounded by Hananiah (28:6) and simply retreated

44. See his *Threat of Falsehood*, 28–29.

45. Ibid., 38–39.

from the scene temporarily when challenged by his counterpart (v. 11). There were likely occasions in Jeremiah's life when he had entertained the prospect that he himself was a false prophet, sent forth by Yahweh with a deceiving spirit (20:7; cf. 1 Kgs 22:13–23; Jer 15:18). Jeremiah had been preaching a message of destruction for the city of Jerusalem for at least fifteen years by this time, and the threats might have worn thin even to him. Could he have been wrong all along?[46]

On this occasion, however, Jeremiah receives further word from Yahweh that fortified him in his confrontation with Hananiah, whose death later that year would have appeared to vindicate Jeremiah's authenticity (28:12–17). The later fulfillment of Jeremiah's vision of judgment and exile for Jerusalem goes far in explaining why we have a book of Jeremiah in the Old Testament and not a book of Hananiah. It was only with hindsight, however, that Hananiah's legitimacy could be dismissed and his claims judged false. In the press of the moment, as Terence Fretheim observes, "the dividing line between true and false prophet is very difficult to discern."[47] If within the biblical canon there is testimony to the difficulty of discerning the work of God in history, we who do not possess the credentials of a Jeremiah might at least hesitate concerning our own capacities.

When it comes to the experience of Habakkuk, it was not competition with another prophet, but conflict with his own sensibilities (themselves formed by prophetic traditions) that created questions concerning God's actions in history. His confrontation was not with another prophet, but with Yahweh himself. A contemporary of Jeremiah's, Habakkuk's message should be read in light of the abuses of justice perpetrated during the reign of Jehoiakim (608–598 BCE). Donald Gowan offers that "the most natural reading of 1:2–4 is to take it as Habakkuk's complaint about the kinds of injustice within Judah that his [prophetic] predecessors had condemned."[48] The prophet's original complaint is a version of "justice delayed is justice denied," and he laments to God, "How long, O Yahweh, will I call for help, and thou wilt not hear?" The persistence of iniquity,

---

46 R. W. L. Moberly, who warns against "psychologizing" Jeremiah, argues that the issues were never in doubt for the prophet. See his *Prophecy and Discernment*, 100–109. The shocking statements in 15:18 and 20:7 seem to indicate more than a measure of uncertainty on Jeremiah's part. In any case, it would have been a confusing matter for those having to decide between alternative prophetic claims.

47. See his *Jeremiah*, 398.

48. Gowan, *Theology of the Prophetic Books*, 93.

destruction, and violence meant, as far as Habakkuk was concerned, that "justice comes out perverted" (1:4).

What is likely Yahweh's response in 1:5–11 is to reassert the long established view that the nations serve as the instruments of divine purpose (1:5) and that it will be (ironically) through a nation whose "justice and authority originate with themselves" (1:7) that Judah will be judged and corrected. For Habakkuk, the prospect of the fierce and arrogant Chaldeans (Babylon) serving as Yahweh's chosen means of discipline seems more than incongruous with what he knows of the divine character and all out of proportion to the relative moral conditions between Judah and Babylon (1:13): "Habakkuk recoils at the thought of YHWH subjecting a covenant people to barbarous soldiers. . . . For Habakkuk, the [proposed] merciless and endless swath of destruction defied rationality."[49]

Habakkuk appears not to have been so quick to tolerate the instrumentality of Babylon as his yoked contemporary Jeremiah. On the other hand, Yahweh seems to recognize the difficulty of the proposal and accepts that it will provoke astonishment and disbelief (1:5). Habakkuk indeed expresses his bewilderment (1:12–17) and hopes for some clarification or correction (2:1); what he is told does not encourage confidence in his ability to thoroughly account for divine providence on the terms afforded by tradition or deliberation: "Behold, as for the proud one, his soul is not right within him; but the righteous man will live by his faithfulness" (2:4). A helpful paraphrase will make clear the significance of this response for the larger concerns pursued here: "The summons is from speculation to action, from questioning to conduct, from brooding to duty. God is attending to his business, and Habakkuk must attend to his. Running the universe is not his task. That burden belongs to God. But Habakkuk has his task, and let him faithfully perform it. Thus he will live in moral sincerity and moral security that righteous living brings in the midst of external calamities. That is the way for a righteous man to live in an evil world."[50] In effect, Habakkuk is cautioned against too great a certainty concerning his capacities fully to discern God's providence and is challenged "to maintain a faithful commitment to God's justice and to persist in its principles, even when such justice appears to be absent in the world around him."[51]

49. Crenshaw, "Theodicy and Prophetic Literature," 250.
50. Calkins, *Modern Message*, 97.
51. Hiebert, "Book of Habakkuk," 642.

The prophetic experience of both Jeremiah and Habakkuk illustrates how difficult, if not at times impossible, it is to determine accurately the precise character of God's governance as displayed through the nations. There is no question that both these prophets operated with the deep conviction that "Yahweh does deal with the nations according to Yahweh's own freedom and passion." While the nations generally are depicted as serving Yahweh's interest with reference to Israel's particular covenant status with God, that is not always the case. Certainly what is the case is that "Yahweh in freedom has the power and capacity to recruit the nations for Yahweh's own purposes . . . even if those purposes run against the expectation of Israel."[52] Even, it might be added, if those purposes run against the expectations of Israel's prophets.

Clearly, these accounts suggest in particular what Richard Bauckham observes in general, that "the biblical portrayal of divine providence cannot be equated with the immanent reason of history because it is contingent on the freedom of God and not open to rational calculation." While Jeremiah and Habakkuk, along with the rest of the biblical storytellers, "recognize the hand of God in the contingency of history, some aspects of history remain intractable to comprehension in these terms."[53] "What do you think of the French Revolution?" someone is supposed to have asked Zhou Enlai. "Too soon to tell," responded the leader of communist China—150 years after the event! There can be no gainsaying the implication of prophetic announcements concerning God's work among the nations: "To put it succinctly," says Fretheim, "God is present on every occasion and active in every event."[54] And yet the character of that presence and the purpose it represents cannot always be clearly discerned. Yes, prophets gained clarity and offered certainty, if sometimes after confusion and false starts. We need to take seriously as well, though, the implications of a closed canon. There were no prophets on the scene to provide the definitive interpretation of the French Revolution, and even now, more than two hundred years later, humility properly cautions against final assessments.

Such humility, however, is sometimes found wanting. It did not take long after the tragedy of September 11, 2001, for confident voices to assert the precise significance of the horrific events, and out of at least some

52. Brueggemann, *Theology of the Old Testament*, 522.

53. Bauckham, "Reading Scripture as a Coherent Story," 49.

54. Fretheim, *God and World*, 167.

expressions of that confidence, major international engagements were pursued. On the one hand, in an interview on Pat Robertson's *700 Club*, baptist preacher Jerry Falwell insisted two days after the terrorist attacks in New York and Washington that God had "lifted the curtain" of protection on an increasingly immoral America and had expressed divine judgment by way of Muslim radicals: "I really believe that the pagans, the abortionists, and the feminists, and the gays and the lesbians who are actively trying to make that an alternative lifestyle, the ACLU, People for the American Way—all of them have tried to secularize America. I point the finger in their face and say, 'You helped this happen.'" Robertson responded, "I totally agree."[55]

In contrast to Falwell's jeremiad, George W. Bush expressed shock that evil terrorists could offer any justification for their attacks on a people whose moral standing is unquestionable. At least Habakkuk drew relative comparisons between the injustices of Judah and the deeper corruptions of the Babylonians. President Bush, though, saw divine providence, not in the use of a wicked force—Osama bin Laden's al-Qaeda—to express divine judgment on the contemporary analog to ancient Israel. Rather, President Bush invoked notions of providence, mission, destiny, and calling to underwrite a plan to use military force to "rid the world of evil."[56]

There are debates as to how explicit President Bush has been in couching the 2003 invasion of Iraq in terms of "God's will."[57] Others have been less restrained. In his 2004 book *American Providence*, Stephen H. Webb approvingly cites Bush's rhetoric of mission and destiny; Webb himself asserts, "God has planted the seeds of freedom, and the mission of America is to nourish those seeds as best she can."[58] What Webb means by "freedom" is that freedom provided in the arena of democratic capitalism, a "theological good [itself] firmly rooted in Christian principles."[59] The twin movements of democratic capitalism and Evan-

---

55. The interview is available for viewing on YouTube. See http://www.youtube.com/watch?v=H-CAcdta_8I.

56. President Bush, Washington DC (The National Cathedral), September 14, 2001; later inserted into the National Security Strategy of the United States of America of September 2002. Text available in Avram, *Anxious About Empire*, 187–215. Much time, of course, has passed since the tragedy of 9/11, though we continue to live with the aftermath. Perhaps enough time has passed, though, to where the religious rhetoric used in response to the event can be evaluated somewhat objectively.

57. See Northcott, *An Angel Directs the Storm*.

58. Webb, *American Providence*, 11.

59. Ibid., 114.

gelical Christianity, Webb offers, must be seen as expressions of God's providential superintendence of human history, and it is the combination of these two "globalisms" that offers the best hope for humanity's future. It is clear to Webb, however, that "the one globalism—American economic power—is, in crucial respects, a necessary prerequisite for the other globalism—American-style Christianity." By way of analogy, Webb suggests, "American commerce is serving God's purpose today just as Roman roads were providential for the expansion of Christianity many centuries ago."[60] While Webb bristles at the further comparisons some have made between the foreign policy agenda of the Bush administration and Roman imperialism,[61] he admits that "America cannot always act democratically on the world stage, even as it acts to increase the number of democracies in the world." Thus, hard decisions must sometimes be made, even unilaterally—for example, "the question of how to handle terrorist states."[62] For the sake of the progress of the gospel, America must take its status as an empire seriously and must be willing to "monopolize the use of violence and thus establish international order so that nations can pursue the trade that is necessary for economic growth. . . . The new world order is the declaration by America that it will monopolize the use of international force for the good of all nations."[63]

Webb firmly believes that the United States of America presently plays the pivotal role in God's providential superintendence of history. America is not the new Israel, Webb is cautious to insist; but "while Israel is the key to history, another nation has undeniably moved to the front pages of current affairs and will stay there for the foreseeable future."[64] Furthermore, Webb demonstrates restraint when he objects to "those on the religious right [who] may be tempted to use providence to baptize every American action on the international scene."[65] Webb, however, rarely cast a critical eye toward President Bush's policies or those of the neoconservative movement that so influenced that administration.[66] Ultimately,

60. Ibid., 145.

61. Ibid., 77–80, 87 n. 14.

62. Ibid., 114.

63. Ibid., 168.

64. Ibid., 7–8.

65. Ibid., 8. Webb (26) points to American involvement in Vietnam, saying, "Whatever God was doing in history, it was not identical with American foreign policy."

66. Webb wrote his work before it became increasingly evident that the arguments used by the Bush administration to justify its invasion of Iraq (presence of WMDs and

it seems that it is in light of what he considers to be the most significant threat to both America and Christianity—the Islamic faith—that Webb gives a green light to President Bush's sense of American mission and calling as displayed in its foreign policy. "Forcing Muslim nations into democratic political orders can accomplish much good in the world, but it needs to be recognized that this goal is theological as well as political," Webb writes.[67]

It must be said that Webb is not the first to be so explicit in his affirmations of the peculiar status of the United States in the purposes of God, nor the first so firmly to support America's military and economic interests in the name of the gospel.[68] Others, however, are not so quick to share Webb's assessment,[69] and criticisms of American imperial designs have surfaced in many Christian circles, while still (as Webb notes) maintaining a hold on some form of America's special providential role in history.[70] In the face of more current events on the economic scene and the continued instability in Iraq and Afghanistan, other voices have put forward the notion of a lesser role for the United States in world affairs.[71] Perhaps the "foreseeable future" of which Webb spoke in 2004 lasted only until the fall of 2008. The present concern, however, is not at all to weigh in on the relative or waning strength of the United States as a world leader, but to make some general observations about appeal to divine providence as the grounds for Christian commitment to this or that mode of action in the world.

---

links with the 9/11 terrorists) were at best weak, and at worst outright fabrications. Webb also wrote before the issues of torture, extraordinary rendition, warrantless wiretapping, and manipulated intelligence surfaced to challenge the moral standing of the administration. More recent affirmations by Webb of George W. Bush as "The Providential President" indicate that these issues have not substantively altered his position. See his "From Prudentius to President Bush."

67. *American Providence*, 139.

68. A standard work on what has been called American "exceptionalism" is Tuveson, *Redeemer Nation*. More recent accounts that critically analyze assertions of America's "chosen" status are Hughes, *Myths America Lives By*, and Hughes, *Christian America and the Kingdom of God*.

69. See the reviews by Bell in *Journal of Church and State*, 228–30; Steffen in *Christian Century*, 33–38; and Beach-Verhey in *Political Theology*, 376–78.

70. See the essays in Benson and Heltzel, *Evangelicals and Empire*; Avram, *Anxious About Empire*; Dorrien, *Imperial Designs*; Taylor, *Religion, Politics, and the Christian Right*.

71. E.g., Bacevich, *Limits of Power*; Johnson, *Nemesis*.

First, conventional use of the doctrine of providence has often served the interests of those with power and is almost always expressed in generic theistic terms, divorced from a particularly Christian understanding of God. Karl Barth long ago lamented "the astonishing fact" that the widely held understanding of God's providence exhibits an "almost total failure even to ask concerning the Christian meaning and character of the doctrine of providence, let alone to assert it." According to Barth, the doctrine of providence as usually upheld highlights abstract themes of a classical theism that presents divine lordship solely in terms of a power expressive of divine wisdom, righteousness, and goodness, but with these traits conceived independently of the explicit christological themes associated with them in the New Testament (see, e.g., 1 Cor 1:18–25; Phil 2:5–11). Thus, the usual construal of Christian belief in providence is ultimately an "empty shell" into which regnant concepts of power and wisdom are poured.[72] Practically what this has meant, according to Charles Wood, is that the doctrine of God's providence has been most serviceable "during that long period of Western Christian history when some version of Christianity was the established religion of the state, and when notions of divine sovereignty and human imperial sovereignty were fatefully assimilated to one another." A convenient appeal to divine sovereignty has regularly served since the period of Constantine to give legitimacy to and sanction "the now-harmonized interests of church and empire."[73] When one sits enthroned, it is always tempting to believe that it is by divine right. It is no accident that President Bush's most frequently used appellation for God, at least in public, was "the Almighty."

Second, it is very difficult to rightly divide the divine intent in current world history. Baptist preacher Jerry Falwell sounds much more like a Jeremiah with the United States playing ancient Judah and al-Qaeda taking the role of the Babylonians. A pious president offers much more the comforting assurances of a Hananiah.[74] The quick and heated response to Falwell's statements suggests that an American public likely echoes the astonishment of a Habakkuk who could not fathom the possibility of a divinely favored nation justly suffering at the hands of an obviously wicked people. If, however, the biblical materials themselves

72. Barth, *Church Dogmatics* III/3, 30–31.

73. Wood, *Question of Providence*, 58–59.

74. For a brief but fair appraisal of George W. Bush's public expression of his personal faith, see Robinson and Wilcox, "Faith of George W. Bush," 215–38. For a more critical assessment, see Wallis, "Dangerous Religion," 25–32.

reflect the ambiguous and fragile character of human discernment of God's engagement in human history, then perhaps Charles Wood's biblical citation with which he concludes his study on divine providence is apt: "O Yahweh, my heart is not proud, nor my eyes haughty; nor do I involve myself in great matters, or in things too difficult for me" (Psalm 131:1).[75] Perhaps it should be with us as it was with Jeremiah, who possessed the willingness to reserve judgment, to wait for further insight, and even to admit to the possibility that there might be false prophets (including him).[76]

A third matter has to do with the fundamental conviction that the primary locus of God's activity and work in the world is the body of Christ, the church, and the church understood in a specific way. Webb is quite certain that God providentially guides human history, not in some general way but in particular events through particular nations. It is this conviction that not only permits but encourages and demands Christian participation in the larger arena of national and international politics. "What special providence properly highlights about God's authority is that it encompasses the political authority of rulers and the ruled." This thoroughly biblical concept, Webb says, requires believers to recognize that, while risky, political engagement is necessary, for "politics and theology are inseparable."[77]

A Christian ethic shaped by the New Testament, though, will challenge the very presence of the conjunction in the phrase "theology *and* politics." There is no question as to the inherently political character of Christian faith. The question is whether the political expression of the Christian faith runs primarily through the halls of state. Webb appears to accept the premise that "the New Testament does not address its audience in terms of a nation or a polis" so the church cannot "withdraw into its own political sphere" but must rather "work toward the transformation of

75. Wood, *Questions of Providence*, 116. No less an advocate of particular providence than John Calvin insists that though we might pray for specific concerns, "what God has determined concerning them is beyond our knowing" (*Institutes*, III.20.38). William C. Placher insists that even for Calvin "there are puzzles" and that according to Calvin "we have to acknowledge the limits of our understanding and seek to trust a God whose nature lies beyond even our imagining." See his *Domestication of Transcendence*, 64.

76. The Bush administration has passed from the scene. The cautions offered here concerning certainty about the providential role of any American president remain appropriate regardless of who inhabits the White House.

77. Webb, *American Providence*, 103–4.

the political."[78] A major finding of current biblical scholarship, however, is that indeed the New Testament *does* address its audience in terms of a nation or a polis (though clearly not in terms of the modern nation-state). The evidence for this will be presented in more detail at a later point. The summary assessment of Michael Gorman concerning the mission of the Apostle Paul, however, is appropriate here: "Paul did not set out merely to save or convert individuals to the gospel but to form communities shaped by the gospel into cruciform [shaped by the cross of Christ], and thereby alternative, theo-political entities."[79]

Webb believes there are clear implications of the Christian faith that permit, even require, Christians to witness to the global lordship of Jesus Christ, particularly with reference to such concerns as "international politics, the fate of nations, and the purpose of limited government."[80] His warning, though, that the point of the church "is not to withdraw into its own political sphere" reveals a basic misunderstanding (one widely shared) that the church *becomes* politically engaged when it concerns itself with what appears overtly political (e.g., the purpose of limited government). The Christian faith, however, is inherently political and believers becomes politically engaged, not first when they participate in the structures and practices of the modern nation-state, but when they join in Paul's doxology, "Blessed be the God and Father of our Lord Jesus Christ, who has blessed us with every spiritual blessing in the heavenly places in Christ" (Eph 1:3). Worship is not the illegitimate "withdrawal" into the church's own political sphere; worship *is* the church's own political sphere.[81]

Thus, we do not first become politically engaged when we seek to determine God's providential role among the nations and then use the power of the nations to assert that role. That effort routinely has more to

78. Ibid., 104–5. Webb engages here with the work of O'Donovan, *Desire of the Nations*.

79. Gorman, *Cruciformity*, 352. Among the important studies in this connection, see those edited by Richard Horsley: *Paul and Politics* and *Paul and the Roman Imperial Order*. Webb is aware of this body of work. He does not engage the substance of the material, though, but only where Horsley addresses current concerns about American imperialism. He does not consider the underlying and more important concerns of a gospel that provides an explicit alternative to the claims and status of the Roman Empire. We are only just now beginning to see the implications of this interpretive stance for ecclesiology and Christian ethics. For one example, see Walsh and Keesmaat, *Colossians Remixed*.

80. Webb, *American Providence*, 107.

81. See Wannenwetsch, *Political Worship*.

do with the power of the nations than it does the radically different power of the gospel. We do not rightly assert the political significance of the Christian faith when we discern in acts of terror either God's judgment or God's permission to respond in kind. That effort regularly fails to honor the gap between God's wisdom and our own and more often sides with a Habakkuk bewildered at the notion that God's providence might not coincide with our own interests. We do not properly enter into the political arena when we champion the interests of one nation and define global interests in those narrow terms. That effort ultimately misunderstands the inherently political character of a church formed in its worship of a crucified Christ in ways that provide a fundamental alternative to the ways of the nations.

Those who share Webb's concern to assert God's providential role in history by supporting the particular policies of this or that administration rightly understand the call of believers to be of positive public significance in a world threatened by evil in its multiple forms. Assertions of God's governance of creation and history certainly raise questions of what God is doing about evil.[82] What was God doing in 9/11? It might very well be too soon to tell. That does not mean, though, that the church is left without a task or bereft of confidence in God's capacity to achieve good in the world through God's people. It does mean that appeals to divine providence cannot be the means by which Christians give absolute legitimacy to their support for and engagement in uncertain enterprises.

Of what use is the doctrine of divine providence, then, if in the midst of things discernment of that providence suffers the constraints of human fallibility? Theologian Jürgen Moltmann offers a helpful distinction: "We must learn to differentiate between the promise of God and the providence of God. The promise of God is not based on the providence of God, but rather the providence of God serves the fulfillment of the promise of God."[83] We might take the thesis of this study as a summary expression of God's promise through the gospel. What is God doing about evil? More than we can know; but we can know that through God's redemptive work, God is creating a people whose lives, sustained in worship, bear witness to God's purpose for creation. God has promised to be at work through a people created and shaped by the gospel for the

---

82. Webb himself raises the question of the relationship between God's providence and the conventional understanding of the issue of theodicy; see *American Providence*, 8–9, 100.

83. Moltmann, *Hope and Planning*, 184.

creation-wide purposes of redemption and reconciliation. The practices and commitments put on display by this people are central to God's purpose and work in this world. Confidence in the providence of God is not confidence that Christians can always discern how God is at work in this or that instance in the long journey toward fulfillment of God's promise. There can be, though, the confidence that the providence of God serves the fulfillment of the promise of God. There should be the confidence among the people of God that their witness to God's purpose for creation is, in God's providence and in spite of what might be appearances to the contrary, employed to significant and redemptive effect in this world.

Believers today engage in debate about all sorts of matters—on how God is at work through events of terror, what God is doing in the economic crises of our day, or what the loss of Arctic summer ice means. All of these are serious issues and demand considered response. For Christians, though, any response must be from within the context of what Christian ethics is all about. With Habakkuk we must first hear a summons from speculation to action, from questioning to conduct, from brooding to duty. Confident in God's providence, we trust that God is attending to the business of managing the universe toward divine ends; with Habakkuk we must attend to our business. Running the universe is not our task. That burden belongs to God. We do, however, have our task, and that is to hear and respond to God's invitation to participate in what God is accomplishing through the gospel, knowing that response to that invitation carries with it the responsibility to walk worthy of our calling.

Towards the conclusion of *The Truman Show*, "Sylvia," one of the "actors" in Truman's life that had sought to enlighten him as to his true circumstances, is watching as Truman deliberates on whether he will remain "in character" or leave the show's set and strike out into the unknown. Christof argues with Truman that he cannot leave: "Truman, there's no more truth out there than in the world I created for you—the same lies and deceit. But in my world you have nothing to fear." In a brief shot of Sylvia, we see her cast her eyes heavenward and her lips mouth a silent prayer for Truman's liberation. By her prayer, Christof is revealed as the false god of false promises who would keep Truman captive. What follows in this study will appear to some as a challenge to many accepted and conventional notions of "the way things are." Sylvia prays that Truman would find the strength to embark on a journey from the familiar to the unknown. For Truman, it would mean a journey of faith. We will see that Ephesians offers a similar challenge.

1

"We Are His Workmanship"

A Theocentric Ethic

"Woe to us if we should be found to be our own creator, inventor, and author of our own future well-being."

JOHANN GEORG HAMANN[1]

"What should I do?" For many, that is the central question of the moral life. That can certainly be an important question in the midst of this situation or that. A coworker steals from the company you both work for. Do you tell the boss? A young couple finds it next to impossible to get pregnant. Is *in vitro* fertilization the solution? A political action committee presses for a state referendum banning gay marriage. Is that the Christian thing to do? The question, "What should I do?" seems to be at the center of so many moral issues.

For others, however, another question has surfaced in discussions of moral philosophy in general and Christian ethics in particular. A strong emphasis on matters of character and virtue finds expression not in the question, "What should I do?" but "Who am I?"[2] The significance of persistent traits expressed across the days, week, months, and years of our lives are of tremendous importance for what the moral life is all

---

1. Letter to F. H. Jacobi, 5 Dec. 1784; cited in Bayer, *Freedom in Response*, 13.
2. See Verhey, *Remembering Jesus*, 3.

about (and will be explored later in this book), but there is an even more important question for the task of Christian ethics.

As important as moral decisions are, Oswald Bayer insists that we should not begin any exploration of Christian ethics with the standard question, "What should I do?" Instead, we should ask, "'What has been given to us?' For human action does not start with itself; it draws its life from freedom that has already been given."[3] Christian ethics begins with neither our action nor our character, but by celebrating the divine initiative and agenda.

In his letter to the Ephesians, Paul offers an ethical vision that begins, not with the question "What should I do?" or even "Who am I?" but by emphasizing what God is doing. That is, the vision of the moral life in Ephesians is fundamentally tied to what it has to say about the character, actions, and will of God made known through Jesus Christ. Clearly this outlook differs from many other approaches to the moral life, particularly any moral strategy that creates and separates something called "ethics" from something called "religion." What this means is that for Christians to talk about the sort of life we believe God intends for humanity, we have to talk about matters that go by the designation "theology."

To emphasize theology, however, is likely to occasion grumbling on the part of some. Gordon Graham observes what he considers to be a general trend of retreat by Western Christianity at the turn of the twenty-first century: "Theologians and believers more generally have lost confidence in the relevance of Christian theology to the explanatory endeavors of intellectual inquiry." Hardly anyone, he insists, "confidently deploys theology in the discussion of intellectual problems in cosmology, evolutionary biology, historiography, jurisprudence, or metaphysics."[4] This abandonment of theology is no more evident, says Graham, than in the discipline called "Christian ethics." In this arena, there is the rejection of a larger theological outlook that could provide any comprehensive frame of reference for an all-embracing vision of reality. Rather, the view of the nineteenth-century mathematician Henri Laplace, that "God is an hypothesis of which the scientist has no need," is now apparently endorsed even by the Christian moralist who would construe Christianity as "but a code by which to live, with, perhaps, 'radical' implications for social criticism as well as for the behavior of individuals."[5]

3. Bayer, *Freedom in Response*, 1.

4. Graham, *Evil and Christian Ethics*, 1.

5. Ibid., 2–3.

What accounts for the willingness to reduce the Christian faith to matters of "ethics," according to Graham, is the widely held assumption that we live in a pluralistic age where the claims of the Christian faith concerning God, Christ, redemption, the Holy Spirit, the Christian community of the church, eschatology, etc., have no public significance. In such a context, if Christianity wants to have any genuine relevance in the world today, it will not be "in any theological-cum-metaphysical explanation of existence and experience that Christian theology has hitherto been thought uniquely to supply." Instead, "if Christianity is to speak to the contemporary world it is [only] in its ethic that a meaningful message is to be found."[6] In this way, as Stephen Long puts it, "The discipline of Christian ethics becomes one more immanent anthropological discourse that incessantly addresses questions of justice, rights, care, autonomy, and the need for religion to have a role in the public square. But seldom does Christian ethics actually engage with the theology of the moral life, that is, with what difference it might actually make for understanding the moral life if the God whom Christian tradition confesses as Father, Son, and Holy Spirit were true."[7]

It is a great irony that for many the obligation Christian faith imposes on us is to seek influence in the world by offering a view of moral practices and obligations independent of the story of God's redemptive work, of the importance of worship and discipleship, of a hope in God's future that rests its confidence in God's past. What Christian ethics must be (some say), if it is to have any contemporary significance in today's pluralistic environment, is anything but Christian. What Christian ethics must be is about positions on this or that issue employing arguments that are expressible in terms that any clear-thinking person can affirm so that such positions can be formulated as policy enacted through legislative means, thus enforceable by the power of the state.[8] Matters of personal agency, the formation of character, the shaping of moral vision, and the painful and sometimes slow acquisition of skills and disciplines that might be needed to sustain a particular form of life are all irrelevant. Arguments that justify policies implemented through the power of the state are all that are needed. Stanley Hauerwas and Samuel Wells describe this as the strategy of "conventional ethics," an effort given over to the task

6. Ibid., 3.

7. Long, *Goodness of God*, 76.

8. A significant example of this approach, represented by Reinhold Niebuhr, will be explored in chapter 3.

of "trying to make a better world without us becoming better people." Hauerwas and Wells insist that "not only is this task impossible, but it is neglecting its chief resource—the way God chooses to form his people."[9] Wells elsewhere describes the ethical enterprise as "about forming lives of commitment, rather than informing lives without commitment."[10] For many, though, the task has become a matter of providing information (telling people what to do) rather than offering transformation (bearing witness to a life-changing gospel). How we have come to this state of affairs requires a look back into important events in European history and philosophy that continue to have significant impact in our world today. Once we have considered features of these forces that have shaped our world, we will hear from Paul in Ephesians how it is that the life God intends for us rests upon God's gifts of grace and peace.

WHERE ARE WE?

Alasdair MacIntyre's "Disquieting Suggestion"

In Walter Miller's *A Canticle for Leibowitz*, the young monk Francis, living in a post-nuclear-holocaust world, discovers fragments of paper with scratch marks on them. Eventually those scratch marks are determined to be from the hand of the blessed Saint Leibowitz, a sacred figure from the distant past. Six hundred years earlier, Leibowitz had actually been an engineer associated with the development of the very nuclear weapons that had caused such widespread destruction. Since the worlds of science, knowledge, and education had all been destroyed, though, there was no context available for deciphering the significance of the various words, formulae, and equations that Francis had discovered. Ceaseless debates follow on the meaning of phrases like "circuit design" and "Transistorized Control System." The debates rage endlessly since there is no shared frame of reference that would make the words intelligible; instead the words are simply employed to advance various viewpoints that seek credibility through association with terms that sound authoritative.[11]

9. Hauerwas and Wells, "Gift of the Church and the Gifts God Gives It," 13–14.

10. Wells, *Improvisation*, 30. Wells describes this outlook as a contemporary expression of the ancient heresy of Gnosticism. Literary critic Harold Bloom has described Gnosticism as the basic feature of contemporary American religion. See his *American Religion*, 49–52.

11. Miller, *Canticle for Leibowitz*. Eventually, though, as the story goes on,

Alasdair MacIntyre uses something like this story as a metaphor for what has occurred in our culture. We still use words like "good," "bad," "right," and "wrong," but there is no longer an agreed-upon frame of reference available to give these words any substance. Endless debates rage over issues like abortion, the death penalty, war, and justice, with all participants using what sounds like the language of morality. Moral language, though, is simply a cover masking the advancement of personal preferences by using language that sounds authoritative. We might still use terms that purport to bear the weight of moral legitimacy, but those words are nothing other than tools we use to communicate our emotional responses to certain experiences.[12] I react negatively to the sight and smell of asparagus. Any strong response I might have to murder or rape or torture, according to the view known as *emotivism*, is perhaps only different in degree, not in kind, from my feelings about asparagus. Matters of moral judgment, in our own confused context, are simply expressions of emotional reaction, no different from matters of taste concerning vegetables or preferences between country and hip-hop.

If we are in a situation similar to that of the young monk Francis, what catastrophe have we experienced that resulted in the loss of the larger frame of reference necessary for understanding moral language? For MacIntyre, the disaster is what he calls "the Enlightenment project." The background, features, and consequences of this era and outlook are essential for us to understand if we are going to read the moral landscape of our own context properly and perceive how different is the vision of the moral life offered to us in the gospel.

Immanuel Kant's Enlightenment Project

One of the ironies of the Enlightenment project is that its influence is so deep and profound that we would resist examining its historical development and cultural significance. Such is the case because a key feature of the Enlightenment project is the notion that history and culture in some ways do not matter. A central assertion of the entire effort was the

---

sufficient "progress" is made in the sciences for humanity to once again threaten its own annihilation.

12. See MacIntyre's *After Virtue*, 1–5. I say that MacIntyre "uses something like" Miller's story, because while the parallels are there, MacIntyre does not cite Miller's book explicitly. I have former student Scott Patz to thank for recognizing the parallels and putting me on to Miller's work.

insistence that as far as morality is concerned the autonomous (self-governing) individual must escape from all those forces that reflect personal history, cultural influence, particular experience, and parochial ties so as to exercise strictly rational judgment to determine moral obligation. The chief representative of the Enlightenment project, Immanuel Kant (d. 1804), expressed this sentiment thus:

> Enlightenment is man's release from his self-incurred tutelage. Tutelage is man's inability to make use of his understanding without direction from another. Self-incurred is this tutelage when its cause lies not in lack of reason but in lack of resolution and courage to use it without direction from another. *Sapere aude!* "Have courage to use your own reason!"—that is the motto of enlightenment.[13]

For Kant, it is not important for us to see ourselves as having been shaped and influenced by cultural, historical, and philosophical movements, traditions from the past, or even family ties. All such factors have to do with contingent (and so not necessary) matters of personal experience and not the pure principles of logic. Kant asks, "Is it not of the utmost necessity to construct a pure moral philosophy which is completely freed from everything which may be only empirical [based on experience] and thus belong to anthropology?" He insists, "The moral law can be found in its purity and genuineness . . . nowhere else than in a pure philosophy."[14] Reliance on tradition, culture, heritage, or any other resource that stems from the contingencies of history would simply be self-incurred tutelage.

For some, Kant's point might seem obvious: "Of course moral obligation must rest on foundations of reason rather than the uncertainties of this or that tradition, this or that cultural bias," they might say. One clear implication of this outlook, which was quite deliberate on Kant's part, was the insistence that matters of morality must not be tied to any particular religious commitments (e.g., Christianity). A basic feature of what MacIntyre calls the Enlightenment project was the concern *to establish a foundation for morality independent of any particular theological outlook.* For Kant, "the ground of moral obligation . . . must not be sought in the nature of man or in the circumstances in which he is placed, but sought *a priori* [before the impact of any particular life experiences] solely in the concepts of pure reason."[15] Religious teachings vary and conflict with one

---

13. Kant, "What Is Enlightenment?" 85.

14. Kant, "Foundations of the Metaphysics of Morals," 5–6.

15. Ibid., 5.

another and rely for their authority on traditional offices of the church or on the competing interpretations of this or that historical figure. The examples and lifestyles of the saints are in and of themselves without sufficient authority to act as appropriate guides for morality. "Even the Holy One of the Gospel must be compared with our ideal of moral perfection before He is recognized as such," says Kant.[16]

Various explanations have been offered for why figures like Kant were so concerned to distance "ethics" from "theology." The most frequently heard argument has to do with the so-called wars of religion of the sixteenth and seventeenth centuries that erupted in the aftermath of the Protestant Reformation. The fragmentation of Christianity, it is said, spawned religiously motivated violence that threatened civic order and social harmony.[17] Philosophers like Kant considered it an important service to society to provide a foundation for ethics independent of any particular religious perspective, precisely because appeal to religion only results in conflict and cruelty. Rather, "a completely isolated metaphysics of morals, mixed with no anthropology, no theology, no physics . . . is not only an indispensible substrate of all theoretically sound and definite knowledge of duties; it is also a desideratum of the highest importance to the actual fulfillment of its precepts."[18] A central goal of the Enlightenment project was to reject any relationship between morality and religion as divisive and to establish a foundation for morality on the basis of universal truths of reason that are available and accessible to all. "Our common human reason," says Kant, ". . . seeks this information in order to escape from the perplexity of opposing claims and to avoid the danger of losing all genuine moral principles."[19]

16. Ibid., 25. It is not the case that Kant did not believe in God. He had been greatly influenced by the pietistic upbringing he received from his parents. It is the case, as we shall explore below, that Kant's moral outlook had dramatic consequences for how God is to be understood in relation to the moral life.

17. Jeffrey Stout expresses this outlook: "Any point of view in which religious considerations or conceptions of the good remained dominant was, in the early modern context, incapable of providing a basis for the reasonable and peaceful resolution of social conflict. Incompatible appeals to authority seemed equally reasonable, and therefore equally suspect, as well as thoroughly useless as vehicles of rational persuasion. . . . But the social consequences were more telling, for they included the devastation of the religious wars." See his *Flight from Authority*, 235.

18. Kant, "Foundations of the Metaphysics of Morals," 27.

19. Ibid., 22. It might be said that the so-called New Atheism represented by the likes of Richard Dawkins testifies to the lingering presence of these concerns. See his *God Delusion*, 262–78.

The standard account for why figures like Kant sought to drive such a sharp wedge between "theology and ethics" has come under significant criticism of late.[20] The task here, though, is to examine what understanding of the moral life Kant derives from such an appeal to the "universal" ("common human reason") rather than the "contingent" (e.g., religion). For it is this account of the moral life, MacIntyre argues, that has ironically led to the emotivism of our day and the moral debates that seem never to find resolution.

What is clear for Kant is that we determine what is good, neither on the basis of character nor consequences, but *by virtue of a good will that uses reason to identify its duty*: "The first proposition of morality is that to have moral worth an action must be done from duty."[21] Kant sees morality as neither *aretaic* (having to do with excellence of character) nor *utilitarian* (with a focus on the consequences of one's actions), but as deontological (from the Greek *deos*, "duty" or "obligation"). Matters of character—Kant mentions courage, resoluteness, and perseverance—are too much like power, riches, and honor; they are not evenly distributed among humanity and can be spoiled by misuse apart from the guidance of a good will. This good will, further, "is not good because of what it effects or accomplishes or because of its adequacy to achieve some proposed end; it is good only because of its willing." The consequences of our actions cannot always be foreseen and are often determined by factors beyond our control. Character and consequences are contingent matters; a will determined to perform duty as guided by universal reason (and only such a will!) "may be esteemed as good of itself without regard to anything else."[22]

---

20. See Cavanaugh, "Fire Strong Enough to Consume"; Cavanaugh, *Theopolitical Imagination*, 20–42. Even more recently, see his *Myth of Religious Violence*. Cavanaugh provides a compelling argument against the standard account of a modern secular state that arose to deliver fragmented Europe from the conflicts of religiously inspired violence. He argues, to the contrary, that the "wars of religion" were themselves expressions of political and economic factors that created a modern state that needed to recast religion as a set of privately held beliefs without explicit political relevance. The conflicts known as the "wars of religion" were so described by *politiques* who had an interest in depicting the state as savior from the irrational violence of religion that should be relegated to the arena of the personal and private. As Cavanaugh puts it, "revulsion to killing in the name of religion [was] used to legitimize the transfer of ultimate loyalty to the modern state" ("Fire Strong Enough to Consume," 397).

21. Kant, "Foundations of the Metaphysics of Morals," 16.

22. Ibid., 9–13. Kant (9) insists that this is true for this sensible world and for any reality beyond this sensible world.

But what counts for this reason? What criteria are available for us to determine our moral duty? MacIntyre summarizes those criteria that seem to be operative for Kant: "It is of the essence of reason that it lays down principles which are universal, categorical, and internally consistent. Hence a rational morality will lay down principles which both can and ought to be held by all men, independent of circumstances and conditions, and which could be obeyed by every rational agent on every occasion."[23] These criteria find expression in what is known as Kant's "categorical imperative," which Kant gives when he says, "I should never act in such a way that I could not also will that my maxim should be a universal law."[24] Kant's statement requires some explanation.

First, Kant wants to underscore what he means by duty with the term "categorical." To this he will contrast the word "hypothetical." We use hypothetical statements all the time when we introduce possible actions and agendas with the word "if": "*If* you want to become a concert pianist, you *should* practice, practice, practice." There is no moral obligation common to all humanity for us to become concert pianists. While someone with such skills may be admired for her musicianship, it would be odd for those of us without such competency to feel shame or guilt for choosing some other course in life. Kant insists, though, that truth-telling or keeping one's promises are actions of a different kind from playing Mozart well. "You *should* practice your piano lessons" is an imperative that makes sense when associated with the hypothetical possibility "if you want to become a concert pianist." There are, however, no "ifs" associated with "You *should* tell the truth." For Kant, telling the truth is a moral duty that is "categorical" in nature. Whether you want to be a concert pianist, a schoolteacher, a small business owner—in whatever situation you find yourself, regardless of the circumstances or consequences—"You should tell the truth." Truth-telling is the moral duty of every rational being.[25]

How does Kant know that? Some of us might point to the Ten Commandments and its prohibition against bearing false witness as authoritative (Exod 20:16). The Apostle Paul urges his readers, "Speak truth, each one of you with his neighbor" (Eph 4:25). But Kant is not going to appeal to divine command or apostolic instruction to argue his point. Morality must find its justification independently of any appeal to religious

23. MacIntyre, *After Virtue*, 45.

24. Kant, "Foundations of the Metaphysics of Morals," 18.

25. See ibid., 31–32, for the contrast between hypothetical and categorical imperatives.

matters. This is where the categorical imperative comes in, however. Kant does not provide us with his own Ten Commandments, or any specific list of moral obligations. What he intends to offer is a way of determining, or testing, whether or not any proposed action is a categorical (not hypothetical) duty.

This test is the categorical imperative: *"Always act according to that maxim whose universality as law you can at the same time will."*[26] In this test may be found the criteria of universality and consistency. According to Kant, what is rational will be both universal and consistent (noncontradictory). Perhaps the best way to understand how these criteria operate for Kant is by way of illustration. If we want to discover whether any proposed action on our part is a moral obligation, we must first state the proposed action in the form of a law, or rule, or maxim. For example, if you need five dollars from a friend but have no intention of paying it back, the maxim might be, "You should promise to pay money back to your friend without any intention of fulfilling the promise," or more briefly, "You should not keep your promises." Kant's theory requires that we state such a maxim in the form of a universal law—"Everyone should at all times in every instance not keep promises."

Now comes the demand for consistency. Kant requires us to be willing to universalize our proposed maxim. Could we actually will promise-breaking to be the universal norm for everybody in every instance? Kant does not believe we could do that. Why? Kant tells us: "I immediately see that I could will the lie but not a universal law to lie. For with such a law there would be no promises at all, inasmuch as it would be futile to make a pretense of my intention with regard to future actions to those who would not believe this pretense or—if they overhastily did so—would pay me back in my own coin. Thus my maxim would necessarily destroy itself as soon as it was made a universal law."[27] It is irrational to will what is inconsistent. To will universal deception is inconsistent with the hoped for gain that lying seeks. How so? Because if lying is the universal law, then it is simply understood by everyone that no promise can be believed and our deceptions either get us nowhere or eventually come back to bite us.

Kant tests several possible actions by the categorical imperative—lying, suicide, a life of self-indulgence, indifference to others in need—and offers that his theory serves as "the canon of the moral estimation of our

26. Ibid., 55.
27. Ibid., 19.

action generally."[28] While he does provide different ways of stating the categorical imperative, his basic assertion should be clear. The categorical imperative provides the individual, autonomous moral agent with everything needed for the moral life.

Almost everything, that is. While Kant insists that what he calls "positive religion" (religious faith that appeals to authoritative revelation) must not serve as the foundation for the moral life, Kant does ultimately make an appeal to God in order to safeguard his moral theory. In fact, Kant must "postulate," or presuppose the necessity of, three truths for his moral theory to succeed. First, he must assert the practical necessity of the freedom of the individual to act according to reason. In contrast to the mechanistic models of human nature that were increasingly popular in the seventeenth and eighteenth centuries,[29] Kant upholds the freedom of the rational agent to act in accordance with duty, otherwise we are reduced to acting solely on the basis of unreliable inclinations. It is only when we act according to reason, for Kant, that we are actually free. Since we are morally obligated to act in accordance with reason, therefore, we must possess some degree of freedom to act in accordance with reason. If this sounds somewhat circular, it is. That is why Kant will "postulate," as a matter of practical necessity, freedom: "The will of a rational being can be a will of its own only under the idea of freedom, and therefore in a practical point of view such a will must be ascribed to all rational beings."[30]

One major problem presents itself to Kant, though, in his insistence on the fundamentally rational nature of morality. Kant believes that as rational beings we can discover and do our moral duty, and this is to be expected from every one of us regardless of circumstances of life or consequences of action. It is the case, though, as most of us have had occasion to find out, that sometimes those consequences can be unrewarding. "Doing the right thing" does not always meet with obvious benefit. Kant is well aware of this. He affirms that "in practical principle we may at least conceive as possible a natural and necessary connection between the consciousness of morality and the expectation of a proportionate happiness as its result."[31] The painful truth, however, is that such a "proportionate happiness" does not always arrive within the confines of "the

28. Ibid., 39–41.

29. Kant ("What Is Enlightenment?" 92) insists that humans are "now more than machines."

30. Kant, "Foundations of the Metaphysics of Morals," 67.

31. Kant, *Critique of Practical Reason*, 342.

world of sense," that is, in the here and now. Furthermore, the ultimate achievement of a "will determined by the moral law" is the realization of the *summum bonum* (the "highest good")—"the perfect accordance of the mind with the moral law . . . a perfection of which no rational being of the sensible world is capable at any moment of his existence."[32]

Here is a problem for Kant. The moral life, he insists, must be established solely on the basis of the universal truths of pure reason. According to Kant, though, fulfillment of one's duty does not always meet with what is to be rationally expected—proportionate reward. Add the recognition that this life of moral obligation will not find ultimate realization in this world and the rationality of the whole system comes under question. How rational is a universe that does not reward rational behavior? How rational is a world that denies fulfillment of what is its only real good—the good will guided by reason?

Along with freedom, therefore, Kant will require two additional "postulates of practical reason"—the immortality of the soul and the existence of God. Thus, according to Kant, while the "critical principles of pure reason" do not allow for such, "the practical interests of morality require . . . God, freedom, and immortality."[33] Kant argues that achievement of the *summum bonum* is itself a practical necessity for the will "determined by the moral law," but since such will not be achieved in the present life, progress toward that goal "is only possible on the supposition of an endless duration of the existence and personality of the same rational being (which is called the immortality of the soul). The *summum bonum*, then, practically is only possible on the supposition of the immortality of the soul; consequently this immortality, being inseparably connected with the moral law, is a postulate of pure practical reason."[34] For Kant, finally, the postulate of immortality "must lead to the supposition of the existence of a cause adequate to this effect; in other words, it must postulate *the existence of God.*"[35] There must be a God, a being powerful enough to ensure the soul's survival of death; otherwise Kant's entire moral philosophy crumbles under the weight of internal inconsistency. So, while God can in no way be appealed to so as to determine the character and content of the moral life, God finally makes an appearance

32. Ibid., 344.

33. Kant, *Critique of Pure Reason*, 10.

34. Kant, *Critique of Practical Reason*, 344.

35. Ibid., 345.

for Kant, in order to secure the character and content of the moral life first achieved without reference to God.

In brief, for Kant, the moral life is primarily the activity of the autonomous individual who discovers and acts on what reason dictates as morally obligatory. The principles of universality and consistency, summarized in the categorical imperative, provide the test for assessing the rationality of any proposed action. While pure reason cannot establish the realities of freedom, immortality, and God, such realities must be "postulated" for the practical reason that the life of moral obligation only makes sense if we regard these postulates as true.

The Failure of the Enlightenment Project

Whatever else may be said of Kant's contribution to the Enlightenment project, he certainly did seek to cover all his bases. Whether he did so in a coherent and sustainable fashion is another thing. He clearly offered a major and influential moral theory that has continued to have great impact on our world. Contemporary philosopher Charles Taylor observes that Kant's moral theory has "bulked large in the self-consciousness of moderns over the last two centuries, and has fed our faith in ourselves as a reforming civilization, capable of reaching higher moral goals than any previous age has."[36] Wyndy Corbin Reuschling notes the affinity that even many evangelical Christians have felt for Kant's outlook, but herself warns of the deleterious effects of a viewpoint that ultimately co-opts both God and Scripture for the pursuit of an agenda where neither God nor the Bible are really necessary.[37] MacIntyre argues that the efforts of Kant and others of his era were inevitable failures and comprise the disaster that has left our contemporary moral landscape mired in confusion. What went wrong?

We might first challenge Kant on his own grounds by asking the simple question, "Does the categorical imperative deliver the goods?" That is, are the criteria of universality and consistency sufficient for safeguarding a rational morality that can adequately guide the good will intent on performing its duty? The quick answer to that is no. MacIntyre gives a number of reasons for the failure.

36. Taylor, *Sources of the Self*, 367.
37. See her *Reviving Evangelical Ethics*, 40–41, 67–72.

First, MacIntyre offers that "many immoral and trivial non-moral maxims are vindicated by Kant's test." We might be willing to hedge our bets on universalizing "Keep all your promises throughout your whole life except one." The true believer might be ready to universalize this: "Persecute all those who hold false religious beliefs." What good would be threatened if we were to insist, "Everyone, everywhere must eat mussels on Mondays in March?" All these proposed maxims pass Kant's test, but few of us would consider matters of mussel eating in March a moral duty. Yet, if Kant's categorical imperative is the exclusive means by which rational acts, and thus our moral obligations, are discovered, on what basis might we object that matters of mussel eating in March are trivial and not in and of themselves of moral significance?[38] To make that judgment would require a reference point beyond the categorical imperative. And yet, Kant insists no such reference point is available.

A second criticism offered by MacIntyre gets to the heart of Kant's claim to provide the foundation for moral obligation strictly on the basis of universal truths of reason. Kant and others of the modern era (e.g., David Hume, d. 1776) made one fateful move in their concern to provide sure and certain grounds for morality—they sought to establish the foundation for morality on the basis of human nature as they understood it. For Kant, that meant human beings defined by the rational will. At the same time, Kant and most other Enlightenment figures were quite traditional concerning the content of the morality they sought to defend— truth-telling, promise-keeping, industry, beneficence toward others, etc. MacIntyre points out, though, that this traditional content of morality actually reflects reliance on a moral outlook fundamentally at odds with the Enlightenment agenda. From the days of ancient Greece throughout the years of Christian-influenced Western civilization, these moral commitments were understood, not to reflect human nature *as it is*, but as challenges to and disciplines of human nature in a necessary process of transformation to a "human-nature-as-it-could-be-if-it-realized-its-*telos* [goal]."[39]

The idea that human beings have one overarching purpose or goal (*telos*), though, is too tied to the contingencies of religious faith in Kant's estimation (this religion believes that humans are destined for the blessed vision of God, that religion believes that humans are destined for

38. MacIntyre, *After Virtue*, 45–46.
39. Ibid., 53.

nirvanic obliteration), so morality cannot rest on some sense of shared *telos*. Instead, the conventional content of morality was to find a new setting within the confines of human-nature-as-it-is. The problem, MacIntyre notes, was that since the injunctions of this conventional morality were "originally at home in a scheme in which their purpose was to correct, improve, and educate that human nature, they are clearly not going to be such as could be deduced from true statements about human nature or justified in some other way by appealing to its characteristics." "Hence," says MacIntyre, "the eighteenth-century moral philosophers engaged in what was an inevitably unsuccessful project; for they did indeed attempt to find a rational basis for their moral beliefs in a particular understanding of human nature, while inheriting a set of moral injunctions on the one hand and a conception of human nature on the other which had been expressly designed to be discrepant with each other."[40] Later critics, such as Nietzsche, would note the arbitrary character of Kant's moral preferences and call his hand on this, identifying Kant as a closet theologian, as it were.[41]

Another problem derives from the Enlightenment abandonment of a sense of shared *telos* for human existence. MacIntyre argues that such a move renders any account of the moral life incoherent, for only when we have a sense of what humans are for do we have a way to offer any moral evaluation. MacIntyre illustrates the connection between purpose and evaluation by pointing to a watch. How do we know if a watch is a good watch? The only way we can know that is with reference to the purpose of a watch. "To call a watch good is to say that it is the kind of watch which someone would choose who wanted a watch to keep time accurately. . . . The presupposition of this use of 'good' is that every type of item which is appropriate to call good or bad . . . has, as a matter of fact, some given purpose or function."[42] If the notion of purpose or function is abandoned, or up for grabs to infinite variety, it becomes difficult to know how to evaluate a watch. For James Bond the criteria might be its explosive effects; for a diva, its fashion value. If there is no definitive sense of what human beings are for, a sense of shared *telos*, then we have lost any frame of reference for moral evaluation of human beings and

40. Ibid., 55.

41. Nietzsche, "The Antichrist," §10. Subsequent citations of this work will be designated *A* followed by a section number. Nietzsche (*A*, §10) taunts that "Kant's success is merely a theologian's success."

42. MacIntyre, *After Virtue*, 59.

their actions. As MacIntyre insists, "Once the notion of essential human purposes or functions disappears from morality, it begins to appear implausible to treat moral judgments as factual statements." Instead, such judgments increasingly take on the appearance of personal preference and statements of moral evaluation simply become "forms of expression for an emotivist self which . . . has lost its linguistic as well as its practical way in the world."[43]

The difficulties with Kant's moral theory identified so far have to do with the inherent plausibility of his outlook. When we insist on raising the issue of "theology and ethics," however, the concerns become even more serious. There have been those, as Nietzsche pointed out, eager to find in Kant a surreptitious path "back to the old ideal"—that is, to a faith that by the eighteenth and nineteenth centuries had faced increasing skepticism and critical assessment among Europe's cultured despisers.[44] Does not Kant, after all, believe in God—even *need* God to give legitimacy to his moral system? Christians need to ask ourselves, though, whether the God revealed in the gospel rightly serves as a prop for any moral system constructed on its own terms and in deliberate distance from the story that reveals the character and intent of the God whose will might not be confined or conformed to the parameters of Kantian rationality. What fruit has the Kantian split between theology and ethics borne?

The concern to drive a wedge between theology and ethics was one (likely the chief) expression of the general concern to escape contingency and particularity in a flight to the universal. How did this work? For one thing, as a function of his denial of the contingent features of character and cultural context, Kant had to narrow what counts as "ethics" to a very specific concern—moral judgment. Kant's concept of ethics looms large whenever and wherever the focus of ethics is reduced to "what should I do?" It is precisely for such a question, however, that the categorical imperative was formulated. Ethics in this view is all about the autonomous individual, who is understood strictly as an abstract will, guided solely by universal reason, determined simply to perform according to the canons of universality and consistency. The focus on decision is necessary because matters of character are denied their significance. "What should I do?" becomes the sole issue without regard to the character of the one asking the question. At least one problem becomes apparent at this point.

43. Ibid., 59–60.
44. Nietzsche, *A* §10.

As Emmanuel Katongole observes, Kant's flight from the world of experience, of tradition, of culture, of heritage, leaves behind "all contingent commitments and engagements, such as being a father, a mother, a soldier or a student, etc." Such a move, Katongole insists, is "to leave behind any interesting reasons for acting one way or the other."[45] Through his suspicion of the contingent, Kant strips human beings of those relationships and commitments that shape identity and character, those features of our lives that have formed our moral selves in one way or the other so that we live one way or another.

To deny the importance of such matters for the moral life is, at the same time, both to make us less and more than what we are. Kant's "unencumbered self," the moral agent stripped of history and context, stands isolated and deprived of the loves, passions, desires, and commitments that remind us of what is at stake in acting one way versus another. On the other hand, this autonomous will guided only by reason, untouched by the contingencies of experience and creaturely existence, Kant elevates to unprecedented heights. Kant insists, "Nothing in the world—indeed nothing even beyond the world—can possibly be conceived which could be called good without qualification except a good will."[46] The language here is quite dramatic. Saint Anselm of the eleventh century had described God as "that beyond which nothing greater can be conceived." Now it is the good will of the autonomous individual that shares that quality.[47] Kant claims that the good will, unconditioned by the limits of history, culture, context—all those features that very much make us who we are—can know for itself how to distinguish good from evil. To some this sounds suspiciously close to the serpent's offer that humanity can leave behind the constraints of our creaturely status and know as God knows. At this point the good will has become "an idol, the self made into a God."[48]

Another way of looking at it, though, is that while Kant has both diminished and exalted humanity, perhaps he has done the same to God. Kant provided a measure of relief for some by his argument on the practical necessity for the existence of God. He even turned upside down the increasingly popular argument against God's existence due to the reality of evil. No longer could it be argued that the suffering of the righteous

45. See his *Beyond Universal Reason*, 23.
46. Kant, "Foundations," 9.
47. Bayer, *Freedom in Response*, 140.
48. Ibid., 144. See also Schneewind, *Invention of Autonomy*, 512–13.

mitigates against God's existence. "If the good suffer, Kant argues, the intrinsic validity of the ethical commandment demands that there be a god who will rectify this intrinsic disorder; otherwise, not only does the existence of god become questionable, but human ethical life itself becomes absurd."[49] We need to be clear, though, about the ramifications of this sort of argument. It is not the case that Kant draws ethical implications from the existence and character of God. "In Kant's world, ethics makes the idea of God possible; the idea of God does not make ethics possible."[50] In this context, God is not the good Creator of a good creation who freely addresses God's creatures with grace and peace. Instead, "He is a concept made by ourselves as an expression of moral resolution and of refusal to come to terms with the way the world is."[51] It might be comforting to postulate a divine being capable of resolving the contradictions of Kantian moral theory. Such a move, however, leads quickly to Ludwig Feuerbach's insistence that the notion of God is simply the projection onto the heavens of humanity failure's to achieve our own ideals. Beyond that is Nietzsche's delightful observation that "the greatest suspicion of a 'truth' should arise when feelings of pleasure enter the discussion. . . . The proof of 'pleasure' is a proof of 'pleasure'—nothing else."[52]

Bernd Wannenwetsch asks the simple question, "Where does ethics begin? With what we do? With our own judgments? Or by acquiescing in what God does, and God's judgment?"[53] We have explored Immanuel Kant's response to this question and MacIntyre's insistence that Kant's project has seriously failed. The effort did not fail simply because it sought to divorce theology and ethics, but the project's failure might display what is at stake when such occurs. As we move to Paul's Letter to the Ephesians, the effort here is not to pit Kant against Paul and to pronounce Paul the winner by default. The concern has been, though, to illustrate the significance of the Kantian move to sever theology from ethics. How profoundly that move has affected our culture can be noticed in the widespread emotivism of our day. The Kantian split between theology and ethics has even determined how many have engaged matters of Pauline ethics. We will need to explore Ephesians with a cautious outlook, bear-

49. Buckley, *At the Origins of Modern Atheism*, 329.

50. Long, *Goodness of God*, 63.

51. Bayer, *Freedom in Response*, 142–43.

52. Nietzsche, *A* §50.

53. Wannenwetsch, *Political Worship*, 5.

ing in mind that we do not live, as Kant suggested, unaffected by our culture, our heritage, or the influence of history, particularly the influence of Kant. Ironically, our confidence that we can lift ourselves above contingency to some disinterested, objective standpoint so as to critically examine all our options, is but one manifestation of the still significant impact of the Enlightenment project.

WHAT IS GOD DOING? CHRISTIAN ETHICS AND THE DIVINE INITIATIVE

Ephesians will not sustain any approach to the moral life separate from the character, actions, and will of God made known through Jesus Christ. Ephesians underscores the divine initiative, and thus the theocentric character of its vision of the moral life, in several important ways.[54] Some of these ways are reflected in the overall shape of the letter, while others are on display in specific things Paul has to say in his letter. One way or another, questions concerning the moral life as presented in Ephesians will be raised in light of the prior question, "What is God doing?"

"Theology and Ethics" in Ephesians?

Peter O'Brien observes and challenges the way in which Paul's Letter to the Ephesians is usually analyzed: "The Letter to the Ephesians falls into two distinct though related halves: chapters 1–3 and 4–6. The first has been loosely called 'theological' or 'doctrinal,' while the second has been referred to as 'ethical,' although neither of these descriptions fully reflects the content of each half or the interplay between them."[55] To some degree, this twofold division does reflect a feature of the structure of Ephesians;

---

54. Richard Burridge argues that Paul's "'God-centered ethics' is more specifically a Christ-centered ethics" and that "there is almost universal scholarly agreement" that Pauline ethics is firmly grounded in his Christology. See his *Imitating Jesus*, 89. We begin with a focus on the theocentric character of Christian ethics, then highlight God's redemptive work in Christ, not because the latter can ultimately be distinguished from the former, but simply to reflect the narrative flow of Paul's teachings as expressed in passages like Eph 1:3–14. Of course, there are those who draw a greater distinction between a theocentric ethics and one informed by God's redemptive work in Christ, but that is not Paul's agenda. See below on James Gustafson's *Ethics from a Theocentric Perspective.*

55. O'Brien, *Letter to the Ephesians*, 66.

the first half of the book clearly contains much material that often goes by the designation "theology" and the second half certainly contains a great deal of what biblical scholars call "*parenesis*"—moral admonition.

It is inadequate to say, though, as Harold Hoehner does, that "Ephesians, similar to other Pauline letters, is divided into two main parts: doctrine or theology (chaps. 1–3) and duties or ethics (chaps. 4–6)."[56] Part of the problem with an analysis of this sort is that it obviously echoes the narrowing of ethics to a Kantian emphasis on "duty" and reflects a view of ethics as concerned primarily with answering the question, "What should I do?" This sort of standard division of the letter into two halves, "theology" and "ethics," all too easily fits into an approach to Christian ethics that draws a Kantian line between the religious features of the letter that can be discarded (chaps. 1–3) and the ethical dimensions that perhaps could be argued for and defended on other grounds (chaps. 4–6).[57]

In fact, this is precisely how some have treated the parenetic sections of the letters of Paul—as conventional moral admonitions that are at best only loosely related to the gospel Paul proclaims in the more "doctrinal" sections of his letters. As Burridge puts it, when we view the material of Paul's letters as divided into doctrine vs. ethics, "the question immediately arises about the relationship of this [ethical] material to the earlier doctrinal teaching and whether it is separate from it."[58] One New Testament scholar, Hans Dieter Betz, voices a common conclusion held by many, "that Paul does not provide [his readers] with a specifically Christian ethic. The Christian is addressed as an educated and responsible person. He is expected to do no more than what would be expected

56. Hoehner, *Ephesians*, 61. Roy R. Jeal even insists on a "disparity between the two halves of Ephesians." See his *Integrating Theology and Ethics*, 8.

57. Jeal's analysis (*Integrating Theology and Ethics*, 8) seems to assume that "ethics" is primarily about "behavioral directions" delivered in a hortatory mode. David G. Horrell seems to be warning against this outlook when he says, "Our much more modern focus on the cognitive dimension of (often privatized) religious faith can lead us to an anachronistic treatment of texts like Paul's letters as primarily documents outlining, correcting, and instructing their recipients about the content of what they are to believe, with certain sections (the 'ethical' sections) concerned with the consequent practical instructions." See his *Solidarity and Difference*, 91. More recently Douglas A. Campbell has voiced an outlook that resonates with much of the present study. See his *Deliverance of God*. Campbell (951 n. 36) insists, "It is difficult to find material in Paul's letters that is *not* in some sense ethical. . . . Even descriptive statements concerning the movements of Paul and his co-workers usually contain ethical implications. Liturgical acts of doxology and prayer implicitly urge imitation as well."

58. Burridge, *Imitating Jesus*, 98.

of any other educated person in the Hellenistic culture of the time."[59] On this view, there is no intrinsic relationship between the gospel Paul proclaims and the way of life envisioned in Paul's letters. If one wants to keep the doctrine and lose the ethics, there will be no harm done to Paul's essential message. Alternatively, one might as well be a Kantian (or in Paul's day, a Stoic) as a Christian in terms of advocating the ethical teachings found in the letters of Paul, for they bear no necessary relationship to Paul's account of God's actions in and through Jesus Christ.[60] An alternative analysis of what Paul is doing, one not so reflective of Kant's agenda, provides a different assessment of what Paul is saying in Ephesians.[61]

Saying and Seeing in Ephesians 1

What if we did not begin with the narrow view of ethics as concerned strictly with "what should I do?" Stanley Hauerwas highlights some concerns that strongly resonate with features of Ephesians that could broaden our understanding of both Paul's letter and the nature of Christian ethics. Hauerwas complains that the focus on "what should I do" in contemporary ethics "has merely mirrored men's illusions of power and grandeur." Targeting Kant, he insists, "By making man's will the source of all value we have turned away from the classical insight of Christian and philosopher alike that the measure of moral goodness ultimately lies outside ourselves."[62] Hauerwas offers a corrective to this conventional approach to the moral life and insists that we begin with matters of vision, not action.

More specifically, Hauerwas wants us to consider the important and inextricable relationship between seeing, saying, and living. "The moral life," he says, "is more than thinking clearly and making rational choices. It is a way of seeing the world." If this is so, though, "once the question

---

59. See his *Galatians*, 292.

60. This approach to interpreting Paul predates Betz, having origins in nineteenth-century biblical scholarship; for discussion see Horrell, *Solidarity and Difference*, 19–24.

61. Over forty years ago one of the most significant works of Pauline ethics exposed the weakness of any approach to Paul that makes hard distinctions between his theology and his ethical instruction. See Furnish, *Theology and Ethics in Paul*, 98–111. That biblical scholars like Hoehner could still find such a division in the letters of Paul testifies to the grip Kant has even now on much of Western civilization.

62. Hauerwas, *Vision and Virtue*, 31. Hauerwas is challenging Kant's reliance on, in MacIntyre's terms, "human-nature-as-it-is."

of the ethical is broadened to include vision, we can comprehend that being a Christian involves more than just making decisions; it is a way of attending to the world. It is learning 'to see' the world under the mode of the divine."[63] We make a fundamental mistake if we approach the moral life first in terms of a set of "Thou shalts" or "Thou shalt nots." The first task of Christian ethics, according to Hauerwas, "is to help us rightly envision the world. . . . In other words, the enterprise of Christian ethics primarily helps us to see. We can act only within the world we can envision, and we can envision the world rightly as we are trained to see." He insists, however, "We do not come to see merely by looking, but must develop disciplined skills through initiation into that community that attempts to live faithful to the story of God."[64] We live in the world in light of the world that we live in. To live in the world faithfully, we must learn to see it truthfully. To see the world truthfully, however, requires a capacity for proper description. To describe properly, further, requires the necessary linguistic skills—skills we only learn through participation in a community itself shaped by a truthful story. In Ephesians, Paul invites his readers to participate in a set of linguistic practices that provides the truthful account of God's relation to the world, enabling his readers to see truthfully and thus to live faithfully.

In fact, emphases on saying and seeing appear consecutively in Ephesians 1. In the opening doxology, or eulogy, of Eph 1:3–14 Paul invites his readers (in 1:3) to respond to God's having initially blessed us (*eulogēsas*) with every blessing (*eulogia*) afforded by the Holy Spirit, by blessing God in return (*eulogētos*).[65] The repetition of the language of "blessing" in English translations of v. 3 is an accurate reflection of the repetition by Paul of terms for speech-acts of praise to God.[66] Paul here encourages proper speech to God in response to how believers have already been addressed by God.

---

63. Ibid., 36, 45–46.

64. Hauerwas, *Peaceable Kingdom*, 29–30.

65. The repeated use of the first-person plural pronouns "us" and "we" (vv. 3, 4, 5, 6, 7, 8, 9, 11, 12, 14) in this passage clearly indicates Paul's concern to invite his readers' participation in voicing the doxology and assuming that the story told here of God's blessings of election, adoption, redemption, forgiveness, and hope is their story.

66. Richard S. Briggs describes "blessing" as one of the archetypal forms of speech-acts in the Bible. See his "Speech-Act Theory," 76. The significance of speech-act theory for understanding Ephesians will be explored more fully in the discussion of the liturgical character of Christian ethics.

Next, in 1:15–23, Paul turns from praise to prayer, and he prays specifically on behalf of his readers "that the eyes of your hearts would be enlightened, that you would know what is the hope of your calling" (1:18). What is interesting to note here is that there are several parallels between the "blessings" God has bestowed on believers, as celebrated in the doxology of 1:3–14, and features of Paul's prayer in 1:15–23.[67] The language of "calling" (*klēsis*) in v. 18, for example, echoes the language of God's choice in 1:4 (*exelexato*). "Inheritance" (*klēronomias*), a term that Paul uses in 1:14 to speak of what believers will one day enjoy, is used in 1:19 to speak of God's present possession of God's people. To see with the enlightened eyes for which Paul prays requires a knowledge of God that depends on the Spirit's gift of wisdom (*sophia* in 1:17), a wisdom Paul had described in the doxology (*sophia* in 1:8) as an expression of God's overflowing grace.

The concern here is not so much with matters of vocabulary, but simply to point out that in the praise of 1:3–14 Paul gives his readers language by which they can, as a community in worship, describe how it is that God has been at work in their lives. In the prayer of 1:15–23 Paul asks God that his readers be able to take this way of describing what God is doing and see how their lives have been drawn into the arena of divine action. Paul invites his readers both to say and see in ways that celebrate and affirm the significance of God's gracious work.

Before we examine in more detail the specific ways in which Paul describes the divine initiative, the ways God is at work in the world and in the lives of believers, the issue of why Paul is concerned with saying and seeing is important for us to consider. It is simply the case that the account offered here of how God is at work in the world is one that was (and is) strongly contested. For Paul's readers to say and see as Paul intends is for them to embrace a vision of reality and a corresponding way of life that creates great distance from the prevailing conventions and practices, the "sacred canopy," of the day. As Hauerwas insists, we do not see merely by looking; we must be trained to see properly; and one of the

---

67. Commentators on Ephesians regularly note the parallels of style and themes (more than have been indicated here) between the doxology of 1:3–14 and the prayer of 1:15–23. See, for example, Lincoln, *Ephesians*, 50. O'Brien (*Ephesians*, 125) says, "The intercession is a prayer for the realization of the blessings of the eulogy [doxology] in the lives of the readers."

most significant demands of truthful speech and vision is to resist the attractive proposal that the conventional is what defines the real.[68]

Among Paul's initial readers the conventional account of "the way things are" held persuasive power over the lives of millions. This account has to do with two intertwined institutions that provided the basic framework for daily existence for the inhabitants of a world dominated by Rome—the related entities of the patron-client system and the imperial cult of the first century. We need to understand the specifics of the praise and prayer of Ephesians 1 as challenging the "sacred canopy" that gave sense and structure to the everyday lives of those among whom Paul's initial readers lived and from which Paul seeks to "dislodge" his readers.

Briefly, the patron-client system of the Greco-Roman world was the system regulating the exchange of goods and services necessary for survival and economic well-being. In a hierarchically stratified set of relationships, clients of lower social status served the interests and public honor of higher-level patrons, while the patrons protected the economic and legal interests of their clients. Of course, the chief patron of all society was the emperor, considered the "Great Benefactor" to whom all the empire owed proper honor.[69] The matter of honor is where the imperial cult comes in. What better way to express honor and loyalty to the emperor (and thus be in line for imperial benefits) than to worship the emperor as a god. The imperial patronage system according divine honors to Caesar constituted the basic lived environment of the first century Greco-Roman world. In fact, "Recent studies by classical historians and archaeologists . . . find that honors and festivals for the emperor were not only widespread, but pervaded the public life, particularly in the cities of Greece and Asia Minor, the very area of Paul's mission."[70]

For those who first read Ephesians, daily life was immersed within a set of claims and practices that intermingled the concerns for survival, participation in society, political power, and the religious environment of emperor worship. Walsh and Keesmaat observe that the symbols of Roman power, the image of Caesar as well as other symbols, regularly confronted the early Christians "in the market, on coins, in the gymnasium, at the gladiatorial games, on jewelry, goblets, lamps, and paintings. The sovereign rule of Caesar was simply assumed to be the divine plan for

68. Hauerwas, *Vision and Virtue*, 102.

69. See Lampe, "Paul, Patrons, and Clients," 488–523.

70. Horsley, "General Introduction," 4.

the peace and order of the cosmos. Of course, this is the way the world works."[71] At least that is what Rome wanted its subjects to believe.

If the conventional practices and beliefs of the wider culture defined everyday reality in terms of the imperial patronage system, with divine honors going to the emperor, then to say and see in accordance with the speech and vision of Ephesians 1 is to undergo a drastic conversion of perspective and commitment. To say with Paul the eulogy of Eph 1:3–14 is to insist that the true source of good is not the emperor, but the God and Father who calls us in Christ to be holy and blameless before him in love (1:3–4). To see as Paul prays that we would see in 1:15–23 is to see that Christ, not the emperor, is enthroned above all rulers and authorities and powers and principalities (1:19–22). Paul asserts that the Christ who died at the hands of the Romans on the most extreme symbol of Roman power is now, by virtue of having been raised from the dead, sovereign over all other power claimants and is God's channel of bestowing divine blessing. This clearly entails a different way of saying and seeing.

For the initial readers of Ephesians to say and see in line with Paul's praise and prayer would obviously set them at odds with conventional assessments of the day as to "the way things are" (this goes far in explaining Paul's location in prison when writing this letter). The challenge might be present for today's readers as well. Our challenge, though, might be of a different sort—at least at first. To read Ephesians in particular, and the New Testament in general, as offering political commentary on the claims of the Roman Empire is a strange experience for many contemporary Christians. We are heirs to an Enlightenment project that did its best to privatize the Christian faith as an inward experience of personal beliefs. It is hard for us to realize that such a concept of "religion" was absolutely foreign to a first-century outlook. What Neil Elliott says of Romans could also be said of Ephesians: "If we do not immediately hear the counter-imperial aspects of Paul's letter, perhaps it is because we are predisposed, by the constricted, privatized, and domesticated contexts in which Paul's letters are most usually read, to perceive in them only a narrow bandwidth of what we consider religious discourse."[72] We are accustomed to the notion of Christianity as all about personal faith that assures of eternal salvation. The Christian faith must certainly be personal and the resurrection of Christ from the dead is the promise of a fel-

71. Walsh and Keesmaat, *Colossians Remixed*, 83.
72. See his *Arrogance of Nations*, 9.

lowship with God that is stronger than death. It is also the case, though, that the resurrection of Christ from the dead is the clearest assertion of a sovereignty superior to and of a different sort than Rome's.[73]

When Rome kills you, you are supposed to stay dead. The resurrection of Christ from the dead is God's vindication of the way of Jesus—a way concerning which Paul has much to say in Ephesians—over the way of Rome. Rome and early Christianity at least shared one common symbol—the cross. Of course, for Rome it was the symbol of Roman peace through Roman power to threaten, intimidate, and brutalize. In Ephesians, as we shall see, it serves to highlight the way of reconciliation through the church's practices of forgiveness, sacrifice, and service. For Rome, the cross was a symbol of what Rome would do to those who challenged Roman order. For Christians, the cross provides the pattern for a gospel order that challenged the claims of Roman beneficence and sovereignty.[74] If we understand Paul's doxology and prayer, though, as asserting claims counter to imperial propaganda, then already in Ephesians 1 Paul offers a language and a vision, a saying and a seeing, that cannot be neatly distinguished as "theology" over against the "ethics" of chapters 4–6.[75]

The Gospel of Grace and Peace

For Christians to live in the world faithfully, we must first describe the world truthfully. It is no small matter that the topic of truth runs throughout Ephesians (1:13; 4:15, 25; 6:14), for it is this true account of the world that Paul offers in Ephesians, not some incidental religious talk that we can safely discard as long as we uphold our allegiance to something called

73. Most of the literature exploring the letters of Paul in light of the imperial context does not give attention to Ephesians, due to doubts as to the Pauline authorship of the letter; see, though, Long, "Paul's Political Theology." Long indicates (2 n. 14) that the "politically subversive understanding of many of the NT documents" has reached something of a consensus among New Testament scholars from "across the theological spectrum."

74. N. T. Wright hints at this polyvalent nature of language concerning the cross: "Brute force, dehumanizing humiliation, shameful death: that was the symbolic message of the cross, and that was the symbol that came, from Paul onwards, to speak of the love of the true God, the love which had somehow conquered the principalities and the powers." See his "Redemption from the New Perspective?" 79.

75. Hauerwas insists that any effort to find such distinctions in Paul's letters "says more about us than it does about Paul." See his Sanctify Them in the Truth, 21.

values or morality or ethics. For Paul, we can only live in the world faithfully as we describe the world truthfully, and that is what he offers in Ephesians 1–3: a way to describe the world truthfully.

What world does Ephesians describe? From the beginning of the book, Paul describes a world in which God is at work to accomplish the divine will. We get a sense of the theocentric tone of Ephesians right from the start of the letter. The mention of grace and peace in Paul's greetings is a conventional feature of his letters (1:2). What is unique in Ephesians is the pairing of these terms at the conclusion of the letter (6:23–24). It is not too much to say that the twin themes of grace and peace identify key concerns of the theocentric emphasis of Ephesians, for they stress both the divine initiative and the divine agenda, announcing God's gracious work to achieve God's ultimate will.[76] The vocabulary of grace and peace appears throughout the book as reminder of the themes that mark its boundaries and reveal its content.[77]

It is artificial, however, to suggest that we can talk about words such as "grace" and "peace" in some abstract manner. "Paul does not think in detached aphorisms or theological slogans, but in large stories, including the one within which he believes himself to be playing a vital role."[78] What we have in Ephesians is a rendering of Paul's message that presupposes and explores the significance of a narrative that begins with creation and moves to a grand fulfillment of the divine purpose for that creation, celebrating what God is doing to achieve that fulfillment and making explicit what role Christ and his followers play in that work.[79]

---

76. John P. Heil's analysis of Ephesians explores the book on the basis of its extensive use of chiastic structure. Chiastic structure is a form of inverted parallelism that can run from the most basic ABA' structure, where the themes paired in A and A' are situated and interpreted in light of the intervening B section, to much more elaborate and extensive patterns. Heil sees Ephesians as replete with chiastic forms. In 1:2, "grace" (A) and "peace" (B) are mentioned. At the conclusion of Ephesians, the order is reversed—first the B theme ("peace" in 6:23), then the A theme ("grace" in 6:24). This ABB'A' structure, Heil suggests, reveals concerns that frame the entire book and thus serve as interpretive guides to its message. See his *Ephesians*, 39.

77. Paul speaks of grace (*charis*) in Eph 1:2, 6, 7; 2:5, 7, 8; 3: 2, 7, 8; 4:7, 29; and 6:24. He refers to peace (*eirēnē*) in 1:2; 2:14, 15, 17 (2x); 4:3; 6:15, 23.

78. Wright, "Redemption from the New Perspective?" 78.

79. "Narrative" and "story" are used interchangeably here. Richard B. Hays offers that we have in the letters of Paul his attempt to demonstrate the "inexhaustible significance [of the story of Jesus] for shaping the life and thought of the believing community." See his *Faith of Jesus Christ*, 27. Hays argues that it is possible to discern a narrative substructure underneath the discursive character of the letters of Paul. While

In a sense, while Paul explicitly affirms that God is the one "who created all things" (3:9), Paul's narrative actually begins before creation. For from "before the foundation of the world" (1:4) God determined that he would call to himself a people that would display his character, "holy and blameless," in this world. It has always been God's intention to have a people in the world that would reflect God's goodness within creation.[80] Who these people are, why they must be holy and blameless, how they can become so, and what their relationship is to the rest of creation are all issues that Ephesians explores in detail.

The opening doxology of 1:3–14 speaks of God's will for creation and does so with language that echoes creation's beginnings as well as indicates its destiny. Specifically, in Eph 1:8–10, Paul declares with fanfare and flourish what he insists is the will of God for "things in the heavens and things upon the earth" (cf. Gen 1:1). For many, talk about "the will of God" evokes questions about inexplicable suffering, uncertainties in relationships, issues of life after graduation, or matters of consumer choice. And for many, talk about "the will of God" remains focused on strictly personal concerns. Paul rarely speaks in such terms and he does not here.[81] Paul's vision is as universal and all-embracing as is imaginable. The will of God has to do with "things in the heavens and things upon the earth," that is, "all things" in the heavens and "all things" upon the earth. In Eph 1:8–10, Paul pulls back the drapes, opens the cosmic window, and lets the light of God reveal the will of God for all of creation.

Paul indicates in v. 10 what this will of God is all about by using two important words. Translators offer "administration" or "plan" or "dispensation" for Paul's use of *oikonomia*, the word from which we

not all have agreed with Hays, the proposal has been a fruitful one for gaining a better understanding of what Paul is doing in his letters. See the collection of essays in Longenecker, *Narrative Dynamics in Paul*. The significance of this narrative emphasis will be explored more fully in the chapter on narrative ethics.

80. Certainly the language of election and predestination is used in Eph 1:4–5. Whether Paul's comments can be enlisted in debates about the predestination of individuals to heaven or hell in a Calvinistic mode or not is another matter. The pronouns of these verses are plural and reflect the emphasis in Ephesians on the church as the one body of Christ, who is, as the Christ, the Elect One. See *Dictionary for Theological Interpretation of the Bible*, s.v. "Ephesians, Book of," by Max Turner. See also Newman, "Election and Predestination," 237–47.

81. As common as the appeal is in contemporary evangelical circles to "God's will" in such personal matters, Furnish makes the point that in the letters of Paul such a view is not present in terms of "any specific act or line of conduct." See his *Theology and Ethics in Paul*, 191.

derive "economy." Paul is not at this point specifically talking about matters of work and money (though such concerns are included), but how it is that God governs God's universe—literally, what is the rule of God's household. And Paul tells us that God's governance has a specific goal. Translators identify that specific goal with various phrases: "to sum up," "to gather together," "to unite"—all giving some sense of what Paul means by *anakephalaiōsasthai*, an impressive term used only one other time in the New Testament. In Rom 13:9 Paul uses it to say that any and every law or commandment finds its sense and purpose only when seen in light of love for one's neighbor. Here it announces God's ultimate will for all of creation and what the divine initiative and agenda are all about. God intends to achieve unity and peace by gathering together all of creation into a universe centered in and reconciled through Jesus Christ. Anything and everything in all of creation will ultimately find its sense and purpose only in and through Jesus Christ.

What we have heard of this story so far should be enough to pique our curiosity for how Ephesians unfolds its message of God's grace and peace. Why a particular people destined from before creation? Why this plan for reconciliation through Jesus Christ? What is God doing, and why? Paul describes this plan for reconciliation as "the mystery" of God's will (v. 9). For us, a mystery is a puzzle that is hard to figure out. Given enough clues, however, we should be able to connect the dots and solve any enigma that comes our way. That is not what Paul means by "mystery." When the devout speak of "the mystery of God's will," sometimes it is with reference to those instances of inexplicable suffering or inequities in life. There are those troubling occasions when we simply do not have a ready explanation for why some things happen as they do. But Paul is not talking about "the mystery" of God's will in that way either. When Paul speaks of "mystery" he speaks of that which we can know only because God has revealed it. It is neither a puzzle nor an exhausting worry; it is what we can know about God's will because God has decided to let us in on it.[82] And here in Eph 1:9–10 Paul offers that God has let us in on what God is doing about evil. God has chosen to pursue the peace and reconciliation of a fractured cosmos through the redemptive work of Christ.

The key to understanding this "mystery," and really the key to understanding the message of Ephesians, is the phrase "the things in the heavens and the things upon the earth." Chrys Caragounis points out that

---

82. O'Brien, *Ephesians*, 109.

these two spheres—the "heavens" and the "earth"—represent two important arenas of confrontation and conflict that Ephesians will repeatedly address. We eventually discover in Ephesians that the "heavens" include the realm of conflict with spiritual forces that are rebellious toward God (6:12) and drag humanity along with them in that rebellion (2:1–3). Paul describes the chief expression of that conflict "on the earth" as the long-established enmity and hostility between Jew and Gentile (2:14–16).[83] What is true of both the heavens and the earth is that they are marked by conflict and rupture, hostility and strife. Ephesians gives an account of this conflict that spans the cosmos and ranges from transcendent powers to ethnic divisions to personal animosities to divided hearts. Paul views the entire landscape of human existence and the broader sweep of creation as one of dislocation and disorder. When we think of such matters we might want to invoke the word "mystery" in our struggle to account for the goodness and justice of God in a fractured world. Paul employs the language of "mystery" to describe what God is doing about that world.

Ephesians is concerned with detailing how God is at work to bring about this reconciliation through Christ. In addition, Ephesians can be understood as offering an invitation to its readers—Paul speaks of God's "calling" (1:18; 4:1)—to participate in that work and as indicating what that participation looks like. The various features of this work of grace and peace will be spelled out in subsequent chapters on Christian ethics as a "redemptive ethic," as an "ecclesial ethic," and so on. At various points we will note how the threats of fracture and hostility erupt in different areas of life, such as in the workplace or the home, and explore how God's final work of reconciliation must be anticipated in the witness of God's people now. At this point, though, we simply need to underscore that what Paul offers in Ephesians 1–3 is a broad account of how God is at work to "unite together all things in Christ, the things that are in the heavens and the things upon the earth." Paul's prayer of 1:17–22 provides us with a way of seeing that this grand work of cosmic reconciliation has very much to do with us.

As we noted earlier, the doxology of Eph 1:3–14 invites us to join with Paul in praising God for what God is doing in this world. God has chosen from before creation to create a people that would reflect his own character in this world. If we join with Paul in doxology, we celebrate

---

83. Caragounis, *Ephesian* Mysterion, 144–46.

with him that it is through Christ's suffering on the cross that we are set free to join with God in God's purpose for the cosmos (1:7).[84] We also celebrate that, though we live in anticipation of the ultimate end toward which God is moving creation (1:10), we are assured of participation in that final achievement by virtue of the presence of the Holy Spirit in our lives now (1:13–14). To say with Paul what he says in the doxology of 1:3–14 is to give joyful response to what he describes as "the message of truth, the gospel of your salvation" (1:13). To put it another way, to join in the doxology is to have accepted the invitation extended by God in his "calling." How what Paul "says" in the doxology relates to the will of God to unite all things together in Christ can be "seen" as we explore Paul's prayer in 1:17–22.

What does Paul pray for here? He prays that we would be able to see the significance for our lives of what we have been saying in the doxology. Specifically, though, he prays that we would know "what is the hope of his calling"—that is, that we would enjoy a profound sense of hope and confidence in light of the invitation to participate in what God is doing in this world. This invitation has everything to do with God's plan for reconciliation and peace announced in 1:10. And this invitation, or calling, has two dimensions to it that relate to the two realms of conflict—conflict in the heavens and upon the earth.[85] Paul's prayer addresses these realms of conflict in reverse order: first, the things upon the earth, and second, the things in the heavens.

The first feature of the calling that Paul wants his readers to understand more deeply has to do with God's invitation to share in the inheritance that is the people of God: "what are the riches of the glory of his inheritance in the saints" (1:18). Paul prays, in effect, that believers would realize how richly blessed they are to be part of the people of God. God's

---

84. O'Brien (*Ephesians*, 105–6) notes that Paul's concept of redemption in 1:7 "connotes liberation from imprisonment and bondage" and has its antecedents in the Old Testament account of "God's mighty deliverance of his people from the bondage of Egypt." Gordon Fee says the echo of the exodus narrative suggests "that the unbeliever is imaged as enslaved to/by sin . . . as Israel was enslaved to Egypt." See his "Paul and the Metaphors for Salvation," 52.

85. It must be said that most commentators identify three petitions in Paul's prayer, each identified by the Greek particle *tis* or *ti*, "what," in vv. 18 and 19. For contextual reasons, I see Paul as offering one petition concerning the calling of his readers, but a calling with two features that correspond to the plan of God identified in 1:10 and to which Paul returns again and again throughout the letter. See Holloway, *Peripateō*, 188, 199.

plan includes the concern to unite all the things that are on the earth. For Paul, the major expression of conflict and division on the earth is the enmity between Jew and Gentile. Paul's gospel, he insists, provides the way in which both Jew and Gentile can be united in one new humanity, establishing and demonstrating peace on the earth (2:11–18). Paul believes that it is the church, the one body of Christ, established without reference to the ethnic, national, and social divisions that mark a fractured world, that now bears witness to the intent of God to unite all things upon the earth. Paul's prayer is that believers would grow in their appreciation and awareness of the significance of their participation in that plan.

The second feature of the calling that Paul wants his reader to understand more deeply has to do with "the surpassing greatness" of God's power at work in the lives of believers, the power supremely expressed in raising Jesus from the dead (1:19–20). God's plan includes the concern to unite all the things that are in the heavens. For Paul, the major expression of conflict in the heavens has to do with the spiritual forces that are rebellious toward God (6:12) and implicate humanity with them in that rebellion (2:1–3). The resurrection of Christ, Paul insists, demonstrates God's decisive triumph over the powers (1:19–22), a triumph enjoyed by believers who, by God's grace and mercy, share the destiny of Christ (2:1–10). Paul believes that new life in Christ sets people free to live life as God intended it from the beginning; that life now bears witness to the intent of God to bring reconciliation to all things in the heavens. Paul prays that believers would grow in their appreciation and awareness of the power of God at work in their lives that enables them to participate in the purpose of God.

God calls us to, invites our participation in, the mystery of God, God's *oikonomia*, God's plan to gather together all things in Christ. To a fractured world, one shattered by hostility and conflict both in the heavens and on the earth, God offers reconciliation. God's gracious initiative is a work of peace that takes shape in the gospel Paul proclaims in Ephesians. What is this gospel all about? It is new life in the one body of Christ. It is new life that participates in the triumph of Christ over the powers in the "heavenlies" by virtue of his resurrection from the dead. It is life in the one body of Christ that effects reconciliation and establishes peace "on the earth" between formerly hostile parties.

Later in Ephesians, Paul will exhort his readers to "walk worthy of the calling with which you have been called" (4:1) and will identify practices that correspond to the gracious reconciling work of God. At times he will focus on practices that relate to life in the body of Christ (4:1–16; 4:25—5:2). Sometimes the focus is on the significance of new life in Christ in comparison to the old, where the rebellious powers still hold sway (4:17–24; 5:3–14). He appears to bring these various aspects of God's reconciling work together in 5:15–21, where contrast between old and new and relations in the body of Christ are both emphasized. What we must remember, though, when we look at the later admonitions in Ephesians, is that before Paul says anything about our ethical practices, he has first invited his readers to adopt a moral language and vision that elicits and enables such practices. He has invited us to describe the world truthfully that we might live in it faithfully. If we say with Paul the truthful account of the world provided in the doxology of Eph 1:3–14, we will see a world in which God is at work to provide new life in the one body of Christ. We will refuse to take the conventional accounts of the world, either of the first or the twenty-first century, for the real, and we will see the world as it is—a world in which God's grace is at work to establish peace.[86] We will understand, then, that Christian ethics is faithful response to God's calling to participate in this grace and peace. We will understand that Christian ethics is theocentric in its concern to highlight and affirm the divine initiative.

Debt and Distance

When we begin an exploration of Christian ethics from a theocentric standpoint, it provides a fundamentally different framework for the moral life than that of the Enlightenment project. A standpoint such as is found in Ephesians "emphasizes the primacy of God's agency over human agency, of grace and gift over personal autonomy and achievement."[87] It

---

86. An important comparison needs to be made here with respect to the perspective of Friedrich Nietzsche. Nietzsche famously distinguished between the world as it is and the world as it ought to be, insisting that the world as it ought to be does not exist and the world as it is offers no grounds for anything but a nihilism that must be overcome by the sheer determination of the will to power. Nietzsche wrongly identifies Christianity with abandonment of the world as it is and hope for the world as it ought to be. See his "Twilight of the Idols," 171. Such an assessment is insufficient to describe what we read in Paul. Ephesians will offer no such "Platonism for the masses." The "world as it is" is the world Paul describes in Ephesians 1–3. It is, though, a world other than as Nietzsche saw it. It is not a finished world; but neither is it an abandoned world.

87. Wadell, *Happiness and the Christian Life*, 21.

affirms the goodness of God and of God's intentions for creation over and against whatever distortions and corruptions of creation we now suffer. It reminds us that we are in over our heads and that we confront challenges personally, communally, and globally that are beyond our own abilities to negotiate, much less even recognize. With such a beginning we resist the prevalent mindset of modernity that we can draw neat distinctions between theology and ethics, salvation and the good life, grace and everyday existence. With such a beginning we confess that "the 'achievement' of good and avoidance of evil" is not our own achievement secured by our ingenuity and determination, but "comes as a gift with which we can at most participate but never create."[88] In this way, we recognize, as Stephen Long says, that "rather than a struggle against vice, the focus of the Christian life is to have one's life reordered toward God's gifts of faith, hope, and charity."[89] The theocentric focus of Christian ethics reminds us that what God is doing about evil is not simply making void what is already empty, but overcoming evil with the good that is God's own self.

Use of the term "theocentric," though, requires acknowledgment of an important debt as well as the admission of some distance. James Gustafson, one of the most significant voices in the field of Christian ethics in the twentieth century, published a two-volume work in the 1980s titled *Ethics from a Theocentric Perspective*.[90] Any reference to a "theocentric ethic" demands appreciation of these two volumes. Most importantly, with his emphasis on "ethics from a theocentric perspective" Gustafson wants to guard against many problems he believes to be all too present in most discussions of Christian ethics in particular and Christian theology in general.

Gustafson believes that the discipline of Christian ethics too often tries to address matters of ethical significance without making it clear what understanding or account of God provides the frame of reference in which the moral life and moral responsibility are to be placed. There are certainly other considerations, but Gustafson insists, "[T]he interpretation of God and God's relations to the world and particularly to human beings, and the interpretation of God's purposes . . . ought to be most decisive" in any attempt at constructing a theological ethic.[91] Far from

88. Long, *Goodness of God*, 107.

89. Ibid., 167.

90. Volume 1, *Theology and Ethics*, was published in 1981; volume 2, *Ethics and Theology*, was published in 1984.

91. *Ethics and Theology*, 143–44.

this being a retreat from the practical matters so many would emphasize in Christian ethics—turning quickly to matters like divorce, economic justice, or same-sex relations—Gustafson insists, "The practical moral question" of ethics from a theocentric perspective is, "What is God enabling and requiring us to be and to do?"[92]

Gustafson laments that so much of what has counted as Christian ethics has been entirely too anthropocentric. The central concerns in traditional approaches to ethics have derived "from purely human points of reference," says Gustafson. "The dominant strand of piety and theology," he insists, "has focused on the grandeur of man," resulting in "a tendency to assume that the intentions and activities of the Deity are primarily oriented toward human benefit."[93] Reflecting a qualified "preference for the Reformed tradition," Gustafson expresses appreciation for what he finds in the works of John Calvin and Jonathan Edwards—a "sense of the powerful Other" that evokes "a sense of awe and reverence, the senses of dependence, gratitude, obligation, repentance, possibilities for action, and direction." For Gustafson, these dimensions of the Reformed tradition make it clear that for those possessed of such a religious consciousness, "morality and religion are . . . inextricably intertwined."[94]

The moral outlook Gustafson associates with a theocentric perspective, though, cannot assume that God exists and acts "exclusively for the benefit of man. . . . The preoccupation with self has to be altered; the proper orientation is not primarily toward self but toward God—to the honoring of God, and to the ordering of life in relation to what can be discerned of the divine ordering."[95] Gustafson offers that we have good reason to possess "a rightly measured confidence in the divine benevolence toward man." "But," he insists, "the benevolence that we know and experience does not warrant the confidence that God's purposes are the fulfillment of my own best interest as I conceive them." He rejects the notion that genuine faith warrants an "ultimate confidence that God intends my individual good as the usually inflated and exaggerated terms portray that good." He dismisses the idea of a faith that "puts God primarily in the

---

92. *Theology and Ethics*, 327.

93. Ibid., 82, 109.

94. Ibid., 167.

95. Ibid., 110.

service of humans" and urges instead a "faithfulness" that "puts human beings in the service of God."[96]

It should be obvious that the approach to Christian ethics offered in this chapter on "the divine initiative" owes much to the concerns expressed in Gustafson's "theocentric ethic." Here too the concern is to shift away from the conventional starting point for many studies in Christian ethics—namely, the question, "What should I do?"—and to ask instead, "What is God doing?" That is certainly where Ephesians places the emphasis. Gustafson similarly and repeatedly insists that the proper starting point of a theocentric ethic is to ask, "What is God enabling and requiring us to be and to do?" Further, his cautions against the common anthropocentric assumptions of much contemporary Christianity are certainly in need of rehearsal.[97] Gordon Kaufmann warns, however, that there is much in what Gustafson has to say that "may sound very like traditional Christian piety. But that would be a mistaken understanding."[98] If we are to speak of a "theocentric ethic," it must be with recognition of the debt owed to Gustafson's own sophisticated and articulate work. There must also be, however, admission of a significant difference from Gustafson's understanding of how God is at work to achieve the divine purpose for creation.

Gustafson is unrelenting in his criticism of anthropocentric religion—"the self-serving, utilitarian, instrumental character of both religious activities and religious ideas." Many Christians would assent to his criticism that at both individual and corporate levels, "We strive valiantly to put God in the service of man."[99] Some might be a little more uncomfortable with his insistence that "we cannot be as certain as the [Christian] tradition has been that man is so centrally, so exclusively, the object of divine beneficence or divine providence."[100]

When Gustafson finally evacuates humanity completely from the ultimate purposes of God for creation, however, we can understand why one critic labels Gustafson's account "post-Christian."[101] Gustafson insists, though, that modern discoveries about the history and evolution of

---

96. Ibid., 202–3.

97. For essays challenging the various ways in which American Christianity likes to make God over in our own image, see Laytham, *God Is Not . . .*

98. Kaufmann, "How Is God to Be Understood?" 17.

99. *Theology and Ethics*, 188–89.

100. Ibid., 188.

101. Maguire, "Review of *Ethics from a Theocentric Perspective*," 257.

life on earth undercut "the anthropocentric centering of value, enforced by the view that the divine intention is finally focused on our species." The scientific understanding of the human species and our small place in the cosmos supports, according to Gustafson, the assertion that "as the beginning was without us, so will the end also be without us."[102] Needless to say, the concerns of Ephesians to speak of the purpose of God embracing a redeemed humanity as the expression of his intent to reconcile a fractured creation grants far too significant a role for humanity for Gustafson's taste. The language of Ephesians detailing the "mystery of [God's] will" (1:9–10) offers much more than Gustafson says we can actually know of divine intentions. Indeed, Gustafson is himself uneasy with the idea that God even has a will ("a capacity to control events comparable to the more radical claims made for human beings") or discernible intentions. "I do not find," he says, "sufficient reasons to move from our perceptions of the purposes of the divine governance to the assertion that these imply an intelligence similar to our own, or a capacity of radical agency similar to certain claims made for human beings."[103]

Ultimately, Gustafson's account of God leads in directions fundamentally at odds with major features of traditional Christian faith. His account leaves no room to speak of God in a personal way and consequently dismisses the significance of God as an agent who calls humanity to partnership, who attends to human prayers, and who wills triumph over the powers of death. "Indeed, in the eyes of some," he says, "I have left out the heart of the matter, the redemptive work of Christ known in the Scripture." Small wonder that Gustafson himself questions whether his view has "left behind so many tenets of the Christian theological tradition that it is beyond the pale."[104] He insists, though, that while his effort will be "unsatisfactory to many adherents of Christian faith and theology. . . . It does . . . form the basis of a theological ethics which I believe bears continuities with the Christian tradition and can be warranted by many human experiences and by data and explanations from some well-established sciences."[105]

---

102. *Theology and Ethics*, 267–68.

103. Ibid., 270–71. Critics have expressed uncertainty as to how or why Gustafson distinguishes between purposes and intentions, the former being even discernable in animals, the latter in neither animals nor God. See, for example, Stout, *Ethics after Babel*, 171.

104. Ibid.,167, 274.

105. Ibid., 279. It is apparent that Gustafson is not concerned to base his

Gustafson's critics are often not able to detect such continuities. Indeed, with such a wide gap between Gustafson's understanding and more traditional beliefs about God, some wonder why he bothers to continue to speak of God at all.[106] The concern here, though, is not to offer a full-blown analysis and critique of Gustafson's entire perspective, but to acknowledge the importance of his assertion that we all too often begin in the wrong place and employ the wrong criteria in pursuing the task of Christian ethics. Approaches among Christians that begin with "what should I do?" usually end by finding semi-Christian justifications for practices that assume settings and commitments that might themselves come under question if we start with Gustafson's question: "What is God enabling and requiring us to be and do?"

Gustafson answers his own question by insisting, "We are to relate ourselves and all things in a manner appropriate to their relations to God."[107] With his minimalist view of God, however, Gustafson will not be of much help in indicating what counts as "appropriate."[108] It is hard to say how he would evaluate particular features of the parenesis in Ephesians 4–6. On the one hand, he insists generally that "the divine governance is not revealed to us in its moral details in the Scriptures." On the other hand, he says, "To be sure, there are commandments that one cannot foresee being broken without moral guilt."[109] What would he

theocentric ethic on any significant engagement with Scripture. He does list Scripture and Christian traditions as two of the four possible sources of authority for the task of theological ethics. He repeatedly makes it clear, however, that he gives priority to human experience (115–20), and insists that whatever we might retrieve from Scripture and Christian tradition "cannot be incongruous . . . with well-established data and explanatory principles by relevant sciences, and must 'be in some way indicated by these'" (257). While he selectively draws on the Gospels to illustrate from the life of Jesus his account of what a "theocentric piety" (dispositions of reverence and awe) might look like, the letters of Paul (along with Hebrews and the book of Revelation) are of little significance for his reconstruction of theology (275).

106. Kaufmann, "How Is God to Be Understood?" 22–23; Stout, *Ethics after Babel,* 178.

107. *Theology and Ethics,* 327

108. As Harry Huebner observes, "It is difficult to see how to determine 'what God enables or requires of us' if we cannot know what God is doing." See his *Introduction to Christian Ethics,* 411. To be fair, in *Ethics and Theology,* Gustafson offers a number of specific proposals for concrete examples of what the practice of moral discernment from within his perspective might achieve. At many points his proposals would find wide support within Christian circles; his comments concerning suicide might be less well received. See *Ethics and Theology,* 187–216.

109. *Theology and Ethics,* 339.

say of Paul's insistence on honesty, hard work, and gracious speech (Eph 4:25–29)? It is hard to imagine any opposition to such concerns, as long as those demands are understood in some general way.

Of course, Paul is not simply concerned with honesty, hard work, and gracious speech. These are not simply abstract moral demands, but (as further discussion will demonstrate) vital practices that must be seen in relationship to God's announced *oikonomia*—the uniting together of all things in Christ (Eph 1:9–10). Gustafson would likely endorse these practices as "fundamental requisites that can be perceived and must be taken into account not only for individual and interpersonal life but also for social institutional life and the life of the species."[110] It is less likely that he would see them in the same terms as did Paul, as practices of the redeemed body of Christ that serve to undergird the life of the community called to bear witness to the power of the gospel to reconcile a fractured cosmos.

There are certainly other features of what we find in Ephesians that would attract Gustafson. The repeated concern to honor or glorify God would certainly meet with his approval (Eph 1:6, 12, 14; 3:21). The peculiar insistence in Ephesians that God's glory is bound up with the divine agenda to create a people—the church—that displays and shares in the glory of God would find less support (3:21).[111]

Gustafson also dismisses the place given to Christ's sovereignty in Ephesians,[112] a move that leaves his "theocentric" emphasis vulnerable to specific criticism. Ephesians insists that the same Christ who is sovereign over all (1:19–22) also embodies the true measure of human existence (4:13), so that, as Richard McCormick says, "the dichotomy between anthropocentricism and theocentricism is a false dichotomy." The view of Christ presented in Ephesians supports McCormick's assertion that "being theocentric means being Christocentric—which means anthropocentric in a way Gustafson cannot admit."[113] At this point, Ephesians

110. Ibid.

111. It is not that Gustafson has no room in his perspective for the Christian community. Its "symbols, myths, rites, and stories" can all function to direct attention away from ourselves and more properly to "the ultimate power on which all things depend" (*Ethics and Theology*, 290–91). These expressions of piety, however, serve only a "social-psychological function" (*Theology and Ethics*, 324) and should not be assumed to be "fully appropriate to human experience and to various things we know about the world" (321).

112. *Theology and Ethics*, 275 n. 65.

113. McCormick, "Gustafson's God," 60.

represents an outlook persistently voiced throughout Scripture—that God has chosen to couple his glory with the divine purpose for humanity. This association surfaces in both awkward and profound ways in the story of Israel (Exodus 32; Ezekiel 36–37) and finds no more surprising expression than when Paul says the glory of God resides in both "the church and in Christ Jesus" (Eph 3:21).

In response to Gustafson's proposals, Stanley Hauerwas insists, "I too want to do ethics from a radically theocentric perspective and I do not understand why beginning with Jesus' life, cross, and resurrection prevents me from doing that."[114] Can we pursue a theocentric ethic that avoids the grotesque domestication and diminishment of God that so often distorts contemporary expressions of Christian faith and practice? Can we pursue an approach to Christian ethics that begins with the right question—not "what should I do?" but "what is God doing?" That is certainly where Paul begins in Ephesians. Such a starting point does not mean the evacuation of humanity from the ultimate purposes of God, though. What Ephesians has to say about Christ makes it clear that it is God's intent to create and embrace a redeemed humanity for the sake of the entire cosmos.

It will mean, however, that we cannot assume that it is God's concern to underwrite our own objectives, institutions, agendas, and systems—ecclesial, economic, political, or otherwise. How often we try to do that will surface in various ways throughout the course of this study. Ephesians will have plenty to say that challenges conventional assumptions sustaining many of our common practices. One area of life where that might be the case is in the world of money, economics, and work. What Paul has to say about such matters in Ephesians only makes sense if we start where Paul does—with the belief that God is at work to reconcile a fractured creation. An examination of what Paul has to say about work in Ephesians will indicate both the importance of starting where Paul does and of making clear that, for Paul, a theocentric ethic certainly embraces a vision for the well-being of those who actually learn what it means to trust in God's wisdom and purpose. Such trust is not a faith that puts God in our service, but a trust in God's faithfulness to include our service in God's purpose.

114. Hauerwas, "God the Measurer," 407–8.

GOD'S *OIKONOMIA* AND OURS

Only because Paul believes we live in a world in which the divine initiative and agenda are evident can he say what he says in Eph 4:28. Because the world described in Ephesians is one bound by grace and peace; because it is a world in which God is at work to gather all things together in Christ; because it is a world in which God grants new life in the one body of Christ, Paul can say, "Let him who steals, steal no longer, but rather let him labor with his hands what is good, in order that he may have something to share with him who has need."

To contemplate this exhortation from our contemporary standpoint is to face several surprises. While we are not too surprised that Paul would speak against theft, we are somewhat (but only somewhat) startled at the suggestion that the earliest Christian congregations included those who needed specific instruction to put their thieving ways behind them. Paul's words are not theoretical; they indicate, instead, "how difficult [some of Paul's readers] found it to break away from the ethical norms of the society from which they had been converted."[115] What is likely most surprising, though, is the justification he gives here for work. Elsewhere Paul can encourage his converts to engage in manual labor, evidently to be able to provide for themselves so as not to be a burden on others (1 Thess 4:11), a practice he personally embodied (1 Thess 2:9). That is not what he calls for here. Instead, "The motive for work is not individual profit but rather communal well-being."[116]

We have seen that Paul speaks of God's plan for the reconciliation and peace of all of creation as God's *oikonomia*—God's economy. While Paul's use of this language is much more comprehensive than reference to what we today speak of as "the economy," we might say that Paul can only say what he says about economic matters in 4:28 because of what he says about God's economy in the broader sense. By the time we get to Paul's moral admonitions in Ephesians 4–6, we have already been told of the immeasurable blessings of God's abundant grace that God, as the great benefactor, bestows on his people. God's governance of God's creation displays the bounty of God; the language of abundance is itself abundant in the book. Paul speaks of "the *riches* of his grace, which he *lavished* upon us" (1:7–8). God is "*rich* in mercy," and "in the ages to come" intends to show through his people "the *surpassing riches* of his grace" (2:4,

115. Best, "Ephesians 4.28," 181.

116. Lincoln, *Ephesians*, 304.

7). It is Paul's honor and task as an apostle "to preach to the Gentiles the *unfathomable riches* of Christ" (3:8), and he prays confidently for his readers on the basis of "the *riches* of [God's] glory" (3:16). David Ford admits, "If I were choosing just one theme to emphasize about the God of Ephesians in relation to salvation it would be that of abundance—the pervasive sense of lavish generosity in blessing, loving, revealing and reconciling."[117]

Two mistakes could be made in light of this language of abundance. One is to enroll Paul in the "health-and-wealth gospel club," whose members insist that God wants us all to be rich, sleek, tanned, and trouble-free. Paul would have to offer a different account of his imprisonment by Roman authorities than he does in Ephesians 3 if he were to promote that sort of message. Another mistake would be to read Paul as some sort of Gnostic dualist whose talk about "spiritual blessings in the heavenly places" (1:3) has nothing to do with the actual, concrete circumstances of our lives.

"Spiritual blessings," though, need to be more precisely identified as "blessings made present in our lives through the Holy Spirit."[118] There is no good reason to draw a hard-and-fast line between the Spirit's involvement in material versus nonmaterial matters. This is true for the Bible as a whole (see Gen 1:2; Ps 104:27–30) and particularly for Paul (see Rom 15:26–27). In addition, we do not need to confuse Paul's use of *toi epouranioi* ("the heavenly places") with some ethereal dimension that has nothing to do with present life in this world. Paul makes it clear that dark forces bent on malice and evil are part of the current environment with which believers must contend (Eph 6:12), and yet these forces dwell *en tois epouraniois* ("in the heavenly places"). That believers have been "raised and seated in the heavenly places in Christ Jesus" (2:6) does not mean they need a change of address form at the post office. It does mean a radical shift in orientation and outlook based on God's redemptive work in Christ. The reference is not so much spatial as it is qualitative. Paul's use of "heavenly places" is concerned with providing an expansive vi-

117. Ford, *Self and Salvation*, 113. Even the literary style of Ephesians exhibits a rhetorical emphasis highlighting abundance. The "pleonastic" (from the Greek *pleon*, "more") style of Ephesians, with its long sentences, piled-up adjectives, and studied repetition, suits this thematic feature of the letter. See O'Brien, *Ephesians*, 6–8; Lincoln, *Ephesians*, xliv–xlvi.

118. Margaret Y. MacDonald says of this phrase, "As is usually true in the NT, the use of the adjective 'spiritual' (*pneumatikos*) refers to the presence and working of the Holy Spirit in God's blessing." See her *Colossians and Ephesians*, 197.

sion of reality that goes beyond the immediate and the apparent.[119] Once again, Paul is concerned that we not confuse the conventional with the real and reduce all experience to the level of the mundane and immanent. Rather, while believers "walk" in the present world with all of its responsibilities, challenges, and threats, that walk is one qualified by the power and present reality of the "new" made possible and present in Christ (Eph 2:10; 4:17–24).[120] God's bestowment of blessing has everything to do with the fulfillment of what God intended for creation from the beginning. "Spiritual blessings" do not leave the realm of creation behind; rather, within the realm of creaturely existence, God meets us with blessing.

We cannot take Paul's language of God's abundance as a guarantee of Wall Street salaries, nor can we restrict the reference to some psychological disposition. What are we to make, then, of this talk of God's abundance and Paul's peculiar outlook concerning work? It means at least this: the understanding of matters of work and economics in Ephesians will not fit within the parameters and expectations of prevailing models, either in Paul's day or our own. The reason is that what Paul really means is something along the lines of what Sam Wells says: the abundance of God's action toward the world "constitutes *everything* his people need to follow him."[121] Only as we understand this can we understand Paul's view of work given in Eph 4:28. We can best approach these issues by exploring three broad assertions springing from Paul's Letter to the Ephesians: (1) God works, (2) God wills work, and (3) God wills work in keeping with God's will.

God Works

M. Douglas Meeks notes that in our present context, "Work . . . is profoundly ambiguous." On the one hand, work "seems to be a curse such

119. Walter Wink says the language of "the heavenlies" in Ephesians speaks to "a heightened awareness, the consciousness of the noumenal realm in which the final contest for the lordship of all reality is being waged." Knowledge of this sort, says Wink, "cannot simply be added to existing knowledge" but "requires an altogether new mind, indeed, a new humanity." See his *Naming the Powers*, 92.

120. Paul's repeated use of *peripateō* in Ephesians (2:1, 10; 4:1, 17; 5:2, 8, 15) needs to be seen in relation to his use of *en tois epouraniois*, for the walking metaphor clearly serves in the letters of Paul to describe life in the present age, qualified by either orientation to the practices and commitments of a world indifferent to God or to a world made new by God's grace; see Holloway, *Peripateō*, 226–27.

121. Wells, *God's Companions*, 5.

that it would be better for people to fold their hands and cease all human activity. On the other hand, works seems to be a blessing associated with the use of work's product and with satisfaction in accomplishment." [122] In the midst of one of the worst economic downturns in U.S. history, attitudes about work could be somewhat mixed. With a nationwide unemployment rate of 9 nine percent, people are lining up by the hundreds and thousands whenever a few job openings are announced. At the same time, recent surveys point to growing dissatisfaction among workers in the United States with work environment and situation.[123] At some workstations, employees display on their computer monitors the years, months, weeks, days, hours, and minutes until retirement. Just about everyone can complete this sentence: "Take this job and . . ." Perhaps we should not be too surprised; some have estimated that the American worker puts in more labor each year than did medieval peasants.[124]

Any current distaste for work is but an echo of ancient sentiments. In fact, in the world in which the Bible was originally produced, there was a fairly uniform outlook voicing a harsh prejudice against work. That perspective was nowhere more clearly on display than in the widely held view that work (understood as manual labor) was beneath the dignity of the gods. The ancient Akkadian creation epic *Enuma Elish* illustrates this supremely.

Enuma Elish is the story of Tiamat and Marduk, in which Marduk slays Tiamat, mother of the gods. Fearful of their mother's wrath because they had murdered their father, Apsu, rebellious gods choose Marduk as their champion to kill Tiamat. Marduk accepts the task on one condition—that upon victory he would be elevated as king of all the gods. Marduk defeats Tiamat and cleaves her body in two; half her carcass becomes the sky above and half becomes the earth below. The assembly of the gods keeps their end of the bargain and proclaims, "O Marduk, thou

122. Meeks, *God the Economist*, 127.

123. See the report on job satisfaction for 2010 at www.conference-board.org. The trend in job satisfaction is clearly downward with only 45 percent reporting that they are satisfied with their job, down from a 61 percent satisfaction report in 1987. The Conference Board reports that "less than 37 percent of workers under the age of 25 are satisfied with their employment situation."

124. According to the "Take Back Your Time" movement's Web site, www.timeday. org. Of course, we should not be surprised if that were the case, since in medieval Europe the church mandated strict observance of Sabbath, holy days, and feast days, observances taking up about a third of the year. What might surprise us is that there was once a day in which the church had such a voice in economic matters.

art indeed our avenger. We have granted thee kingship over the universe entire."[125] That was just fine—except what good is it being king unless you have a nice palace? The question arises, how will this palace get built? Labor is not something for which the gods are suited. What good is it being a god if you have to work for a living? Marduk has the solution:

> Blood I will mass and cause bones to be.
> I will establish a savage; "man" shall be his name.
> Verily, savage-man I will create.
> He shall be charged with the service of the gods
> That they may be at ease![126]

The disdain of labor was not exclusive to the ancient Near East. Prominent voices from ancient Greece express a similar view. In that setting, work was considered a threat to the greater goods in life of friendship, civic duty, and contemplation. The one skilled in the mechanical arts, according to Plato's Callicles, has his place in society, but "you would not wish to give your daughter in marriage to his son."[127] Plato's student Aristotle explains: "The citizen must not lead the life of mechanics or tradesmen, for such a life is ignoble, and inimicable to virtue. Labor robs persons of the leisure to participate in political and military activities as well as moral and intellectual pursuits, all of which are appropriate only to free citizens. Neither must they be husbandmen, since leisure is necessary both for the development of virtue and the performance of political duties."[128] Work, according to Aristotle, precludes the time and freedom required for the acquisition and display of genuine virtue. In this view, one cannot work hard and be a virtuous person.

For both Plato and Aristotle, there is a higher calling in life than that of manual labor—the life of contemplation. To avoid a life of active productivity was not to permit indolence and sloth, however. It is through the contemplative life of the mind that "we come closest to the true form of divine life and thereby achieve the highest possible degree of human happiness."[129] This preference for the *vita contemplativa* over

---

125. *Enuma Elish*, IV.13–14. Text in Pritchard, *Ancient Near East*.

126. *Enuma Elish*, VI.5–8.

127. Plato, *Gorgias*, 512b.

128. Aristotle, *Politics*, 1328b–1329a.

129. Hardy, *Fabric of This World*, 11.

the *vita activa* would become a mainstay of Christian piety and devotion in the Middle Ages, embodied in the routines of the monastic orders.[130]

And yet, God works. Douglas Meeks insists, "It has to be said, over against every attempt to make God a workless supreme being, that according to the biblical narratives God the Economist works. . . . God is not the distant emperor or city-state king living the life of leisure while expecting God's people to do all of God's hard work. Human beings are not made, as in the Sumerian and Babylonian myths, to do the arduous work of the gods."[131] The biblical materials are filled with images for God drawn from the world of labor: God is the farmer that "planted a garden toward the east, in Eden" (Gen 2:8). God is the potter that forms Israel as clay in God's hands (Jer 18:1–6). Hosea appeals to a sickened Israel to seek no physician other than Yahweh (Hos 5:13). And, of course, everyone knows that "the Lord is my shepherd" (Ps 23:1). In creating the cosmos, in forming and restoring a people, in guiding them and protecting them from danger, God is at work.

Ephesians, in particular, employs the language of labor with reference to God in several important instances. God's *oikonomia* (1:9–10) has as its foundation and vehicle the cross and resurrection of Christ. According to Paul, the resurrection of Christ from the dead is the chief measure of the "surpassing greatness" of God's power and actively puts on display the strength and might of God (1:19). In the resurrection of Christ from the dead, the means by which God expresses his redemptive grace and triumphs over the powers, God was at work.[132]

Paul will use a number of images in Ephesians to describe the nature and purpose of this redemptive work. Many of those images reinforce this picture of God at work. If the church is being built as a temple (2:19–22), then God is its architect and master builder. Perhaps most charming is Paul's depiction of believers as God's "workmanship, created in Christ Jesus for good works" (2:10). Here Paul describes believers as God's *poiēma*. While that word looks and sounds similar to our English word

---

130. See *Summa Theologica*, II.2, 183, art. 1–2. For Thomas Aquinas, love for neighbor, displayed in the active life, is subordinate to love for God, expressed in the contemplative. We will need to see, though, that there was more appreciation for the active life of labor even in the medieval monastic orders than is often recognized.

131. Meeks, *God the Economist*, 137.

132. Paul even uses the word *energeian* (v. 19), translated as "working," to describe God's "power in action" (Hoehner, *Ephesians*, 271). Of course, our English word "energy" derives from this Greek term.

"poem," Paul does not have the art of poetry in mind here. Rather, the language echoes the Old Testament account of God's work of creation. The Greek translation of the Old Testament, the Septuagint, uses *poiēma* to speak of "the work of thy hands" (Pss 19:1; 92:4; 143:5), to refer to "that which is made" by God (Isa 29:16), or to the product of divine effort (Eccl 3:11; 7:13). In Ephesians, Paul explains what it means to be God's *poiēma* with the phrase "created in Christ Jesus" to underscore that God's provision of new life in Christ must be seen in light of God's original work of creation. What God intended from the beginning of creation finds its fulfillment and realization in Christ. In the gift of new life in Christ that creates a new people fashioned and built "into a dwelling of God in the Spirit" (Eph 2:22), God is at work.

Why does God work? We have a ready answer for why we work (we want to eat, don't we?), one that will require further reflection. Why, though, does God work? One of the prominent theological dimensions of Ephesians is what has been called its incipient trinitarianism. That is, we find in Ephesians, not a fully reflective and philosophical account of God as Father, Son, and Holy Spirit, but an easy and uninhibited moving back and forth of references to the Father, the Son, and the Holy Spirit.[133] For example, in 3:14–19 Paul prays to the Father that believers would be strengthened through the Spirit for the sake of the indwelling of Christ. In something of a confessional acclamation in 4:4–6 Paul affirms faith in one Spirit, one Lord, one God and Father of all. The understanding of God as Trinity reminds us that God has never suffered from lack of fellowship. There has been from eternity the abundant love between Father and Son, bound together by the Holy Spirit. God did not create, nor does God redeem because of some lack within God. God's works of creation and redemption are, as Ephesians repeatedly emphasizes, expressions of God's superabundant grace. God works, not because God has to, but out of the overflowing abundance of God's grace and mercy. God is not constrained to work by circumstances outside of God. God works because of who God is, and God's work reveals who God is—the God of grace and

---

133. Michael J. Gorman insists that "although Paul does not have a fully developed theology of the Trinity, such language is nonetheless appropriate." What Gorman says of Paul in general is particularly significant for Ephesians: "Believers know and are known by God the Father, who has adopted them. They live 'in' the crucified but now exalted Christ, who also lives in them. They are empowered to live in Christ, as God's children, by the Spirit." See his *Apostle of the Crucified Lord,* 139; see also Hoehner, *Ephesians,* 106–7, who describes Ephesians as "the Trinitarian letter."

mercy who seeks to bless God's creation in ways measurable only by the "surpassing greatness of his power."

The significance of the work of the triune God for our work might be explored in any of a number of ways.[134] Christian confession of the Trinity should at least affirm this: while our culture might harbor a measure of ambiguity about work, God works; and if God works, there must be some essential goodness, some fundamental dignity, something basically right about work. Many Christians go about their work lives with various degrees of uncertainty as to how God relates to those tasks that demand more and more of their waking hours. David W. Miller reports of the "Sunday-Monday gap," where for many Christians the "Sunday worship hour bears little to no relevance to the issues they face in their Monday workplace hours." According to Miller, "workers, businesspeople, and other professionals often feel unsupported by the Sunday church in their Monday marketplace vocations."[135] One reason for this felt gap might be that there is very little said in our churches about matters relating Christian faith to economics and work.[136] There is no guarantee that a view of work informed by Ephesians will support anything and everything that goes on in the marketplace. A beginning point for any discussion of such matters, though, needs to be the simple observation that God works.

God Wills Work

There certainly was an ecclesial preference for the *vita contemplativa* over the *vita activa* throughout the Middle Ages. We do not need to imagine, though, that even the monks in the monasteries of Europe managed to avoid manual labor. In fact, certain monastic orders built the requirement of work into their daily routines. The value placed on work only went so far, but there was the understanding that work was part of the will of God for the brothers of the Benedictine Order, for example. The Rule of Saint Benedict (d. 543 CE) speaks of "the Daily Manual Labour":

---

134. See also Meeks, *God the Economist*, 132–34.

135. See his *God at Work*, 9–10.

136. One survey indicates that among those regularly involved in worship services of one sort or another, only about 40 percent hear a sermon relating matters of Christian faith and discipleship to issues of work and economics in a given year. See Wuthnow, *God and Mammon in America*, 55–56.

Idleness is enemy of the soul. And therefore, at fixed times, the brothers ought to be occupied in manual labour; and again, at fixed times, in sacred reading. Therefore we believe that both these ought to be arranged thus: from Easter until the 1st of October, on coming out of Prime they shall do what labour may be necessary until the fourth hour. From the fourth hour until about the sixth, they shall apply themselves to reading. . . . But, if the needs of the place or poverty demand that they labour at the harvest, they shall not grieve at this: for then they are truly monks if they live by the labours of their hands; as did also our fathers and the apostles. Let all things be done with moderation, however, on account of the fainthearted.[137]

Much from this rich passage is noteworthy: the effort at finding balance between the *vita contemplativa* and the *vita activa*, the concern for meeting material needs, the concern to view work in the light of an inherited tradition of the Christian faith, and the demand that work not become burdensome and oppressive. Most interesting is the implication that work is here seen as a vital instrument in the task of spiritual formation and as a safeguard against the soul's dread enemy of idleness. Saint Benedict obviously believes that God wills work.[138]

Clearly, Paul's admonition in Eph 4:28 assumes as much, as do other features of the letter. There is, however, an important and necessary qualification and warning needed at this point. It is certainly the case that language of the will of God concerning work has been and remains a powerful tool granting license to degradation, oppression, and injustice in the arena of work.[139] It is not for nothing that Karl Marx, in his vehement criticism of the working conditions of early European capitalism, described religion as the "opium of the people," a powerful narcotic capable of numbing the pain of oppression and exploitation.

There is a long history of the use of religious language to provide justification and force to economic arrangements determining who does what work, and for what reward. One of the earliest efforts at this comes

137. Text in Bettenson, *Documents of the Christian Church*, 123.

138. Michael Banner offers that the Rule of Saint Benedict addresses the question, "What is it to live well?" and responds by giving attention to "a vertical dimension which directs us towards God, and a horizontal dimension which directs us towards our neighbor." See his *Christian Ethics*, 11–12.

139. One of the major concerns of Meeks's *God the Economist* is to explore how "God concepts, albeit highly secularized in the modern world, have grounded and modeled society's prevailing concepts of work" (127).

from Plato (d. 348 BCE). Plato's ideal republic would manifest a threefold division of society: philosophers rule, an auxiliary class of soldiers and teachers enforce and inculcate the laws established by the philosophers, and a working class provides for the material needs of the city. The question arises as to how people might be convinced to bear "the toils and pains and conflicts prescribed for them" by their station in life. Plato, through the mouth of Socrates, offers "one of those needful falsehoods of which we lately spoke—just one royal lie" with which to address the citizens of the city: "Citizens, we shall say to them in our tale, you are brothers, yet God has framed you differently. Some of you have the power to command, and in the composition of these he has mingled gold, wherefore also they have the greatest honor; others he has made of silver, to be auxiliaries; others again who are to be husbandmen and craftsmen he has composed of brass and iron." It is vital that members of a particular class observe the duties and roles proper to their station: "For an oracle says that when a man of brass or iron guards the State, it will be destroyed." Here a religious tale is proffered to foster a belief that "will make them care more for the city and for one another."[140] In this story, station and function in life are divinely ordained and may be neither challenged nor changed.

While he invokes Paul rather than Plato, the Protestant Reformer Martin Luther offers a similar analysis concerning what eventually came to be called "vocation." Luther had himself been a monk of the Augustinian order, but he underwent a radical change of outlook that initiated major changes in European history and the history of Christianity. The 1520s in Germany were years of great unrest and economic turmoil. The rise of a money economy and the effects of famine served to fan flames of rebellion. When Luther's challenge to ecclesial authorities was taken by some to justify an egalitarian challenge to social order, the reformer was quick to respond. He called on the "robbing and murdering hordes of peasants" to "stop claiming you have the Christian law on your side." In case the peasants refused to listen, though, he admonished the princes of the land to "smite, slay, and stab, secretly or openly, remembering that nothing can be more poisonous, hurtful, or devilish than a rebel."[141]

Luther, though, sought to provide a more substantive basis for social order than merely the threat of force. His view of vocation functioned

---

140. Plato, *Republic*, 414–15.

141. Cited in Lindberg, *European Reformations*, 165–66.

toward this end. In a misinterpretation of 1 Cor 7:17–24 Luther reads Paul's statement, "Only, as the Lord has assigned to each, as God has called each, in this manner let him walk," as demanding a fixity of status and station in life. If you are born into peasantry, a peasant you must remain. If your father was a craftsman, you should not seek a higher position in society than what such a role offers. According to Luther, "God assigns to each man his toil in accordance with his powers and in keeping with his calling. . . . To each one God has assigned his portion. . . . [God] wants you to do your duty happily in accordance with your assigned task and leave other things to other people."[142]

Luther's view of calling marks both a broadening and a narrowing of the concept of vocation. During the Middle Ages, language of calling or vocation was associated strictly with ecclesial and religious roles, such as priest, monk, or nun. Luther rejects that view and broadens the concept to include farming, brewing, milking, and so forth. On the one hand, this serves to ennoble what had often been viewed as menial and insignificant work. Yet Luther also employs the concept to restrict and narrow people's opportunities and to undergird prevailing assumptions about the social order of his day.

Another great Protestant Reformer of the sixteenth century, John Calvin, takes Luther's view of vocation a step further, refusing to restrict calling to a matter of inherited status. Calvin furthered the growing preference for the *vita activa* over the *vita contemplativa* Luther had expressed. Rejecting any notion of God's omnipotence as of "the empty, idle, and almost unconscious sort," Calvin insists God's power is of "a watchful, effective, active sort, engaged in ceaseless activity."[143] Those made in the image of God do not best reflect that image in a life disengaged from the activities and responsibilities of daily life, but in active fulfillment of a divine calling. Indeed, "The Lord bids each one of us in all life's actions to look to his calling." This calling, according to Calvin, is determined not by inherited status; rather, "each individual has his own kind of living assigned to him by the Lord as a sort of sentry post, so that he may not heedlessly wander about throughout life." Calvin does not provide an exhaustive list of all the possible vocations to which God might call an individual. Attention to God's calling to "various kinds of living," though,

142. Luther, *Notes on Ecclesiastes*, 98, cited in Jensen, *Responsive Labor*, 35. For a reading of 1 Corinthians 7 that offers an alternative to Luther's, see Holloway, *Peripateō*, 70–81.

143. Calvin, *Institutes*, 1.xvi.3.

is a basic feature of the Christian way of life. "It is enough if we know that the Lord's calling is in everything the beginning and foundation of well-doing."[144]

While Calvin's notion of calling is not defined by inherited status, there is still the insistence that calling is fixed and that status and station in life are not to be resisted. "A man of obscure station," says Calvin, "will lead a private life ungrudgingly so as not to leave the rank in which he has been placed by God." That station might bring "discomforts, vexations, weariness, and anxieties," but "no task will be so sordid and base, provided you obey your calling in it, that it will not shine and be reckoned very precious in God's sight." For Calvin, there is a "singular consolation" in knowing that in any "cares, labors, and troubles" occasioned by obedience to one's calling, God is "the guide in all these things."[145]

It is hard to overstate the significance of the shift in perspective represented by Luther and Calvin on the issue of calling and vocation. When Luther and Calvin broadened the idea of vocation from the limited arena of religious office, they highlighted the spiritual value of the everyday and affirmed the interpenetration of the sacred and profane. As Charles Taylor puts it, "The denial of a special status to the monk was also an affirmation of ordinary life as more than profane, as itself hallowed and in no way second class."[146] The ramifications of this shift have been far reaching. It should be obvious, though, that their language of God's calling can be put to use in ways that require workers to resign themselves to any and every harsh circumstance endemic to their socioeconomic condition. With respect to Calvin's contributions, in particular, it is not simply his understanding of calling that has functioned in this way. His larger outlook on divine sovereignty with respect to the doctrines of election and predestination, it has been argued, has also had significant impact. Specifically is this the case with respect to how work is viewed in the context of capitalism. In fact, according to some analyses, capitalism likely would not have developed apart from the influence of John Calvin.

Immediately prior to his discussion of "the Lord's calling a basis of our way of life," Calvin discusses the relationship between the hope of

---

144. Ibid., III.x.6.

145. Ibid. It is tempting to cite Stanley Hauerwas's words concerning Pope John Paul II's *Laborem Exercens* in connection with Calvin at this point: "His account has all the marks of the kind of things that those who no longer have to work feel they need to say about those who do." See his "Work as Co-Creation," 117.

146. Taylor, *Sources of the Self*, 217–18.

eternal life and "outward conduct of life" in the present. Calvin's doctrine of election—the assertion that God chose before creation those who would know salvation or damnation—offered no explicit assurance of knowledge now of one's status later. One could, however, demonstrate the signs of one's elect status in the conduct of daily life. Such a life demands, for example, that one "indulge oneself as little as possible; but on the contrary, with unflagging effort of mind to insist upon cutting off all show of superfluous wealth, not to mention licentiousness." Keeping to "the rule of moderation" insures "considerable progress in the Lord's school." A proper account of one's stewardship in life requires "abstinence, sobriety, frugality, and moderation." Excess, pride, ostentation, and vanity are all condemned.[147]

One of the founders of modern sociology sees in Calvinism the ingredients necessary to the development of capitalism. Max Weber took note of "the idea of the necessity of proving one's faith in worldly activity" in the particular way taught by Calvin.[148] He saw in the ongoing influence of Calvinism the formation of a culture that prized hard work as an arena of divine activity as well as one that promoted the virtues of simplicity, thrift, and frugality. When such qualities combine there is bound to result a prosperity that makes possible accumulation of vast sums of capital. "When the limitation of consumption is combined with this release of acquisitive activity," says Weber, "the inevitable practical result is obvious: accumulation of capital through ascetic compulsion to save."[149] The inevitable accumulation of enormous amounts of capital made available the resources necessary to fund the dramatic shift away from the feudal economies of medieval Europe to the capitalist economies of our modern era.

We should not imagine that Weber presents the market understanding of economics and work as Christian in character. He does argue, however, that the influence of Calvin and his Puritan heirs "favored the development of a rational bourgeois economic life; it was the most important, and above all the only consistent influence in the development of that life."[150] Weber remarks as well, though, how the very principles of market economics, touted as the necessary mechanisms of nature,

147. Calvin, *Institutes*, III.x.4–5.
148. Weber, *Protestant Ethic*, 121.
149. Ibid., 172.
150. Ibid., 174.

eventually crowded out any of the restraining influences of Christian virtue. The "purely religious enthusiasm" fueled economic development through its "ascetic educative influence." Then, he says, "the intensity of the search for the Kingdom of God commenced gradually to pass over into sober economic virtue; the religious roots died out slowly, giving way to utilitarian worldliness."[151] Weber argues that what had its cultural origins in an environment elevating work to the status of "calling" is "now bound to the technical and economic conditions of machine production which to-day determine the lives of all individuals who are born into this mechanism . . . with irresistible force." In an earlier day, "The Puritan wanted to work in a calling; we are forced to do so." By Weber's day, the world of work had become an "iron cage."[152]

If there is in Weber a sober sense of the burdens of work, his account offers perhaps only a realistic appraisal of work in our contemporary environment, as did the first major theorist of the free market—Adam Smith. For Smith, work is a necessary evil that is justified only by its instrumental value in prospering a nation as a whole.[153] By "instrumental" is meant that Smith views work, not as something good in and of itself, but of value only on account of its capacity to provide the means by which goods and services—"the necessaries and conveniences of life"—can be obtained. God might work as an expression of who God is, but man works because he has to; and in doing so he must "always lay down" some "portion of his ease, his liberty, and his happiness."[154] Smith is well aware that work can be onerous and that, particularly with respect to "inferior

151. Ibid., 176. That did not mean complete silence among religious voices concerning the world of work and economics. It simply meant that "God-concepts" once again came to serve prevailing economic arrangements, whatever the character of those arrangements. Weber (178) describes how in his day the "literature of almost all denominations is saturated with the idea that faithful labour, even at low wages, on the part of those whom life offers no other opportunities, is highly pleasing to God."

152. Ibid., 181. Weber's historical and conceptual analysis has been widely challenged, but his assertion that in the United States work is concerned primarily with "the pursuit of wealth, stripped of its religious and ethical meaning" and that for many work now possesses "the character of sport" (182) rings true. See Hughes, *End of Work*, 33–60.

153. Smith, *Wealth of Nations*, 1. It is critical to note the significance of the title of Smith's volume. He offers an account of the "wealth of nations," not individuals. Capitalism is not concerned with how any particular individual fares in the marketplace. The "mechanisms" of the market function in a utilitarian manner, justified with reference to the greatest good for the greatest number.

154. Ibid., 14.

employments" (he identifies the trade of butcher as "a brutal and odious business"), "the sweets of labour consist altogether in the recompense of labour."[155]

Miroslav Volf identifies a significant tension in Smith's view of work at this point: "Individually, the goal of every person is to avoid working because anthropologically, work is something clearly negative. Societally, however, the goal is to increase the quantity and quality of work because economically, work is something thoroughly positive; it is the primary factor in economic growth on which the whole progress of society depends."[156] Work is needed for the sake of "the wealth of nations," but Smith believes work threatens the freedom of the individual. Smith believes it is a *free market* characterized by the division of labor that best resolves this tension. If work must be done, the burdens of work are best offset by making work as efficient as possible. According to Smith, "The greatest improvement in the productive powers of labour, and the greater part of the skill, dexterity, and judgment with which it is anywhere directed, or applied, seem to have been the effects of the division of labour."[157] The division of labor, whereby goods and services are produced by those particularly skilled at more and more discrete tasks, affords the individual with more vocational choices (one can become a butcher, a brewer, or a baker) and greater opportunity to perfect a particular skill by not having to master many in order to survive. The focus on a narrower set of skills enables a worker to be more efficient and thus in a position to forfeit less ease and liberty while being more productive.

If the division of labor, though, is supposed to lessen the onerous character of work in a capitalist context, Smith himself indicates that the mechanism might even have the opposite effect. Where division of labor and efficiency of production are priorities, "the employment of the far greater part of those who live by labour, that is, of the great body of people, comes to be confined to a few very simple operations, frequently to one or two." In such a situation "skill and dexterity" appropriate to the task will certainly improve and work become more efficient. "But the understandings of the greater part of men," recognizes Smith, "are necessarily formed by their ordinary employments." What, then, might happen to "the man whose whole life is spent in performing a few simple

155. Ibid., 52.
156. Volf, *Work in the Spirit*, 50–51.
157. Smith, *Wealth of Nations*, 3.

operations?" Such a person, he says, "has no occasion to exert his understanding" and "generally becomes as stupid and as ignorant as it is possible for a human creature to become." While such a person certainly becomes quite efficient and skilled "at his own particular trade," such benefits are inevitably "acquired at the expense of his own intellectual, social, and martial virtues."[158] Smith is confident, however, that the mechanisms of the market, left to themselves, will achieve, as if "by an invisible hand," the general well-being of society as a whole.[159]

Smith leaves us with an irresolvable contradiction in his view of work. The division of labor functions to ameliorate the necessary evil of work as a threat to liberty and ease. At the same time, though, the demands of market efficiency mean that "all the nobler parts of the human character may be, in a great measure, obliterated and extinguished in the great body of people," surrendering them to a "drowsy stupidity."[160] While we need to remember that capitalism offers no guarantees to the individual concerning success and meaningful work, the notion that their sacrifices serve the greater good seems hardly sufficient to assign to the majority of a nation's workforce the duty of self-imposed alienation. For Adam Smith, evidently, such "is the price . . . societies have to pay for being economically advanced and civilized."[161]

A full-scale critique of capitalism is not the concern here. What must be noted, however, is how, even in the disenchanted world of the "free" market,[162] "God-concepts" still function in nontheological form to underwrite prevailing assumptions about work. Meeks offers, for example, that the doctrines of divine providence and salvation have been secularized into "internal laws of progress" that operate "naturally" (Smith's "invisible hand") when market mechanisms are allowed to run without interference. The modern "success ethic," Meeks says, "is the

158. Ibid., 340–41.

159. Ibid., 194.

160. Ibid., 341. Volf insists that, despite numerous attempts by defenders of Smith, "This contradiction defies all attempts at a solution" (*Work in the Spirit*, 208 n. 49).

161. Volf, *Work in the Spirit*, 54.

162. Part of what is meant by "free" is the insistence that matters of economic exchange operate without the interference or regulation of any concerns or values outside of the economic arena. Hughes (*End of Work*, 46) describes the modern market as "a supposedly value-free space of pure utility, opposed to the traditional and the theological."

individualized theory of progress writ small, in the life of the individual."[163] Combined with a laissez-faire approach to the market (matters of economic exchange are self-regulating and need no additional constraint or regulation by government or the church), the success ethic argues that one's economic well-being is entirely a matter of one's own making and holds out the promise of sufficient reward to compensate for any rigors encountered on the way. While the success ethic does not necessarily invoke the name of God for its legitimacy, Meeks argues that behind the ideologies of laissez-faire economics and the contemporary success ethic "is the *faith* that the mechanisms of the price system . . . can best fulfill the utilitarian calculus" that draws us to the pleasure of material comfort and away from the pain of poverty.[164]

From Plato's republic to Adam Smith's free market there is the recognition that work that is burdensome and personally unrewarding will fall to the greater part of any population. Again and again, whether it is Plato's myth of the metals, Luther and Calvin's doctrine of calling, or Smith's confidence in an "invisible hand," religious or quasi-religious appeals have been made to underwrite social conditions and work situations recognized as hurtful and dehumanizing. Is there not danger in invoking God's will in the economic arena? Does the assertion that God wills work not play into the hands of those eager to grant divine legitimacy to social and economic arrangements that privilege some at the expense of others?

Certainly Paul's Letter to the Ephesians has been used in that way. What more abusive work relationship could there be than that between master and slave? Does not Paul himself provide sanction and support to such abuse when he demands, "Slaves, be obedient to those who are your masters according to the flesh" (6:5)? Does not his qualifying phrase "as to Christ" render such obedience a religious obligation? What have been called the New Testament "household codes" have obviously been used to insist on a divine pattern establishing a relationship between the "ruler" and the "ruled." Pro-slavery advocates in the nineteenth-century

163. Meeks, *God the Economist*, 141–42.

164. Ibid., 140; emphasis mine. Perhaps the most overt expression of the secularization of God-concepts in the economic arena is Andrew Carnegie's essay "Wealth," in the June 1889 edition of *The North American Review*. For Carnegie, the "gospel of wealth" offers four basic laws: (1) individualism, (2) private property, (3) accumulation of wealth, and (4) competition. According to Carnegie, these features offer "the true Gospel concerning Wealth, obedience to which is destined to solve the problem of the Rich and the Poor, and to bring 'Peace on Earth, among men Good Will'" (671); cited in Betsworth, *Social Ethics*, 69–70.

American South employed such texts in precisely that way.[165] Contemporary critics deplore "an impoverishment [in the household codes] which allowed gross injustice to flourish in Christian countries through the centuries."[166] A closer examination of the Ephesian household code awaits us. For the present, however, it might be offered that Paul is not addressing the legitimacy of the Greco-Roman household, but how it is that believers might behave within that context. It was an important question: "Can one be a slave and act like a Christian?" That is a different question from whether or not the institution of slavery is legitimate. It is one thing for a believer to serve Christ in less than ideal, even oppressive, circumstances. Who is responsible for those circumstances and what is required of them is another matter altogether.

Still, God wills work. The God who works has created believers in Christ Jesus "for good works" (2:10). When many hear the phrase "good works" they might assume Paul refers here to obvious acts of Christian ministry in evangelism and missions. Habitat for Humanity or summer missions—those are good works. Accounting, making furniture, managing a restaurant, driving a school bus—that's just work. We do need to note, though, that Paul prepares here for the extensive parenesis of chapters 4–6. He does not spell out in 2:10 what counts for those "good works," but "its implications will be taken up and amplified in the exhortatory sections of the letter."[167] Nestled within those sections is that notice with which our exploration of work began—"Let him work with his hands what is good" (4:28). "Good works" is more than about work; Paul discusses a number of matters in chapters 4–6. Paul does talk about work, however, and it must be viewed within the context of the life that God has intended for us from the beginning.

That is something of the point behind Paul's specific language that believers are "*created* in Christ Jesus for good works." Later in Eph 4:24 Paul again speaks of the new life of believers in terms of creation. We are called to "put on the new self," which "has been *created* in righteousness and holiness of the truth." The significance of this link between creation and redemption will be more fully explored in the next chapter; let it be stressed here, though, that God's work of redemption in Christ is not a renunciation of what God began in creation, but its fulfillment. Because

---

165. For an examination of how the Bible was used in such arguments, see Swartley, *Slavery,* 31–64.

166. Davies, "Work and Slavery," 347.

167. O'Brien, *Ephesians,* 180.

of the arduous features of much of our work, we perhaps forget that work is not simply a feature of a fallen world. The sin of the garden looms over our work whenever we suffer its toilsome and futile dimensions (cf. Gen 3:17–19). But from the beginning it was not so: "The Lord God took the man and put him into the garden of Eden to cultivate it and keep it" (2:15). God willed work from the beginning. Yet, God's work of new creation does not merely return us to the status of the garden; rather, the divine initiative of grace and peace offers the realization of that to which the garden was but the prelude.

God Wills Work in Keeping with God's Will

Many would likely support the theses so far offered; that God works and that God wills work are useful beliefs that can go far in motivating a workforce, particularly when the work in question can itself be so unrewarding. Paul's admonition that slaves serve their masters "not by way of eye-service, as men-pleasers, but as slaves of Christ, doing the will of God from the heart" (Eph 6:6) might sound one way to slaves and another to masters. Still, God wills work. Does Ephesians offer any resources for seeing work other than as a necessary evil, or for placing a check on the demands of the workplace that can otherwise be so harsh?

Here, as they say in Texas, we must go from preaching to meddling. "Meddling" might be the description given for any efforts to bring considerations into the economic arena from those Smith identifies as "do-gooders," those who insist on imposing constraints and regulations on matters of economic exchange in an attempt to alleviate the brutalities of the workplace. Smith's vision permits each and every individual to pursue his or her own self-interest, constrained only by the competition of others also in pursuit of their self-interest. The worker engaged in such pursuit "intends neither to promote the public interest, nor knows how much he is promoting it. . . . He intends only his own gain." Smith's confidence was, though, that the worker "is in this, as in many other cases, led by an invisible hand to promote an end which was no part of his intention."[168]

---

168. Smith, *Wealth of Nations*, 194. Volf (*Work in the Spirit*, 53) says, "Smith shared the liberal belief in the harmony of self-interest with the good of civil society" whereby "the 'invisible hand' transformed self-interested rational labor of individuals into a system of mutual service." The 2008 turmoil in world markets led some to question Smith's premise. See Irwin and Paley, "Greenspan Says He Was Wrong," for a report on former Federal Reserve chairman Alan Greenspan's reflections on such matters.

Any intentional intrusion of noneconomic considerations from some other quarter (e.g., church or state) only threatens the fine balance of market forces that, left to themselves, will in the long run resolve any of the problems encountered in the market.

Any number of responses to this outlook have been provided. A fundamental question, left unresolved by capitalist theory, though, gets to the very heart of many current debates and bitter divisions in contemporary American culture. Let us suppose that Smith is correct about matters of economic exchange, that they function most efficiently, productively, and beneficially when the market is left to operate according to its own internal mechanisms. That assumption offers no guidance for determining what goods are to be assigned to the arena of economic exchange and what goods are exempt. Stephen Long observes that "whether all things should be assigned a monetary value . . . they obviously can be."[169] Many important areas of life—sexual relations, body organs, the procreation of children, matters of health—all of these are important "values," and some of them (e.g., health) have already been largely placed in the arena of market considerations. Might it be merely a matter of time before the distribution of body organs or unwanted children are subject to market forces? For many, sexual relations are of a different character than commercial goods. Should prostitution be legalized and controlled only by the principles of supply and demand? Should access to marijuana or cocaine?

The assurance of capitalist theory is that market forces simply express the laws of nature and it is not nice to fool Mother Nature with unwarranted meddling from outside the market. Long's point is that "economists constantly mistake what is made at a particular social and historical moment for a natural fact."[170] It is a social fact that for many health care has been priced out of their reach. It is a matter of social preference that most in Dallas, Texas, favor private over public modes of transportation. These are not natural facts like the law of gravity. The basic point here is that to argue against the intrusion of "nonmarket" considerations into the market ignores the reality that what is assigned to the mechanisms of market exchange and what is "protected" from such are decisions made apart from the market. Admittedly, the prospect of profit for some goods might be tempting; but the very subjection of some

---

169. Long and Fox, *Calculated Futures*, 38.
170. Ibid.

goods to the market violates the very nature of those goods. It might be tempting for a professor to distribute *A*'s in a class to the highest bidder; accrediting agencies would view the practice as a fundamental distortion of what counts for a university education. The reality is that commitments reflecting a sense of what is good and what is not are already at work in the market setting; to assume that the market simply operates on the basis of natural forces and should be exempt from "meddling" is to ignore the impact such commitments already make in our economic behavior.

The powerful assertion of market ideology is that economics operates as a self-contained, discrete sphere of life. Other cultural enterprises are all worthwhile and have their place; their place, however, is not to interfere within the realm of the economic. Religion has its proper domain in the arena of the spiritual. Economics has its proper domain in the arena of the material.[171] Unfortunately, even many Christians seem to observe this sharp divide, treating economic choices as a separable arena of life, only loosely tied to any faith commitments. On the basis of extensive survey data exploring the influence of religious convictions on economic habits in the United States, Robert Wuthnow concludes, "When we are influenced by our faith, we are more likely to say we feel better about what we do than to do anything differently. We do not look to the churches to tell us what career to pursue or what purchases to make but to tell us that whatever choices we have made are OK. Our spirituality is little more than a therapeutic device. . . . We have domesticated the sacred and stripped it of authoritative wisdom by looking to it only to make us happy."[172]

As Long says, though, "Christian theology must refuse this forced spatialization and confess that the relationship between God and the

---

171. The influence of Kant should be apparent in this outlook; see Hughes, *End of Work*, 38–39.

172. Wuthnow, *God and Mammon in America*, 5–6. Wuthnow describes one survey respondent as "typical of the majority of church members who largely keep work and faith in separate compartments" and quotes him as saying, "I don't allow my value system to be dictated by the church. I have to take responsibility for my own decisions" (55). When respondents were asked if they had in the last year thought about how their faith relates to their work, 60 percent of those who attended weekly religious services said they did so. Wuthnow says the figure indicates "that many people are at least interested in making their faith relevant to their work. It also indicates that many people have learned to compartmentalize the two" (55).

world is discovered in the ordinary, material reality of everyday life."[173] As we have seen, Paul's Letter to the Ephesians offers a language and a vision, a saying and a seeing, concerning God's *oikonomia* that is as universal and all-embracing as is imaginable (1:9–10). The cosmic sovereignty of Christ over all powers (1:19–23), the admonition to work what is good (4:28), Paul's insistence that masters cannot do with their slaves as they please (6:9)[174]—all these features indicate that a walk worthy of God's calling will embrace the arena of the everyday and encompass even those hours that are claimed by the market. God wills work in keeping with God's will. What might be some features of such work?

Even if we confine ourselves to Ephesians, we will still have plenty to challenge us concerning work in keeping with God's will. This will has everything to do with the divine initiative of grace that pursues the divine agenda of peace. That means, of course, that if we are to ask what we should do about work, we must first ask what God is doing and how our work might participate in and reflect the work of God. Only when we view work in this light can we understand Paul's astonishing insistence: "Let him work with his hands what is good, that he may have something to give to the one who has need."

We also need to place Paul's admonition in 4:28 in the context of the immediate passage—a paragraph that extends from 4:25 to 5:2 and that concerns at least two major issues. The first concern has to do with the specific character and shape of new life in Christ lived in contrast to the "former manner of life" (4:17–24). The second concern is reflected in the repeated language of "one another" in 4:25—5:2, stressing relationships in the Christian community. Paul's peculiar admonition concerning work has everything to do with new life in the one body of Christ.[175] But this passage alludes to another scriptural context that we must also take into consideration. In Eph 4:25 Paul exhorts his readers, "Speak truth, each

---

173. Long, *Goodness of God*, 85.

174. Again, the household codes of the New Testament do not underwrite the household structure that prevailed in the Greco-Roman context, but insist that within that context the demands of God's calling must find expression. That Paul tells masters what they can and cannot do with what was considered their property O'Brien calls "outrageous" (*Ephesians*, 454).

175. See Fowl, "Making Stealing Possible," 164–76. Fowl (168) insists, "This entire passage is directed towards maintaining the common life of the church. These are not demands addressed to isolated individuals to make of what they will. Rather, they are admonitions to a community about how they must talk and live with each other in order to maintain their unity and faithfulness under Christ."

one of you with his neighbor," a citation of Zech 8:16. When Paul cites an Old Testament passage he is not proof-texting—quoting a verse out of context so as to make a point entirely unrelated to the original context. Rather, by what Richard Hays calls the literary device of *metalepsis*, Paul generally wants to create "a broad interplay" between the text cited and its current use, "encompassing aspects of [the text employed] beyond those explicitly echoed."[176] The connections between Zechariah 8 and Ephesians 4:25—5:2 are many and can inform our exploration of what this passage has to say about work.[177]

The prophet Zechariah portrays the life of a community to come established by God's grace and blessed with God's peace. A people *once* scattered and under divine wrath *now* know God's saving intervention and peace (Zech 8:7–8, 10–12). While the prospect might seem far-fetched to some, it is not too difficult for God to form a people who, though they *formerly* lived in alienation and futility, will *now* know peace and prosperity (8:6, 11–12) and relationship with God "in truth and righteousness" (8:8).[178] Zechariah mentions many of the characteristics of a saved people living in covenant with God. Their hands are to be strong for work in the temple and in the fields (8:9, 12–13). As a community they are to speak truth and practice peace (8:16); indeed, they are to "love truth and peace" (8:19). Their worship will be marked by "joy, gladness, and cheerful feasts for the house of Judah" (8:19). All this they enjoy because God has "purposed in these days to do good" on their behalf (8:15). The confidence of the prophet is that a community so shaped by God's grace and peace will exhibit before the nations a way of life such that "many peoples and mighty nations will come to seek the Lord of hosts," recognizing the presence of God in their midst (8:20–23). As far as Paul is concerned, new life in the one body of Christ is the arena in which the prophetic hope finds its realization.[179]

176. Hays, *Echoes of Scripture*, 20.

177. Yoder Neufeld (*"Put on the Armour of God,"* 133–34 n. 128) says, "Zechariah 8 has many notable points of contact with Ephesians . . . the brief citation of Zech 8:16 in Eph 4:25 is but the tip of the iceberg in terms of the role Zech 8 plays in the thought of the author of Ephesians."

178. On this "once"-"formerly"/"now" pattern in Ephesians, see Tachau, *"Einst" und "Jetz" im Neuen Testament*, 125–26, 138; Holloway, *Peripateō*, 189, 211. Paul mentions relationship with God "in righteousness and holiness of the truth" in Eph 4:24, immediately prior to his citation of Zech 8:16 in 4:25.

179. According to O'Brien (*Ephesians*, 338), "What is predicated of the eschatological future of God's people in terms of new Jerusalem language in the Old Testament

Paul's use of the Old Testament here has profound implications for how Christians should understand the role of work in our lives. For starters, it is important to note that the prophet's depiction of the eschatological community includes an account of strong hands *at work*. On account of the resurrection of Christ from the dead, Paul understands the church, as those raised and seated with Christ (2:4–6), to be this community. Far from seeing work merely as a consequence of the sin of the garden, though, work is seen in light of the fulfillment of God's intent for creation. Paul is certainly aware of the distortions of work and matters of economic exchange that sin brings into the arena of human toil. His warnings against greed (4:19; 5:3), his admonition to thieves (4:28), and his recognition of the capacity of the abuse of power found, for example, within the master-slave relationship (6:5–9) all testify to his recognition that in the world of work things can and do go wrong. What is God doing about it? Through God's redemptive work, God is creating a people whose lives, sustained in worship, bear witness to God's purpose for work. Work is not an alien feature to God's intent for creation, and so the will of God for work includes its renewal for the sake of witness to the power of the gospel to transform all of life.

That renewal will be a witness to the capacity of God to bless abundantly so that those blessed by God can bless others. Zechariah underscores the divine agency and agenda behind fruitful vineyards and productive lands: "I will save you that you may become a blessing," declares the Lord of hosts, with a concluding admonition: "Do not fear; let your hands be strong" (Zech 8:12–13). This account explains how it is that Paul can give his peculiar reasoning for why the thief needs to quit his thieving ways and work with his hands what is good—"so that he may have something to give to the one who has need." And this account indicates how work must be for believers a witness to new life in the one body of Christ.

How is it that Paul can say what he says about work? Why work? We have a ready answer to that question, one informed by the demands of the market and its underlying anthropology. Smith reveals that anthropology as of an autonomous individual motivated by rational self-interest. Why do people work, asks Smith? "It is not from the benevolence of the butcher, the brewer, or the baker that we expect our dinner, but from

---

passage is picked up by Paul in relation to the 'new person', God's new community in Christ upon whom the ends of the ages have come."

their regard to their own interest," he has famously said.[180] This bottom-line conviction about human nature is the foundation and repeated reference point for the entire market understanding of work. Its mechanisms of pricing, competition, supply and demand, determination of wages, production and distribution of goods and services all reflect this premise concerning the human condition—we are all locked in a battle of self-interested competition in a context of scarcity.

Paul's admonition to the thief does not reflect Adam Smith's assumptions. Rather, his words reflect a competing vision for how God seeks to order work in the lives of believers in the broader context of their participation in a community that bears witness to the divine initiative of grace and peace. Specifically, Paul does not begin with the assumption of scarcity as the prior economic condition that must be negotiated. That is the starting point, however, for standard approaches to economics. "Capitalist economics assumes scarcity," Long observes, "not as an empirical analysis of the natural. It functions in economics as a metaphysical claim."[181] Limit, loss, distress, deprivation—these were the circumstances known by a people who had lived life outside the arena of divine justice and mercy (Zech 7:8–14). A refusal to practice justice, kindness, and compassion had sunk a society to the point of crippling economic distress (8:10). But such scarcity was the result, not the prior condition, of their economic practices.

Paul's words about the motivation for work—"in order that he may have something to give to the one having need"—reflect the peculiar tension of New Testament eschatology that assumes the believing community lives within the present conditions of a world in need of redemption as participants in and witnesses to the redemption Zechariah envisioned. The present conditions of constraint and limit occasioned by the economics of scarcity contribute to the reality that there are those "having need." That believers are encouraged to work, driven not by the threat of scarcity but by a commitment to generosity, assumes participation in a broader reality characterized by God's abundance. "Work with his hands" does not testify to a broken creation where work is merely the consequence of sin. That there are still those "having need" does remind us that the world yet awaits its full redemption. "In order to give" reminds Christians that

180. Smith, *Wealth of Nations*, 7.
181. Long and Fox, *Calculated Futures*, 41.

our work can serve as a witness to "many peoples and mighty nations" that God is in our midst even now (Zech 8:21–23).

Neither Zechariah nor Paul, however, present work as the only mark of a redeemed people. Zechariah depicts a new Jerusalem in which rest and play are present in its streets (Zech 8:4–5). These activities "suggest a pleasant existence, life in which the citizens of the city are not always pressed by concerns for finding food, shelter, and clothing."[182] Fasting becomes feasting with joy and gladness in this scene of bounty (8:19). For Paul as well, there is more to new life in the one body of Christ than work. The little phrase "good works" in 2:10 hints at what Paul describes in great detail in Ephesians 4–6, and there is much more to this life than work. Paul talks about our relationships with one another as believers in worship and in service; he talks about basic qualities of life such as honesty and fidelity; he warns against conforming to the patterns of behavior and thinking of an unbelieving world; he encourages households to bring the basic standards of Christian practice like service and love into the domestic arena; he encourages us all to allow the love of God in Christ to serve as the measure of our lives as we learn to be kind to one another, tenderhearted, forgiving each other just as God in Christ has forgiven us; he too describes a scene of joyful worship and celebration in which the Spirit of God is present to guide and make us wise. There is more to this new life in Christ than work.

The work Paul does envision, then, is not driven by the threat of scarcity into a frantic and ceaseless demand for acquisition and accumulation. In fact, twice Paul singles out the economic sin of greed as one of the chief marks of a life lived in separation from God (Eph 4:17–19; 5:3–5).[183] The life of restless acquisition and accumulation fueled by the fear of scarcity is the antithesis of the life of play, worship, and generosity sustained by a restful trust in God's abundance. If, for believers, work

---

182. Petersen, *Haggai and Zechariah 1–8*, 300.

183. In Eph 5:3 and Col 3:5, Paul associates greed (Greek: *pleonexia*, "have more") with both sexual license and idolatry. Brain S. Rosner has pointed out that this association is characteristic of biblical teaching on greed and identifies it as "a typical sin of the gentiles, a vain folly and an evil desire that leads to other sins and ought to be treated with the greatest vigilance since it evokes stern divine judgment." See his *Greed as Idolatry*, 174. The connection with idolatry identifies the greedy as "as those with a strong desire to acquire and keep for themselves more and more money and possessions, because they love, trust, and obey wealth rather than God" (129). The association with sexual immorality invests greed with the sense of selfish gratification and abusive use of others that sexual license displays (see O'Brien, *Ephesians*, 360).

must be a witness to new life in the one body of Christ, then there are some things work must not be. Work must not be the defining feature of our lives, for example. This assertion drives Hauerwas's criticism of John Paul II's *Laborem Exercens*, that the papal encyclical elevates work to a role and status in our lives that it ought not to bear: "Attributing greater significance to work risks making it demonic, as work then becomes an idolatrous activity through which we try to secure and guarantee our significance, to make 'our mark' on history."[184] That work often becomes the defining feature of our lives is itself too often due to this restless quest for acquisition and accumulation, whether the quest is by the ones doing the hard work or the ones for whom the hard work is done.

Paul's words about work will sound strange to many ears and even unrealistic to those for whom the conventional defines the real. Believers situated in the modern West live under the intense supervision of cultural forces that encourage shopping as a patriotic duty. The "sacred canopy" that defines the boundaries of expectation measures success in terms of acquisition and accumulation. Work is the necessary evil that must be endured so as to enjoy the freedom to ceaselessly pursue those things that make life worthwhile (at least those things we are told will make life worthwhile). The challenge for those who know new life in the one body of Christ concerns how to pursue work in keeping with God's will in the midst of a cultural environment that invests work with a very different significance.

Zechariah does not abstract his vision of strong hands and fruitful vineyards from the wider setting of a community whose practices reflect God's work of grace and peace. The prophet speaks of life in a community committed to truthful speech, restorative justice, joyful worship, and a common life that displays the presence of God. Neither does Paul abstract his words about work from other commitments that characterize new life in the one body of Christ. Work in keeping with God's will for work permits both rest and generosity. Such an approach to work, though, faces the relentless demands of our culture to define ourselves and our work otherwise. And here, "the problem is that we lack the personal resources to resist the seductions of a culture in which more is always better and in which status is always measured by possessions."[185] But Paul is not offering advice to the isolated individual faced with the demands of heroic

---

184. Hauerwas, "Work as Co-Creation," 115.

185. Verhey, *Remembering Jesus*, 313.

self-denial. He speaks to participants in a community where the demands of one practice only make sense and are only made possible by that participation and by shared commitments to several practices that reinforce one another. This is the point Stephen Fowl makes when he observes the relationship between Paul's words about work and their setting in Ephesians: "What this passage . . . indicates . . . is that Christians' abilities to speak truthfully with each other, to offer edifying and gracious words, to be angry without sinning, and so forth, are directly connected to issues about how they acquire and hold wealth."[186]

The reverse is true as well: how Christians acquire and hold wealth is directly related to the nature of our participation in a community that has learned to speak the truth, that knows how to deal with conflict in ways that lead to resolution and reconciliation, that offers edifying and gracious words, and that embodies the very way of Christ in a community of love and forgiveness. Only in such a community characterized by such practices are our lives shaped in ways to see work's proper place. Only in such a community can we learn to say and see in ways that challenge and overcome the standard assessment of the role of work. We live in the world in light of the world we live in. Work in keeping with God's will becomes a reality not as we live in Kant's world of autonomous individuals guided by Smith's rational self-interest. Believers know, though, that we live in a world marked by the divine initiative of grace in pursuit of the divine agenda of peace. As we participate in the community shaped by that reality, we can then participate in work in keeping with God's will for work.

186. Fowl, "Making Stealing Possible," 174.

2

"Created in Christ Jesus"

A Redemptive Ethic

> "The only philosophy which can responsibly be practiced in the face of despair would be the attempt to contemplate all things as they would present themselves from the standpoint of redemption. Knowledge has no light but that shed on the world by redemption."
>
> T. W. ADORNO[1]

Years ago a student asked on the first day of a class in Christian ethics, "Do you believe that there is a morality for everybody?" He was concerned that his professor might be a moral relativist, one who does not believe in moral truths that hold across time and cultures and to which are all accountable. The professor could tell his response did not satisfy: "I believe that there is a gospel for everybody." The student's audible groan suggested his worst fears had been confirmed—"My Christian ethics professor does not believe there is a morality for everybody." His concern perhaps reflects the thinking of many Christians: the idea that "Christian ethics" can proceed in some way without reference to the gospel, the glad announcement that through God's redemptive work in Christ a work of new creation takes place, the transformative reality in which believers participate and to which they bear witness in the world. The student likely held a view, maintained in some circles, that the gospel

1. Adorno, *Minima Moralia*, 18.

that *is for everybody* is *all* about going to heaven, that God's work of re-demption through Christ is understood primarily in "forensic" terms; that is, that it is all about getting a "not guilty" verdict one day before the seat of divine judgment.

To put it crassly, some think redemption is simply about "fire insur-ance" and that the gospel has to do only with the next life and not too much with this one. Such a view evokes one of the criticisms Friedrich Nietzsche (1844–1900) leveled against Paul's presentation of the gospel. Nietzsche's objections to the Christian faith are many; one of his com-plaints, though, is that the Christian doctrine of "salvation by grace, through faith, apart from works" (see Eph 2:8–9) was detrimental to the notion of vibrant action in the world. According to one interpreter, Ni-etzsche considers "faith" as "that which modern man professes hypocriti-cally without having a thought of doing anything about it—except going to communion." In particular, the Apostle Paul is guilty of advocating a split between faith and action. He is "the man who made it possible for pagans the world over to persist in their own way of life while calling themselves Christians."[2]

Nietzsche's antipathy toward the Apostle Paul, which we will ex-plore more fully, is as deep as it is misguided. We have to admit, however, that he is not alone in his criticisms and not without evidence provided by the too frequent failures of Christian practice. Samuel Wells laments, "Christians may engage in the most damaging of public practices while still assuming that thinking 'the right things' about salvation or having a 'close personal relationship' with God ensures that righteousness remains with them."[3] From the 1940s comes a challenge from the Jewish writer Joseph Soloveitchik, who describes what he often saw among Christians in his day:

> [The religious man] praying in his house of worship. . . , repeat-ing over and over . . . not my will be done, only Thine—is not at that moment a this-worldly man, possessor of riches and chat-tels, estates and factories, who drives his impoverished workers ruthlessly, and whose hands are often stained with the blood of the outcast and the ill-gotten gain wrung from the hands of the unfortunate. For him the world of prayer and the world of

2. Kaufmann, *Nietzsche*, 343. Nietzsche (*A*, §38) speaks of those who are "anti-Christians through and through in their deeds" who "still call themselves Christians and attend communion."

3. Wells, *Improvisation*, 40.

> reality have nothing to do with each other. . . . The heavenly
> kingdom does not come into the slightest contact with the
> earthly kingdom. . . . The man in the sanctuary and the man in
> the marketplace are two separate and distinct personalities who
> have absolutely nothing in common with one another.[4]

A rabbi living in Poland and Germany in the 1920s and 1930s surely had sufficient opportunity to witness evil and injustice perpetrated by those who identified themselves as Christians.

Christian ethics nonetheless asks, "What is God doing about evil?" A faithful response to that question will insist that God responds to evil through and by God's redemptive work. What, however, is meant here by God's "redemptive work"? In the most general terms, as J. Richard Middleton has put it, "In Scripture, redemption is conceived most fundamentally as the reversal of the fall and the restoration of God's good purposes from the beginning."[5] In the Old Testament that redemption came to expression in God intervening on behalf of an enslaved people and delivering them from the murderous hands of Pharaoh. In the New Testament it means God acting through Christ to deliver from the bondage to sin, the world, and the destructive forces of the powers, and in granting new life in the body of Christ.

How does this redemptive work relate to the moral life God intends for humanity? In Ephesians, before there is any concern to identify specific moral norms or expected patterns of behavior, there is first the account of God's redemptive work through Christ. Loyola ethicist Roberto Dell'Oro insists that "Christian ethics will be concerned only *derivately* with moral norms; in the first place, Christian moral discourse will point to the renewed existential condition of human freedom made possible by God's self-communication (grace). To be 'in Christ' (*en Christo*), to use a Pauline expression, is the ontological condition for being able to do (to act) like Christ."[6] What moral exhortation Paul offers in Ephesians he offers to those whom he describes as "in Christ," a phrase he uses in

---

4. Soloveitchik, *Halakhic Man,* 92–93; cited by Reno, "Redemption and Ethics," 28–29.

5. Middleton, "New Heaven and a New Earth," 75.

6. Dell'Oro, "Theological Anthropology and Bioethics," 21. Dell'Oro continues to contrast what he calls "a biblical understanding of moral life" with "a scholastic version of natural law heavily shaped by the epistemological presuppositions of modern rationalism." That contrast is appropriate in any discussion of Christian ethics as a redemptive ethic, but we will take up the issue of natural law in a subsequent chapter on Christian ethics as liturgical in character.

Ephesians at least thirty-three times.[7] Klyne Snodgrass warns that "no simple definition of 'in Christ' will do" and that "each occurrence must be analyzed individually and in context."[8] The general sense of the phrase, though, indicates that Paul addresses his readers as those whose lives, identity, relationships, conduct, speech, and destiny are all shaped by their relationship with God as made possible through Jesus Christ. In Ephesians, Paul will offer a redemptive ethic whereby the life God intends for humanity is the life made possible through Jesus Christ.

Is there a morality for everybody? There is a gospel for everybody. O'Donovan would address the fears of the student mentioned earlier and respond to Nietzsche by insisting, "A belief in Christian ethics is a belief that certain ethical and moral judgments belong to the gospel itself."[9] O'Donovan insists as well, though, "Christian ethics must arise from the gospel of Jesus Christ. Otherwise it could not be *Christian* ethics."[10] We will explore how Paul's vision of the moral life God intends "for everybody" has everything to do with God's redemptive work in Christ. To gain a better understanding of what is at stake in this discussion, though, we will need first to examine Nietzsche's attack on Paul's understanding of redemption and morality. By examining Nietzsche's complaints we will have occasion to highlight certain features of what we will find in Ephesians concerning what it means to be "created in Christ Jesus."

NIETZSCHE'S INDICTMENT

One of the earliest writings we have from Nietzsche comes from a journal entry dated 1858, when he was fourteen years old. The son of a minister (who died when Nietzsche was not quite five years old), young Friedrich was often called "the little minister" by schoolmates. The influence of his

---

7. See Best, *Ephesians*, 153–54. The qualification "at least" reflects the different totals achieved by some scholars counting "in the Lord" phrases found in Ephesians (e.g., Eph 6:1).

8. Snodgrass, *Ephesians*, 47.

9. O'Donovan, *Resurrection and Moral Order*, 12. Richard Burridge (*Imitating Jesus*, 347) identifies the strategy the student was likely reflecting and insists "the common practice of quoting just the ethical teachings or Jesus' and Paul's sayings about moral issues without regard to their context within the *gospels* and letters is a *genre* mistake." I would add that quoting such teachings or sayings without regard to their context within the *gospel* is a *theological* mistake.

10. O'Donovan, *Resurrection and Moral Order*, 11.

upbringing in an environment of deep Lutheran piety is evident: "I have firmly resolved within me to dedicate myself forever to His service. May the dear Lord give me strength and power to carry out my intention and protect me on life's way. Like a child I trust in His grace: He will preserve us all, that no misfortune befall us. But His holy will be done!"[11] One of his last writings, *The Antichrist*, written thirty years later, concludes with this sample of vitriol: "I call Christianity the one great curse, the one great innermost corruption, the one great instinct of revenge, for which no means is poisonous, stealthy, subterranean, small enough—I call it the one immortal blemish of mankind" (A, §62). A lot can happen in thirty years.

What did happen is a matter of debate. It is clear that by 1865, during his first year of theological studies at the University of Bonn, his assessment of the faith in which he had been reared had undergone quite a transition. In that year he would write to his sister that it is no great achievement "simply to accept everything that one has been brought up on and that has gradually struck deep roots." There is indeed much comfort in resting content with "what is considered truth in the circle of one's relatives and of many good men." However, he asks, "Is it decisive after all that we arrive at *that* view of God, world, and reconciliation which makes us feel most comfortable?" Nietzsche counseled his sister, "If you wish to strive for peace of soul and pleasure, then believe; if you wish to be a devotee of truth, then inquire . . ."[12]

It is likely that several factors were involved in Nietzsche's "revaluation" of his inherited faith. The death of his father and a younger brother no doubt haunted him as examples of the threats to meaning in life. Indications are that relationships with his mother and sister were not good. His educational experience at Bonn solidified what had been a growing antagonism toward Christianity. His encounters with the theory of Feuerbach (that Christian belief is the projection onto some

---

11. Cited in Benson, *Pious Nietzsche*, 18.

12. Nietzsche, "Letter to His Sister," 29–30. Nietzsche here commits a couple of logical fallacies. The "genetic fallacy" occurs when a belief is spurned or accepted merely on the basis of its origins. Simply because a belief originates either in the quest for comfort or the pursuit of truth is neither here nor there. A belief can be true without regard to the intent of the one holding the belief. Nietzsche also presents here a "false dichotomy," the presentation of two mutually exclusive options as if they were the only options available. A belief can both be true and comforting; we do not have to accept Nietzsche's either/or premise. But, of course, such errors in logic are of little concern for Nietzsche.

transcendent reality—God—of what are mundane—human—character-istics and values), with the philosophy of Arthur Schopenhauer (reality is the expression of a blind and impersonal "will-to-life"), and with an abysmal European Christianity are all among those factors that produced the one who described himself as "the Antichrist."[13]

This is not the place for a full-scale analysis and point-by-point refutation of any and every criticism of the Christian faith raised by Ni-etzsche.[14] The task here is to highlight the central points of attack by Ni-etzsche on Christianity which have much to do with the present concern for understanding Christian ethics as a redemptive ethic. For with respect to Nietzsche, at the core of his criticism is his assertion that the Christian doctrine of redemption, expressed chiefly by the Apostle Paul, produces a morality that is fundamentally dehumanizing and contrary to human nature—a morality of decadence. Oddly enough, Nietzsche was himself consumed with the relationship between redemption and morality; it is clearly the case that the presentation of this relationship by the Christian-ity with which he was familiar repulsed him. He will offer, then, what he considers to be a "life-affirming" alternative. We engage Nietzsche not to defeat Nietzsche and then declare Paul the winner, although there is value in exposing some of the incoherencies and misrepresentations involved in Nietzsche's attacks. Rather, the concern is once again to underscore the significance and substance of a basic feature of Christian ethics by way of contrast with a clear alternative.

While Nietzsche hardly presents anything resembling systematic re-flection, there is a general thrust to his outlook that Karl Löwith suggests

13. Some theologians, wanting to enlist Nietzsche as partner, suggest his argument is not so much with Christianity as it is with a degraded Christianity accommodated to its European setting. Helmut Thielicke, for example, argues that in attacking Christi-anity, "Nietzsche is not just fighting decadence; he is also fighting a degenerate view of God. . . . When Nietzsche thinks that he is speaking of Christ, he is speaking of an im-age of Christ distorted by the church." See his *Evangelical Faith*, 1:251. It is important to ask detractors of the Christian faith what it is that they do not believe. It might be the case that informed believers will share to some degree in that disbelief. It is also im-portant to remember, though, that Nietzsche considered himself embroiled in a fight to the death against Christianity (*A* §62). That he is understood as "enemy," however, is all the more reason to engage him in dialogue. See Green, *Theology, Hermeneutics, and Imagination*, 112–14. For an account of the "abysmal" character of the European Christianity of Nietzsche's day, see Kierkegaard, *Attack upon Christendom*.

14. A growing number of works give extended treatment to the issues. See, for ex-ample, Fraser, *Redeeming Nietzsche*; S. N. Williams, *Shadow of the Anti-Christ*; Benson, *Pious Nietzsche*; and Hovey, *Nietzsche and Theology*.

includes three dominant and related assertions. Nietzsche's narrative begins with "the death of God, in its midst the ensuing nihilism, and at its end the self-surmounting of nihilism in eternal recurrence."[15] The significance of these ominous and forbidding elements of Nietzsche's alternative "evangel" will become clearer as we allow them to guide our exploration of his assault on a redemptive ethic.

The Death of God

One of the most famous passages in all of philosophical literature is the tale of the madman in Nietzsche's *Gay Science*: "Haven't you heard of that madman who in the bright morning lit a lantern and ran around the marketplace crying incessantly, 'I'm looking for God! I'm looking for God!'" The indifferent bystanders are provoked to laughter and offer a mocking response: "Has he been lost, then? asked one. Did he lose his way like a child? asked another. Or is he hiding? Is he afraid of us? Has he gone to sea? Emigrated?" The madman addresses the amused but indifferent crowd: "'Where is God?' he cried. I'll tell you. *We have killed him*—you and I. We are all his murderers."[16]

Several matters are important to note here. First, Nietzsche is not describing the demise of some omniscient, omnipresent, omnipotent, eternal Being at the hands of mere creatures. Nietzsche does not here comment on the existence or nonexistence of a supernatural Supreme Being that we designate "God." Nietzsche is unconcerned with arguments for or against the existence of God. In fact, one of the reasons he cites for why he is "so clever" is that he never cluttered his mind with "questions that do not amount to anything. . . . 'God,' 'immortality of the soul,' 'redemption,' 'beyond,' are simply ideas that I have not paid any attention to or devoted any time to, even as a child."[17] Nietzsche's dismissal of the

15. Löwith, *From Hegel to Nietzsche*, 193.

16. Nietzsche, *Gay Science*, §125. Subsequent citations of this work will be designated *GS* with a section number.

17. Nietzsche, "Why I Am So Clever," 85. Subsequent citations of this work will be designated *EH* with a page number. Nietzsche's assertion here is more rhetorical than factual. His thoughts were consumed with these matters. Fraser (*Redeeming Nietzsche*, 13) says Nietzsche's opposition to Christianity reminds us, though, "that one can reject Christianity without being all that interested in the philosophical question of God's existence. . . . Nietzsche is among the few atheists who genuinely understands that to attack . . . the Christian faith, one operates on an entirely different level from that of rational-philosophical demonstration."

Christian faith has its origins other than in argument: "What decides against Christianity now is our taste, not our reasons" (*GS* §132). He even goes so far as to assert, "We deny that God is God. . . . If someone were to *prove* this Christian God to us, we would believe in him even less" (*A* §47).

What, then, is Nietzsche's madman doing? Nietzsche reflects here something of the influence of Feuerbach, with respect to the notion that ideas of God represent a projection into the transcendent realm of human aspirations and values. Humanity has created God as a guarantor of its interests and morality. But what does Nietzsche's madman say? "We have killed him—you and I. We are all his murderers." Nietzsche's madman subsequently indicates what has truly occurred with this cataclysmic deicide:

> How were we able to drink up the sea? Who gave us the sponge to wipe away the entire horizon? What were we doing when we unchained this earth from its sun? Where is it moving to now? Away from all suns? Are we not continually falling? And backwards, sidewards, forwards, in all directions? Is there still an up and a down? Aren't we straying as through an infinite nothing? Isn't empty space breathing at us? Hasn't it got colder? Isn't night and more night coming again and again? . . . God is dead. God remains dead. And we have killed him. How shall we console ourselves, the murderers of all murderers! (*GS* §125)

The crowd by now has moved from mockery to silence; they stare in astonishment at the madman, who departs, saying, "I have come too early; my time has not yet come." The madman's message is only partly understood, with some of it being obvious to those in the marketplace and some of it remaining obscure. The crowd mocks because his assertion of the death of God is considered unnecessary. The sophisticates of Nietzsche's day did not need to be told of God's absence. This they had long affirmed. What they failed to understand were the consequences of this turn of events. As Hovey says, "Christian Europe had yet to come to terms with the cultural consequences of the fact that it had jettisoned Christianity."[18] Nietzsche's *Human, All Too Human* will later explain, "There will never again be a life and culture bounded by a religiously determined horizon."[19] The horizon that had provided orientation and

---

18. Hovey, *Nietzsche and Theology*, 47.

19. Nietzsche, *Human, All Too Human*, §234. Subsequent citations of this work will be designated *HH* with a section number.

boundaries has been wiped away. The common reference point for the world's order and life's meaning is gone.

What aggravated Nietzsche and why the madman was ahead of his time is that few, if any, recognized the character of the crisis. "God" had been the creation of humanity in its efforts to grant legitimacy to commitments and values. A decadent Christianity, by denying those commitments and values, had "murdered God"; the lingering problem was the vain effort by many to pretend as if life could go on unchanged and the same values "honored." As Anthony Kenny puts it, "Nietzsche had no patience with those thinkers . . . who tried to preserve Christian morality while denying the Christian faith." As "a coherent and complete view of things" you cannot "break off one of [Christianity's] principal concepts, the belief in God," and carry on with something like "traditional values" as if everything else could continue as before.[20] Nietzsche himself insists, "When you give up Christian faith, you pull the rug out from under your right to Christian morality as well. . . . Christianity is a system, a carefully considered, *integrated* view of things. If you break off a main tenet, the belief in God, you smash the whole system along with it: you lose your grip on anything necessary."[21]

Nietzsche detected the lingering aftereffects of decadent Christianity all around him: "After Buddha was dead, they still showed his shadow in a cave for centuries—a tremendous, gruesome shadow. God is dead; but given the way people are, there may still for millennia be caves in which they show his shadow.—And we—we must still defeat his shadow as well!" (*GS* §108). He speaks of what he calls "religious after-pains," complaining that "however much one may believe one has weaned oneself from religion, the weaning has not been so complete that one does not enjoy encountering religious moods and sentiments without conceptual content, for example in music." What greatly bothered him, though, was the enduring presence of such "after-pains" when philosophy seeks

20. Kenny, *New History of Philosophy*, 4:309; see also Hovey, *Nietzsche and Theology*, 64.

21. Nietzsche, *Twilight of the Idols, or How to Philosophize with a Hammer*, 194. Subsequent citations of this work will be designated *TI* with a page number. While we might wince at the word "system," Christians must agree with Nietzsche that the account of God's will in Eph 1:9–10 to "unite all things together in Christ" calls for an "integrated view of things." Such a commitment makes talk of "traditional values" or a "morality for everybody" that can be separated and justified independently of the gospel all the more troubling. Even Nietzsche knew better than that.

to demonstrate "to us the justification of metaphysical hopes and the profound peace of soul to be attained through them" (HH §131).[22]

Nietzsche sensed among modern philosophers a clandestine support for the church when they uphold in one way or another "the *lie* of 'the moral world order'. . . . And what does 'moral world order' mean? That there is a will of God—once and for all—relating to what human beings do and do not do; that the value of a people, of an individual, can be measured by how much or how little each one obeys the will of God"(*A* §26). He detected the "lie of 'the moral world order'" in any and every attempt to project a realm of ideals that serves to challenge and judge the real world. That realm is perhaps "the world we revere." *This* world, though, is "the world which we live, which we—are."[23] Nietzsche took great pains to draw a fundamental contrast between the "true world" of ideals, known by faith (Christianity) or philosophical speculation (Plato, Kant), and the "apparent world" (i.e., "reality"), and to insist that with the death of God we are rid of the "true world" and thus our illusions (*TI* 171). "The 'apparent' world is the only world: the 'true world' is just a *lie added on to it . . .*" (*TI* 168).

We need to be clear about what Nietzsche's assertion concerning the death of God entails. He makes it clear in his *Notebooks* where he observes, "Morality, now without sanction, is no longer able to preserve itself. The moral interpretation is finally let go—(though feeling continues everywhere to be full of the aftershocks of Christian value judgement—)." For Nietzsche, we might try to maintain reverence for that "true world." We are confronted with a choice, however: "It remains for us to abolish either our reverence or ourselves" (*N* §2[131]). It is naïve to believe we have any other choice. What this means, though, is that, according to Nietzsche, one way or the other, humanity is confronted with the challenge of nihilism.

22. He likely has figures such as Immanuel Kant in mind. When Nietzsche in this same section warns that "scientific philosophy has to be very much on its guard against smuggling in errors on the basis of need," we are probably meant to recall Kant's three postulates of "practical reason": God, freedom, and the immortal soul. See *GS* §335.

23. Nietzsche, *Writings from the Late Notebooks*, §2[131]. Subsequent citations of this work will be designated *N* with a section number.

Nihilism and the Genealogy of Christianity

In one of his notebooks from 1887, Nietzsche tells us what he means by "nihilism": "the goal is lacking; an answer to the question 'Why?' is lacking. What does nihilism mean?—That the highest values are devalued" (*N* §9[35]). Nietzsche would later describe a number of activities that are supposedly "goal-oriented": "the 'fulfillment' of a highest canon of morality in all that happens, the moral order of the world; or increasing love and harmony in the interaction of beings; or coming closer to a general state of happiness; or even setting off on the path to a general state of nothingness—any goal is still a meaning." All these efforts, however, represent only "the long *squandering* of our strength, the torment of the 'In vain.'" Why? "What all these kinds of ideas share is that the process aims to achieve something:—and now it is realized that becoming aims for nothing, achieves nothing. . . . Hence, disappointment about a supposed purpose of becoming as a cause of nihilism" (*N* §11[99]).[24]

Several matters are bundled together here. We must begin, though, with the recognition that for Nietzsche, Christian faith and practice represent the chief expression of and response to the brutal truth of the "In vain." Christianity is both cause and effect of nihilism. As effect, Christianity is a decadent response to the threat of the meaningless of existence; as cause it promotes beliefs and values concerning some "true world" that say "no" to everything in this one. "Nihilist and Christian: this rhymes, it does more than just rhyme . . ." (*A* §58).[25] In *A* §15 he asserts, "In Christianity, morality and religion are both completely out of touch with reality." Whatever feature of Christianity we consider—"soul," "redemption," "grace," "punishment"—for Nietzsche, "This entirely fictitious world can be distinguished from the world of dreams . . . in that dreams reflect reality while Christianity falsifies, devalues, and negates reality." Nietzsche objects most strongly to the Christian understanding of God: "God as a god of the sick, God as spider, God as spirit—is one of the most corrupt conceptions of God the world has ever seen. . . . God having degenerated into a contradiction of life instead of its transfiguration and eternal yes! God as declared aversion to life, to nature, to the will to life! God as the formula for every slander against 'the here and now,' for every lie about

24. Nietzsche speaks of life and all of existence as "becoming" to indicate life as a dynamic reality of constant flux and change, in contrast to "being," which implies reality as static and fixed.

25. The terms *nihilist* and *Christ* do rhyme in Nietzsche's German.

the 'beyond'! God as the deification of nothingness, the canonization of the will to nothingness! . . ." (A §18).

We better understand Christianity as both cause and effect of nihilism when we consider how Nietzsche distinguishes two types of nihilism: active versus passive.[26] Passive nihilism exhibits "a decline and retreat of the spirit's power," and "as a sign of weakness" it abandons formerly held goals and values as "no longer appropriate" and "no longer believed." It responds to the "truth" that "there is no truth; that there is no absolute nature of things" with a search for "everything which revives, heals, soothes, benumbs." These aids come "to the fore in a variety of disguises: religious, or moral or political or aesthetic, etc." Active nihilism responds to the loss of meaning with "an increased power of the spirit" and "may be a sign of strength." As such, it abandons previous "goals" as "no longer appropriate"; but, in contrast to "weary nihilism that no longer attacks," active nihilism "achieves its maximum force as a violent force of destruction." Michael Gillespie explains the contrast: "Passive nihilism is a form of resignation in the face of a world without God. . . . Active nihilism, by contrast, is not content to be extinguished passively but wants to extinguish everything that is aimless and meaningless in a blind rage; it is a lust for destruction that purifies humanity." Passive nihilism "wants to go out not with a bang but a whimper," whereas active nihilism intends to go down swinging.[27]

Both forms of nihilism are pathological, but Nietzsche clearly prefers one to the other. For Nietzsche, "Nothing would be more useful or more to be encouraged than a thoroughgoing practical [active] nihilism. . . . What, on the other hand, is to be condemned in the sternest terms is the ambiguous and cowardly compromise of a religion such as Christianity; more precisely, such as the church: which instead of encouraging death and self-destruction, protects everything ill-constituted and sick and makes it propagate itself."[28] The value of active nihilism is precisely in its

26. For what follows see N §9[35].

27. Gillespie, *Nihilism Before Nietzsche*, 179-80.

28. Nietzsche, *Will to Power*, §247. Subsequent citations of this work will be designated *WP* with a section number. Kaufmann's edition of *The Will to Power* is an earlier presentation of the same general material as found in the *Writings from the Late Notebooks* volume later edited by Bittner. The value of these materials for interpreting Nietzsche is notoriously debated. Bittner presents his volume as an improvement on Kaufmann's, but his claims have been contested. See the review of Bittner's work by Aydin and Siemens in *The Journal of Nietzsche Studies*, 94-104. Bittner omits the passage presently cited. Aydin and Siemens claim such omissions reflect Bittner's concern

destructive capacities. Nihilism is, as such, "a pathological *intermediate state*." Its active expression, however, "is not just a contemplation of the 'In vain!', and not just the belief that everything deserves to perish: one puts one's hand to it, one makes it perish . . ." (*N* §11[123]).[29] In other words, as Gillespie observes, active nihilism has "an instrumental value. It levels the ground for a new creation by instituting a monstrous logic of terror that destroys European morality."[30] We will eventually explore the character of that "new creation"; we need first, however, to trace Nietzsche's assessment of Christian faith and practice as "passive nihilism."

Nietzsche insists, "One cannot sufficiently condemn Christianity for having devaluated the value of such a great purifying nihilistic movement . . . through the idea of the immortal private person: likewise through the hope of resurrection: in short, through continual deterrence from the *deed of nihilism*, which is suicide—It substituted slow suicide: gradually a petty, poor, but durable life; gradually a quite ordinary, bourgeois, mediocre life, etc." (*WP* §247). What is the fault of Christianity? It stands in the way of the pursuit of life in the face of nihilism.

For those who have heard Jesus say, "I am the way, the truth, and *the life*," Nietzsche's complaint is perplexing. Nietzsche actually has, in some ways, a measure of admiration for Jesus.[31] His animosity toward the early church and the Apostle Paul, however, knows no bounds. Nietzsche displays the influence of much nineteenth-century German Protestant liberalism when he draws a hard-and-fast distinction between Jesus the simple Galilean, whose own life exhibits the character of a "free spirit," and early "Christians" such as Paul who turned the "glad tidings" embodied in the life of Jesus into a set of "concepts . . . known for what they are, the most malicious counterfeits that exist to devalue nature and natural values" (*A* §38).[32]

---

to present a particular philosophical portrait of Nietzsche. The quest for the historical Nietzsche continues.

29. While the qualifier "active" does not appear in this note, comparison with the passage in *N* §9[35] makes this application appropriate.

30. Gillespie, *Nihilism Before Nietzsche*, 179.

31. For assessments of Nietzsche's rendering of Jesus, see S. N. Williams, *Shadow of the Anti-Christ*, 187–90; Hart, *Beauty of the Infinite*, 118–25; and Murphy, *Nietzsche, Metaphor, Religion*, 111–26. Murphy surveys several different assessments of Nietzsche's understanding of Jesus.

32. Nietzsche's difficulty in keeping terms straight indicates the contrast he draws between Christ and Christianity: "Even the word 'Christianity' is a misunderstanding," he insists. "There was really only one Christian, and he died on the cross. The 'evangel'

When Nietzsche speaks of Paul as "the first Christian," he means to credit him with the invention of what we call Christianity.[33] And while Nietzsche insists he never attacks people and claims not to "hold individuals to blame for the disaster of millennia" (*EH* 82–83), he certainly directs specific charges against the apostle. Nietzsche's account of the origins and expression of Paul's apostleship reveal his specific complaints against Christianity as cause and effect of nihilism; according to Nietzsche, Paul is the apostle of *ressentiment*.

Nietzsche uses the term *ressentiment* to describe the feelings of revenge and hatred held by the powerless and weak against the strong and powerful. Robert C. Solomon calls it "a bitter emotion based on a sense of inferiority and frustrated vindictiveness."[34] Religion is, according to Nietzsche, the fearful response of frail humanity before the ominous, arbitrary, and uncertain powers of the natural order. "The believer in magic and miracles reflects on how to *impose a law on nature*—: and, in brief, the religious cult is the outcome of this reflection." Religion is driven by one concern: "how can the *weaker* tribe nonetheless dictate laws to the *stronger*, dispose of it, regulate its actions (so far as they affect the weaker)?" (*HH* §111). This concern establishes the basic pattern for how Nietzsche interprets religion in general and Christianity in particular. Paul's apostleship and proclamation reflect a similar pattern.

How so? Paul's apostleship was a power grab driven by the desires for revenge and *ressentiment*. Frustrated by his failure to observe the law of Moses adequately, Paul sees in the cross of Christ a means by which he can, at the same time, absolve his tortured conscience as well as feed "his extravagant lust for power" (*D* §68).[35] According to Nietzsche, what

---

died on the cross. What was called 'evangel' after that was the opposite of what *he* had lived: a '*bad* tidings,' a *dysangel*" (*A* §39).

33. *Daybreak*, §68. Subsequent citations of this work will be designated *D* with a section number. In *A* §42 Nietzsche says that Paul "*invented for himself a history of the first Christianity*."

34. See his "One Hundred Years of *Ressentiment*," 95. Nietzsche employs the French *ressentiment*, as no German word adequately expressed his intent.

35. Nietzsche suggests that Paul's conscience was bothered by a whole host of transgressions: "he [Paul] hints at enmity, murder, sorcery, idolatry, uncleanliness, drunkenness and pleasure in debauch." Nietzsche further draws a comparison with the struggles of Martin Luther along these lines (*D* §68). In making this comparison, Nietzsche reveals his reliance on an understanding of Paul that can no longer be sustained. Paul's own testimony in Phil 3:2–6 and Gal 1:13–14 hardly reveals a soul tortured over noncompliance with God's law. Our exploration of Paul's message of redemption in Ephesians will need to bear in mind that whatever Paul's view was, its

really happened on the road to Damascus (see Acts 9) was not an encounter with the resurrected Jesus, but a moment of genius on Paul's part. The story of a crucified and resurrected savior could serve as a message of redemption that provides promises of both forgiveness of sins and immortality. "With the idea of becoming one with Christ all shame, all subordination, all bounds are taken from [the soul], and the intractable lust for power reveals itself as an anticipatory reveling in *divine* glories" (*D* §68).

As far as Nietzsche is concerned, Paul, an "appalling fraud" and "genius in hatred," devalued all of what was valuable about the life of Jesus by fabricating any number of doctrines that enabled him to establish a "priestly tyranny" over the gullible. Nietzsche lists "the doctrines of judgment and return, the doctrine of death as a sacrifice, and the doctrine of the resurrection" as together comprising a gospel that "becomes the most contemptible of all unfulfillable promises, the *outrageous* doctrine of personal immortality." It is this doctrine of personal immortality that indicates, according to Nietzsche, the nihilism that is at the heart of Christianity. He insists, "When the emphasis is put on the 'beyond' rather than on life itself—when it is put on nothingness—, then the emphasis has been completely removed from life." For Nietzsche, "the enormous lie of personal immortality destroys all reason, everything natural in the instinct,—everything beneficial and life-enhancing" (*A* §§41, 43).

Why does this emphasis on "personal immortality" provoke such a strong response from Nietzsche? This doctrine serves several corrupt interests, according to Nietzsche. First, Nietzsche says the Apostle Paul holds this prospect out "as a reward" (*A* §41), suggesting it plays a role in a system of carrots and sticks by which Paul exercised his "priestly tyranny." In playing the role of priest, Paul employs the concepts of guilt and punishment to evoke "a feeling of total depravity" among people upon whom Paul would then shine "a beam of divine mercy, so that, surprised and stupefied by this act of grace," they would give "vent to a cry of rapture" and ultimately assume a posture of servility, which (within Christianity) "assumes the appearance of a virtue" (*HH* §§114–15). People need first to be made unhappy by way of the concepts of sin, guilt, and punishment so that they would seek resolution in the only place possible—in the offer of immortality held out by Paul. Paul's power grab is

---

focus was not on a law-induced sense of guilt. One of the more recent challenges to any reading of Paul through the experience of Martin Luther may be found in Watson, *Paul, Judaism, and the Gentiles*, 28–50.

complete (see *A* §§26, 47). Fraser clarifies Nietzsche's outlook on Christianity in general at this point: "Christianity is . . . a protection racket of metaphysical proportions. It offers security as the price of acquiescence." While "it offers empowerment to those who are weak and vulnerable it does so in such a way as to secure their dependence and weakness rather than overcome it. It makes a virtue of weakness and vulnerability so as to enslave people into a power structure that is engineered by a religious establishment obsessed with its own control."[36]

Apart from serving the "hidden agenda" of Paul, there are several aspects of this "doctrine of personal immortality" that clearly outrage Nietzsche. For one thing, he sees the doctrine as a chief expression of the "anti-life" character of Christianity. To accept the "enormous lie of personal immortality" is to abandon any true concern for this world, "so that there is no *point* to life anymore, *this* [lie] now becomes the 'meaning of life'" (*A* §43). In *Ecce Homo* he insists, "The concept of the 'beyond,' the 'true world'" was "invented to devalue the one world there is,—to deprive our earthly reality of any goal, reason or task." The concepts associated with this doctrine, concepts such as "'soul,' 'spirit,' finally 'immortal soul'" were all likewise "invented to make the body despised, to make it sick . . . to treat as frivolous all the things about life that deserve to be taken very seriously" (*EH* 150). *Ressentiment* also comes to expression in this doctrine by way of its "'egalitarian' dimensions." Paul's "doctrine of personal immortality" employs "the *ressentiment* of the masses as its *main weapon* against . . . everything on earth that is noble, joyful, magnanimous, against our happiness on earth." Paul accomplishes this by waging "a deadly war on every feeling of respect and distance between people." How? By "granting immortality to every Tom, Dick, and Harry," Paul has unleashed "the most enormous and most vicious attempt to assassinate noble humanity." By the great leveling work of salvation by grace, "the aristocraticism of mind has been undermined at its depths by the lie of the equality of souls." The end result of this *ressentiment* of the masses "is rebellion of everything that crawls on the ground against everything that has height: the evangel of the 'lowly' *makes* things lower . . ." (*A* §43).[37] Paul's doctrine, permitting "the most fatal kind of self-presumption ever,"

36. Fraser, *Redeeming Nietzsche*, 83.

37. Nietzsche lists democracy and socialism as corrupt heirs of Christianity's emphasis on a doctrine of equality that weakens the strong and preserves "the failures," leaving us with a "surplus of unsuccessful cases." See his *Beyond Good and Evil*, §§62, 202. Subsequent citations of this work will be designated *BGE* with a section number.

the notion that all of humanity stands "equal before God," blinds people from seeing "the abysmal disparity in order of rank," the absence of which breeds "the European of today," described by Nietzsche as "a herd animal, something full of good will, sickly and mediocre" (*BGE* §62). Finally, the doctrine of the immortal soul figures in one more expression of *ressentiment* and revenge—the doctrine of recompense or judgment. Nietzsche mocks theologians such as Tertullian (second century CE) and Thomas Aquinas (thirteenth century CE) who accentuate the blessedness of the saints in heaven at the expense of the damned in hell. If Dante's inscription over the gateway to hell read, "Eternal love created me as well," Nietzsche insists a better inscription would read, "Eternal *hate* created me as well."[38]

One matter should be clear. Nietzsche evaluates Christian beliefs in terms of their cultural and practical impact and in this respect finds them fundamentally flawed.[39] Christianity, particularly as expressed by the Apostle Paul, is the vengeful response of the weak to the meaninglessness of life and serves only to worsen the condition of sick humanity. According to Nietzsche, "Christianity needs sickness. . . . making things sick is the real intention behind the church's whole system of salvation procedures. . . . nobody gets 'converted' to Christianity,—you have to be sick enough for it." Citing Paul's words in 1 Cor 1:26–28—"The weak things of the world, the foolish things of the world, the base things of the world, and the things that are despised, hath God chosen"—Nietzsche insists, "Christianity is based on the rancor of the sick, the instinct against the healthy, *against* health" (*A* §51).

Nietzsche is clearly interested in "health." This could be considered either ironic or understandable in light of the poor health from which he suffered throughout most of his life. His focus on health, however, has more to do with culture than with physiology. And in terms of the well-being of culture, for Nietzsche, "the expulsion of Christianity from conscience, consciousness and culture is the absolute precondition of the health of humanity."[40] This health would not be the absence of suffering; one of the faults of Christianity is that it seeks to console the sufferer, "to refresh, to soothe, to narcotize" (*GM* §3:17). Nietzsche faults Christian morality in general and the virtue of compassion in particular for the

---

38. Nietzsche, *On the Genealogy of Morality*, §1:15. Subsequent citations of this work will be designated *GM* with a section number.

39. A note at *TI* 189 indicates that for Nietzsche, culture is "what matters most."

40. Williams, "Dionysus against the Crucified, Part II," 141.

tendency to sustain those by whom society as a whole is weakened: "The weak and the failures should perish: first principle of *our* love of humanity. And they should be helped to do this. What is more harmful than any vice?—Active pity for all failures and weakness—Christianity" (*A* §2).[41] "What is bad?" Nietzsche asks. "Everything stemming from weakness." "What is good?—Everything that enhances people's feelings of power, will to power, power itself" (*A* §2).

For Nietzsche, Paul's message of redemption represents "the perspective of a nihilistic philosophy that inscribed the *negation of life* on its shield." Its attendant ethic of compassion and altruism expresses a "slave morality" that uses the language of good and evil in a disingenuous way to enable the weak to gain power over their betters (*GM* §10). This sample of passive nihilism finds "the world ugly and bad" only to make "the world ugly and bad" (*GS* §130). Nietzsche's concern, he insists, is to provide a "life-affirming" alternative to Christian decadence. What is needed, he insists, is a "revaluation of all values" (*A* §62). The prescription for health he offers is his alternative soteriology of "eternal recurrence."

Eternal Recurrence: Nietzsche's Psychological Reality of "Redemption"

After all we have heard from Nietzsche, it might seem odd to hear him speak of redemption in any way. Many students of Nietzsche, though, have begun to realize just how "religious" he was and how driven by religious issues his writings are. Fraser argues that what Nietzsche said of European culture as a whole reflects his own outlook as well: "It seems clear to me that the religious instinct is indeed in vigorous growth—but that it rejects the theistic answer with profound mistrust" (*BGE* §53). In fact, Fraser insists, "Nietzsche is obsessed with the question of human salvation.... [His] work is primarily soteriology: experiments to design a

---

41. The German term translated "pity" here is *Mitleid*. The word "compassion," "to suffer with," more closely corresponds to the German than does "pity." Nietzsche considers the practice of compassion to have devastating consequences: "when they gave comfort to the suffering, courage to the oppressed and despairing, a staff and stay to the irresolute ... with a good conscience, as a matter of principle ... [they] work[ed] at the preservation of everything sick and suffering, which means in fact and truth at the *corruption of the European race*" (*BGE* §62). Compassion, according to Nietzsche, simply multiplies the amount of misery in the world and covertly provides moral cover for feelings of superiority (*A* §7; *D* §§134–35).

form of redemption that would work for a post-theistic age."[42] Nietzsche's account of redemption is one he fashions for a world that has had to reckon with the death of God. He offers such an account in his doctrine of "the eternal recurrence."

For us to understand what this doctrine is all about, we have to relate the theme to other aspects of Nietzsche's thought. We need, for example, to note that one of the driving forces behind his attack on the relationship between redemption and the moral life in Paul is his quest for a "healthy morality" governed by "an instinct for life" (*TI* 174), and a particular understanding of "life" at that. From his *Notebooks*, we have this definition: "But what is life? Here a new, more definite version of the concept 'life' is needed. My formula for it is: life is will to power" (*N* §2[190]). Nietzsche's concept of "the will to power" is another one of those debated issues in Nietzsche scholarship; there are even suggestions that Nietzsche provides no single explanation of the notion, but several.[43] At the risk of oversimplification, however, we will focus on how Nietzsche sees the will to power operating in its most concrete terms. It is not a sight for the timid:

> Life itself is *essentially* a process of appropriating, injuring, over-powering the alien and the weaker, oppressing, being harsh, imposing your own form, incorporating, and at least, the very least, exploiting,—but what is the point of always using words that have been stamped with slanderous intentions from time immemorial? Even a [civic] body within which . . . particular individuals treat each other as equal (which happens in every healthy aristocracy): if this body is living and not dying, . . . [i]t will have to be the embodiment of will to power, it will want to grow, spread, win dominance,—not out of any morality or immorality, but because it is *alive*, and because life *is* precisely will to power. (*BGE* §259)

Nietzsche insists he is simply offering as a statement of fact that "'exploitation' does not pertain to a corrupt or imperfect or primitive society: it pertains to the essence of the living thing as a fundamental organic function, it is a consequence of the intrinsic will to power which is precisely the will of life." He mocks voices promising some future society "in which

---

42. See Fraser, *Redeeming Nietzsche*, 2.
43. See Clark, "Nietzsche's Doctrines of the Will to Power," 139–49.

there will be 'no more exploitation'—that sounds to my ears like promising a life in which there will be no organic function" (*BGE* §259).[44]

What is the will to power? We make a mistake if we read into this phrase a psychology of intent or subjective desire ("I could lose twenty pounds, if I just had enough *willpower*"). Neither should we suppose that Nietzsche "is speaking of a human willing that aims at power over other persons as its ultimate end."[45] Such interpretations are too narrow and grant too much significance to conscious motives for Nietzsche's taste. The will to power is much more basic and more broadly displayed. Nietzsche believes he has "succeeded in explaining our entire instinctual life as the development and ramification of one basic form of will—as will to power," so that "one could trace all organic functions back to this will to power . . . one would have [then] acquired the right to define *all* efficient force unequivocally as: *will to power*. The world seen from within, the world described and defined according to its 'intelligible character'—it would be 'will to power' and nothing else—" (*BGE* §36). Nietzsche is concerned here to present all of material reality—and that is the only reality there is—as an ever-changing assembly and reassembly of force or energy, without goal, without purpose, without any direction. The will to power is simply the expression of force against resistance that any and every organism employs, not in pursuit of any particular end or goal, but strictly as the expression of power.[46] The will to power is not evaluated in light of how it is used for good or ill; good and ill are evaluated in terms of the will to power. How does Nietzsche define what is good? As everything that enhances the will to power. How does he define what is bad? As everything stemming from weakness (*A* §2).

Certainly the will to power finds expression in pursuit of various goals or objectives. The will to power is not measured, though, by its success in attaining those goals or objectives. Satisfaction of desire is not primary; expression of power is. What Nietzsche says in this regard might seem counterintuitive at first: "The satisfaction of the will is not the cause of pleasure. . . . instead, that the will wants to move forwards, and again and again becomes master of what stands in its way: the feeling

44. See also *GM* §2:11.

45. Richardson, *Nietzsche's System*, 19.

46. Hovey (*Nietzsche and Theology*, 85) explains: "The will to power always functions as an activity that is only realized in action rather than being realized in the satisfaction of its desires. . . . What the will to power desires . . . is not a state at all; satisfaction is found in its exercise rather than the outcome of its exercise."

of pleasure lies precisely in the unsatisfaction of the will, in the way it is not yet satiated unless it has boundaries and resistance . . ." (*N* §11[75]). But if "*this world is will to power—and nothing besides*" (*N* §38[12]), then satisfaction of desire would spell the end of existence—the end of what it means to be a human being: "And you too are this will to power—and nothing besides" (*N* §38[12]).

At one level, Nietzsche's doctrine of the will to power operates in a descriptive manner, as simply an account of "the way things are." Yet, Nietzsche also insists that one must *become* what one is; so, the concept of will to power also serves as a demand for creativity in the task of the revaluation of all values. With the "death of God" and the consequent dismantling of Christian morality, there is now the freedom to replace old tablets of law with new. The title character of Nietzsche's *Thus Spoke Zarathustra* announces as his message, "Willing liberates because willing is creating: thus I teach. And you should learn *only* for creating."[47] In this work Zarathustra complains of those who sit among the broken tablets that once offered divine laws and who now cry out, "Why live? All is vain!" What is needed, insists Zarathustra, is "a *new nobility*, which is the adversary of all rabble and all despotic rule and which writes anew the word 'noble' on new tablets" (*TSZ* 162–63). Who will have courage and vitality sufficient to offer this new creation? Here Nietzsche speaks of "the *Übermensch*," the overman, the one who overcomes and signals "the way to new dawns" (*TSZ* 158).

Nietzsche's *Übermensch* has often been misunderstood as representing the ideals of brutality and cruelty associated with the Nazi movement.[48] The *Übermensch* is better understood as a symbol of what Nietzsche offers as the only type of redemption available in a world without God, defined strictly in terms of the will to power: eternal recurrence. While some interpreters maintain the connections are tenuous, Kaufmann argues, "Nietzsche's philosophy of power culminates in the dual vision of the overman and the eternal recurrence."[49] How might they

47. Nietzsche, *Thus Spoke Zarathustra*, 165. Subsequent citations of this work will be designated *TSZ* with a page number.

48. Such an association has to do with Nietzsche's sister, Elisabeth Förster-Nietzsche. Her personal relationship with Adolf Hitler facilitated the incorporation of elements of Nietzsche's thought into the dominant strain of German nationalism. All this took place years after Nietzsche's death in 1900. See Cate, *Friedrich Nietzsche*, 574–76.

49. Kaufmann, *Nietzsche*, 307. David B. Allison concurs that the concepts of the overman, eternal recurrence, and the will to power are all interrelated. See his

be related? Zarathustra exclaims, "Behold, I teach you the overman! The overman is the meaning of the earth. Let your will say: the overman shall be the meaning of the earth! I beseech you, my brothers, remain faithful to the earth and do not believe those who speak to you of extraterrestrial hopes" (*TSZ* 6). The overman represents commitment to "an ideal the pursuit of which does not entail the negation of our earthly life, but on the contrary permits to affirm it."[50] The embrace of eternal recurrence is the character and measure of this affirmation.

What, though, is eternal recurrence? One feature should be obvious. Nietzsche's doctrine is an explicit alternative to the Christian hope of eternal life as understood by Nietzsche: "Do not believe those who speak to you of extraterrestrial hopes!" When we remember Nietzsche's view that Paul taught something called the "doctrine of personal immortality" and that in his view this doctrine is a major expression of the life-negating character of Christianity, we can assume that Nietzsche intends eternal recurrence to be life-affirming and very much grounded in experience of this world. Such a doctrine would have to express something other than the *ressentiment* Nietzsche detects in Christian faith. Here, precisely, is the function of Nietzsche's eternal recurrence: to be able to embrace life fully—past, present, and future—without *ressentiment* or regret, as the highest expression of the affirmation of life.

There are elements of Nietzsche's writings that indicate he at least flirted with the idea of "a cosmology according to which everything that is has already been and is fated to be again, exactly as it was."[51] The presentations of eternal recurrence in *The Gay Science* and *Thus Spoke Zarathustra*, however, offer what amounts to a moral challenge to see whether or not one has the stuff of the *Übermensch*. How so? In *The Gay Science*, Nietzsche presents a thought experiment that serves as a test for assessing one's level of self-affirmation. What if a demon were to say to a person at the lowest point of his life, "This life as you now live it and have lived it you will have to live once again and innumerable times again; and

---

Reading the New Nietzsche, 119. With respect to the idea of the eternal recurrence, once again there are competing interpretations as to what precisely Nietzsche means. For a detailed analysis of five different interpretations, see Reginster, *Affirmation of Life*, 205–22.

50. Reginster, *Affirmation of Life*, 250.

51. Ibid., 205. Most of this sort of emphasis is found in the material unpublished during his lifetime but later collected and presented as *The Will to Power*; see *WP* §§1063–66. Those familiar with *The Matrix* movie series will detect there the presence of this Nietzschean theme. See Lawrence, *Like a Splinter in Your Mind*, 82.

there will be nothing new in it, but every pain and every joy and every thought and sigh and everything unspeakably small or great in your life must return to you, all in the same succession and sequence—even this spider and this moonlight between the trees, and even this moment and I myself. The eternal hourglass of existence is turned over again and again, and you with it, you speck of dust!" (*GS*, §341). Fraser interprets this offer as asking, "Is your self-regard sufficiently free from regret that it enables you to affirm (that is, love) all about yourself and your personal history and the world in which you live, including especially all those moments of pain and heartbreak, of fear and anxiety?"[52]

Nietzsche outlines two responses to the prospect of eternal recurrence. "Would you not throw yourself down and gnash your teeth and curse the demon who spoke thus? Or have you experienced a tremendous moment when you would have answered him: 'You are a god and never have I heard anything more divine.'" The question is, as Nietzsche states it, "how well disposed would you have to become to yourself and to life *to long for nothing more fervently* than for this ultimate confirmation and seal?" (*GS* §341). What would an embrace of eternal recurrence look like? It would look like the full affirmation of everything that has occurred to produce the present moment, whether the present moment is one of joy or sorrow, delight or misery, song or sigh. It would look like the will to affirm anything and everything that has happened in one's life and world to bring about the present state of affairs. Anything less and *ressentiment* and revenge, negation and regret allow the weakness of passive nihilism to consume our lives. Zarathustra voices the proper sentiment: "To redeem what is past in mankind and to recreate all 'It was' until the will speaks: 'But I wanted it so! I shall want it so—' This I told them was redemption, this alone I taught them to call redemption—" (*TSZ* 158).

We better grasp the point of eternal recurrence if we recognize, as Benson points out, that Nietzsche's use of the term "redemption" is "the exact opposite of its usual meaning." The underlying assumption behind Paul's use of "redemption" is that there is a problem that must be addressed, a wrong situation that must be set right. "Conversely, redemption for Nietzsche means not thinking there is something wrong in the first place: if we can call it 'redemption,' then it is in effect a redemption *from* redemption."[53] This point is made the more clear when we see that

---

52. Fraser, *Redeeming Nietzsche*, 110.

53. Benson, *Pious Nietzsche*, 51; see also Fraser, *Redeeming Nietzsche*, 77.

one way in which Nietzsche expresses the significance of eternal recurrence as an "anti-redemption" mode of redemption is with the concept of *amor fati*—love of fate.

A Christian understanding of redemption will affirm that things can and do go horribly wrong and that God is at work to set things right. Nietzsche offers an understanding of redemption in a world without God and, therefore, without any frame of reference for what setting things right might look like. There is no "human-nature-as-it-could-be-if-it-realized-its-*telos*." There is only "human-nature-as-it-is." There is no "true world," only this world. If redemption is to be found, it will be within the finite conditions of whatever state of affairs greets us in life. Nietzsche seeks to make a virtue out of necessity by calling for a joyful embrace of whatever has thus far contributed to the present moment. "To redeem those who are the past and to recreate all 'it was' into 'thus I willed it!'—only that would I call redemption" (*TSZ* 110; see also *TSZ* 112). In *Ecce Homo*, Nietzsche announces his "formula for human greatness" as "*amor fati*, that you do not want anything to be different, not forwards, not backwards, not for all eternity. Not just to tolerate necessity, still less to conceal it—all idealism is hypocrisy towards necessity—, but to *love* it" (*EH* 99; see also *GS* §276).

We discover the rigors of the demand of eternal recurrence, though, when we realize that the demon's reference to "this spider and this moonlight between the trees" are tokens of a more comprehensive incorporation of all events everywhere and throughout time that intertwine to make the present moment what it is and the one confronted with the challenge of eternal recurrence who she is. The challenge in saying "yes" to eternal recurrence is in recognizing that to say "Yes to one joy" is also to say "Yes to all pain. All things are enchained, entwined, enamored—if you ever wanted one time two times, if you ever said 'I like you, happiness! Whoosh! Moment!' then you wanted everything back!—Everything anew, everything eternal, everything enchained, entwined, enamored, oh thus you *loved* the world—" (*TSZ* 263).

Nietzsche's eternal recurrence is a thought experiment, "a litmus test for the worth of our lives,"[54] to test the measure of our capacity to affirm life regardless of circumstances. It is important to note, though, that "Nietzsche's thought makes no appeal to a judgment of goodness conceived

---

54. Welshon, *Philosophy of Nietzsche*, 187.

as a transcendent or metaphysical standard."[55] The only standard is the standard of eternal recurrence, to which we say either "yes" or "no." Nietzsche's doctrine does not permit selection or assessment or sifting through for the good parts. There might be those moments or encounters we would rather do without. Zarathustra himself has to come to grips with the discomfiting prospect that to embrace eternal recurrence is to welcome once again into his life a "great surfeit of human beings": "alas, human beings recur eternally! The small human beings recur eternally!" (*TSZ* 177). We are to understand it as the measure of Zarathustra's stature as "the teacher of eternal recurrence" that he can affirm, "I will return to this sun, with this earth, with this eagle, with this snake—not to a new life or a better life or a similar life: I will return to this same and selfsame life, in what is greatest as in what is smallest, to once again teach the eternal recurrence of all things" (*TSZ* 178). The only standard for assessing the value of life is life's affirmation at any cost, even the cost of having to tolerate again and again those the very thought of whom makes Zarathustra nauseous.[56] Those who pass the test of eternal recurrence will take into account the heights and depths, the joys and the sorrows, and, willing to embrace them all, are able to say, "Was *that* life? Well then! One more time!" (*TSZ* 125).

Nietzsche says the doctrine of eternal recurrence is the central concern of his most important work *Thus Spoke Zarathustra* (*EH* 123).[57] It is an idea, Nietzsche believes, made possible by the death of God and made necessary by the nihilism that is both cause and effect of Christianity. As Nietzsche's alternative to Paul's redemptive ethic, eternal recurrence provides an ethic of the affirmation of life that has as it fundamental value . . . the affirmation of life.

Evaluating the Revaluator

Robert Solomon offers that "it is no surprise that conservative Yale philosopher Brand Blandshard once threw Nietzsche (one of his books, that

---

55. Ansell-Pearson, *How to Read Nietzsche*, 75.

56. There are indications that Nietzsche considered his mother and sister as the only possible arguments against his doctrine of eternal recurrence (see *EH* 77).

57. For Nietzsche's assertion that *TSZ* is his most important work see *EH* 72 where he says, "With it, I have given humanity the greatest gift it has ever received. . . . it is also the most *profound* thing to be born out of the innermost richness of the truth."

is) across the room."[58] Nietzsche would probably have delighted in that response and would have seen it as one more indication of his genius: "the fact that people do not hear me these days, that they do not know how to accept anything I say, these facts are not only understandable, they even strike me as the way things should be" (*EH* 100). To attempt any critique of Nietzsche is to risk being placed among the "scholarly cattle" by the one who called himself "the anti-jackass *par excellence*" (*EH* 101–2). It is perilous to evaluate one who insists that any objections to his views simply reveal an inability to rise to the heights necessary to recognize his wisdom.

There may indeed be wisdom here, and of a sort that Christians might need to consider. Though not accepting Nietzsche's entire program of revaluation of *all* values, there might be some value in attending to some of his criticism of Christianity.[59] We do not need, for example, to accept his Feuerbachian analysis of the origins of belief in God to ask if any of our ideas about God are ever themselves projections of our own preferences, prejudices, and predilections. Rodney Clapp warns against a "malleable and shape-shifting god" who "is always who 'we' want god to be."[60] Are our images of God ever simply a mirror image of ourselves writ large on the heavens? Is the measure of our beliefs that which provides comfort and the assurance that God functions to underwrite our own practices and projects?

We do not need to endorse wholesale Nietzsche's assessment of Christian moral vision to recognize that Christian language and teaching have been used for centuries to satisfy the quest for power. We do not have to look far to see evidence of Nietzsche's contention that the invocation of Christian morality often operates in ways that serve the partial interest of parties in power: rich over poor, white over nonwhite, male over female, straight over gay. The capacity to invoke "the will of God" as cover for self-interest is, despite the third commandment, as common as it is deplorable, and few of us can declare ourselves innocent in this regard.

58. Solomon, *Living with Nietzsche*, 8.

59. Hovey (*Nietzsche and Theology*, 4) insists, "The Christian ability to listen to Nietzsche as welcoming a stranger while also not letting what he 'meant' have the final word will be a function of the strength of Christian devotion and the force of our conviction that the gospel is true."

60. Clapp, "God Is Not 'A Stranger on the Bus,'" 24.

We do not need to accept Nietzsche's accusation that Paul's gospel of redemption expresses *ressentiment* and rage against life to admit that Christians past and present often portray to the world a witness that is lifeless apart from the strength needed to vent hostility and fear against forces we cannot control. Stephen Williams wonders, "Perhaps Nietzsche attacked a Christianity whose vision had become so severely blinkered, a faith which allowed for too little in the way of joy and beauty, and so distorted eternity and wisdom."[61]

There are, however, legitimate criticisms to be raised against Nietzsche's account of the Christian faith and against the alternative "evangel" he offers. Any number of issues could be highlighted to demonstrate that Nietzsche's broadsides are sometimes aimed at caricatures, misunderstandings, or outright misrepresentations of the teachings of Paul. Benson suggests, "Nietzsche's portrait of Paul is . . . composed of (1) a more or less 'orthodox' reading of Paul, (2) a highly distorted reading of those writings, and (3) Nietzsche's own invented 'psychology' of Paul. The result is not simply that one is unable to trust what Nietzsche says about Paul but also that one begins to wonder how much of Nietzsche's account of Paul is really about *himself.*"[62] In one of his many discussions of Kant and his categorical imperative, Nietzsche wonders, "What do claims like this tell us about the people who make them?" (*BGE* §187). When Nietzsche describes the rhetoric and practices of Christianity as disguised *ressentiment* and a cloaked pursuit of power, what might we be learning about Nietzsche himself?[63]

Some of the response to Nietzsche's assessment of Paul's account of a redemptive ethic will have to wait for our engagement with this theme in Ephesians. Before that, however, one central feature of Nietzsche's alternative gospel needs further examination and evaluation—his doctrine of eternal recurrence. A standard criticism of Nietzsche's general outlook is that it is highly individualistic.[64] Julian Young has recently argued, however, that Nietzsche expresses what might be called a "romantic

---

61. S. N. Williams, "Nietzsche Contra Christianity, Part II," 150.

62. Benson, *Pious Nietzsche*, 134. Of Nietzsche's treatment of Paul, Hart (*Beauty of the Infinite*, 120–21) says, "One could scarcely conceive of a diatribe that could succeed better at being at once so unbalanced and so platitudinous." For an extensive rebuttle to the idea that Paul is the inventor of Christianity, see Wenham, *Paul*.

63. Hart (*Beauty of the Infinite*, 123) suggests Nietzsche's *The Antichrist* is itself "a strategy of *ressentiment.*"

64. S. N. Williams, "Nietzsche Contra Christianity, Part I," 231.

communitarianism" in which a healthy society practices a healthy ethos sustained by the worship of healthy gods, much as could be found in "the life- and humanity-affirming characteristics of Greek religion."[65] Exploration of the doctrine of eternal recurrence suggests, I believe, that what we have with Nietzsche is the worst possible combination of an emphasis on an aristocratic individualism with a profound recognition of the "entwinement" of the individual in a world society.

Young offers that Nietzsche's doctrine of eternal recurrence functions somewhat as a theodicy. We remember that eternal recurrence asks us to affirm all there is and has been as the measure of self-affirmation in a world where "all things are enchained, entwined, enamored" (*TSZ* 263). The doctrine serves as a theodicy in the sense that "*to long for nothing more fervently*" than the eternal recurrence (*GS* §341) "is to affirm that there is no possible way in which the world could be better than it is."[66] The notion that eternal recurrence functions as something of a theodicy is to say that Nietzsche means to offer this mode of "redemption" as a way of confronting "the horror of existence."[67]

Nietzsche asserts that great misery and suffering are inescapable in our world. He speaks as well, though, of the "profound delusion" maintained by those (like Socrates) who think we can penetrate to the depths of life's horrors in order to change them.[68] Ultimately, however, no real changes can be made to alter the basic structure of reality, which is defined by conflict and the tragedy of meaningless suffering. Nietzsche holds in contempt "that morality of the herd animal . . . which strives with all its force for a universal green-pasture happiness on earth, namely security, harmlessness, comfort, easy living . . . and . . . takes suffering itself as something that absolutely must be abolished" (*N* §37[8]). Such efforts are delusional and fail to embrace the affirmation of life *as it is* as demanded by eternal recurrence.

For someone like Nietzsche, though, who knew significant and irremediable physical suffering throughout most of his life, to affirm life in all aspects can be an expression of courage and the mark of a certain nobility of character. Nietzsche refused (he says) to allow his suffering to get the best of him. To seek solutions or cures when none can be found

65. Young, *Nietzsche's Philosophy of Religion*, 191–92.

66. Ibid., 200.

67. Kain, "Nietzsche, Eternal Recurrence, and the Horror of Existence," 49–63.

68. Nietzsche, *Birth of Tragedy and Other Writings*, §15. Subsequent citations of this work will be designated *BT* with a section number.

is only to invite *ressentiment.* "Born from weakness," however, "*ressentiment* is most harmful to the weak themselves. . . . To accept yourselves as a fate, not to want to 'change' yourself—in situations like this, that is reason *par excellence*" (*EH* 81–82). To try to reduce suffering when it cannot be reduced is to become a slave to that suffering. By embracing the idea of eternal recurrence, however, Nietzsche "broke the stranglehold [suffering] had on him. He ended his subjugation. He put himself in charge. He turned all 'it was' into a 'thus *I* willed it.'"[69]

Perhaps the stoic embrace of eternal recurrence is the best that can be expected in a world in which God is dead. There is a side to this embrace, however, that is not so noble, and the full significance of Nietzsche's doctrine is not recognized until this side is known. Eternal recurrence demands, we remember, not simply the endless repetition of one's own life. Since "all things are enchained, entwined, enamored" (*TSZ* 263), to "accept any part of our self, then we accept our entire self, and all the world as well; and if we reject any part of it, then we reject our entire self, and all the world with it."[70] The nobility and courage required to embrace eternal recurrence for one's self must be confident enough to embrace it on behalf of the entire world. It must will eternal recurrence even, as Zarathustra realized, for the "great surfeit of human beings" (*TSZ* 176). Zarathustra's nobility might shine through when he is willing to tolerate the sorrow and nausea he suffers due to those "small human beings" who weary him so. Is that, however, the final measure of Nietzsche's "theodicy"?

Theodicy was also on the mind of a writer familiar to Nietzsche: Fyodor Dostoevsky. In Dostoevsky's *Brothers Karamazov* atheist Ivan belittles the faith of his younger brother Alyosha.[71] Alyosha is a novice monk in the Russian Orthodox Church and Ivan wants to persuade him of the foolishness of such a calling. So, he repeats tales of senseless suffering, particularly the suffering of children who have done nothing to deserve their pain. Ivan details the torture of a five-year-old girl, beaten by

---

69. Kain, "Horror of Existence," 57.

70. Nehamas, "Eternal Recurrence," 129.

71. Dostoevsky, *Brothers Karamozov*, 121–27. It is fairly certain that Nietzsche was familiar with *The Brothers Karamazov* and comparisons have been made between Nietzsche's outlook and Dostoevsky's at many points; see Hubben, *Dostoevsky, Kierkegaard, Nietzsche, & Kafka*, 127–34. There is evidence, though, that Nietzsche viewed Dostoevsky as representative of the slave morality he criticizes. See, for example, Stoeber, "Dostoevsky's Devil," 33 n. 27.

her parents "till her body was one bruise. Then, they shut her up all night in the cold and frost in a privy, and . . . they smeared her face and filled her mouth with excrement, and it was her mother, her mother did this." Ivan demands of his brother, "Do you understand why this infamy must be and is permitted? Without it, I am told, man could not have existed on earth, for he could not have known good and evil. . . . Why, the whole world of knowledge is not worth that child's prayer to 'dear, kind God'!"

Ivan later admits, "I recognize in all humility that I cannot understand why the world is arranged as it is. . . . [But] if all must suffer to pay for . . . eternal harmony, what have children to do with it, tell me, please?" In light of the reality of senseless evil Ivan rejects the faith that his brother represents and insists, "I must have justice, or I will destroy myself. And not justice in some remote infinite time and space, but here on earth, and that I could see myself. I have believed in it. I want to see it, and if I am dead by then, let me rise again, for if it all happens without me, it will be too unfair." Ivan rejects a system of harmony and moral order that requires the torture of children. He apparently was familiar with theodicies that operate so efficiently that evil and suffering are somehow made to fit in with God's plans. Our subsequent exploration of Ephesians will attempt to address whether the gospel provides a response to Ivan's demand to see justice here on earth. We have to wonder, though, how Ivan would respond to Nietzsche's attempt at "theodicy." For in Nietzsche's account such infamy is not merely "permitted," it is required if Zarathustra or any *Übermensch* is to embrace eternal recurrence.

The thought experiment of eternal recurrence requires the will to welcome endlessly the same life in the same world with the same sequence of events that in their entwinement achieve the present moment with the present self. To will anything else is to indulge senseless regret, vain aspiration for change, and to reject those events and circumstances necessary to who we have become. It is one thing, though, for Zarathustra to embrace eternal recurrence for himself and another to will that for the victims of torture. The apparent nobility of accepting the rigors of eternal recurrence loses its attraction when we discover its true cost. Nietzsche's resounding "yes" to life rings hollow when uttered on behalf of the abused child. If this is Nietzsche's alternative to a redemptive ethic, we might employ Paul's sentiment about "a different gospel, which is really not another" (Gal 1:6–7).

It is finally insufficient, though, to challenge Nietzsche for the implications of his doctrine of eternal recurrence in terms that Nietzsche would likely dismiss as mawkish sentimentalism. Since for Nietzsche these are all matters of taste and not reasons, a different strategy must be applied in addressing him and those under his influence. Williams insists, "It is surely in the presentation of an alternative vision that the power of riposte must lie. . . . Philosophy of Nietzsche's kind is met by religious visions, not philosophical analysis."[72] What we find in Ephesians concerning a redemptive ethic can perhaps provide that alternative vision.

EPHESIANS AND A REDEMPTIVE ETHIC

Ephesians uses a variety of metaphors to describe God's work of redemption through Christ.[73] One matter to note, though, is that as is the case throughout Scripture, the vision of the moral life given in Ephesians 4–6 is one that corresponds to the character of God's redemptive work through Christ as described in Ephesians 1–3. In Eph 4:1, Paul urges his readers to "walk worthy of the calling." That calling is the invitation to participate in God's redemptive work, and the walk "worthy" of that calling is one measured by the character and nature of that work. A Christian ethic formed and informed by what we find in Ephesians will be a redemptive ethic. Of course, this is precisely what Nietzsche attacks. We gain a better understanding of the features of this redemptive ethic from Ephesians as we respond to some of the specifics of Nietzsche's complaints. It might be the case that engagement with Nietzsche's errors provides ways for a better understanding of what Ephesians has to offer.

A More or Less "Orthodox" Reading of Paul

Nietzsche's list of the doctrines he rejects will sound familiar to most Christians: "the doctrines of judgment and return, the doctrine of death as a sacrifice, and the doctrine of the *resurrection*." This last one is the basis, according to Nietzsche, for "the most contemptible of all unfulfillable promises, the outrageous doctrine of personal immortality" (*A* §41)—a doctrine that Nietzsche understands in terms of "a state after death" enjoyed by "immortal souls." It is, of course, the emphasis on the "'beyond'

72. S. N. Williams, "Nietzsche Contra Christianity, Part I," 241–42.

73. Indeed, "redemption" is itself one of those metaphors. See Fee, "Paul and the Metaphors for Salvation," 52–55.

rather than on life itself" that marks for Nietzsche the nihilistic character of Christian faith (*A* §43), and it is Paul who is largely responsible for inventing this "method of priestly tyranny" (*A* §42).

Nietzsche could hardly be faulted for narrowing the Christian faith to a few simple terms: 1) God is the holy and righteous creator of all things who demands conformity to his law; 2) humans are unable to conform to God's law and are thus sinners who deserve eternal judgment; 3) as an expression of divine grace, Jesus died on the cross, taking the punishment for sin that humans rightly deserve; 4) confessing faith in Jesus provides assurance that when a believer dies, he will receive a "not guilty" verdict from God, and his soul will enjoy eternal bliss in heaven with God. This summation generally reflects the basic beliefs of what has come to be known as "the Lutheran Paul"—Paul as read and understood on the basis of the experience and teachings of the great Protestant reformer of sixteenth-century Germany, Martin Luther.[74] Whether the points listed here are a sufficient or adequate rendering of Luther's theology is a legitimate question; that in some circles Protestant Christianity has been reduced to these beliefs is undeniable. Nietzsche himself insists (in a passage faulting Luther), "To reduce Christianity, to reduce being a Christian to a set of claims taken to be true, to a simple phenomenalism of consciousness, is to negate Christianity" (*A*, §39). If we bring Paul's Letter to the Ephesians into the conversation, at least at this point, we would have to agree with Nietzsche.

If we go further, though, and compare Nietzsche's narrow understanding of Christianity with what we find in Ephesians, "the unfathomable riches of Christ" proclaimed by Paul (Eph 3:8) will offer a substantially different account of the Christian faith that contrasts greatly with Nietzsche's. Ephesians, for example, will not support the understanding of the human condition or of the cross of Christ presupposed by Nietzsche. For one thing, the view of the human condition in the Christianity presupposed by Nietzsche is not as profoundly troubling as presented in Ephesians. Nietzsche considers the Christian view of sin and guilt merely as a matter of the failure to meet the demands of divine law. He assumes, as well, a widely (but not universally) held interpretation

---

74. For a more detailed "portrait" of "the Lutheran Paul," see Westerholm, *Perspectives Old and New on Paul*, 88–97. Benson (*Pious Nietzsche*, 121–22) and Fraser (*Redeeming Nietzsche*, 33–34) affirm the role of Luther in Nietzsche's understanding of Christianity.

of Jesus' death on the cross.[75] Nietzsche understands the cross of Christ to trade on the matters of guilt and punishment (*A* §§33, 49) and that the cross is held by Christians to be a "*guilt sacrifice*, and in fact in its most revolting barbaric form, the sacrifice of the *innocent* for the sins of the *guilty*! What gruesome paganism!" (*A* §41). Nietzsche objects to the interpretation of the death of Jesus on the cross that is commonly known as the "penal substitutionary theory of atonement," a view formalized by John Calvin in the sixteenth century and the default position held in many evangelical circles since then. In this view, God's justice is viewed as retributive and demands satisfaction for human failure to measure up to God's law: this accounts for the "penal" language. No human act can sufficiently meet the demands of infinite justice, so God's retributive anger is redirected toward Jesus on the cross, who suffers the divine wrath instead of us: this accounts for the "substitutionary" language.

Some question whether the penal substitutionary theory of atonement has a genuinely biblical basis.[76] Others challenge it on moral grounds: Timothy Gorringe says its retributive view of justice underwrites our modern dysfunctional criminal justice system;[77] Brown and Parker ask, "Is it any wonder that there is so much abuse in modern society when the predominant image of the culture is of 'divine child abuse'?"[78] Whether the theory finds general biblical support or not, Ephesians presents a very different understanding of the death and resurrection of Jesus. Particularly is this the case when we realize that a penal substitutionary interpretation has no real need for the resurrection of Jesus from the dead, the key element of Paul's announcement of divine triumph in Ephesians. If the central issue is God exhausting God's wrath on an innocent victim, then the resurrection is something of an unnecessary add-on.[79]

75. Throughout church history a number of different models for interpreting the saving significance of Jesus Christ have been developed. For a helpful overview, see Peters, "Six Ways of Salvation," 223–35.

76. See Green and Baker, *Recovering the Scandal of the Cross*, 11–34.

77. See his *God's Just Vengeance*, 83–219. "Wherever Calvinism spread," says Gorringe, "punitive sentencing followed" (140). The dysfunctional character of the American criminal justice system has been widely documented. For a Christian analysis, see Logan, *Good Punishment*. Logan provides extensive evidence to support his assertion that "in the United States today, the current practice of imprisonment as a means of reducing criminality and securing public safety in fact does just the opposite, maintaining and even promoting criminality" (17).

78. Brown and Parker, "For God So Loved the World?" 26.

79. Weaver, *Nonviolent Atonement*, 54. See also Campbell, *Deliverance of God*, 76–77.

Paul certainly talks about "trespasses and sins" in Eph 2:1, but they are merely the overt expressions of the more fundamental problem of human captivity to destructive powers that are beyond our capacity to manage. While the language has been variously interpreted, when Paul describes his readers as having once walked "according to the *aeon* [age] of this world" (2:2), he likely has in mind a view of world history that was basic to his outlook as a Jew taught by his scriptures.[80] His emphasis on the resurrection of Christ from the dead makes this certain.

Paul's Apocalyptic Gospel

Jewish "apocalypticism" begins where the Bible begins, with the conviction that God is the good Creator of a good creation.[81] The people of Israel were acutely aware, however, that we do not live in the unblemished blessing of Genesis 1, but in a world where things can and do go horribly wrong. Israel believed, however, that God had created and covenanted with them to be the means by which God's initial purpose for the goodness and blessing of creation would ultimately be achieved and that the "wrongness" that mars God's creation would be set right. Israel's role in this redemptive process was to be a "kingdom of priests and a holy nation" (Exod 19:6) by living according to God's will embodied in the law of Moses. In this way Israel was to serve as a witness to the nations of God's will for all of creation. Israel, however, knew such wrongness firsthand in its own sinfulness and in the oppression and violence Israel suffered at the hands of others. Rather than a holy Israel serving as a channel of God's blessings to the nations, the nations served to threaten the very existence of a sinful Israel. Such problems raised the question of whether God's original intent for creation would ever be fully realized. Jewish

---

80. Some interpreters understand Paul's use of *aeon* in v. 1 to refer to a Greek deity. See, for example, Yee, *Jews, Gentiles and Ethnic Reconciliation*, 49–50. Yee argues that Paul is wanting to stress his Jewish monotheistic outlook by highlighting his readers' former commitment to idolatry. Most commentators, however, see in Paul's use of *aeon* here an indication of Paul's reliance on his Jewish perspective on history. See Holloway, *Peripateō*, 190.

81. The literature on Jewish apocalyptic is vast and ever increasing. For a brief discussion of these features, see Wright, *New Testament and the People of God*, 299–301. For its role in Paul's thought, see Wright, *Paul in Fresh Perspective*, 40–58; de Boer, "Paul and Apocalyptic Eschatology," 345–83; de Boer, "Paul, Theologian of God's Apocalypse," 21–33.

apocalypticism is a significant response to this question, assuring of God's faithfulness and righteousness and of Israel's special role in history.

A central feature of Jewish apocalypticism is the division of history into two distinct ages. There is the present evil age in which Israel suffers oppression at the hands of the Gentiles; the reality of death is the chief sign that the present age and its malignant powers persist in their oppressive reign. Israel's task during this age is to remain faithful to its identity as the covenant people of God by observing God's law. There is, however, the age to come in which God will vanquish all forms of evil, will restore Israel to glory and honor, and the will of God will come to full expression throughout a healed and restored creation; for many Jews, the coming of Israel's Messiah (God's agent for accomplishing all this), the welcoming into covenant of Gentiles, the resurrection of the dead and the vindication of the righteous are the great signs of the dawn of the age to come, or what is sometimes called (particularly by Jesus) "the kingdom of God."

Another major feature of Jewish apocalypticism is the division of creation into two realms: the heavens and the earth. The popular use of this language can lead to much confusion about what we find in Ephesians and elsewhere in the Bible (e.g., the book of Revelation). We must not understand "the heavens" as the place where God lives and to which we hope to go when we die. Jewish apocalyptic (and the New Testament in general) sometimes uses the language of "the heavens and the earth" to speak more of orientation and understanding than of location. N. T. Wright emphasizes this when he says, "Within the twofold created universe, humans have the capacity to investigate things on earth; but only God, and perhaps other beings like angels, have the capacity to understand, and (should they wish) to reveal to mortals, the things in heaven."[82] What takes place in revelation is God's act of revealing (Greek, *apokalyptō*) what otherwise remains hidden and inaccessible as "mystery."[83]

---

82. Wright, *Paul in Fresh Perspective*, 51.

83. This understanding of "the heavens and the earth" is on clear display in Rev 13:8 where it describes those who worship "the beast" as "all who dwell on the earth" (cf. 13:12, 14). That the phrase indicates matters of orientation and understanding and not location is clear from the fact that the saints who refuse to worship the beast suffer at his hands (13:7, 15). Obviously, the saints are well within the "earthly" grasp of the beast to do them harm. "Those who dwell on the earth" are those whose vision, understanding, and orientation in life are limited by the immediate and the apparent and do not accept the truth of the revelation given through John's vision as to the genuine character of the beast. G. K. Beale says the phrase refers throughout the book of Revelation to "unbelieving idolaters." See his *Book of Revelation*, 290.

Apocalypticism is one of the chief ways by which Scripture explains what God is doing about evil.[84] The problem of evil presupposed by Paul is a much more serious issue than can be addressed by assuaging human guilt through an offer of forgiveness. Pauline scholar J. Louis Martyn insists, "The root trouble lies deeper than human guilt, and it is more sinister. The whole of humanity—indeed the whole of creation—is, in fact, trapped, enslaved under the power of the present evil age. This is the background of God's invasive action in sending Christ, in his declaration of war, and in his striking the decisive blow against the powers of the present evil age."[85] Paul's letters are thoroughly apocalyptic, and the gospel he proclaims presupposes 1) the division of history into two ages with the expectation of God's ultimate triumph over evil in the age to come, and 2) the distinction within creation between the heavens and the earth and that God reveals through Christ both the character of God's triumph over evil and what is necessary to participate with God in that triumph.[86]

There are, however, significant modifications of this apocalyptic outlook in Paul. In the opening chapter of Ephesians, Paul indicates that he will be retelling the story of Israel from the standpoint of belief in Jesus as Israel's Messiah.[87] Echoes of the Old Testament story of election (1:4), redemption (1:7), and inheritance (1:14) frame the opening doxology. With its assertion of the resurrection of *Christos* (Greek for "the Messiah") from the dead, however, Paul's prayer insists that creation is now witness to the triumph of God over "all rule and authority and power and dominion and every name that is named, not only in this age but also in the one to come" (1:20–21). The language here is thoroughly apocalyptic,

84. De Boer ("Paul and Apocalyptic Eschatology," 350) insists, "Apocalyptic eschatology is fundamentally concerned with God's active and visible rectification (putting right) of the created world (the 'cosmos'), which has somehow gone astray and become alienated from God."

85. Martyn's comments reflect his engagement with Paul's Letter to the Galatians, but they pertain to basic features of Paul's gospel that appear in Ephesians as well. See his *Galatians*, 105.

86. "Paul's understanding of Christ and his saving work," says de Boer, "is permeated from beginning to end . . . by the categories and the perspectives of apocalyptic eschatology" ("Paul and Apocalyptic Eschatology," 346–47). R. Barry Matlock cautions against an imprecise and overgeneralized understanding of what counts as "apocalyptic eschatology." See his *Unveiling the Apocalyptic Paul*, 247–316. Anthony Thiselton responds, "But many points in the teaching of Jesus and Paul . . . derive at least initially from axioms familiar in the apocalyptic literature of the day." See his *Hermeneutics of Doctrine*, 544.

87. Wright, *Resurrection of the Son of God*, 236–37.

with the astonishing assertion, though, that with the resurrection from the dead of a crucified Messiah—the hope of Israel—the kingdom of God is in some respects already upon us.

On the other hand, Paul still speaks of the age(s) to come (1:20; cf. 2:7), and in Ephesians he clearly indicates his anticipation of a still future "day of redemption" (4:30; note also his talk of a future "inheritance" in 1:14). Furthermore, while God "has made known to us the mystery of his will, . . . the summing up of all things in Christ, things in the heavens and things upon the earth," the ultimate realization of this awaits "the fullness of the times" (1:9–10), and the present is still a time marked by conflict and the need for vigilance (6:10–18). This "already"/"not yet" tension is characteristic of what we find in Paul and is something that will need more discussion down the road. For now, it is critical, though, that we understand what Paul says in Ephesians as representative of an apocalyptic outlook, but one transformed by the conviction that Jesus the crucified Messiah has been raised from the dead. At the very least, this emphasis requires us to broaden our understanding of redemption from a focus on the individual soul's prospects for immortality to the cosmic dimensions of heaven and earth embraced by God's intent to set things right. Ivan Karamazov is not alone in his demand for justice "here on earth." Such a concern is at the very heart of Paul's apocalyptic vision of redemption.

We live in the world in light of the world we live in. Paul has already invited his readers to adopt a new way of describing the world through doxology and has prayed for eyes to be opened by "a Spirit of wisdom and revelation" (*apokalypseōs*) to see the world as it truly is—a world in which God is at work to redeem and triumph over evil. How so? Ephesians describes Christ as the divine warrior, Israel's Messiah engaged in cosmic conflict to defeat those powers arrayed in hostility against the purposes of God in the world. Of course, this divine warrior achieves victory over the powers by the surprising means of suffering crucifixion at their hands (cf. 1 Cor 2:6).[88] By virtue of having been raised from the dead, however, Jesus has triumphed over the ultimate threat posed by the powers and

---

88. The pseudepigraphal *Psalms of Solomon* (first century BCE) anticipates a warrior king who, as "the Lord Messiah," would "purge Jerusalem from Gentiles who trample her to destruction." This "son of David" would "smash the arrogance of sinners like a potter's jar" and "shatter all their substance with an iron rod." An expectation held by some during this period was of a Messiah who would cause the Gentiles to suffer. That the early church proclaimed a Messiah who suffered at the hands of the Gentiles was at the least counterintuitive (see 1 Cor 1:18–25).

has been established as sovereign over any and all forces that bear on the well-being of God's creation (Eph 1:20–22).[89] This sovereignty is effective specifically on behalf of those who believe (1:19) and make up the church, the body of Christ (1:23).

Timothy Gombis asks, "If Christ has been so exalted, what are his triumphs, or in what way has he demonstrated his superiority over these supposedly vanquished powers?"[90] To address this concern we will need to explore two matters. First, how does the resurrection of Jesus from the dead have any bearing on anyone else but himself? Or, perhaps, what is the present impact of God's triumph over evil? Second, what specifically does this triumph of the divine warrior look like? Or, perhaps, what is the present character of God's triumph over evil? These are matters that Paul addresses in the second chapter of Ephesians, where he details the character of new life in the one body of Christ.

Created in Christ Jesus: The Poetics of Grace

One of the deficiencies of the penal substitutionary theory of atonement is that the impact of the cross of Christ is focused chiefly in one direction—at the mollification of God; Jesus' suffering on the cross functions to placate the wrath of an angry God whose holy will has been violated. God, in this view, at the same time shows himself to be merciful, in that he has sent his Son to suffer the punishment sinful humans deserve. Jesus suffers *instead* of us. That the significance of the cross of Christ is directed chiefly toward effecting something of a change in God's disposition toward sinful humans rather than a change in the disposition of sinful humans toward God has resulted, though, in what J. Denny Weaver describes as an ahistorical and a-ethical dimension to this view of the cross: "It is an a-ethical atonement image—it projects an understanding of salvation that is separated from ethics. That is, salvation in [this

---

89. Heil (*Ephesians*, 86 n. 23) indicates the universal scope of this sovereignty, describing v. 21 as "a comprehensive statement specifying that regardless of designation or title a ruling power may have whether in heaven or on earth, it is inferior to Christ who is at the right hand of God." The specific character of these powers has yet to be discussed (see the next chapter on "An Ecclesial Ethic"), but Heil offers the helpful suggestion that here the powers are "spiritual agencies in the heavenly realm standing behind any earthly or human institutions" (*Ephesians*, 86, n. 24). This definition ascribes a properly spiritual identity to forces that operate in concrete historical structures.

90. Gombis, *Triumph of God in Christ*, 62.

substitutionary model] does not envision a change in status in history or in life on earth."[91] Of course, this is precisely the understanding of the Christian faith that Nietzsche attacks.

A significant problem for this understanding of the redemptive work of Christ is that Paul routinely employs what has been called "participatory" language in his discussions of the saving significance of Christ. Paul *never* says Christ died on the cross "instead of us"; he regularly indicates that believers have died and been raised to new life "with Christ" and so are understood to be "in Christ."[92] At the core of Paul's message of redemption is, as Richard Hays puts it, "the apocalyptic significance of the cross and the inclusion of the faithful in the Messiah's destiny."[93] Paul's use of participatory language insists that what has been achieved in the death and resurrection of Jesus is precisely directed toward the situation in which sinful humanity finds itself so that it indeed effects "a change in status in history or in life on earth" in the lives of those who make up the believing community—those who are "in Christ."

It is Paul's "in Christ" and "with Christ" language that indicates the present impact of God's triumph over evil through Christ, specifying how his resurrection from the dead has any bearing on anyone but himself. This participatory language has been interpreted in a number of ways. That it is central to what Paul has to say is clear; what exactly he intends us to understand by it is less so.[94] He does not likely intend us to imagine some personal, mystical absorption into the divine whereby our own identity is lost. Dunn insists, "Being in Christ is not any kind of mystical removal from the real world of every day. On the contrary, it becomes the starting point and base camp for a quite differently motivated and directed life."[95] That is certainly what Paul seems to stress in the opening doxology of 1:3–14. Every blessing of the Spirit that God bestows, God bestows "in Christ" (1:3). God determined before the foundation of the

---

91. Weaver, "Narrative *Christus Victor,*" 9.

92. For statistical information on the use and distribution of these phrases in the letters of Paul, see Dunn, *Theology of Paul the Apostle,* 402–3.

93. Hays, "Crucified with Christ," 239.

94. The centrality of this motif for understanding Paul's message of redemption has long been recognized; a number of recent studies have underscored this emphasis. For example, Tannehill, "Participation in Christ," 223–37; Gorman, *Inhabiting the Cruciform God,* 41–86; Campbell, *Quest for Paul's Gospel,* 56–68; and Campbell's more recent *Deliverance of God.*

95. Dunn, *Theology of Paul the Apostle,* 411.

world to create a people to be holy and blameless as they are found "in him" (1:4). Redemption is found "in him" (1:7). So is the purpose of God (1:9), the uniting of all things "in Christ" (1:10). Why all this centers on Christ Paul underscores in his prayer that moves imperceptibly into the celebration of 1:19–22. All centers on Christ because he has triumphed over the powers through his cross and resurrection. Having suffered the full extent of their threat, the resurrected Christ now reigns supreme over any challenge to God's purpose for creation and exercises that sovereignty on behalf of those who, as they are "in Christ," are the body of Christ. What is true for Christ is true for those who are "in Christ."

What, though, is the character of this triumph? Because believers share in Christ's triumph over those powers that stand opposed to God's purpose for creation, they enjoy new life in the one body of Christ. Paul first highlights the gracious gift of new life in Eph 2:1–10; he then emphasizes, in 2:11–22, that basic to this new life is participation in the one body of Christ. Both portions of Ephesians 2 clarify the significance of the redemptive work of Christ: the present discussion concentrates on the "new life" emphasized in 2:1–10; our next chapter will focus on the "in the body of Christ" dimensions of 2:11–22.

We learn in Eph 2:1–10 that the redemptive work of Christ cannot be reduced to the narrow vision assumed by Nietzsche. The issues are much more involved than that of absolution of guilt so the soul can enjoy immortal bliss. In vv. 1–3, Paul wants his readers to look back on their lives prior to faith in Christ to see that such life, by comparison, can only be counted as spiritual death. From the standpoint of faith in Christ, the former life is now viewed as one of disobedience to God and subjection to destructive powers that dominate the present evil age in opposition to God. The review is intended, not to give Christians a sense of moral superiority over unbelievers, but to set in relief what is recounted in 2:4–7: a narrative of the grace and mercy of God that gives new life through including believers in the life and destiny of Christ.[96]

Two matters are significant here. First, there is a strong emphasis on God's love and mercy. God is "rich in mercy because of his great love with

---

96. O'Brien (*Ephesians*, 158) observes, "The gravity of [the readers'] previous condition . . . serves to magnify the wonder of God's mercy. The past is recalled not because the emphasis falls upon it, but in order to draw attention to God's mighty action in Christ." While the explicit language of the "once"/"now" motif is not used in 2:1–10, the twofold "once" with the strong "but" of v. 4 makes its implicit force evident. The motif functions in general to highlight both the power and grace of God in transforming the lives of believers.

which he has loved us" (v. 4). Believers have been saved by grace (vv. 5, 8), God's rich kindness that will display God's redemptive mercy throughout the ages (v. 7). Second, there is a repeated emphasis on sharing in the experience of the resurrected Christ. Paul uses three compound verbs that begin with the prefix *syn-* (Greek = "with") to indicate that those who are "in Christ" have been joined by God to the history and destiny of Christ. God has made believers "alive together with Christ" (*synezōopoiēsen*, 2:5). Thus, as Christ has been raised from the dead (*egeiras*, 1:20), so has God raised believers from the dead *with* Christ (*synēgeiren*, 2:6); as Christ has been "seated in the heavenlies" (*kathisas . . . en tois epouraniois*, 1:20), so has God "co-seated" believers "in the heavenlies" *with* Christ (*synekathisen en tois epouraniois*) by virtue of their status "in Christ" (2:6). What is true for Christ is true for those who are "in Christ."[97]

With his familiar insistence "for by grace you have been saved . . . it is the gift of God" (v. 8), Paul emphasizes once again that the wonder of new life in Christ comes entirely at the divine initiative. It is the passage as a whole, however, that informs us as to what it really means to be "saved." Paul's account of what it means to be saved can only be understood in light of its immediate setting and in light of the echoes of the exodus story of the Old Testament. In the Old Testament, the paradigmatic act of divine salvation is the deliverance of Israel from Egyptian bondage.[98] In Ephesians, deliverance is from the old life characterized by bondage to sin, the flesh, and spiritual powers that hold humanity captive to the norms and standards of the present evil age. To be saved is to know new life in Christ, who has triumphed over those destructive powers. And just as God delivered Israel from bondage for the purpose of witness to the world of God's intent for all of creation (Exod 19:4–6), so God, by joining believers to the history and destiny of Christ, delivers believers from bondage for the purpose of witness to the world of God's intent for all of creation. Thus, Paul rounds out this passage by way of summary: "For we are his workmanship, having been created in Christ Jesus for the purpose of good works which God previously prepared that we should walk in them" (Eph 2:10). While salvation is in no way the result of any human achievement, but comes entirely by grace, salvation is certainly for the

97. Lincoln, *Paradise Now and Not Yet*, 147–48.

98. The verb used in v. 8, *sōzein*, "to save," is frequently used in the Septuagint to describe God's gracious intervention on behalf of the people of Israel to deliver them from threat; it is used with specific reference to the exodus event in Deut 33:29 and Ps 106:8, 10, 21, 47.

purpose of setting sinful humanity free to enjoy life as God intended it from the beginning, a life shaped by God's will.

It is interesting that Paul uses the language of "creation" in his account of what God's work of redemption through Christ is all about. To be saved is to be "*created* in Christ Jesus." Paul's description of believers as God's "workmanship" also employs "creation" language. *Poiēma*, "workmanship" or "craftsmanship," a term used only one other time in the New Testament (see Rom 1:20, "the things having been made"), is used in the Septuagint (e.g., Pss 91:4; 142:5) to refer to what God has made. In this light, we might say that believers are participants in the poetics of grace— God making all things new in love and mercy.

The twofold use of "creation" language, coupled with Paul's employment of *peripateō*, the walking metaphor (vv. 2, 10), lends emphasis to a feature of Paul's apocalyptic gospel that is often missed in discussion of Ephesians. The dramatic insistence in Ephesians 2 that believers presently share in the life of the resurrected Christ is one of the major reasons many New Testament scholars cast doubt on its Pauline authorship. The letter so emphasizes present fulfillment of God's saving work, many argue, that no room is left for the future orientation Paul stresses in his other letters (cf. 1 Thess 4:15–18; 1 Cor 15:12–58).[99] The contrast is overstated,[100] and a significant feature of Paul's account of salvation in Ephesians 2:1–10 is left unattended, leaving us with the truncated version of the gospel accepted by many but scorned by Nietzsche. With the convergence of Paul's apocalyptic emphasis on the power of the resurrected Christ present in the lives of believers, a description of salvation in terms of "creation," and his use of *peripateō* all interrelated in one passage, we have the elements for the formulation of the redemptive ethic that stands as the heart of this study.

The significance of this convergence can best be understood by exploring the relationship between these three elements. Paul's use of "creation" language is often taken as further emphasizing Eph 2:8–9:

99. Jeal (*Integrating Theology and Ethics*, 138) even insists, "Ephesians 2 is so fully 'realized' that it seems to leave no room for an ongoing 'earthly' existence." A major feature of his work is the argument that there is no clear theological relationship between gospel and ethics in Ephesians. Our analysis argues against Jeal's position.

100. Gorman (*Apostle of the Crucified Lord*, 503) says, "These supposedly radical differences from the authentic Paul depend in part on a misreading of the undisputed letters and in part on a misreading of Ephesians." We have already seen that Ephesians clearly maintains a future orientation in its expectation of the "day of redemption" (4:30). See Gräbe, "Salvation in Colossians and Ephesians," 300–301.

that salvation is a divine gift that leaves no room for human boasting. Lincoln says, "Just as humans contributed nothing to their own creation so also they contributed nothing to their new creation; both are God's work."[101] That is only a partial explanation for why Paul uses the language of creation to talk about new life in Christ; the apocalyptic setting of this discussion and his use of *peripateō* emphasize a particular quality of the "new creation" that is God's achievement in redeeming through Christ.

Certainly an apocalyptic outlook expresses deep awareness of the brokenness of the present evil age. That sense of brokenness is sometimes so overwhelming, though, that in some examples of Jewish apocalyptic God's creation is so swallowed up by evil that the only remedy is to scrap the whole thing and start all over.[102] That is not, however, Paul's understanding. In Rom 8:18–25, Paul expresses his expectation, not of cosmic annihilation, but of the transformation of a suffering creation keyed to the ultimate redemption of our physical bodies (8:23)—the resurrection of our bodies vouchsafed by God having raised Jesus from the dead (8:11). As we have already seen, in Ephesians Paul anticipates, not the replacement of the heavens and earth by a completely different act of creation, but the "uniting of all things in Christ" (1:10). Paul is second to no one in his appreciation for the dark shadow of futility that hangs over all of creation and every human project; but his bright insistence is of the faithfulness of God to bring to fulfillment what God has intended from the beginning. What Bernard Och says of the hopes of the people of Israel, Paul insists is coming to pass in the reality of the cross and resurrection of Israel's Christ: "Redemption is understood as the implementation of creation and the actualization of the order and goodness of creation. Through redemption, God realizes those fundamental purposes for life and blessing inherent in the creation of the world."[103]

We might qualify what Och has said in one important aspect. O'Donovan affirms that the resurrection of Christ from the dead "tells us of God's vindication of his creation and so our created life" and that "in the resurrection of Christ creation is restored and the kingdom of God dawns."[104] O'Donovan also insists, however, "We must go beyond

---

101. Lincoln, *Ephesians*, 114; see also O'Brien, *Ephesians*, 178.

102. This is perhaps the view held by the community associated with the Dead Sea Scrolls. See Cook, *Apocalyptic Literature*, 40–42; but see Martinez, "Apocalypticism in the Dead Sea Scrolls," 189–90.

103. Och, "Creation and Redemption," 227.

104. O'Donovan, *Resurrection and Moral Order*, 13, 15.

thinking of redemption as a mere restoration, the return of the *status quo anti*. The redemption of the world, and of mankind, does not serve only to put us back in the Garden of Eden where we began. It leads us to that further destiny to which, even in the Garden of Eden, we were already directed."[105] Theologians have a lovely way of putting this: "*Endzeit ist mehr Urzeit*"—"the end time is *more* than the early time." What God does in the cross and resurrection of Christ is not just return us to Eden. If that were the case we would remain forever susceptible to the serpent's voice and subject still to the threat of the powers. "Put succinctly," Reno says, "the Christian view of redemption endorses rather than cancels the intrinsic goodness of creation. . . . At the same time, redemption entails a transformation rather than a simple affirmation of the created order."[106] This transformation is underway in the community made up of those "created in Christ Jesus."

What is the significance of this affirmation/transformation, continuity/discontinuity of creation effected in the Christian apocalyptic announced by Paul? That God's work of redemption through Christ embraces all of creation is evident (see also Col 1:13–20). The apocalyptic character of a gospel that announces God's triumph over the present evil age by means of the cross and resurrection of Christ, however, tells us that everything is now different. N. T. Wright insists the resurrection of Jesus from the dead changes everything: "If it happened, it matters. The world is a different place from what it would be if it did not happen."[107] In what way? Why does Paul stress *kainos* ("new") in association with *anthropos* ("humanity"), as in Eph 2:15 and 4:24?

Stanley Hauerwas makes an interesting set of observations about the character of apocalyptic theology and its significance for the task of Christian ethics. "Those who emphasize apocalyptic are often accused," he says, "of failing to do justice to God as creator."[108] In some circles within theological ethics, "creation talk often serves as a means for the domestication of the Gospel." How does this happen? "Appeals to creation often are meant to suggest that all people, Christian or not, share fundamental moral commitments that can provide a basis for common action." While that might sound appealing or helpful as a basis for moral agreement

---

105. Ibid., 55.

106. Reno, "Redemption and Ethics," 27.

107. Wright, *Resurrection of the Son of God*, 714.

108. Hauerwas, "Creation as Apocalyptic," 110.

on important matters, Hauerwas warns, "These appeals to creation too often amount to legitimating strategies for the principalities and powers that determine our lives."[109] The search for the "lowest common denominator" that permits cooperation in a pluralistic environment frequently serves as cover for a readiness to accept too quickly "the way things are" as representative of the created order. The challenge of Paul's apocalyptic gospel is its refusal to confuse the conventional with the real, a confusion that tempts too many "American Christians . . . to accept, with despair and relief, the inevitability and thus the goodness of things as they are."[110]

For those "created in Christ Jesus," though, there can be no such resignation to the inevitability of things as they are. They are themselves living testimony to the power of the gospel to effect transformation. We dare not, however, narrow this transformation to the dimensions of personal piety. To be "created in Christ Jesus" is to participate, not simply in personal transformation, but to recognize that personal transformation itself takes place through participation in the cosmic sovereignty of Christ. That Christ's sovereignty is established over "all rule and authority and power and dominion" (1:21), however, requires, as Hauerwas puts it, the "authentic Christian mode . . . of taking seriously Christ's lordship over the public, the social, the political." This enables a resistance to the standard insistence that we live in a closed system of causal relations that leaves no room for the *kainos*, but only for the *anthropos*. The "way things are" is always open to the dramatic intervention of a God "who cannot be excluded from creating new possibilities for our lives through our lives."[111] "Created in Christ Jesus" entails the apocalyptic affirmation of God's good creation, effects its liberation from the futility imposed upon it by the powers, and its transformation toward what God intended from the beginning. Critical in that transformation is the witness of that community created in Christ Jesus. That witness brings us to the third element essential to the character of Paul's redemptive ethic—his use of *peripateō*.

Ephesians 2:1–10 offers a contrast between two ways of life, preparing the way for the steady contrast between two different types of

109. Ibid.

110. Ibid., 114. And so, reports in the spring of 2009 indicate that the majority of regular church attenders in the United States support the use of torture as a method of "enhanced interrogation" of terror suspects. For the data see http://pewforum.org/docs/?DocID=156.

111. Ibid., 109.

existence traced throughout the second half of the book.[112] Prior to God's provision of new life in Christ, Paul's readers "walked" (*peripateō*) in the world according to the pattern and norms of the present evil age (2:1–3). Paul announces as the purpose of God's gracious work of redemption that those who have been "created in Christ Jesus" are to walk (*peripateō*) in the "good works, which God prepared beforehand" (2:10). Many contemporary English translations (e.g., NIV, NRSV) mistakenly assume Paul employs a "dead" metaphor with his use of *peripateō* and render the verb as "live," obscuring the metaphor of movement and embodiment.[113] Paul's frequent use of this metaphor (thirty-two times in all the Paulines; eight times in Ephesians) serves to remind believers that the Christian life is one lived very much in the present age with all of its challenges, responsibilities, and temptations; and yet it is a life that knows the transformative impact of Paul's apocalyptic gospel by which believers participate in Christ's triumph over the powers.[114]

112. Best, "Two Types of Existence," 139–55.

113. That *peripateō* was for Paul not a "dead" metaphor (one whose association with its "source domain" had receded into the past) is clear from the fact that it simply was not used very often at all outside the letters of Paul in the way Paul uses it. Commentators frequently assume Paul derives his usage from the Hebrew Scriptures (where *halak*, "to walk," is used some two hundred times in a figurative sense; e.g., Mic 6:8), by way of the Septuagint (e.g., O'Brien, *Ephesians*, 157 n. 14; Lincoln, *Ephesians*, 94). The Septuagint, however, only uses *peripateō* in this way about four times, while the term most frequently employed in the Septuagint to translate *halak*, *poreuomai*, is never used by Paul in the figurative sense. Paul certainly derives his use of the walking metaphor from Scripture; for whatever reason, though, that he chose a term rarely used elsewhere to convey a familiar image suggests the importance of the metaphor for him and that its use is intentional and significant. See Holloway, *Peripateō*, 1–27.

114. A partial survey of Paul's use of the metaphor other than in Ephesians shows its association with such concerns as sexual fidelity in marriage, honesty in business matters, and diligence in labor (1 Thess 4:1–12); relationships of love, mutual respect, and peace in Christian fellowship (1 Cor 3:3; Rom 14:15); and the capacity to use any and every social status as an opportunity for expressing Christian identity (1 Cor 7:17–24). A walk "in newness of life" (Rom 6:4) presents the members of one's body to God as instruments of righteousness (Rom 6:12–19), is empowered by the Holy Spirit to live in a way that pleases God (Rom 8:1–11), and bears the Spirit's fruit in order to support and sustain Christian fellowship (Gal 5:15–26). It is a cruciform life that finds its basic pattern in the self-giving service of Jesus (Phil 3:17; cf. 2:5–11). As newness of life lived by the power of the Spirit, it is life that knows the power and presence of the age to come. That it is, however, a "walk" in newness of life is the reminder that this life is still one of expectancy and hope (Rom 13:11–14) in which we "walk by faith, not by sight" (2 Cor 5:7). The underlying theme of Paul's use of *peripateō* throughout his letters it that of life in the present age conditioned by the presence and power of the coming age. Other than greater frequency, its use in Ephesians differs is no significant way.

How is the transformative impact of Christ's triumph over the powers made known and visible in the world? How is God's intent to affirm and restore creation to its divine purpose expressed in the present? When those who are "created in Christ Jesus" walk in "good works," the way of life God has intended for humanity from the beginning,[115] they demonstrate in the midst of the present evil age the reality of Christ's triumph over the powers and display here and now what God will bring to universal realization in the age to come.

Two final aspects of Paul's use of *peripateō* will highlight the significance of what Paul is saying here and will provide some response to Nietzsche's attack on Christian ethics as a redemptive ethic. First, when Paul describes salvation as deliverance from a walk dominated by the powers of the present evil age and in terms of participation in the new creation that enlivens those "created in Christ Jesus" to walk in good works, he anticipates with the phrase "good works" the basic content of what we find in Ephesians 4–6. There the repeated use of *peripateō* (4:1, 17; 5:2, 8, 15) ties together Paul's moral admonitions as one long expansion of his brief reference to "good works" in 2:10.[116] This connection lets us know more precisely how those "created in Christ Jesus" participate in and demonstrate to the world the triumph of God through Christ. The dispositions, virtues, and practices that characterize "the worthy walk" (4:1) are the concrete, visible measures by which the church bears witness to the powers (3:10) of how God is at work in the world to demonstrate the gospel's triumph over evil. And how is that? By the formation of lives that walk in humility, gentleness, patience, and forbearing love (4:1–2), qualities that sustain and support "the unity of the Spirit in the bond of peace" (4:3). By fashioning a people who refuse to echo back to the world its own ways of futility, spiritual callousness, and self-centeredness but instead offer witness of the goodness for which God created us in the beginning (4:17–24). By molding lives after God's own image, that image chiefly seen in the self-offering of Christ, but seen derivatively in the vital graces of daily life: honesty, generosity, mutual encouragement, and the reconciling practices of forgiveness and mercy (4:25—5:2). By putting on

---

115. Jeal (*Integrating Theology and Ethics*, 144) argues that as the good works are "prepared beforehand" (*proētoimasen*) the walk in good works is itself predetermined, so that "believers appear to be reduced to existence as mere automata of God." Gombis (*Triumph of God in Christ*, 73 n. 93) suggests Paul's language "need not point to determinism, but merely indicates that God has created his people for righteous living."

116. Holloway, *Peripateō*, 196–99.

display the life-giving light of Christ in the midst of a world of darkness (5:3–14), through a people enabled by the Holy Spirit to offer a visible contrast to the world's foolishness (5:15–18).

A second point serves to reinforce and clarify the first. This walk in "good works" is carried out by those who have been made alive together with Christ, raised with Christ, and seated with him "in the heavenly places in Christ Jesus" (2:6). We earlier explored Paul's language of "the heavenly places" and recognized that Paul does not want us to consider ourselves as removed from the present realm of responsibilities, challenges, tasks, and temptations. Indeed, Paul makes it clear in Eph 6:12 that, far from exempting believers from conflict, sharing in the resurrection life of Christ introduces believers into God's conflict with evil in a radically new and significant way—instead of the captivity presupposed in Eph 2:1–3. To be "seated in the heavenly places" is to be made aware of the larger reality in which life is lived and thus to know what is genuinely at stake in responding to God's calling. To be "created in Christ Jesus" is to have responded to God's calling to participate in God's restorative act of new creation. It is to join with God in what God is doing to unite all things together in Christ in triumph over the powers that serve to threaten and endanger the well-being of God's good creation. To know new life in Christ is to know that things can and do go horribly wrong, but that God is at work through Christ to set things right. By the poetics of grace, God enlists and enables believers to participate in that restorative act. Paul's insistence that believers have joined with Christ "in the heavenly places" is no retreat from this world and its challenges, but the reminder that those challenges can be faced with a confidence born of Easter's confrontation with and triumph over death.

It is crucial to note, however, how this conflict is waged. Paul's admonition in Eph 6:10–20 is for believers to "put on the whole armor of God." Another way of putting that might be simply to say that we are called to engage in the conflict with evil using the same strategy as employed by God. Put in a yet different way, God's way of engaging in conflict with evil is to use a people who demonstrate to the world the formation of a community that puts on display the new life made possible by Christ's triumph over the powers through death and resurrection. While the temptation is always there (and history testifies to an all-too-easy surrender at this point) to echo back to the world its own strategies for managing conflict, Paul offers an analysis of what God is doing about evil that requires believers to follow a different path. After all, we are called to "walk no longer as the Gentiles walk" (4:17), so we should not be terribly surprised that we are challenged to confront evil in a manner markedly different from the ways most of humanity has done so most of the time. What is that strategy? It has everything to do with truth and righteousness and a gospel of peace and faith and prayer and proclamation. It has everything to do with a way of life, community, speech, and witness that testifies to new life in the one body of Christ. This strategy has to do with the concrete expression of the way of the gospel in lives that have been "created in Christ Jesus." Paul sums up that way of life with an account of "good works which God prepared beforehand that we should walk in them" (2:10).[117]

What is God doing about evil? What of Ivan Karamazov's demand to see justice "here on earth"? New life in Christ is not life that leaves this world behind. Popular reception of apocalyptic thought often fosters retreat from life and refuses to take seriously the crisis the gospel provokes by the eruption of the new in the midst of the old. In such cases, Nietzsche's complaint is fairly accurate: "When the emphasis is put on the 'beyond' rather than on life itself . . . , then the emphasis has been completely removed from life" (*A* §43). Christian apocalyptic, though, does not permit such a retreat. Lincoln neatly summarizes the larger point we have been pursuing: while "Paul's Christian apocalyptic is defined both by the future and by the recent past," it is primarily "about what happens when the life of the age to come has been made available through Christ's resurrection and how that life . . . works itself out on earth in the present."[118] That life is described in terms not of "the beyond," but as having been "*created in Christ Jesus.*" It is not about the eternal bliss of an "immortal soul" (a phrase made problematic by the fact that it never appears in the Bible), but about the contrast between a "walk" determined by the destructive powers regnant in the present evil age (2:1–3) and a "walk" transformed through God's invasion into the present by the power of the resurrected Christ, who makes possible life as God intended it from the beginning (2:10). We have uncovered many points of contrast between Nietzsche's narrow account of redemption through Christ and what Paul has to say in Ephesians. The contrast between a focus on Christ as a "guilt offering"

---

117. Thus, the call to "divine warfare" in 6:10–20 needs to be seen as conclusion to and summary of the parenesis beginning in 4:1. As Yoder Neufeld ("*Put On the Whole Armour of God,*" 110) says, "It constitutes the climax of the parenesis of the letter, indeed, of the letter as a whole." See also Wild, "Warrior and the Prisoner," 284–98.

118. Lincoln, *Paradise Now and Not Yet,* 179.

and Paul's apocalyptic gospel that celebrates the death and resurrection of Christ as a triumph over the powers, a triumph in which believers share, is apparent. Nietzsche's complaint, however, that the Christian doctrine of redemption is all about the individual soul's immortal bliss, a doctrine in Nietzsche's estimate that leads to indifference and rejection of the significance of life in this world, also finds challenge and correction in Paul's account of redemption. Paul's account of salvation in Ephesians 2 cannot be narrowed to the minimalist terms presumed by Nietzsche. Of course, there are Christians who have narrowed the Christian faith to the thin account Nietzsche attacks. When and where that is done, their argument is not with Nietzsche, however, but with Paul himself.

THE MEASURE OF CHRIST: PAULINE ANTHROPOLOGY AND THE NEW EUGENICS

Paul's Letter to the Ephesians reveals a redemptive ethic that gives great attention to life in this world. Far from being anti-life, Paul's apocalyptic gospel has everything to do with what it means to be "*created* in Christ Jesus." How, though, might this redemptive ethic actually affect human life at its most vulnerable points? If this redemptive ethic is all about life as God intended it from the beginning, what significance does it have when God's intentions for life's well-being seem most threatened? Every one of us eventually faces those situations where the boundaries of life appear uncertain and what constitutes life's goodness becomes difficult to discern. Any ethic that insists it has something to say about what it genuinely means to be human will have to accept such circumstances as a test of its capacity to redeem the tragic. Nowhere is this more of a challenge than in the complex array of issues known cumulatively as "bioethics." In ever increasingly complicated areas of life and death, the very definitions of life and death seem elusive and the parameters for what counts as human existence are contested. Shakespeare's Ophelia opined, "We know what we are, but know not what we may be."[119] Were we to update her sentiment, she might very well say, "We have no idea what we are, and what we may be is entirely up for grabs."

The ambiguities are no more apparent than in the prospects of what some call "the new eugenics," the concern to make full use of biomedical technologies such as genetic diagnosis and engineering to fundamentally

119. *Hamlet*, Act IV, Scene V.

alter and "improve" the human condition. While many bioethical issues merit our attention, it is the case that the vision, commitments, and intellectual heritage contributing to the outlook of the new eugenics are present and influential across the entire spectrum of bioethical issues. To account for the aspirations of the new eugenics is to go far in explaining the understanding of what it means to be a human being that reigns in current discussions and practices ranging from abortion to physician-assisted suicide and many of the technological interventions in between. There are prevailing sentiments and perspectives dominating our ideological landscape that drive not only the quest for "designer children," but sanction in our culture both the demands for and expectations of life without blemish as well as the demands for and expectations of death without inconvenience.

We will first explore the new eugenics, placing it in historical context in comparison with the "old eugenics" of the early decades of the twentieth century. To understand what the new eugenics offers we must also examine the promises and possibilities of biomedical technology as applied in matters of human reproduction and health.[120] We only properly understand the character of the new eugenics, though, as we perceive in its aspirations the ultimate expression of an agenda of technological mastery over nature that reaches back to the period of early modernity and the influence of figures such as Francis Bacon and René Descartes. After surveying the character and concerns of the new eugenics, we will need to return to Ephesians to inquire as to what Paul has to say there concerning the fundamental question at stake in any and every concern related to bioethics in general and the new eugenics in particular: what does it mean to be a human being? At that point, the work of contemporary American philosopher Calvin O. Schrag will serve as a heuristic tool, providing the means for a fresh analysis of Pauline anthropology as found in Ephesians. What this analysis brings to light will provide a means for evaluating some of the major claims, presuppositions, and implications of the new eugenics in light of what Ephesians has to say about God's intent for human well-being.

---

120. I am going to use the term "reproduction" in this discussion, instead of the more theologically suitable "procreation," as an indication of the shift in character of the act of human "begetting" within an ever increasingly technological context. See Meilaender, *Bioethics*, 10–24.

The New Eugenics

On June 26, 2000, President Bill Clinton announced the completion of the first draft of the sequencing of the human genome, the result of a ten-year, 2.7 billion dollar effort known as the Human Genome Project. President Clinton expressed something of the magnitude of the achievement: "Today, we are learning the language in which God created life. We are gaining ever more awe for the complexity, the beauty, the wonder of God's most divine and sacred gift. With this profound new knowledge, humankind is on the verge of gaining immense, new power to heal. Genome science will have a real impact on all our lives—and even more, on the lives of our children. It will revolutionize the diagnosis, prevention and treatment of most, if not all, human diseases."[121]

The former president rightly identifies the endeavor as one having to do with "gaining immense, new power" and that a revolution in human medicine is underway. The Human Genome Project is just one expression of the ongoing quest of technological mastery over nature that has given us everything from antibiotics to zygote intrafallopian transfer (a type of *in vitro* fertilization). We have become so accustomed to routine announcements from the scientific community of this or that breakthrough that we simply live with the expectation voiced by President Clinton—that through the patient and determined application of medical technology, we will eventually be able to diagnose, prevent, and treat most, if not all, human diseases. To voice any concerns about this rosy future is to invite comparison to the Luddites of the nineteenth century, who are dismissed as irrational opponents of the inevitable and beneficial march through human history of technological triumph.

Concerns, however, have been voiced. Specifically, some fear we have entered an era in which subtle, but no less real, forces of compulsion are increasingly at work to fashion a world in which the quest for human perfection by technological means actually serves to threaten fundamental goods of human existence. Some fear the advent of a new eugenics. Others believe the new eugenics is already upon us. What is meant, though, by "the new eugenics?"

The term "eugenics" was first coined by Francis Galton, Charles Darwin's cousin, in 1883, who defined eugenics as "using our understanding of the laws of heredity to improve the stock of humankind." According to

121. From a White House press release dated 06/26/2000. See http://www.genome.gov/10001356.

Galton, the goal of eugenics is "to give the more suitable races or strains of blood a better chance of prevailing over the less suitable than they otherwise would have had."[122] Galton himself advocated what is called "positive eugenics," the encouragement of reproduction by those who possess the "superior endowments" perceived as desirable for the improvement of the human species. Others would call for "negative eugenics," the concern to limit reproduction by—or even eliminate—those who possess traits considered a threat to the progress of human civilization.

Negative eugenics is often viewed in association with the Nazi Germany of the 1930s. Informed by Nietzsche's warnings of a decadent Europe and against the nihilistic influence of Christian compassion for the weak, it is argued, the Nazis unleashed a brutal economy of selection by which the "useless eaters" of society were targeted for eradication.[123] The shadow of the "old eugenics," those harsh and coercive policies aimed at improving the human race by ridding the world of undesirables, we would like to keep at a distance, "usually safely on the other side of a wide intellectual and cultural gap."[124] The truth is, though, as Amy Laura Hall puts it, "The eugenics movement was germinated in a relatively elite, academic version of scientific racism from the previous century, but it took root in the heartland of America," with the urging and complicity of Protestant clergy and laity eager to present themselves as well-educated citizens supportive of a civic order needing to protect itself from "the unsafe, the unsound, and the insane."[125] That protection would take the form of laws prohibiting interracial marriage and permitting the forced sterilization of those identified as mentally ill or "criminally insane." Between 1907 and 1930, twenty-eight states passed laws allowing forced sterilization. Although there were voices of protest against these laws in some (mainly Roman Catholic) quarters, the Supreme Court sanctioned

122. Cited in Soulen, "Cruising toward Bethlehem," 108–9.

123. One of the goals of many Nietzsche scholars is to challenge this association between Nietzsche and the Nazis (see, e.g., Kaufmann, *Nietzsche*, 284–306). Clearly, Nietzsche abhorred German nationalism; however, that his ideas were appealed to by Hitler himself cannot be denied. See Whyte, "Uses and Abuses of Nietzsche in the Third Reich," 171–94.

124. Hall, "To Form a More Perfect Union," 76.

125. Ibid., 78–83. Hall's essay highlights the role of mainline Protestant clergy and laity in the eugenics movement in early twentieth-century America. For an account of the role of evangelicals in this movement, see Durst, "Evangelical Engagement with Eugenics," 45–53. Durst describes evangelicals of this period as "apathetic, acquiescent, or at times downright supportive of the eugenics movement" (45).

such laws in 1927. Justice Oliver Wendell Holmes, writing on behalf of the court, argued in *Buck v. Bell,* "It is better for the world, if instead of waiting to execute degenerate offspring for crime, or to let them starve for their imbecility, society can prevent those who are manifestly unfit from continuing their kind. The principle that sustains compulsory vaccination is broad enough to cover the cutting of Fallopian tubes. Three generations of imbeciles are enough."[126]

Many factors eventually served to diminish the appeal of eugenics programs in the United States. The proper response of revulsion to Nazi eugenics programs, a growing recognition that environment plays a critical role in determining how genes are expressed, and greater attention to Mendelian principles of genetics were among the reasons enthusiasm for such programs waned.[127] If the "old eugenics," though, with its overtones of racism and taint of coercion, has fallen out of cultural favor, a "new eugenics . . . seems to be emerging almost spontaneously from existing cultural trends."[128] Coupled with significant advances in medical technology, these cultural trends account for a set of practices such that "while it may be that no one deliberately or consciously intends a eugenic goal for the population as a whole, the result may well be the same."[129] We will survey the practices first and then seek to account for the cultural trends that have permitted the rise of the new eugenics.

The very technologies and practices that offer so many apparent goods and benefits for human well-being are the same technologies and practices that present the threat of the new eugenics. The last fifty years have seen some of the most revolutionary advances in medical technology in all of human history, specifically as they relate to human reproduction. In 1978, the first "test tube" baby, Louise Brown, was born in England. Through the process of *in vitro* fertilization (IVF), whereby egg and sperm are combined in a laboratory dish to produce a zygote (fertilized egg) that can then be transferred to a woman's uterus, women who experience difficulty in becoming pregnant can significantly increase

126. Cited in Hall, "To Form a More Perfect Union," 76–77.

127. It needs to be said, though, that a program of forced sterilization, primarily of impoverished African-American women, endured from the 1930s into the 1970s in North Carolina. See the report by *The Winston-Salem Journal,* "Against Their Will: North Carolina's Sterilization Program." Online: http://www.journalnow.com/specialreports/againsttheirwill/.

128. Soulen, "Cruising toward Bethlehem," 109.

129. Song, *Human Genetics,* 50.

their chances.[130] Of course, the process does require the removal of many eggs from a woman's ovaries and a ready supply of sperm. For the sake of efficiency, generally several (eight to ten) eggs will be fertilized, though not all resulting embryos will be transferred to the uterus. Again for the sake of efficiency (if the initial attempt at IVF is not successful, for example), extra embryos may be *cryopreserved* (frozen) for subsequent efforts.[131]

A number of moral concerns arise from the process of IVF itself. What is the status of those frozen embryos? For those who believe the embryo enjoys the rights of full personhood from the "moment of conception" (really, a process that can take about twenty-four hours), the notion of discarded embryos is profoundly troubling. The variety of relationships that might result from the process also raises questions. It is possible that a child might be "produced" for a couple who, for understandable reasons (issues of inheritable diseases, for example), make use of donor eggs and/or sperm and enlist a surrogate to carry the child to term. In such circumstances, a child could have up to five "parents." While birthdays and Christmas might offer a bonanza to the child, clarifying the many social relationships could be tricky.[132]

It is when coupled with new genetic technologies, however, that IVF both offers would-be parents greater assurance of healthy babies as well as introduces heightened concerns regarding the new eugenics. A number of clinical practices make IVF an almost inevitable eugenic practice. The first of these is *preimplantation genetic diagnosis* (PGD). While not necessarily a part of the IVF process, the demand for efficiency and an environment where cost is a significant concern means it "only makes sense" to screen the embryos available for uterine transfer for the most viable. If the concern is that of passing on inheritable diseases, available embryos will naturally be screened for the presence of genetic abnormalities. The mapping of the human genome has only accelerated the pace of discovery of relationships between specific diseases and genetic dysfunction, with

130. An explanation of the process accessible to nonspecialists is *Assisted Reproductive Technologies: A Guide for Patients* (2008), published by the American Society for Reproductive Medicine. Online: http://www.asrm.org/Templates/SearchResults. aspx?q=assisted%20reproductive%20technologies%20a%20guide.

131. A fertility clinic that offers a 1 in 3 success rate for live birth resulting from one IVF cycle is at the high end of performance measures. When one cycle can cost upwards of $30,000, the issue of efficiency becomes significant.

132. See Meilaender, *Bioethics*, 15–22.

about 4,500 diseases being linked to mutations in single genes to date. Theoretically, several options are possible if any such abnormalities are detected. Routine practice is the selection of the more favorably disposed embryos for implantation. It is projected that gene therapies will one day be able to correct such abnormalities, even at the embryonic stage, by replacing defective genes with those that function properly. Since such therapies are not yet available, the conventional practice is the careful selection of preferred embryos; others are either discarded or placed in cold storage.

Of course, genetic testing is not bound to the practice of IVF. A sample of the amniotic fluid surrounding the growing baby can be drawn and tested for signs of any genetic disorders. Since the number of inheritable diseases detectable through genetic diagnosis is far greater than available therapies, the general assumption is that detection of serious genetic abnormality will lead to the "therapeutic abortion" of the fetus.[133] What counts for "serious genetic abnormality" is itself an open question. The influence of cultural prejudices in this arena "is already amply documented by the selective abortion of female fetuses in many Asian countries, where the number of 'missing girls' in India alone is estimated to be as high as forty million or more."[134] In some cultural contexts, to be a female is evidently to suffer an inherent genetic disadvantage.

As indicated, the promise of gene therapy outdistances reality at present and research has known both setback and success. In September 1999, a relatively healthy eighteen-year-old test subject, Jesse Gelsinger, died in a gene transfer study conducted at the University of Pennsylvania. Subsequent investigation revealed an inadequate oversight system, resulting in calls for greater superintendence of clinical research.[135] On

133. One recent study reveals that in England and Wales, in approximately 45 percent of the cases where prenatal tests indicated Down syndrome the pregnancy was terminated. See the 2008 report of the Wolfson Institute of Preventative Medicine: http://www.wolfson.qmul.ac.uk/ndscr. Data in the United States offers up to a 90 percent abortion rate; see http://blogs.discovermagazine.com/gnxp/2008/09/down-syndrome-and-abortion-rates/.

134. Soulen, "Cruising toward Bethlehem," 113. Boston Globe columnist Jeff Jacoby cites a UNICEF report that calculates that "7,000 fewer girls are now born in India each day than nature would dictate, and 10 million have been killed during pregnancy or just after in the past 20 years." While the statistics are not nearly as startling, he reports a growing trend in this practice in the United States as well. See his "Choosing to Eliminate Unwanted Daughters."

135. For discussion of the incident and its aftermath, see Walters, "Human Genetic Intervention," 375–80.

the other hand, in April 2009, word came that one gene therapy study had been successful in providing some level of sight for children that had been born blind.[136] It is the case, at any rate, that the future of medicine is one thoroughly bound to genetic science, and indications are that "we are on the cusp of achieving . . . the power to bring vast domains of human life once subject to necessity or fate within the scope of human technical intervention."[137]

The promise of genetic technology comes in a number of forms. The basic idea of gene therapy in general is that a gene related to a particular disorder is removed from its cell and replaced by a properly functioning version of the same gene. When the cell with its properly functioning genes reproduces sufficiently, the pancreas (for example) that was not producing adequate amounts of insulin will now do so. Gene therapy, however, could be directed at two different kinds of cells. First, there is *somatic cell* therapy in which cells in the bodily tissues or organs of a particular patient are subject to treatment. There is also, however, the prospect of *germline* therapy, in which the reproductive cells that develop into egg or sperm and would carry heritable disorders to future generations are targeted. Germline therapy, because it would not only affect every cell in the initial recipient but also would modify the genes passed on to future generations, seems a much more economical and efficient strategy. Rather than having to repeat corrective measures whenever inheritable disorders become manifest, "over a long period of time, germline gene transfers could decrease the incidence of certain inherited diseases that currently cause great suffering."[138] Given the fact that all of us carry within our cells a number of defective genes that may or may not come to phenomenological expression,[139] germline therapy in effect proposes an eventual revision of human nature, with disease and disorder a thing of

136. See the press release of the Institute of Ophthalmology at University College London: http://www.ucl.ac.uk/media/library/Genetherapyblind.

137. Soulen, "Cruising toward Bethlehem," 104.

138. Chapman, "Genetic Engineering and Theology," 78.

139. This reflects the difference between *genotype* and *phenotype*, a reminder that the presence of a genetic marker for a particular disorder does not mean it will come to physiological expression. This is a theme of the 1997 film *Gattaca*, in which the genetic profile of the film's protagonist, Vincent, renders him a "de-generate." Just because his profile reveals the presence of genetic indications for a variety of health and psychological problems (e.g., heart disease), though, does not mean those problems would manifest themselves.

the past. The implicit endeavor is to gain control of the evolution of the human species in order to deliver humanity from disease and suffering.

Gene therapy is concerned with addressing genetic abnormalities that interfere with people's ability to enjoy a "normal" human existence. Tay-Sachs disease, Huntington's disease, cystic fibrosis, Down syndrome, and Duchene muscular dystrophy are among the many inheritable maladies that seriously affect individuals, their families, and wider society and that, researchers suggest, might one day be eliminated through gene therapy. Why stop there, though? An old television commercial offering the promise of a more "regular" digestive experience insists, "Doctors say 'normal' is what's normal for you." Some are not content with the prospect of simply employing genetic technologies for the sake of addressing disease and disability. "As is evident from the ready association in the tabloid imagination of the new genetics with designer babies and the like. . . . the possibility of genetic enhancements, of positive genetic engineering, opens out a future in which people may be able to choose for themselves or their children bodily alterations at a fundamental level."[140] If how we define disease and disability is a reflection of cultural preferences anyway, why bother discriminating between therapy and enhancement? In a culture that affirms personal sovereignty over one's own body, it might be argued that genetic technologies should not be limited to achievement of an approximate and ultimately arbitrary "normalcy." Robert Song suggests that as medical science hones its skills at gene therapy, the broader cultural context will gradually render any distinction between therapy and enhancement irrelevant: "In the context of a widespread popular belief in the significance of genetics for personal identity, a mentality that looks for technological solutions to problems, and an economic environment which rewards those who find such technological solutions, the tendency of the culture as a whole becomes clear. Whatever the immediate problems, the theory and potential practice of genetic enhancement is not going to disappear."[141]

---

140. Song, *Human Genetics*, 41.

141. Ibid., 63. Some downplay any differences between therapy and enhancement to argue that if we are free to do the one we should be free to do the other. Others blur the lines in order to cast suspicion on the whole enterprise of genetic medicine, or at least to insist that the issues of the use of such technology cannot be reduced simply to deciding between therapy and enhancement. See The President's Council on Bioethics, *Beyond Therapy*, 13–15.

The technologies of IVF, PGD, and the prospects of genetic engineering together hold out the promise of a world where fewer and fewer lives are marked by crippling disease or significant disability. Already these technologies have functioned to decrease the number of children in the United States born with severe disabilities. Of course, the reason for that is the use of PGD to screen out unfavorable embryos and the common use of "therapeutic abortion" to prevent the live birth of "defective" children. Refinement of genetic technologies, however, would diminish the need for such crude methods of "negative" eugenics.

Why even burden this vision with the label "new eugenics"?[142] Clearly there are major differences from the "old eugenics." Most obviously, there is no explicit resort to the power of the state to impose a singular vision of which children should be considered "worthy a place in our midst."[143] We will instead enjoy "a new era of 'laissez-faire' eugenics," Soulen argues. "It will operate not through direct state coercion but through the cumulative effect of many private decisions by parents who have access to genetic information."[144] Others suggest, however, that while the element of overt coercion by the state is largely absent from the current scene, there are powerful influences at play in our culture that provide subtle forms of coercion expressed in prevailing attitudes toward disability. The widely held assumption that to be disabled is to suffer leads some to conclude, in the name of compassion and benevolence, that "to live with a disability is to have a life not worth living."[145] If the creation of a life that is destined only to suffer can be avoided, then it is only right to do so. When PGD and other forms of genetic diagnosis are available, along with the services of abortion clinics, some believe "it may become increasingly unacceptable to decide to give birth to a child who is known to have a particular disease."[146] When costs associated with caring for such individuals are taken into consideration, we need to understand

142. We might remember Nietzsche's complaint about the negative connotations he believed others would hear in his account of the will to power: "Why should one always have to employ precisely those words which have from of old been stamped with a slanderous intention?" (*BGE*, §259).

143. A phrase from a 1927 essay by the Reverend C. L. Dorris, advocating community oversight of permissible pregnancies. Cited in Hall, "To Form a More Perfect Union," 90.

144. Soulen, "Cruising toward Bethlehem," 110.

145. Ibid., 117.

146. Song, *Human Genetics*, 24.

that insurance companies will be more and more interested in requiring prospective parents to submit to a range of tests to see if any child of theirs might suffer from "preexisting conditions." There are already reports of insurance companies insisting they would pay for the abortion of children having been diagnosed with genetic anomalies, but not for the live birth and care of such children.[147] Song insists, "To pretend that there is never any kind of coercion involved in current genetics or obstetrics is simply self-deceiving."[148]

Regardless of the level of coercion at work in these matters, "eugenics" is still the proper term to describe the use of genetic technology "to improve the stock of humankind" (to invoke Galton's definition). While the coercive element is not essential to its definition or practice, many believe that the natural inclinations of parents to have a child of their own—a child that is healthy—and to give that child the best start in life will more and more bow to the promises of technology in the context of powerful cultural expectations and economic pressures.[149] The new eugenics is already culturally present.

It is a cultural condition, however, that has a lengthy heritage. It is important that we understand what factors have been involved in the development of an outlook that experiences no moral reservation at aborting fetuses that test positive for genetic conditions that for much of human history called for special care and treatment. It is important that we understand the origins and development of this movement, for it is a movement that has brought us to the point where, concerning humanity's future, what we may be is entirely up for grabs.

As far back as the twelfth century, Europe's monastic orders provided the setting in which, according to David Noble, there developed "a connection between the mundane and the celestial, between technology and transcendence."[150] The "mechanical arts" were even conceived as a divine bestowment aiding humanity in the recovery of its lost estate. The late Middle Ages and the early modern period saw an increasing sense of the "mechanization of nature" above which there reigned a free human consciousness that could turn its rational skills toward the technological mastery of nature for the sake of humanity's improvement. One piv-

---

147. Hook, "Genetic Testing and Confidentiality," 128.

148. Song, *Human Genetics*, 55.

149. Ibid., 63.

150. Noble, *Religion of Technology*, 16.

otal figure joining "applied science" to a millenarian view of humanity's growing dominion over nature was Francis Bacon (1561–1626). Bacon considered the "useful arts" of technology and engineering to be essential to humanity's dominion over creation and thus "rehabilitation of past glory and primeval bliss."[151] What this would manifest, according to Gerald McKenny's account of the "Baconian project," would be the elimination of suffering and expansion of the realm of human choice: "in short, to relieve the human condition of subjection to the whims of fortune or the bonds of natural necessity."[152] It hardly needs stressing, though, that Bacon's biblically inspired vision was one of ameliorative recovery, not of heedless transformation. The mechanical arts—technology—would serve humanity's restoration, not boundless revolution.

It fell to René Descartes (1596–1650) to strengthen the account of a distinct and free mind over against a subordinate and inferior material order that includes the human body. For Descartes, what is essential to human existence is a mind, the *res cogitans* ("thinking thing"), fundamentally distinct from the body, the *res extensa* ("extended thing"). The immortal mind is godlike, incorporeal, and exists solely to think: "What then am I? A thing which thinks." And what is more, "I am not a collection of members which we call the human body" (*Meditation* II). And yet for Descartes there is still some sort of relationship between mind and body, "For the mind depends . . . on the temperament and disposition of the bodily organs" (*Discourse on Method*, VI). The distinction and relationship between the two makes possible and necessary a program of mastery over nature applied through medicine. For Descartes, the divine mind of humanity has the task of investigating nature through a "practical philosophy by means of which . . . we can . . . render ourselves the masters and possessors of nature" (*Discourse on Method*, VI). Included in this mastery of nature would be the human body, which Descartes considers "as being a sort of machine . . . built up and composed of nerves, muscles, veins, blood, and skin," distinguishable from the mind so as to come under its sovereignty (*Meditations*, VI).

This Cartesian dualism of a free and independent mind imposing its sovereign will over a mechanized nature—including the human body—establishes and represents a modernist account of technological mastery over nature that seeks to understand its principles so that humans might

151. Ibid., 50.

152. McKenny, *To Relieve the Human Condition*, 2.

"enjoy without any trouble the fruits of the earth and all the good things which are to be found there" as well as the "preservation of health . . . the chief blessing and the foundation of all other blessings in this life" (*Discourse on Method*, VI). Descartes offers a disembodied mind seeking mastery over nature so as to fulfill, in some manner, the task of stewardship. Be that as it may, Descartes' distinction between mind and body has, as we shall see, eclipsed for much of modernity the emphasis on embodiment in biblical anthropology; it has also bred all manner of consequences in any number of contemporary practices, not least in matters related to bioethics.

The contemporary scene is heir, however, not just to Descartes' modernist mind-body dualism. Schrag warns against what he calls the postmodern self marked by "multiplicity, heterogeneity, difference, and ceaseless becoming, bereft of origin and purpose."[153] And here we will need briefly to trace a path from Descartes, through Nietzsche, to the present.

The nineteenth century would see a steady "process of the naturalizing of the soul," challenging the Cartesian notion of a human mind that stood free and independent of the material order. "At the beginning of the nineteenth century, most progressive intellectuals still held that humans had been made in the image of God. By the end of the century . . . most held that humans had been made in the image of biology and society."[154] With Charles Darwin on the one hand and Karl Marx on the other, we have the insistence that not only are humans completely immersed in the natural order, but every aspect of human consciousness, "including not only mundane, day-to-day reflections, but law, morality, religion, and philosophy, is but a reflection of underlying social relations, which are wholly material."[155] The total impact of this shift in human self-understanding is certainly beyond narration here, but its effect on any tendencies toward a postmodern anthropology can be traced to some degree.

It should be no surprise that the naturalization of the human would ultimately lead to the loss of the very idea of a fixed, stable self or of the idea of the normatively human. If the "natural" world is constructed, then so is the "self" that does the constructing. With his reliance upon a thoroughly biological account of all life, Nietzsche insists that any sense

---

153. Schrag, *Self After Postmodernity*, 8.

154. Martin and Barresi, *Rise and Fall of Soul and Self*, 201.

155. Ibid., 211.

of a unity of consciousness that would account for the human subject is a useless fiction. The notion of a unitary self represented by the little word "I" is simply the result of the bewitchment of language, and we do not need to mistake grammar for reality. "It may even be said that here too, when we desire to descend into the river of what seems to be our own most intimate and personal being, there applies the dictum of Heraclitus: we cannot step into the same river twice" (*HH* §2:223). The absolute rejection by Nietzsche of any sense of teleology—whether theological (e.g., Christianity), philosophical (e.g., Hegel), or biological (e.g., Darwin)—leaves only a world of constant and purposeless motion, a whirlwind of pure natural energy overwhelming any and all stability, boundaries, and subjectivity. Without purpose or goal there is no stable self in the world any more than there is a stable world beyond what language falsely creates. While this loss of *telos* and subjectivity might be the occasion for nihilistic despair by some, unbridled rage and lust by others, for the Nietzschean *Übermensch* the loss of a false equilibrium provides every opportunity for life's realization, its "instinct for growth, for endurance, for the accumulation of force, for *power*" (*A* §6). Of course, this growth and accumulation is completely without purpose, guidance, direction, or intent. It is simply the will to power, and the only "given" in this world is the world of our desires and passions. "We cannot get down or up to any 'reality,'" Nietzsche insists, "except the reality of our drives" (*BGE* §36).

From Bacon we have learned that our increasing technological sophistication will enable us to eliminate human suffering and expand our freedom. From Descartes we have the superior soul ascendant over the belittled body, a prioritized mind over diminished stuff. Nietzsche celebrates the arbitrary self, ever seeking power in a world artificially constructed and entirely without inherent meaning, a world that can and must bend to the demands of the will to power. I do not mean to suggest that the new eugenics is a conscious result of theorists drawing on these various philosophical resources, or that these resources represent the only influences on our contemporary cultural context.[156] These perspectives, however, have all contributed to a cultural environment in which

---

156. An interesting inquiry would be an investigation of John Locke's view of property, detailed in his *Second Treatise on Government*, as that which results from the combination of one's labor with natural resources. Does his philosophy of what C. B. Macpherson calls "possessive individualism" underwrite the modern insistence that our bodies are our own to do with as we please and to manipulate as we will? See his *Political Theory of Possessive Individualism*, 197–221.

the aspirations of biomedical technology express and reflect a particular outlook on what it means to be human.

What view of the human self derives from this mixture of influences? The modern and the postmodern converge in many ways (assuming they are all that different to begin with). At this point of determining the *humanum* we are left with disembodied consciousness, aspiration without restraint, a bundle of fleeting desires claiming absolute autonomy to create or destroy, a fluid self resistant to the notion of intrinsic limits, willing to accept only those confinements required by any temporary technological constraints. This anthropological outlook funds a number of contemporary perspectives and practices. With respect to the new eugenics, Song sees this outlook as providing a surrogate form of salvation, an alternative set of doctrinal commitments that give sanction to the unbridled use of technology in the pursuit of human existence beyond the constraints of finitude and mortality. Its doctrine of creation "conceives nature [including our bodies] as raw material for technological manipulation." Human beings are understood "in terms of self-defining freedom above the contingencies of bodily life." Eschatological hope "lies in the dream of escape from finitude, and locates the means of salvation to that end in the application of technical reason and the 'power of modern science.'"[157] That this alternative gospel has its attractions and its benefits for addressing significant matters of human suffering cannot be denied. Can particular benefits be rightly enjoyed while we erect barriers to the broader drift towards the new eugenics? Only if we have some sense of what counts for genuine human well-being will we have a frame of reference available for discerning between what resonates with God's work of redemption in Christ and what effectively functions for so many as its substitute.

University of Chicago Professor Jean Bethke Elshtain suggests that "we need powerful and coherent categories and analyses that challenge cultural projects that deny finitude, promise a technocratic agenda that ushers in almost total human control over all of the natural world, including those natures we call human, push toward an ideal of sameness through genetic manipulation and self-replication via cloning, and continue with the process of excision of bodies deemed unworthy to appear among us and share our world." She insists we must cultivate a rich language of opposition, "like that embodied in Christian theological

---

157. Song, "Human Genome Project as Soteriological Project," 178–79.

anthropology."[158] Calvin Schrag's anthropological analysis helps retrieve resources from Ephesians that are significant both for our dialogue with concerns in bioethics and for offering the sort of Christian theological anthropology Elshtain believes is necessary to challenge the new eugenics.

New Eugenics or New Creation?

Elshtain uncovers the implicit agenda of the new eugenics: "With the widespread adoption of prenatal screening, now regarded as routine, so much so that prospective parents who decline the panoply of procedures are treated as irresponsible, we see at work the presumption that life should be wiped clean of any and all imperfection, inconvenience, and risk. Creation itself must be put right."[159] The question is no longer, "What is God doing about evil?" For many, that inquiry has been abandoned. In some circles, theodicy now takes the shape of anthropodicy as humanity seeks to set things right on its own terms.[160] The centerpiece of that anthropodicy is clearly not God's redemptive work through Christ; it is rather the salvific role that medical technology has assumed in the context of the Baconian project of relief from suffering and the expansion of freedom. Points of specific comparison between a Pauline anthropology developed in dialogue with Schrag will make clear the contrast between the new eugenics and new creation in Christ.

Schrag insists the human self conforms neither to the canons of Cartesian modernity (the ahistorical, disembodied self), nor to the account of a Nietzschean postmodernity (the self defined solely in terms of drives ever in flux), but is best understood in terms of narrative temporality. The self exists at "the crossroads of speech and language" as a "who" that "has already spoken, is now speaking, and has the power yet

158. Elshtain, "Body and the Quest for Control," 170–71.

159. Ibid., 165.

160. Hauerwas (*Naming the Silences*, 59–64) suggests how such a shift allows for the new eugenics. "Sickness creates the problem of 'anthropodicy' because it challenges our most precious and profound belief that humanity has in fact become god. Against the backdrop of such a belief, we conclude that sickness should not exist" (62). But if the suffering and disabled persist in reminding us of the limitations of the human condition, how should we employ our technological sophistication to eliminate such sickness and disability? Hauerwas suggests such thinking concludes, "It would almost be better to eliminate the subjects of such illness rather than have them remind us that our project to eliminate illness has made little progress" (63).

to speak, suspended across the temporal dimensions of past, present, and future."[161] In Ephesians, Paul offers participation in doxology (1:3–14), adoption of transformative speech that would situate the self in a narrative temporality: joyful immersion in the story of a prior calling to holiness (1:4), present participation in divine redemption and forgiveness through the death on the cross of Jesus Christ (1:7), and confidence in the Holy Spirit's ability to secure believers for their participation in the ultimate realization of the divine purpose (1:13–14). The view of the human self formed in this narrative setting will differ greatly from understandings shaped by more current alternatives.

For one thing, medicine plays a different role depending on the narrative setting in which the practices and goals of medicine are situated. The opening doxology of Ephesians invites participation in the redemptive work of God that embraces past, present, and future in the purpose of God to unite all things together in Christ. Whether that vision has always been properly appropriated, some version of it has provided the context for the practice of Western medicine for most of its development, simply because it provided the reigning paradigm for interpreting the fortunes and misfortunes of the human journey. What that vision did mean for the concerns of medicine and human well-being is that the physical health of a person was seen in relationship to other goods considered of greater significance. That is not to say that health was not considered important. To use the language of Bonhoeffer, however, goods such as health were considered of *penultimate* significance in relation to matters of *ultimate* significance—the *telos* for all creation intended by God.[162] Joel Shuman illustrates how matters of health and medicine might be viewed within the context of this narrative: "Physical health is in this scheme an admittedly important good, but it cannot be regarded as the ultimate good." In this light, Shuman explains, the Christian faith "holds that it is possible

---

161. Schrag, *Self After Postmodernity*, 17. Subsequent references to this work will be indicated by parenthetical references.

162. Bonhoeffer, *Ethics*, 146–70. Bonhoeffer, who had witnessed firsthand the fruits of the old eugenics, indicates what occurs when the relationship between penultimate and ultimate is inverted. "One supposes with rational means one can create a new, healthy humanity. At the same time, health is held to be the highest value to which all other values must be sacrificed. The rationalization and biologization of human life unite in this vain undertaking, which destroys the right to life of all that is created and thereby, finally, destroys all human community."

to be physically healthy without living well, or to live well in the relative absence of health."[163]

This relationship between the penultimate good of health considered in view of the ultimate good of the cosmic drama of redemption accounts for the Christian church's long history of establishing and maintaining hospitals and of believers entering the medical professions with a sense of calling and mission, while still insisting that the removal of suffering is not the supreme good. In a world where illness and disability persist, this tension should remain important, for, as Song suggests, "It has generated on the one hand a deep commitment to healing and caring for people in their need, and on the other a willingness to accept suffering and to look for good and hints of meaning in it."[164]

What happens, though, when this narrative of God's work of redemption, which for so long provided the setting for the practice and goals of medicine, is replaced by the modernist narrative? Hauerwas describes the modernist narrative as that which assures us "that since we are unencumbered by any received story, we are truly free to fashion *de novo* any narrative we wish and thus make (and remake) of ourselves whatever we will."[165] This is the narrative that prescribes for medicine the twin tasks of eliminating human suffering and maximizing individual freedom to no other purpose than that which each of us might choose for him or herself, without regard to the constraints of time, embodiment, or community, committed only to transcending the limitations inherent in our status as creatures.

As we have seen, central to this modernist narrative is a dualism that draws a hard-and-fast distinction between mind (*res cogitans*) and body (*res extensa*) where the true self is the free and independent mind that seeks mastery over nature, the material world that includes the body. The modernist narrative defines and seeks redemption as liberation from creation and the body. Schrag contends, however, for an affirmation of the body as constitutive of the self since the self enabled by narrative temporality will demonstrate a unity over time through an ethos, a character revealed in consistency of action by an *embodied self*. "The speaking and narrating subject announces itself in full bodily attire," says Schrag. "It

---

163. Shuman, *Body of Compassion*, 83.

164. Song, *Human Genetics*, 13.

165 Hauerwas, *Wilderness Wanderings*, 26.

is in the phenomenon of the self in action . . . that the role of the body moves into prominence" (44).

Likewise, the body is central to new life in Christ, new life that is known in some measure in present embodied experience and that becomes manifest precisely in what we do as embodied selves. Paul elsewhere clearly affirms that believers await the full redemption of our bodies (Rom 8:23; 1 Cor 15:20–58) and says in Ephesians that believers live in confident anticipation of that inheritance (1:11–14). As we have seen, however, that Paul describes salvation in terms of being raised with Christ even in the midst of the present evil age (2:4–7) indicates that God's redemptive work exhibits deep affirmation of an embodied existence that is included in what it means to be "created in Christ Jesus." For Schrag, the embodied self becomes present through "various gestural comportments—the handshake, the caress, the kiss, the laugh, the cry, the intimidating stare" (55). For the Apostle Paul, the embodied self has to do, for example, with such mundane responsibilities as truth-telling to a neighbor (4:25), working with one's hands so as to meet the needs of others (4:28), and careful use of the mouth for the sake of encouragement of others (4:29).

The alternative soteriology of the new eugenics bears on embodiment in many different ways. Alan Verhey traces a suspicion of the body back to the early days of the modern discipline of bioethics in the work of one of its initial voices—Joseph Fletcher.[166] Fletcher, employing the language of Jewish philosopher Martin Buber, contrasts the essential identity of a person, a *thou*, with that which is "over against us" as an *it*: "Physical nature—the body and its members, our organs and their functions—all of these *things* are a part of 'what is over against us.'" Fletcher demonstrates his clear reliance on a Cartesian dualism by saying, "Freedom, knowledge, choice, responsibility—all these things of personal or moral stature are in us, not *out there*. Physical nature is what is over against us, out there. It represents the world of *its*. Only men and God are *thou*; they only are persons. . . . What is simply given in nature has no moral value; it is without character since it neither exerts nor requires any moral choice of decision."[167] While Fletcher insists, "We ought not to ignore or disregard or flout what is, simply because it is unchosen," for him, clearly what defines humanity in its essential character is the capac-

166. Verhey, *Strange World of Medicine*, 73–75.
167. Fletcher, *Moral and Medicine*, 211.

ity for choice: "This is the radical difference between man and that nature with which he lives and moves and shares his being. Self-consciousness marks the frontier between *thou* and *it*."[168]

Fletcher wrote before many of the major advances that have made the new eugenics possible, but it certainly seems the case that, operating within the same general orientation, he would heartily approve of current trends; he even exhibits some features of the overtly coercive tendencies of the old eugenics. When he argues for a policy of compulsory sterilization so the community can defend itself against "the continued procreation of feeble-minded or hereditarily diseased children,"[169] or when he argues for (even involuntary) euthanasia, rejecting "a purely vitalistic doctrine of man's being,"[170] we hear the strains of the modernist narrative's suspicion of the body. For Fletcher and for the new eugenics, "What matters morally is intelligence and choice (and the control they provide over objects of our understanding and choosing). The body does not really count for much. The body is manipulable nature, over which persons may and must exercise control, mastering nature and human nature for the sake of rational choices to benefit persons."[171] This is a view of what it means to be a human being that differs greatly from a Pauline anthropology, one that licenses a very different set of practices and commitments concerning what counts as a "person."

Of course, when "person" is defined so narrowly, then the character of community is reshaped as well, for to be a self is to be a self in community. Schrag declares that the narrative identity of the embodied self always finds expression as a communal self: "The acting self is always embedded in social practices that reclaim a tradition and invoke remembrance of things past in anticipation of future practices yet to be performed" (73). For Schrag, not only are narrative temporality and embodied action basic to what it means to be human, but "community is constitutive of self-hood" (78). For Paul, community is constitutive of salvation. The next chapter on Christian ethics as an ecclesial ethic will highlight this emphasis in more detail. Let it be said in anticipation, though, that in Ephesians a vision is offered for individual flourishing in a setting where each member of the body of Christ, the church, finds

168. Ibid., 213–14.
169. Ibid., 168.
170. Ibid., 187.
171. Verhey, *Strange World of Medicine*, 75.

strength from and contributes to the well-being of the entire community (4:16) created and called to embody God's reconciling peace in the world (2:11–22). The well-being and growth of the whole is thus determined by practices that demonstrate care for the other (4:32—5:2) and by the insistence that all believers are servants to all other believers (5:21). The self of Ephesians, created by participation in God's story of redemption, embodies activity in a way of life that makes genuine community possible.

The new eugenics offers a message of technological redemption that highlights the autonomous individual pursuing self-defined good with bodies subordinate to and even dispensable with respect to that pursuit. What sort of community derives from the modernist narrative that prioritizes the disembodied mind over the fragile and susceptible body? What sort of community do we create when PGD and genetic testing are used to screen out of existence those bodies that do not meet whatever specifications currently define "normal"? What sort of community do we create when those with access to expensive technologies fashion for themselves children protected from certain disadvantages and favored with selected advantages? Elshtain warns that the use of available technologies has already narrowed our definition of humanity and diminished "a felt responsibility to create welcoming environments for all children." In addition, "The proliferation of genetic testing," she says, "will most certainly have discriminatory effects because it puts everything under the domain of choice and parents of children with 'special needs' become guilty of irresponsible behavior in 'choosing' to bear children and burdening society in this way."[172] In general, as Hans Reinders puts it, "People with disabilities perceive the implicit message of clinical genetics to be that they are living less valuable lives."[173] How could it be otherwise when the growing consensus is that children with disabilities ought never to have been born?

Usually, those who depict the attractions of utopian societies insist that the benefits of technology will be shared by all. In the case of the new eugenics, however, the "all" that would enjoy such benefits would be those whose existence has precisely meant the refusal of existence to those deemed unworthy. The redemptive ethic of the new eugenics is not one that seeks "to make people better or more fortunate. Rather it seeks better or more fortunate people. . . . To the degree that eugenics can be

---

172. Elshtain, "Body and the Quest for Control," 161–62.

173. See his "Life's Goodness," 163.

said to confer benefits at all, it does so not by *improving* the condition of those who are needy, but rather by *selecting for existence* those for whom life can be expected to go well."[174] And so the new eugenics does form community of a sort; it is simply the community of the marketplace, where autonomous individuals are free to make whatever consumer choices meet their own interests and selective requirements. We need to realize, though, that in such an environment, children are not welcomed into the world unconditionally, but as products that will be judged in terms of how they meet certain specifications. Song speaks of "a mindset of commodification" that treats "children as objects, capable of being manufactured (extremely crudely at first, no doubt, but with increasing sophistication over time)." He warns of a cultural drift such that "instead of children being accepted for themselves with an unconditional love that is willing to embrace them, whatever their capacities, there is a real risk that love becomes conditional on their meeting certain performance standards."[175]

In contrast, Schrag insists that the self in true community genuinely permits the other his or her "intrinsic integrity, so that in seeing the face of the other and hearing the voice of the other I am responding to an exterior gaze and an exterior voice rather than carrying on a conversation with my own alter ego" (84). It is in this sense that "community and conformity are alternative modalities of being with other selves" (88). Thus we see that the new eugenics by definition cannot create true community. For in allowing the existence of only those who from the embryonic stage must pass tests of acceptability and whose existence is welcomed only conditionally, the demands of conformity foreclose on the possibility of community without exclusion or of relationships with those who are not necessarily our own alter egos.

In contrast, Ephesians describes a relational self immersed in a communal context in which barriers that exclude are broken down and practices of peace serve to sustain a community called to exhibit God's work of reconciliation—a reconciliation that forms us into agents of God's mercy and insists that with God there is no partiality (6:9). The story of self and salvation in Ephesians differs strongly from the vision of the new eugenics and provides a completely different foundation for a distinctive form of community. The new eugenics reflects a competing

174. Soulen, "Cruising toward Bethlehem," 114.

175. Song, *Human Genetics*, 24–25.

mode of redemption and offers only a greater source of division in a world already threatened by the human capacities for racism, discrimination, subjugation of the other, and exclusion of the stranger. Christians need to ask themselves if, in reliance on IVF, PGD, and technologies of genetic testing, they want to participate in practices that serve to foster forms of community fundamentally at odds with what God intends to create through the gospel.

Of course, the drive toward these practices is the desire by parents for a healthy child of their own who has the best start in life possible. The fears behind this drive are understandable, and obviously the technologies of the new eugenics promise a certain sort of freedom from what would otherwise limit or even imprison. The very goal of the Baconian project is to offer relief from suffering and to expand the reach of human freedom. That is a project, however, that has no logical conclusion within a modernist narrative that affirms no *telos* to human existence other than what each individual chooses for him or herself. It is a project that, ironically, offers only a limited range of possibilities when it comes to its understanding of freedom. The new eugenics offers the promise of *transcendence*—transcendence of a sort, however, that has one set of metrics, qualities such as physical prowess, longevity, or intellectual ability. Its concerns are measured in terms of recognizable disabilities or enhancements that are physiological in character, genetically based, and theoretically controllable through technology.

Schrag certainly understands the self as confronted and drawn by the transcendent. For him, this transcendence is critical for the formation of the authentic self in freedom and responsibility in three ways. First, it "occasions a standpoint for a critique and evaluation of beliefs and practices" into which we might otherwise find ourselves uncritically absorbed. Second, the transcendent "supplies the conditions for the unification"—we might say the coherence—of our participation in a variety of "culture-spheres," pursuits in various arenas of life such as science, morality, art, and religion. Third, transcendence "provides resources for the transfiguration of the dynamics of self and societal formation" (124). Ultimately, for Schrag, it is only as we are challenged by something like the New Testament account of the love of God as grace and gift that we can become selves in relationship with others in ways that provide coherency to those disparate activities that otherwise threaten to fracture and dominate our lives (141–46).

Followers of Christ need to consider that the quest for transcendence cannot be determined by the standard concerns addressed by the new eugenics. Physical prowess, long life, and heightened intelligence might be considered gifts received along with the appropriate task of stewardship. But they must not be confused with those qualities that reveal genuine engagement with true transcendence. For Paul, that true transcendence is Christ himself, and the measure of that engagement is the appearance in the lives of his followers of qualities emphasized when Paul says, "Be kind to one another, tenderhearted, forgiving one another just as God has forgiven you in Christ" (Eph 4:32). The measure of engagement with true transcendence is not the acquisition of advantage over others through our mastery of nature, but the demonstration of humility, gentleness, patience, and forbearing love in response to God's calling (4:1–2)—qualities precisely suited for the task of bearing with the frailties and finitude that will continue to mark our lives to various degrees until the day of our final redemption. If the new eugenics promises transcendence of our frailties and finitude as human beings, then it is only as we create a world where frailty and finitude are not permitted. As Soulen suggests, its promised transcendence "requires us to exercise a preference for the sort of fellow human beings we will have, namely, the kind who will be least likely to trouble us with their infirmities in the first place."[176] The gospel offers a transcendence, on the other hand, that makes possible a gracious acceptance of those whose lives call for humility, gentleness, patience, and forbearing love, whose presence in our midst is a reminder to us all of our infirmities (of one sort or another) and of our common need for the transcendent gifts of God's mercy and love.

That transcendence, however, is both gift and task. At this point, the task transcendence occasions is a critique and evaluation of beliefs and practices into which we might otherwise be uncritically absorbed. Transcendence further supplies the conditions for the unification and coherence of our participation in various culture-spheres. In our present context, the task is unavoidable for those committed to the Christian faith. Rather than being uncritically absorbed into the beliefs and practices of the new eugenics, believers must evaluate on what basis and to what extent participation in the pursuits of health and mastery over nature represented by the current culture-sphere of biomedical technology coheres with the narrative, practices, and community formed by the

176. Soulen, "Cruising toward Bethlehem," 114.

gospel. Paul offers a redemptive ethic that at one time provided the narrative in which the pursuits of health and human well-being found their penultimate value, placed as they were within larger aspirations for participation in God's cosmic work of redemption. Now that the alternative narratives of modernism and the Baconian project have achieved regnant status in the spheres of health, medicine, and biotechnology, it is critical that Christians be all the more vigilant as to whether they have placed their hopes in the new creation or the new eugenics.

3

"New Life in the One Body of Christ"

An Ecclesial Ethic

"The church does not have a social ethic; it is a social ethic."

STANLEY HAUERWAS[1]

We have looked at many features of Paul's vision for life as presented in Ephesians. We have done so in comparison with competing accounts of the moral life offered by Kant and Nietzsche. We understand better the significance of Paul's emphasis on the divine initiative and agenda when we contrast that with Kant's project of establishing morality independently of any particular religious outlook. We understand better the importance of Paul's insistence that redemption through Christ makes possible life as God intends when we contrast that with Nietzsche's attack on the Christian faith as "anti-life."

We need to remember, though, that these concerns are part of the larger concern of asking, "What is God doing about evil?" The question reminds us that the task of Christian ethics is to explore in what concrete ways God is at work to bring to realization the life God intended for humanity from the beginning. By God's gracious initiative God intends to achieve peace, the reconciliation of a broken creation through new life in Christ. What does this look like? How precisely is God at work to redeem a broken creation through new life in Christ? God is creating a people.

1. Hauerwas, *Peaceable Kingdom*, 99.

Christian ethics is *theocentric*. It begins with the divine initiative. Christian ethics is *redemptive*. It gives center stage to God's offer of new life in Christ. Christian ethics, however, is also *ecclesial*, for there is no redemption that does not incorporate the believer into the one body of Christ.[2]

Bernd Wannenwetsch describes as "the most important shift in recent ethical theory" what he terms "the recontextualization of ethics." In a move away from the search for ideal principles (such as Kant's categorical imperative), alternative approaches now give attention to matters such as "virtue, the emotions, friendship, the role of tradition in shaping communities, and so forth."[3] Alasdair MacIntyre's *After Virtue* has certainly played a role in effecting the shift noted by Wannenwetsch. MacIntyre concludes his challenge to the Enlightenment project's quest for a universal morality independent of any particular religious outlook by recommending the formation of small-scale communities that enable participants to develop those virtues and habits of life appropriate to the practices and beliefs of a shared tradition.[4]

Some have labeled MacIntyre a "communitarian."[5] "Communitarianism" highlights what might be taken as a sociological truism, "that our ethical thinking and living take place in a particular, historical social formation."[6] A Christian ethic, however, will not be content simply to recognize the importance of community. "I fear all appeals for community as an end in itself," says Hauerwas, since some community contexts (such as the family or the state) can end up serving as idolatrous substitutes for a community formed by the worship of God.[7] What is the case, though, is that a Christian ethic, one shaped by the divine initiative and agenda expressed through God's redemptive work, will be an *ecclesial ethic* in which the church (*ekklēsia*) serves as the primary setting for the formation and practice of and witness to life as God intends.

This ecclesial dimension, while (as we shall see) integral to Paul's understanding of what God is doing about evil, has not been a major feature of what counts as "Christian ethics" for many. If Wannenwetsch

2. A slight revision of Cyprian's "*extra ecclesiam nulla salus*" ("Outside the church there is no salvation").

3. Wannenwetsch, *Political Worship*, 1.

4. MacIntyre, *After Virtue*, 263.

5. MacIntyre himself is reluctant concerning the designation; see his "I'm Not a Communitarian, But . . ." 91–92.

6. Long, *Goodness of God*, 25.

7. Hauerwas, "Communitarians and Medical Ethicists," 158.

can announce a recent shift in ethical theory that attends once again to matters of social setting and community context for the formation and expression of the moral life, there are still major voices in the field of Christian ethics that place little emphasis on the church as fundamental to the character and task of Christian ethics. While not solely responsible for the relative inattention given to the identity and role of the church in Christian ethics, a chief representative of such an approach would be Reinhold Niebuhr. In order to appreciate better the ecclesial dimension of what we find in Ephesians about the moral life God intends, we need to look at an approach to Christian ethics where such a concern is barely present.

REINHOLD NIEBUHR AND THE ECLIPSE OF ECCLESIOLOGY

Reinhold Niebuhr is the most significant figure of twentieth-century American Christian social ethics. The word "social" should be understood precisely: Niebuhr's focus was largely on matters of public policy, international relations, economic matters, and politics. "He did not write about lying," James Gustafson observes.[8] From 1928 to 1960 he taught at Union Theological Seminary in New York City. He wrote voluminously, lectured ferociously, and engaged fiercely in all manner of public debates, serving as counselor to denominational agencies, member of institutional boards, and even in an advisory capacity to the State Department during the Truman years. Serious illness in 1952 slowed his public activities considerably; he continued writing even after his retirement from teaching. He died in 1971 at the age of seventy-nine.[9] A bibliography of his published works extends to 268 pages![10]

In terms of his influence, a few measures indicate his continued impact. In a 2007 interview, then Senator Barack Obama identified Niebuhr as "one of my favorite philosophers."[11] While few know its origins,

8. Gustafson, "Theology in the Service of Ethics," 30. Gustafson needs to be more precise. Niebuhr regularly wrote about the dangers of self-deception.

9. Several biographies are out on Niebuhr. See, for example, Fox, *Reinhold Niebuhr.*

10. Robertson, *Reinhold Niebuhr's Works.* The secondary literature on Niebuhr is enormous. A few of the important treatments of Niebuhr are Brown, *Niebuhr and His Age;* Crouter, *Reinhold Niebuhr;* Gilkey, *On Niebuhr;* Halliwell, *The Constant Dialogue;* Harries, *Reinhold Niebuhr;* Harries and Platten, *Reinhold Niebuhr & Contemporary Politics;* Kegley, *Reinhold Niebuhr;* Lovin, *Reinhold Niebuhr* and *Reinhold Niebuhr and Christian Realism;* Rice, *Reinhold Niebuhr Revisited;* Stone, *Professor Reinhold Niebuhr.*

11. Brooks, "Obama, Gospel and Verse."

millions have echoed Niebuhr's "Serenity Prayer": "O God, give us the serenity to accept what cannot be changed, the courage to change what should be changed, and the wisdom to distinguish one from the other."[12] In other matters, Hays says, "What appears to be commonsense political ethics to the majority of Protestant churchgoers today is actually a popularized version of Niebuhr's Christian realism."[13] We will have to explore what is meant by "Christian realism," how it finds practical expression, and whether or not this outlook coheres with the ecclesial character of a Christian ethic that draws on Ephesians as a primary resource.

Reinhold Niebuhr's "Christian Realism"

Among Niebuhr's many avenues of expression, one of his favorites was preaching. Before his years as professor at Union, he served from 1915 to 1928 as pastor of Bethel Evangelical Church in Detroit, Michigan. As time went by he preached less and less in churches and more and more in seminary and university chapels. He would still say in 1959, "I am a preacher and I like to preach."[14] Most of his published works are substantive historical and theological analysis of concerns that sound the recurring themes of his "Christian realism." One of his sermons, though, provides significant access and insight into those themes, the substance of which can be further traced in his weightier works.

In 1960 Niebuhr preached from a biblical text he believed gave expression to central features of his outlook. His sermon "The Wheat and the Tares," based on Jesus' parable in Matt 13:24–30, was preached at Union not long before his retirement.[15] In the King James Version read by Niebuhr, the parable reads as follows:

12. For discussion as to the origins of this prayer, see Brown, *Niebuhr and His Age*, 112–13. For his own comments about this prayer, see Niebuhr, "View of Life from the Sidelines," 251–52.

13. Hays, *Moral Vision of the New Testament*, 215.

14. As quoted by his wife, Ursula, in her "Introduction," 1. His daughter suggests that in the age of Billy Graham and Norman Vincent Peal her father's willingness to broach difficult subjects made him less palatable in most church settings. Sifton, *Serenity Prayer*, 316–17.

15. The sermon, as printed in *Justice & Mercy* (51–60), was preached February 28, 1960. Niebuhr preached similar sermons on the same biblical text on other occasions. A similar sermon is the focus of analysis by Cartwright in his *Practices, Politics, and Performances*, 25–38. Cartwright suggests that "Niebuhr finds an authorization for his 'interpretation' of Christian ethics' in Jesus' parable" (29). That the sermon in

Another parable put he forth unto them, saying, "The kingdom of heaven is likened unto a man which sowed good seed in his field. But while men slept, his enemy came and sowed tares among the wheat, and went his way. But when the blade was sprung up, and brought forth fruit, then appeared the tares also. So, the servants of the householder came and said unto him, "Sir, didst not thou sow good seed in thy field? From whence then hath it tares?" He said unto them, "An enemy hath done this." The servants said unto him, "Wilt thou then that we go and gather them up?" But he said unto them, "Nay; lest while ye gather up the tares, ye root up also the wheat with them. Let both grow together until the harvest; and in the time of the harvest I will say to the reapers, 'Gather ye together first the tares, and bind them in bundles to burn them; but gather the wheat into my barn.'"

Toward the end of his sermon on this passage, we get an indication of the significance of Jesus' parable for Niebuhr's outlook: "Thus human history is a mixture of wheat and tares."[16] Niebuhr's Christian realism evaluates human nature and history in light of a biblical insistence on the *moral ambiguity* of all human action. In contrast to other modes of analysis that lead to either naïve optimism or unyielding despair, Niebuhr insists that a biblical outlook best makes sense of human experience and history.[17] The parable's emphasis on the intermingling of wheat and tares—good and evil—affords Niebuhr with the opportunity to expound on fundamental features of "the drama of human history" (*WT* 53). The evidence of his-

---

Justice & Mercy was preached so late in his career suggests that the themes present reflect Niebuhr's mature and considered position. The same Union sermon appears in Niebuhr, *Essential Reinhold Niebuhr*, 41–48. That this is one of two sermons in a collection so titled is some indication of its significance for understanding Niebuhr.

16. Niebuhr, *Justice & Mercy*, 59. Subsequent references to this sermon will be designated *WT* with a page number.

17. Niebuhr's use of the Bible is an important study in its own right and will occupy us below. For analysis see Hays, *Moral Vision of the New Testament*, 215–24; Siker, "Reinhold Niebuhr," 8–24. John Howard Yoder describes an important feature of Niebuhr's use of the Bible for his arguments on human nature: "He continued to believe that the best way to read the Bible is by submitting it to our modern Western judgment of what makes sense, rather than by subjecting ourselves in any heteronomous way to its authority. . . . Whether the human nature in question is individual or social, Niebuhr's understanding of it developed from examining his contemporary reality. Then he discovered that the Bible had said something similar. . . . Niebuhr did not say that this understanding of human nature is right because it is in the Bible. . . . He said that it is right because it makes sense." See his "Reinhold Niebuhr's 'Realist' Critique," 285, 289.

tory and experience read from the perspective of biblical testimony provides an understanding of the human condition best described using one
of Niebuhr's favorite words: tension. Tension and paradox are constituent
features of what it means to be a human being, and what it means to be a
human being is central to Niebuhr's engagement with Jesus' parable and
to his entire perspective.

Niebuhr's sermon actually begins with a reflection on Psalm 90,
a psalm that employs images of a roaring flood and withering grass to
describe human frailty before overwhelming forces (vv. 5–6). The psalm's
emphasis on the brevity of life provokes Niebuhr to say, "We are like
corks that bob up and down in the river of time" (*WT* 52). The psalmist, though, provides Niebuhr with the opportunity to draw an implicit
emphasis from the text concerning the human situation: "Man is indeed
like a cork that is drawn down the river of time, carried away as with a
flood. But he could not be altogether that, because he knows about it; he
speculates about it as the psalmist does, and about the significance of it"
(*WT* 52–53).

This complex situation of being both immersed in history and
yet sufficiently above it to reflect on its significance lies at the heart of
Niebuhr's broader understanding of the human story. It is this complex
situation that provides the focus for Niebuhr's most notable work, the
published version of his 1939 Gifford Lectures at the University of Edinburgh, *The Nature and Destiny of Man*.[18] In those lectures Niebuhr offers
what he considers to be "the Christian view of man." In contrast to a
naturalism that immerses humanity entirely in the material order, and to
an idealism that elevates humanity to the realm of pure rationality, what
Niebuhr describes as "the biblical view" insists that humans are created
by God as a unity of body and spirit in the image of God (*HN* 12–18).[19]
The very phrase "created in the image of God" (cf. Gen 1:26–27) contains within it the tensive elements inherent in human experience. That
humans are "created" underscores our finitude and "involvement in the
necessities and contingencies of the natural world." We *are* like corks that

18. Published in two volumes: vol. 1, *Human Nature*, and vol. 2, *Human Destiny*.
Niebuhr's "man," offered decades before the concerns of gender politics, is certainly
generic in reference. Subsequent references to these works will be designated *HN* and
HD respectively.

19. Niebuhr regularly achieves and presents his views by way of contrast with other
perspectives that are generally polar opposites of one another. A helpful discussion of
"polemics and dialectics" as basic to Niebuhr's methodology is Ayers, "Methodological, Epistemological, and Ontological Motifs," 153–74.

bob up and down in the river of time. That humans are created "in the image of God," however, "emphasizes the height of self-transcendence in man's spiritual stature" (*HN* 150). So, like the psalmist, we have the capacity to note, reflect on, and respond one way or another to our situation. By his appeal to Psalm 90, Niebuhr takes the opportunity to express a central feature of his theological ethic: the anthropological assessment of our finitude and freedom, our peculiar status as creatures who enjoy the capacity for self-transcendence.[20]

This paradoxical condition is the will of God and as such reflects the goodness of God's intent for creation. Indeed, this condition is the basis for what is unique about humanity—our capacity for genuine creativity as an expression of our desire to transcend the limits of our finitude. In his sermon Niebuhr exclaims, "We admit that we are creatures." In addition, though, "We know that we are unique creatures, that God has made us in his image, that we have freedom to do something that nature does not know, that we can project goals beyond the limitations, ambitions, desires, and lusts of nature" (*WT* 55).

This delicate balance of finitude and freedom, though, has the result of not only stimulating creativity but also provoking anxiety. That humans exist "at the juncture of nature and spirit . . . involved in freedom and necessity" puts us in a position similar to the sailor halfway up the ship's mast, "with the abyss of the waves beneath him and the 'crow's nest' above him. He is anxious about both the end toward which he strives and the abyss of nothingness into which he may fall" (*HN* 181, 185). Anxiety, for Niebuhr, makes possible positive expressions of creativity as we seek meaning beyond merely material existence, but also provides the occasion for temptation to sin as we pursue destructive ways of negotiating the tenuous balance of freedom and finitude.

While Niebuhr is careful to insist that "anxiety is not sin," he also says, "It is not possible to make a simple separation between the creative and destructive elements in anxiety" (*HN* 183–84). On the one hand, "Anxiety is the inevitable concomitant of the paradox of freedom and finiteness in which man is involved." On the other hand, "Anxiety is the internal precondition of sin." There is always the possibility "that faith

---

20. Niebuhr scholar Robin Lovin observes that Niebuhr's focus on human nature as central to his understanding of Christian ethics "is an idea deeply rooted in Western thought, at least as far back as Aristotle, that the way human beings ought to live depends on the capacities and limitations that they have by nature." See Lovin, "Reinhold Niebuhr's *The Nature and Destiny of Man*," 496.

would purge anxiety of the tendency toward sinful self-assertion," and so cannot itself be identified with sin. Such "faith in the ultimate security of God's love," however, ". . . is a possibility only if perfect trust in divine security has been achieved." Niebuhr's judgment, though, is that "no life, even the most saintly, perfectly conforms to [Jesus'] injunction not to be anxious" (*HN* 182–83).

The result of such failure, sin, comes to expression in two different ways, reflecting failure one way or the other to negotiate the tensions inherent in being creatures of finitude and freedom. Sin expresses "the inclination of man, either to deny the contingent character of his existence (in pride and self-love) or to escape from his freedom (in sensuality)." For Niebuhr, the sin of sensuality "represents an effort to escape from the freedom and the infinite possibilities of spirit by becoming lost in the detailed processes, activities and interests of existence, an effort which results inevitably in unlimited devotion to limited values" (*HN* 185).

Sensuality and pride are certainly related to one another (both are idolatrous), but it is the sin of pride to which Niebuhr gives most of his attention: "Man falls into pride when he seeks to raise his contingent existence to unconditioned significance" (*HN* 186). In "The Wheat and the Tares," he describes this as our readiness to see ourselves as transcendent over the river of time: "This is the strategy of detachment, according to which we all have our private airplanes, spiritually speaking, and these spiritual airplanes have indeterminate altitude records. There is no limit to how high you can go" (*WT* 54). In an earlier work Niebuhr had already made explicit the connection between anxiety and self-aggrandizement: "Man is destined, both by the imperfection of his knowledge and by his desire to overcome his finiteness, to make absolute claims for his partial and finite values. He tries, in short, to make himself God."[21] "Playing God to the universe," says Niebuhr, "can be very exhilarating but very irresponsible" (*WT* 54).

Such self-glorification is our chief sin. Pride, according to Niebuhr, becomes manifest in the egotism of the individual in his quest for power, when he pretends his finite knowledge is ultimate and final, and when his virtue or moral achievements become the occasion for self-righteous

---

21. Niebuhr, *Interpretation of Christian Ethics*, 52. Subsequent references to this work will be designated *ICE*. Niebuhr will later distance himself from some of the concerns of this work, but its pervasive criticism of overly optimistic anthropologies remained a constant for Niebuhr. See his "Reply to Interpretation and Criticism," in Kegley, *Reinhold Niebuhr*, 510–11.

intolerance of others (*HN* 188–203). The individual's capacity for self-transcendence, though, while certainly complicit in these sins of pretension and pride, also makes it possible to rise above mere self-interest. The parable of the wheat and the tares reminds us of the peculiar paradox of the human condition: "Consider how much . . . evil and good, creativity and selfishness, are mixed up in actual life" (*WT* 56). We do not need to believe, however, that the image of the wheat and tares allows us to assess some actions or attitudes as strictly wheat (good) and some solely as tares (evil). It is not as simple as that: "How curiously are love and self-love mixed up in life, much more complexly than any scheme of morals recognizes" (*WT* 56). The same action—writing a novel, for example—can be an act of both creativity and vanity.

Even if there is the possibility for an individual to rise above mere self-interest, as when motivated by what Niebuhr calls "the religious spirit of love," a "distinction between group pride and the egotism of individuals is necessary . . . because the pretensions and claims of a collective or social self exceed those of the individual ego" (*HN* 208). For a number of reasons, according to Niebuhr, the love and self-denial we might express in intimate relationships are not reproducible on larger scales. The central thesis of Niebuhr's *Moral Man and Immoral Society* is "that group relations can never be as ethical as those which characterize individual relations."[22] A repeated target of Niebuhr's criticism is the naïveté of a modern liberalism that expects the steady progress of human civilizations, so that we build for ourselves social structures and institutions that will one day embody perfect reason (secular liberalism) or perfect love (Christian liberalism). Instead, Niebuhr's assessment of the drama of history, one he describes as "abhorrent to the modern mood," is "that the possibilities of evil grow with the possibilities of good, and that human history is therefore not so much a chronicle of the progressive victory of the good over evil, of cosmos over chaos, as the story of the ever-increasing cosmos, creating ever-increasing possibilities of chaos"

---

22. Niebuhr, *Moral Man and Immoral Society*, 83. Subsequent references to this work will be designated *MMIS*. Yoder cautions against any misunderstanding of the title of this volume: "Niebuhr did not mean to say that individuals are moral and society is immoral; he meant to show that institutions face greater difficulty in being moral. Each person is partly evil, but institutions magnify our sinfulness more than they magnify our virtue. . . . Society's structures escalate the impact of selfishness and pride. Therefore we have less reason to hope for peace in the world than for peace and progress in one-to-one relationships." See his "Reinhold Niebuhr's 'Realist' Critique," 288; see also Niebuhr, *Man's Nature and His Communities*, 22.

(*ICE* 60). The Christian realist will not view history as the arena in which human effort conquers the consequences of human pride. "Where there is history at all there is freedom; and where there is freedom there is sin" (*HD* 80).

The sin of group pride, says Niebuhr, finds its chief expression in the collective impulses of the nation-state, since "the national state is most able to make absolute claims for itself, to enforce those claims by power and to give them plausibility and credibility by the majesty and pano-ply of its apparatus." The symbols and expressions of power by the state have an inevitable result: "The temptation to idolatry is implicit in the state's majesty" (*HN* 209). The dangers of such an idolatry are especially troublesome when coupled with religious language and symbols: "subtly compounded with a few stray Christian emphases . . . a religiously sancti-fied self-idolatry is more grievous than its secular variety."[23] Regardless of its ideology, however, "No politically crystallized group has . . . ever ex-isted without entertaining, or succumbing to, the temptation of making idolatrous claims for itself. . . . Sinful pride and idolatrous pretension are . . . an inevitable concomitant of the cohesion of large political groups" (*HN* 210).

Typical expressions of national pride include such dispositions and practices as lust for power, contempt toward other nations, "and finally the claim of moral autonomy by which the self-deification of the social group is made explicit by its presentation of itself as the source and end of existence" (*HN* 211). While these attitudes are an affront to God and a threat to world order and harmony, the Christian realist, Niebuhr in-sists, will simply have to recognize that at the level of group behavior "the limitations of the human imagination, the easy subservience of reason to prejudice and passion, and the consequent persistence of irrational ego-ism . . . make social conflict an inevitability in human history, probably to its very end" (*MMIS* xx).

In keeping with the paradoxical condition of human existence, we need to recognize the tensions within the penchant for national self-ag-grandizement. The ambiguities show up in many different ways. Niebuhr insists, for example, that "the pride of nations is, of course, not wholly spurious." Claims to embody values that transcend national identity and immediate interests need to be taken seriously. What inevitably occurs, however, is that unconditioned claims are made for what are really the

23. Niebuhr, "Idolatry of America," 97.

parochial interests of the nation, so that while "nations may fight for 'liberty' and 'democracy,'" for example, "they do not do so until their vital interests are imperiled." All too often, "The nation claims a more absolute devotion to values which transcend its life than the facts warrant." Alternatively, "it regards the values to which it is loyal as more absolute than they really are" (*HN* 213).

The pretensions of the group characterize all nations, but it would be a mistake simply to cite the Apostle Paul—"For there is no distinction: for all have sinned, and fall short of the glory of God" (Rom 3:22, 23)— and refuse then, out of some false humility, to make moral judgments. Niebuhr would have us distinguish between "the equality of sin and the inequality of guilt" (*HN* 219–27). We would take the wrong lesson from Jesus' parable if we refused the obligation of "making rigorous distinctions between right and wrong, between good and evil" (*WT* 55). We must distinguish between wheat and tares. The parable does caution us, however, "that while we have to judge, there is a judgment beyond our judgment, and there are fulfillments beyond our fulfillments," and that to imagine our own judgments are final is itself a great evil (*WT* 56).

Christian realism will have to "deal with the 'nicely calculated less and more' of justice and goodness as revealed in the relativities of history." There is a difference "between the oppressor and his victim," and while "it is quite necessary and proper that these distinctions should disappear at the ultimate religious level of judgment, yet it is obviously important to draw them provisionally in all historical judgments. The difference between a little more and a little less justice in a social system . . . may represent differences between sickness and health, between misery and happiness in particular situations" (*HN* 220).

Reinhold Niebuhr's Christian realism provides what many consider to be a quite pessimistic estimate of the human condition. Humans, created in the image of God, exist at the juncture of nature and spirit. This condition produces an anxiety, which, though the source of great creativity, also inevitably produces the sins of sensuality and pride. While at the individual level the moral constraints of a religious temperament can somewhat offset the worst effects of our condition, at the group level we simply have to recognize that other dynamics are in effect. As Niebuhr puts it, "It may be possible, though it is never easy, to establish just relations between individuals within a group purely by moral and rational suasion and accommodation. In inter-group relations this is practically an impossibility. The relations between groups must therefore always be predominately political rather than ethical." At the group level, the issues are not morality, but power (*MMIS* xxii–xxiii).

Niebuhr's account of human nature and history, expressed in both his sermon and his more substantive works, reflects a concern to interpret the human condition with reference to biblical concepts and symbols. His analysis is a dark one. Does he believe the Christian faith offers any hope for the relief of this condition? Charles Mathewes asks, "How does Niebuhr's diagnosis of our tragic situation, as powerful and sobering as it is, help us with the fundamentally practical task of seeking to sustain realistic hope for our lives in the world?"[24] Another way of asking the question is, "What does Niebuhr believe God is doing about evil?"[25]

Love, Justice, and the Fulfillment of History

Niebuhr concludes his sermon with the recognition that his account of the moral ambiguity of human nature and history could lead to despair and cynicism. What he wants to achieve, however, is a realistic balance of humility and confidence: "From the standpoint of biblical faith we do not have to despair because life is so brief, but we must not pretend to more because we are so great." The finitude and freedom of those created in the image of God provide the opportunity to discern "a mystery and meaning beyond our smallness and our greatness, and a justice and love which completes our incompletions, which corrects our judgments, and which brings the whole story to a fulfillment beyond our power to fulfill any story" (*WT* 59).

For Niebuhr, the ambiguity of our condition means that neither cynical pessimism nor naïve optimism is realistic. It means we can never sanctify "the relative values of any age or any era" and we must admit to the incompleteness of "every historical achievement."[26] This is not a recipe for inaction, though, but for responsible action. Robin Lovin seeks

---

24. Mathewes, *Evil and the Augustinian Tradition*, 120.

25. This is not the way Niebuhr himself would put the question (see Gustafson, "Theology in the Service of Ethics," 43). Niebuhr's exploration of "the nature and destiny of man," though, clearly examines the issues from within a theological frame of reference, even if, as Gustafson indicates (44), the ethical and political vision Niebuhr offers seems to regulate what theological resources he permits to function and how. For Niebuhr's entire project as a response to the problem of evil, see Lovatt, *Confronting the Will-to-Power*, 192–99.

26. Niebuhr, "Optimism, Pessimism, and Religious Faith," 16.

to strike the right tone of Niebuhr's intent: "Niebuhr's purpose is always to give Christians a way of thinking that will enable responsible moral choices." For Niebuhr, says Lovin, "that means being realistic about the possibilities and limitations of all action, so that our efforts are not wasted on sentimental gestures that fail to touch the real problems, or self-righteous demands that ignore our own involvement in the problems we are trying to solve."[27] What responsible moral choices require, Niebuhr insists, is a proper understanding of the relationship between love, justice, and the fulfillment of history as providing the necessary frame of reference in which meaningful action can be discerned and taken.

What Niebuhr has to say about these matters must be understood against the backdrop of the tumultuous events of the mid-twentieth century: the threats of German nationalism and the spread of Stalinist communism.[28] Niebuhr believed that only by reference to Christian symbols and concepts could a meaningful account of history be given that could sustain responsible action in a troubled world. In this context, Niebuhr argues 1) that history cannot be seen as bearing within itself its own intelligibility but finds its meaning only with reference to Christ; 2) that Christian love *cannot* be appealed to as a practical strategy for responsible action; and 3) that we must strive to create structures and institutions willing to use force in order to safeguard minimal standards of justice that permit as much equality and freedom as possible.

Christ as the Meaning of History

Given the dire condition of humanity, the ambiguities of history, and the constant threats of evil suffered and practiced, can life have any meaning at all? Is there something beyond brute power that can guide responsible action in such as world as ours? Is there a greater sovereignty at work in history other than what seems to be at work in such destructive ways? "The Christian faith," Niebuhr insists, "begins with, and is founded upon, the affirmation that the life, death, and resurrection of Christ represent

27. Lovin, *Reinhold Niebuhr*, 23; see also Mathewes, *Evil and the Augustinian Tradition*, 133.

28. Indeed, some of the lectures that comprise *Human Destiny* were delivered as German bombs rained down on a British naval base close to Edinburgh. Niebuhr seemed oblivious to the commotion, but the large crowds that assembled to hear him did grow uneasy at the sounds of nearby anti-aircraft fire; see Fox, *Reinhold Niebuhr*, 191.

an event in history, in and through which a disclosure of the whole meaning of history occurs, and all of these questions are answered."[29] We can
explore the significance of Niebuhr's assertion by examining on what
basis Niebuhr offers it, how this truth comes to expression, and what difference it makes for responsible human action.

First, as is regularly the case with his mode of argumentation,
Niebuhr offers his Christocentric interpretation of history in the face of
what he considers to be inadequate alternatives. Niebuhr contrasts what
he calls "the Biblical-Christian sense of history" with two major alternatives within Western civilization. On the one hand is the approach of
"Greek classicism which equated history with the world of nature and
sought emancipation of man's changeless reason from this world of
change" (FH 14–15). Plato, for example, represents an approach that
seeks to find life's meaning by rising above the chaos and instability of
history through the use of reason to "disassociate what is regarded as a
timeless and divine element in human nature from the world of change
and temporal flux" (FH 16). The result of this outlook is the pursuit of
"mystical forms of otherworldliness" that finally deny "the meaningful-
ness of history" (HD 14).

On the other hand, Niebuhr challenges the modernist assertion that
history is the solution to its own problems; that is, that we participate
in a historical process that moves toward emancipation from ambiguous
existence by endowing humanity "with the freedom and the power of
unambiguous mastery over his own nature" (FH 30). In Niebuhr's estimate, the modern world has arrogantly "sought redemption by regarding
the process of history itself as a guarantor of the fulfillment of human
life" (HD 320). Behind this effort is the woeful error "of overestimating
the measure of human freedom" as well as of naming that freedom as an
inherent good.[30] The tragic result of this hubris is typified for Niebuhr

29. Niebuhr, *Faith and History*, 26. Subsequent references to this work will be
designated *FH*. These questions might seem to shift from more individual concerns
for personal meaning to larger concerns for the meaning of history *in toto*, but for
Niebuhr (*FH* 218), while there are (as we have seen) distinctions between individual
and group dynamics, there are also "obvious similarities between individual and collective life, which create analogies between the fate of individuals and nations." It is
also obvious, though, that Niebuhr's attention, as time passed, was directed chiefly
to national and international concerns. Still, Niebuhr insists, "Each individual transcends and is involved in the historical process. In so far as he is involved in history,
the disclosure of life's meaning must come to him in history" (*HD* 36).

30. Mathewes (*Evil and the Augustinian Tradition*, 114) notes the implications of

in the story of the Tower of Babel in which, in response to humanity's pride, God confuses the languages and scatters humanity over the face of the earth (Gen 11:1–9). The dangers of such division in a nuclear age are apparent.

The classical view of history results in an escape from responsibility in the world. The modern view of history endangers the world itself with its arrogant assumptions of mastery. In contrast to these alternatives, "The New Testament makes the startling claim that in Christ history has achieved both its end and a new beginning." Christ is the "end" of history in that "in his life, death, and resurrection the meaning of man's historic existence is fulfilled." What that means for Niebuhr is that in Christ God's sovereignty has been revealed as both the source of judgment over humanity's sin and rebellion and as the source of mercy and forgiveness. That Christ is the "new beginning" affirms that with the faith that apprehends in Christ the meaning of life there is also a repentance that makes renewal of life possible (*FH* 139). What difference this claim makes for responsible action in the world can best be understood by understanding the way, according to Niebuhr, the "Biblical-Christian sense of history" comes to expression.

Niebuhr's understanding of the significance of the life, death, and resurrection of Christ must be seen in light of what he calls his "mythical method" of interpretation, an understanding of biblical motifs and concepts that, according to Niebuhr, reflects neither the biblical literalism of Christian orthodoxy nor the outright dismissal of these motifs by liberalism. For Niebuhr, the main story line of the Bible must not be taken merely as narrating events within history. These motifs depict a dialectical relationship between the temporal and the eternal in which "the eternal is revealed and expressed in the temporal but not exhausted in it."[31] The biblical accounts of Adam and Eve, the serpent in the garden, the incarnation of Christ, Jesus' atoning death on the cross, the resurrection of Christ, and matters such as the second coming, the last judgment, and the coming kingdom of God are all to be understood as "primitive

---

these assumptions. In a supposedly secular environment, these assumptions actually reflect "a theological claim, the expression of modernity's belief that humanity is on its own, in a morally vacant universe, and must save itself. On this view, what is evil is what obstructs the expansion of human control. The human will cannot be bad; only what limits it is wicked." In this understanding, human finitude is not the occasion for evil, as Niebuhr holds; it is itself evil. See *FH* 47.

31. Niebuhr, "As Deceivers, Yet True," 4.

religious and artistic symbols"; they are not to be taken literally, nor are they to be dismissed because they do not meet modern scientific measures of validity: "It is important to take Biblical symbols seriously but not literally" (*HD* 50). To take the biblical symbols literally is to suppose that they fit within the constraints and limitations of human history and finitude. "Christianity," however, "does not believe that the ground and fulfillment of existence is self-derived or self-explanatory."[32] The setting of human history and finitude is by itself one of incoherence and meaninglessness. To insist that the biblical myths and symbols fit into such a setting is to strip them of their power to effect transformation. If the symbol of the return of Christ, for example, "is taken literally the dialectical conception of time and eternity is falsified and the ultimate vindication of God over history is reduced to a point in history" (*HD* 289). One pragmatic expression of such a move would be the effort to build a utopian society that falsely believes it can achieve the fulfillment of eternity within time. Such an effort denies the constraints of our finitude and leads inevitably to the destructive consequences of pride. If, on the other hand, the symbol of the return of Christ is "not taken seriously the Biblical dialectic is destroyed" along with any sense of the relationship between eternity and history. Such loss deprives history of any sense of purpose the symbol otherwise provides (*HD* 50). Niebuhr stresses the pragmatic consequences of such a move: "If we declare 'history' to be totally meaningless, we also absolve the individual of responsibility for the health of the various collective enterprises, cultures, and civilizations which make up the stuff of history."[33]

To understand the biblical accounts of creation, sin, incarnation, redemption, and so on, as myth, however, does not mean that what the Bible has to say is not true. The myths of the Bible, according to Niebuhr, can only be true and effective for us as myth, and not as events at some distant point in the past or the future. Since we are finite and God is transcendent, any testimony to God available to us will of necessity be in the form of myth that enables us to see, but only as "through a dark glass" whereby we "penetrate sufficiently to the heart of the mystery" but not so as "to be overwhelmed by it."[34]

---

32. Ibid., 3–4.

33. Niebuhr, "Reply to Interpretation and Criticism," 516.

34. Niebuhr, "Mystery and Meaning," 238.

We need to understand, then, that Niebuhr's entire approach to human nature and action is closely bound to his understanding of the Bible as providing us with profound myths that represent "an understanding of the transcendent and the infinite in the terms of the creaturely and the finite."[35] As Dennis McCann says, Niebuhr's "'mythical method of interpretation' determines the agenda and assures the coherence of his proposal for an 'independent Christian ethic.'"[36] That we cannot reduce biblical myths and symbols to literal events in history reminds us of the depths of existence that transcend our finitude. "It is," says Niebuhr, "the genius of true myth to suggest the dimension of depth in reality and to point to a realm of essence which transcends the surface of history" (*ICE* 7). That we must rely on myth for discerning meaning and purpose in history underscores the limits of our capacity for self-transcendence and our ultimate inability to make sense of history by ourselves. Myth, then, is the most adequate means for describing reality, "For the reality which we experience constantly suggests a center and source of reality, which not only transcends immediate experience, but also finally transcends the rational forms and categories by which we seek to apprehend and describe it."[37]

Biblical myths and symbols reflect the quality of tension and paradox at the core of human existence and history. They are well suited, Niebuhr believes, for providing the context in which responsible moral action may be discerned and achieved in a morally complicated world.

35. Gilkey, *On Niebuhr*, 62.

36. McCann, "Hermeneutics and Ethics," 29.

37. Niebuhr, "Truth in Myths," 31. There is present an ambiguity or variance in whether there are actual historical events behind the major symbols and concepts Niebuhr finds in the Bible. He clearly does not see in the stories of Adam, Eve, and a serpent-tainted garden actual history. He further plainly states (*Beyond Tragedy*, 290), "The idea of the resurrection of the body can of course not be literally true." On the other hand, there are certainly events in the history of Israel and in the life and ministry of Jesus of Nazareth that he takes as historical. His concern, though, is to insist that the story of Christ become, "by the apprehension of faith, something more than a mere event," but "an event through which the meaning of the whole of history is apprehended and the specific nature of the divine sovereignty is revealed" (*FH* 141). It is a mistake to assume, though, that by "myth" Niebuhr intends to speak of a false story "invented to explain some truth, or social historical, institutional, or natural phenomenon." See Ayers, "'Myth' in Theological Discourse," 201. Eventually, Niebuhr expressed regret that he had ever used the term "myth," because of the word's "subjective and skeptical connotations"; but that does not mean he has any interest in defending the notion of an empty tomb on Easter morning (Niebuhr, "Reply to Interpretation and Criticism," 514–15).

The symbols of atonement and consummation, for example, reveal significant truths concerning the character and limitations of responsible moral action. The symbols of the cross of Christ and of his return expose the seriousness and depth of human sinfulness. That Jesus was crucified not by criminals, but by representatives of institutional justice and piety, reveals the corruption of "every majesty or virtue" expressed within history (FH 143). The eschatological symbols associated with the return of Christ (e.g., the "Anti-Christ," the last judgment) provide a frame of reference by which all claims to have attained perfection (individually or collectively) within history are falsified. They reveal all human achievements as morally ambiguous (as both "wheat and tares") and refute all claims to the effect that history is its own redeemer (HD 292–93).

On the other hand, the symbols of atonement and eschatology reveal possibilities for human action that challenge any resignation to the status quo. While the cross is the symbol of judgment over all acts that bear the marks of human pretension, the cross, as the expression of divine suffering on behalf of humanity, also reveals a mercy beyond law and judgment that calls for imitation: "The Christian faith affirms that the same Christ who discloses the sovereignty of God over history is also the perfect norm of human nature" (HD 68). While the return of Christ symbolizes the Bible's refutation of utopian claims, the New Testament's language of a return of the Messiah and a last judgment symbolizes the truth that "each moment of history stands under the possibility of an ultimate fulfillment," a hope grounded "not in human capacity but in divine power and mercy, in the character of the ultimate reality which carries the human enterprise."[38]

The destabilizing effect of Niebuhr's rendering of biblical teaching, the moral ambiguity he highlights in the human condition, the delight in paradox, and the concern to elicit meaningful action in a world of threat all work together to a particular end for Niebuhr—to encourage responsible action in a complicated world, where both the individual and society are willing to live with ambiguity for the sake of modest gain. He mocks the notion that we can achieve the resolution of history within history, but he insists that the reality of evil must be taken seriously. We will bob along as corks in the river, but we have enough of a grasp of mercy and justice not to be totally overwhelmed by the flood.

38. Niebuhr, "As Deceivers, Yet True," 24.

Given the tensions inherent within Niebuhr's own outlook, is there available any specific guidance concerning concrete action in our morally complicated world? The answer to that question, not surprisingly, is yes and no.

The *"Impossible Possibility"*

Niebuhr was the one-time heir of a movement in American Christianity known as the "Social Gospel." The Social Gospel movement, led by figures such as Walter Rauschenbusch (1861–1918), a German Baptist pastor in the New York City neighborhood of Hell's Kitchen, put forward the teachings of Jesus as inspired guidance for both individual and social life. Jesus' teachings and personal example were held up as the solution to the social injustices of a modern industrialized economy; not only individuals but also institutions would come under the law of love. Niebuhr's early years as pastor in Detroit exhibited the influence of this outlook as he confronted the harsh economic realities imposed by Henry Ford's business practices on many of his parishioners.[39] By the time he wrote *Moral Man and Immoral Society* in 1932, however, he had come to reject the notion that human egoism at whatever level could be "progressively checked by the development of rationality or the growth of religiously inspired goodwill" or that with time such goodwill could "establish social harmony between all the human societies and collectives" (*MMIS* xii).

Is there, then, no room for love in Niebuhr's Christian realism? Niebuhr insists on several matters at this point. First, Jesus' love command, concretely expressed on the cross, serves "as the norm of human nature" that "defines the final perfection of man in history." Niebuhr describes the love of Christ, "His disinterested and sacrificial agape, as the highest possibility of human existence." Christ represents a divine love "which seeketh not its own" and "where the sinful rivalries of ego with ego are transcended" (*HD* 68, 72, 73). The cross is the measure of this love, and Niebuhr "unremittingly polemicizes against all attempts to water down the force of [Jesus'] radical teachings or to assimilate them to any sort of prudential ethic."[40]

---

39. A taste of Niebuhr's evaluation of Ford may be found in "How Philanthropic Is Henry Ford?" 98–103, where Niebuhr laments (102) the American mind's habit of investing "its heroes with moral qualities they do not possess" and its eagerness to believe "that the big man is also the good man."

40. Hays, *Moral Vision of the New Testament*, 216; see, for example, *ICE* 29.

Second, according to Niebuhr, the law of love in some ways reflects something basic to human nature. "The real structure of life," says Niebuhr, "the dependence of man upon his fellowmen for instance," indicates that humans have been created in such a way that their very survival depends on "both organic and loving relations between them." Any fulfillment of what it truly means to be a human being, what Niebuhr calls "the freedom of the self," depends on the realization of Jesus' command to love the neighbor "as thyself" (*HN* 275, 295).

Third, that such love must take the form of a command—"thou shalt"—is not to be overlooked. Niebuhr analyzes the significance of this "law" in characteristic fashion. Any fulfillment of the "law of love" would reflect "an ultimate condition of complete harmony between the soul and God, its neighbour and itself in a situation in which this harmony is not a reality." If such a condition were a reality there would be no need for the law in the first place. Obviously, the law presupposes a state of human sinfulness that needs correction or restraint by such a command. On the other hand, "If there were not some possibility of sensing the ultimate perfection in a state of sin the 'thou shalt' would be irrelevant" (*HN* 286). The love command exposes the finitude and freedom and "the contradiction between man's essential nature and his sinful condition" that Niebuhr incessantly observes, a condition he suggests "is insoluble from the standpoint of man's own resources and can be solved only from the standpoint of God's resources" (*HN* 288).

Fourth, even with God's resources, though, it is doubtful as to whether the genuine demands of the law of love can find concrete expression within history. Niebuhr insists that the law of love is an "impossible possibility." Not only do our selfish anxieties make it difficult to meet "the needs of the other without concern for the self," even if such sacrificial love is possible between two individuals, the introduction of third parties brings competing interests into play, which "requires a rational estimate of conflicting needs and interests" (*HN* 295, *HD* 248). So, while "love is the primary law" of humanity's nature and the bonds of fellowship it enables are a basic requirement of social existence, "the love commandment is . . . no simple historical possibility" (*HD* 244, 247). This is especially the case, of course, with respect to the behavior of social groups like nations. With regard to the sentiments of the Social Gospel movement, for example, Niebuhr insists, "The demand of religious moralists that nations subject themselves to 'the law of Christ' is an unrealistic demand, and the hope that they will do so is a sentimental one. . . . No nation in history has ever been known to be purely unselfish in its actions" (*MMIS* 75).

For Niebuhr, the love of God revealed in the self-giving of Christ on the cross is the norm of human existence. The law of love embodied in the cross, though, "represents a transcendent perfection" that serves more to clarify the "obscurities of history" and to define "the limits of what is possible in historical development" than as a strategy for concrete action in history (*HD* 86). Consequently, Niebuhr suggests, "The modern pulpit would be saved from much sentimentality if the thousands of sermons which are annually preached upon [biblical texts calling for the practice of love] would contain some suggestions of the impossibility of these ethical demands" (*ICE* 28). If it is the case, though, that the demands of such love transcend any capacity for fulfillment within history, what then is the relevance of an impossible ethical ideal (*ICE* 62–83)? Niebuhr's understanding of the relationship between love and justice is an effort to answer that question.

Justice and the Approximation of Love

The love command, expressed by and embodied in Christ, calls for an ethic contrary to the natural self-regarding egocentrism of humanity. According to Niebuhr, such an ethic "does not deal at all with the immediate moral problem of every human life—the problem of arranging some kind of armistice between various contending factions and forces. It has nothing to say about the relativities of politics and economics, nor of the necessary balances of power which exist and must exist in even the most intimate social relationships" (*ICE* 23–24). Christian love is without relevance in terms of providing any direct strategy for specific action in the social arena. That does not mean, though, that the love command is entirely without significance for social relations. That significance has to do with the tensive relationship between love and justice, a relationship with both positive and negative dimensions. Why the tension?

We must remember that social institutions and collective relations are for Niebuhr inherently conflictual. In an important essay from 1953 he describes "the moral realities of man's collective life" in terms of "their bewildering confusion of coercion, conflict of self-interest, domination and subordination."[41] It is the task of government "to prevent competitive

41. Niebuhr, "Christian Faith and Social Action," 236. Subsequent references will be designated *CFSA*.

self-seeking from degenerating into anarchy." Despite popular notions to the contrary, we cannot regard such self-seeking as harmless; nor can we, however, be uncritical toward the coercive power of government meant to guard against chaos. The Christian faith bears a public relevance in these matters, especially as it challenges any illusions "about our ideals and structures or about any of the realities of the community" (*CFSA* 230–31). For Niebuhr, "The real problem of a Christian social ethic is to derive from the Gospel a clear view of the realities with which we must deal in our common or social life, and also to preserve a sense of responsibility for achieving the highest measure of order, freedom and justice despite the hazards of man's collective life" (*CFSA* 236). The norm of love serves both to foster that sense of responsibility and to enable that clarity.

To examine the relationship between love and justice, it is best to have some sense of what counts as justice for Niebuhr. Gustafson suggests that while Niebuhr "does not develop a theory of justice," it functions for him as "basically a principle of equality."[42] Indeed, the issue of equality (as also freedom) looms large in Niebuhr's account of justice and it indicates something of the relationship between love and justice: "Equality is always the regulative principle of justice; and in the ideal of equality there is an echo of the law of love." Alternatively, in circumstances of inequality "between those who enjoy inordinate privileges and those who lack the basic essentials of the good life it is fairly clear" that the religious vision "which holds love to be the final law of life" has been diminished (*ICE* 65, 80). For Niebuhr, "Equality as a pinnacle of the ideal of justice implicitly points towards love as the final norm of justice" (*HD* 254).

Niebuhr insists, however, that "the attainment of complete social equality in society is impossible." For example, history teaches "that privileged members of the community invariably use their higher degree of social power to appropriate an excess of privilege not required by their function; and certainly not in accord with differences in need." The tension, then, between "the validity of the principle of equality on the one

---

42. Gustafson, "Theology in the Service of Ethics," 33. In *Human Destiny* (254), Niebuhr affirms liberty and equality as two "universal 'principles' of justice." In that work he analyzes only equality, believing such analysis "will serve to reveal the validity of both as transcendent principles of justice." In a later essay he notes the tensions that arise in different contexts between these two emphases: "The principle of 'equality' is a relevant criterion of criticism for the social hierarchy, and the principle of 'liberty' serves the same purpose for the community's unity." He suggests a necessary dialectical relationship between them when he says, "Neither principle can be wholly or absolutely applied without destroying the community." See his "Liberty and Equality," 186.

hand and the impossibility of realizing it fully on the other, illustrates the relation of the absolute norms of justice to the relativities of history" (*HD* 255).[43] This recognition, however, must not inhibit responsible action. The Christian realist will live with the tension: "The positive relation of principles of justice to the ideal of brotherhood makes an indeterminate approximation of love in the realm of justice possible. The negative relation means that all historic conceptions of justice will embody some elements which contradict the law of love" (*HD* 256). Love and justice stand, then, in a dialectical relationship. Justice is the approximation of the non-calculating demands of the love commandment. Such love achieves relative embodiment in the ongoing quest for justice.

The biblical norm of love, reflecting the natural affinity within humanity for community, finds expression within the conditions of human sinfulness in the form of systems and rules of justice that provide structured and specific ways to extend the sense of obligation towards the other that love evokes (*HD* 248). Such systems and rules must be made concrete in particular contexts through legal enactments that serve as "the instruments of the conscience of the community, seeking to subdue the potential anarchy of forces and interests into a tolerable harmony" (*HD* 257). Because reason is always partial and mingled with inordinate self-regard (especially at the group level), all efforts at establishing such systems and rules suffer tendencies toward distortion that threaten both individual and communal well-being in the form of either tyranny or anarchy. "These twin evils, tyranny and anarchy, represent the Scylla and Charybdis between which the frail bark of social justice must sail" (*HD* 258). The biblical norm of love, however, motivates ongoing commitment to guard against these dangers, seeks specific structural instruments by which they might be avoided, and stands in judgment over each and every partial achievement in the effort.

What particular institutional structure might best reflect and serve the tensions inherent in human nature that both enable and threaten social justice? One of Niebuhr's most well-known aphorisms answers, "Man's capacity for justice makes democracy possible; but man's inclination to injustice makes democracy necessary."[44] Niebuhr's carefully

43. For a Niebuhrian analysis of how difficult the attainment of "complete equality in society is," see Lovin, *Reinhold Niebuhr and Christian Realism*, 219–25; on the tensions between liberty and equality, see p. 226 in that same work.

44. Niebuhr, *Children of Light*, vi. Subsequent references to this work will be designated *CLCD*.

balanced statement reflects the characteristic themes of his basic view of human nature. It is this view of human nature that Niebuhr says is lacking in traditional accounts of democracy, a lack that has left democracy weak and vulnerable. Published in the waning months of World War II, Niebuhr's *The Children of Light and the Children of Darkness* offers a balanced defense of democracy in the face of the idealism of those who believed self-interest could be brought "under the discipline of a more universal law and in harmony with a more universal good"—the "children of light"—and the cynicism of those who "know no law beyond the self" and operate strictly by "the power of self-interest"—the "children of darkness" (*CLCD* 14–15). Democracy requires a view of human nature, says Niebuhr, that combines transcendent aspirations for justice with a shrewd realism about power: "The children of light must be armed with the wisdom of the children of darkness but remain free of their malice. They must know the power of self-interest in human society without giving it moral justification." Those who would preserve democracy, Niebuhr urges, must seek such balance "in order that they may beguile, deflect, harness and restrain self-interest, individual and collective, for the sake of the community" (*CLCD* 34).

"Ideally," says Niebuhr, "democracy is a permanently valid form of social and political organization which does justice to two dimensions of human existence: to man's spiritual nature and his social character, to the uniqueness and variety of individual life and to the common necessities of all men" (*CLCD* 10). Niebuhr does not suggest, though, that democratic institutions are free from the ambiguities of human nature. Indeed, "The whole development of democratic justice in human society" has depended upon the recognition of such ambiguities (*HD* 268). The value of democracy is not as a means, therefore, for achieving permanent solutions in the quest for justice, but as a "method of finding proximate solutions for insoluble problems" (*CLCD* 83). What democracy provides, through "the principle of the equilibrium of power," is a set of procedures meant to check and balance power within government and between government and individuals. For Niebuhr, not only do democracies stand as a power of restraint against inordinate self-interest when one neighbor threatens another, but "it is the highest achievement of democratic societies that they embody the principle of resistance to government within government itself." With a balance of power built into a constitutional framework, government can be "so conceived that criticism of the ruler becomes an instrument of better government," without such criticism giving way to anarchy (*HD* 268).[45]

Democracy, then, reveals humanity at its best and its worst. Its genius is its capacity to provide for approximate expressions of "the law of love as a final imperative," while taking seriously "the persistence of the power of self-love in all of life . . . particularly in the collective relations of mankind." The principle of the equilibrium of power in democratic societies is the concrete recognition of "both the law of love as the final standard and the law of self-love as a persistent force," enabling "Christians to have a foundation for a pragmatic ethic in which power and self-interest are used, beguiled, harnessed and deflected for the ultimate end of establishing the highest and most inclusive possible community of justice and order" (*CFSA* 241).

The social harmony afforded by the balance of power, however, is fragile and susceptible to any number of threats. The same "vitalities" and passions that make democracy possible and necessary—religious impulses, ethnic pluralism, and economic self-interest, for example—can threaten the fabric of society. Thus, "One of the greatest problems of democratic civilization is how to integrate the life of its various subordinate—ethnic, religious and economic—groups in the community in such a way that the richness and harmony of the whole community will be enhanced and not destroyed by them." Niebuhr argues, for example, "Religious ideas and traditions . . . are the ultimate source of moral standards from which political principles are derived." Yet, "Religio-cultural diversity may prove the most potent source of communal discord, because varying answers to the final question of the meaning of life produce conflicting answers on all proximate issues of moral order and political organization" (*CLCD* 87–88).

According to Niebuhr, the second task of a community is to prevent the power by which community is achieved from becoming tyrannical. The first task, however, "is to subdue chaos and create order" (*CLCD* 120–21). The threats posed by religious pluralism cannot be ignored. There is, however, a religious solution to the problems raised by religious diversity. Such a solution actually "requires a high form of religious

---

45. If democracy's traditional defenders were too optimistic about human nature, pessimists (e.g., Thomas Hobbes) fashioned antidemocratic political theories that looked to a strong state as sovereign over rivalries that threatened the peace of the community. Their error, according to Niebuhr (*CLCD* 36–37), was the failure "to provide checks against the inordinate impulses to power, to which all rulers are tempted."

commitment," and that is for "each religion, or each version of a single faith . . . to proclaim its highest insights while yet preserving an humble and contrite recognition of the fact that all actual expressions of religious faith are subject to historical contingency and relativity." This humility, says Niebuhr, is simply the recognition of "the difference between divine majesty and human creatureliness, between the unconditioned character of the divine and the conditioned character of all human experience." While "religious toleration through religiously inspired humility and charity is always a difficult achievement," such toleration is ultimately only the natural expression of any genuine religious faith that encourages "men to moderate their natural pride, and to achieve some decent consciousness of the relativity of their own statement of even the most ultimate truth" (*CLCD* 93–95).

Niebuhr provides no criteria by which religious devotees may distinguish between their faith's "highest insights" and those elements that express "historical contingency and relativity."[46] What he advises, however, suggests that the integrity of any particular faith is subject to critique on the basis of the prior integrity of national identity and harmony: "Whenever the religious groups of a community are incapable of such humility and charity, the national community will be forced to save its unity through either secularism or authoritarianism" (*CLCD* 95). What Niebuhr seems to make clear is that democracy, while best defended on the basis of selected features of Christian doctrine, must be ready to defend itself against any other features that might elevate Christian commitment beyond commitment to the national community that permits Christianity's qualified presence. Ironically, what Niebuhr calls for, in effect, is for Christians "in the name of supporting democracy" to "police their own convictions to insure that none of those convictions might cause difficulty for making democracy successful."[47]

Niebuhr's readiness to assess and subordinate features of Christian faith and identity in light of the prior identity of and faith in democratic society raises important concerns for any analysis of his contribution to the field of Christian ethics. It must be obvious, though, why Niebuhr was so popular in many circles in the 1940s and 1950s. His frank appraisal of the depth of human sinfulness and his appreciation for the "nicely

46. There are other problems with Niebuhr's approach to the issues of religious pluralism; see McClay, "Reinhold Niebuhr and the Problem of Religious Pluralism," 218–33.

47. Hauerwas, "Democratic Policing of Christianity," 105.

calculated less and more" to be found in the relative accomplishments of human action, underwrote the willingness on the part of Western democratic powers to use whatever means were available to place a check on German nationalism and the spread of Stalinist communism. While the demise of the Soviet Union occasioned something of a decline of interest in Niebuhr in the 1990s, the events and aftermath of September 11, 2001, spurred a variety of appeals to Niebuhr, who had in 1940 urged action "to prevent the triumph of an intolerable tyranny."[48] Niebuhr's brand of "Christian realism" provided for many a clear-eyed analysis of the threat of Muslim radicalism and the determination to act as needed.[49] Others appealed to Niebuhr's warnings against national pride to challenge immodest claims by the Bush administration that it would rid the world of evil.[50] The irony of diametrically opposed appeals to Niebuhr has itself not gone unnoticed.[51] There has been, in any case, a revival of interest in Reinhold Niebuhr. Given the renewed attention to his legacy, evaluation of his outlook is important in light of the claim here that Christian ethics is necessarily ecclesial in character. For Niebuhr's own claim is that for the Christian faith to have public relevance it must be through some means other than the church as the primary setting for the formation and practice of and witness to life as God intends.

Whose Justice? Which Reality?

The concern here is not at all to question the personal faith of Reinhold Niebuhr.[52] It is, though, to raise questions about the adequacy of his outlook in terms of a Christian ethic concerned with what God is doing about evil and to contrast his view with the approach drawn here from Paul's Letter to the Ephesians.

---

48. Niebuhr, "To Prevent the Triumph of an Intolerable Tyranny," 272–77.

49. For example, Beinhart, "Fighting Faith," 17–29; McClay, "Continuing Irony of American History," 20–25; Elshtain, *Just War against Terror*, 106–11.

50. For example, Bacevich, "Prophets and Poseurs," 24–37; Finstuen, "This American Mess," 11–12.

51. See Elie, "Man for All Reasons," 82–96; McCorkle, "On Recent Political Uses of Reinhold Niebuhr," 18–41.

52. Some defenders of Niebuhr seem to suggest that any serious criticism of Niebuhr's outlook is tantamount to an attack on Niebuhr himself; see Fackre, "Was Reinhold Niebuhr a Christian?" 25–27.

Niebuhr has been evaluated from a variety of perspectives. A liberation theology originating in South America sees Niebuhr's "realistic" assessment of all claims to justice as a cover for self-interest as effectively silencing the poor and powerless.[53] Some feminist theologians have seen his analysis of sin as primarily expressed through pride as "illuminating" and yet as "inappropriate for women," who see in such an emphasis justification of an androcentric view of God sanctioning hierarchy.[54] Detractors and defenders of Niebuhr fasten on any number of concerns to diminish or enhance his legacy.[55] The concern here is strictly to ask whether Niebuhr has neglected an emphasis that is actually far more fundamental to the task of Christian ethics than he either recognized or was willing to admit.

It is clear to most interpreters of Niebuhr that the church plays no significant role in his understanding of Christian ethics. While it has been suggested this lacuna simply reflects the contingencies of biography and career path,[56] Niebuhr himself hints at other reasons. In response to one critic's observation of Niebuhr's "critical omission" of the New Testament's presentation of the church "as God's instrument for continuing his atoning work in Christ," Niebuhr admits the criticism is justified: "But when I see how much new evil comes into life through the pretensions of the religious community, through its conventional and graceless legalism and through religious fanaticism, I am concerned that my growing appreciation of the Church should not betray me into this complacency."[57]

Niebuhr's criticisms of the church are many and frequently on target. Wendy Dackson suggests his criticisms indicate "an 'outsider ecclesiology' which describes the Church from the standpoint of those who are not its members."[58] Niebuhr himself says that after his years as pastor in Detroit "the life of the local church was *terra incognita* to me."[59] While his participation might have been minimal, his criticisms suggest familiarity.

53. See Lovin, *Reinhold Niebuhr and Christian Realism*, 212–13.

54. Hampson, "Reinhold Niebuhr on Sin," 46–60.

55. A balanced overview of recent attempts is offered by Lovin, "Reinhold Niebuhr in Contemporary Scholarship," 489–505.

56. A suggestion made to me by Robin Lovin in personal conversation, October 30, 2009.

57. The charge is leveled by Wolf, "Reinhold Niebuhr's Doctrine of Man," 324–25. Niebuhr's response is in his "Reply to Interpretation and Criticism," 513.

58. Dackson, "Reinhold Niebuhr's 'Outsider Ecclesiology,'" 88.

59. Niebuhr, "View of Life from the Sidelines," 254.

Dackson argues that Niebuhr highlights two significant failures of the church: the failure of arrogance and the failure of foolishness.[60] The failure of arrogance finds multiple expressions but chiefly stems from the sense of privilege and authority the church takes upon itself as the "repository of a revelation which transcends the finiteness and sinfulness of men." In its arrogance, the church shows itself no different from the state in its capacity to "become the vehicle of collective egoism" (*HN* 217). The failure of foolishness is primarily the failure to recognize the ongoing power of self-interest, not only in the world in general, but even within the lives of the faithful, resulting in "an unrealistic view of the world."[61] Such foolishness results in moralistic attempts to improve society by an imperfect people, an arrangement that usually creates resentment on the part of those targeted for reform (*MMIS* 80). For Niebuhr, the failures of pride and foolishness are twin reminders of how "the sad experiences of Christian history show how human pride and spiritual arrogance rose to new heights precisely at the point where the claims of sanctity are made without qualification" (*HD* 122).

Such complaints might suggest that Niebuhr's relative inattention to the role of the church was contingent on the perceived inadequacies of the church as merely another human institution.[62] It is surely the case that Niebuhr saw no ontological distinction between the church and any other social group, and thus the church, like any other social group, displays all the ambiguities of the human condition. In Niebuhr's outlook, "The church stood in no privileged position in relation to humanity's essential condition."[63] It would be a mistake to assume, however, that the diminished place given to the church by Niebuhr derives solely from its obvious failures. After all, the state fares no better, in Niebuhr's estimate, in terms of its capacity to achieve genuine justice in the world. The absence of any significant role for the church in Niebuhr stems less from personal disillusionment than from features inherent in his basic perspective.[64] Let us first document that absence before offering any explanation for it.

60. Dackson, "Reinhold Niebuhr's 'Outsider Ecclesiology,'" 93–100.

61. Ibid., 97.

62. For more on Niebuhr's assessment of the church, particularly in the United States, see Rice, "Niebuhr's Critique of Religion in America," 317–37.

63. Moulaison, "Theology, Church and Political Change," 181; see also Mathewes, *Evil and the Augustinian Tradition*, 138 n. 56.

64. Stanley Hauerwas insists "the absence of the church in Niebuhr's work" is not an accidental oversight, but is in fact "integral to Niebuhr's theology and his ethics." See his *With the Grain of the Universe*, 137.

One way of getting at the issue of the eclipse of ecclesiology in Niebuhr is to examine how he engages Scripture in support of his "Christian realism." His frequent citations of Scripture in works such as *The Nature and Destiny* of Man suggest an effort to ground his outlook in a biblical frame of reference. In fact, as Hays says, "Niebuhr cannot be considered a careful reader of the New Testament. His interest lies in big theological ideas and themes, not in close exposition of biblical texts. He tends to treat texts as illustrative material rather than as the generative source of his theological reflection."[65] As Siker puts it, "Niebuhr's . . . writings . . . contain endless generic references to the biblical doctrine of this or the biblical concept of that. . . . Yet almost never does he provide any exegetical analysis to support his assertions."[66] The significance of this loose engagement with Scripture can be seen in how he puts biblical language to use in association with core concerns of his entire project.

At the heart of Niebuhr's "Christian realism" is his basic anthropological account of humans as the complex mixture of finitude and freedom. Human beings are creatures capable of self-transcendence; to be human is to know contingency and creativity in such a way that results in the anxiety that inevitably produces the pride and sin that make democratic institutions necessary. While Niebuhr enlists a variety of biblical images in support of his claims, three figure significantly in his discourse that when examined more closely would point in a direction other than that taken by Niebuhr. These are 1) "created in the image of God," 2) "the wheat and the tares," and 3) "the children of light and the children of darkness."

Niebuhr admits, "The Biblical doctrine that man was made in the image of God and after His likeness is naturally given no precise psychological elaboration in the Bible itself" (*HN* 151). That does not, however, keep Niebuhr from applying a psychological interpretation to the language of Genesis 1. Niebuhr is not alone in his appeal to this language to identify that which distinguishes human beings from other creatures.[67] The issue is whether the biblical focus is on the fragile combination of finitude ("created") and freedom ("image of God") that Niebuhr sees as

---

65. Hays, *Moral Vision of the New Testament*, 220.

66. Siker, "Reinhold Niebuhr," 14.

67. David Kelsey says the concept of "image of God" has been "traditionally understood to be some essential structural feature of human beings that constitutes them as distinctively human and distinguishes them from animals who do not exhibit God's image." See his *Eccentric Existence*, 895.

constitutive of human existence. Niebuhr's appraisal of anxiety as the motivating force behind both human creativity and destructive power is insightful. Does he miss something, however, by reading into the biblical text his psychological analysis of the human condition?

Interpretation of what Gen 1:26–27 means by "image of God" is hindered by the fact "that there is virtually no explanation of the term within the Old Testament."[68] A wider embrace of biblical testimony indicates, though, that Niebuhr (with countless others) makes a mistake when he uses the language of Genesis 1 to describe "a general property of human beings as God's creatures." "Exegetical debates," David Kelsey warns, "are simply too inconclusive to warrant giving 'image of God' the central, anchorlike role it has traditionally played in theological anthropology's account of what human being is."[69] Brueggemann even insists, "The notion of humanity in the 'image of God' plays no role in Old Testament articulations of humanity."[70] That does not mean, though, that the phrase plays no significant role in Scripture as a whole. New Testament use of the "image of God" motif, however, moves in quite a different direction than does Niebuhr, while extending the trajectory of thought from the Old Testament.

The Old Testament indicates that those made in the image of God are called to represent the divine sovereignty over the rest of creation—that is, humans are created for the purpose of a covenant relationship with God that serves God's will on behalf of all creation (Gen 1:28). The failure in the garden to adhere to God's will places every aspect of the relationship between God and humanity, humans and one another, and humans to the rest of creation in jeopardy (Genesis 3). Scripture insists, though, that God has not abandoned the divine purpose for all of creation and calls an Israel to serve as witness to the nations of what that purpose is all about (cf. Exod 19:5–6). Prophetic voices in the Old Testament testify both to Israel's failures in this respect and to a hoped-for Messiah that would restore Israel and bring that witness to fruition.[71]

Paul's Letter to the Colossians is very specific that the "image of God" finds ultimate expression in Israel's Messiah, the Christ, "the image [*eikōn*] of the invisible God, the first-born of all creation" (Col 1:15),

68 Childs, *Old Testament Theology in a Canonical Context*, 97.

69. Kelsey, *Eccentric Existence*, 2:896, 900.

70. Brueggemann, *Theology of the Old Testament*, 452.

71. This narrative summary relies broadly on Wright, *Climax of the Covenant*, 18–41.

by whom "all things were created" and through whom all things will be reconciled (Col 1:20). For the present, Christians are those who have now been reconciled "in his fleshly body" that is the church (1:21–24), a new humanity defined not by the divisions that drive human conflict, but by a work of renewal "according to the image of the One who created him" (3:10–11).[72] While the "image" language is not explicit, the same emphases are found in Ephesians where Paul describes the purpose of God as the ultimate uniting of all things in Christ (1:9–10), a goal presently anticipated in the new humanity that is his body (2:15–16), the new humanity created in the likeness of God (4:24), the church called into being to bear witness to God's intent to unite all things in Christ (3:10). In the New Testament, "image of God" cannot be reduced to an anthropological reference. With Christ as its major reference (see also 2 Cor 4:4; Heb 1:1–3), through whom the reconciliation of creation takes place, a reconciliation presently embodied in the church, "image of God" functions as shorthand for the narrative of God's redemptive work that includes God's decision to create a people called to live in ways that currently express what God ultimately intends to achieve for all of creation—what God intended for creation from the beginning (cf. Rom 8:29). Is Niebuhr wrong to describe humans as troubled by the tensions between finitude and freedom? Not necessarily; it is simply that when he uses the language of "created in the image of God" to render this psychological assessment, he occludes the ecclesial emphasis in that phrase offered by the broader canonical witness.

Niebuhr also fails to observe the ecclesial element within Jesus' parable of the wheat and the tares. We have seen that Niebuhr finds in this parable biblical support for his basic view of the human condition. All of human history reflects the inescapable mixture of good and evil. Each and every act, by the individual or the group, testifies to the misery and ecstasy of humanity as witness to the creative and the destructive powers unleashed by our anxious condition. It is foolish to think we can make ultimate distinctions between wheat and tares; no final resolution of human injustice is available within history. It is certainly foolish to think the church can pretend to be a separate people, clearly distinguished in the world as those who live solely by disinterested love rather than willful self-interest. Within history "we must make provisional distinctions,"

---

72. See Kelsey, *Eccentric Existence*, 2:956–67 for extended discussion of the "Christ-hymn" of Colossians 1.

Niebuhr says, "but we must know that there are no final distinctions" (*WT* 59).

Niebuhr severely misreads Jesus' parable. His error stems, as Cartwright has shown, from his refusal to engage with Jesus' own "interpretation" of the parable given in Matt 13:36–43.[73] Niebuhr interprets Jesus' parable as highlighting the moral ambiguity that inscribes every human action. He particularly has in mind a warning to Christians that they too suffer the admixture of evil and good, particularly when they would "violate the parable" and make "premature judgments . . . about themselves and each other" (*WT* 56). In effect, Niebuhr echoes a reading of the passage given by Augustine in the fifth century and magisterial reformers of the sixteenth century. Those readings drew on the parable to deny any need for maintaining discipline within the church for the sake of bearing a distinctive witness in the world.[74] Niebuhr's reading assimilates all of humanity into the same moral ambiguity depicted by wheat and tares growing indiscernibly together, leaving no room at all for a church that bears some unique status and mission.

The interpretation of the parable given in 13:36–43, however, makes it clear that "the field" in which both "wheat and tares" grow is not the church, but "the world." The "wheat" represents the fruit of "the good seed," the community of those who have responded favorably to the proclamation of the kingdom of God—"the sons of the kingdom"—while the "tares" represent those who have not so responded—"the sons of the evil one" (13:38). Whatever the larger intent of the parable, a clear distinction is made in the interpretation of 13:36–43 between a community formed by favorable response to the proclamation of the gospel and those who have not (at least, not yet) so responded. The move by Niebuhr to use the imagery of "wheat and tares" to describe a moral ambiguity shared to the same degree by both the Christian community and the rest of humanity may be accurate social analysis, but it is not good biblical interpretation and fails to acknowledge the ecclesial element within the parable.[75]

73. Cartwright, *Practices, Politics, and Performance*, 32. It is possible that Niebuhr ignores the interpretation of the parable given in Matt 13:36–43 as the Gospel writer's own addition and not original to Jesus, the standard position of biblical scholarship in Niebuhr's day. Niebuhr makes no mention of the interpretation one way or the other.

74. Ibid., 30–33.

75. Klyne Snodgrass says, "The parable is not about the mixed character of the church but about the fact that the righteous and sinners coexist in the world—even when the kingdom is present. The church is indeed of mixed character, tragically so, but that is not what Matthew's parable is about." See his *Stories with Intent*, 204. The

Niebuhr exhibits the same tendency in his use of what he calls "a scriptural designation" of "the children of light and the children of darkness." We recall that Niebuhr uses the imagery to contrast those who believed self-interest could be brought "under the discipline of a more universal law and in harmony with a more universal good"—the "children of light"—with those who "know no law beyond the self" and operate strictly by "the power of self-interest"—the "children of darkness" (*CLCD* 14–15). Niebuhr criticizes the children of light, the naïve defenders of liberal democracy, as not appreciating the power and enduring presence within themselves of the self-interest the children of darkness unabashedly pursue. Substantive defense of democracy cannot afford such naïveté and must not be hesitant to harness the power of self-interest in the pursuit of approximate justice.

Strictly speaking, the Bible nowhere uses the phrase "children of darkness." Paul, though, does make use of "children of light" (Eph 5:8; cf. "sons of light" in 1 Thess 5:5), and the juxtaposition of "light" and "darkness" to indicate a moral contrast is a common enough biblical device. Paul's use of "children of light" in Ephesians, however, serves a very different agenda from Niebuhr's. Coupled with the "once"/"now" motif and explicit calls to abstain from what Paul considered characteristic sins of the Gentile world (sexual immorality and idolatry; 5:3–7), Paul intends to generate "the solidarity of a particular community, depicted as a pure and holy community, standing in sharp distinction from the evil world in which it is located." That Paul uses such language in the context of admonition, however, certainly indicates that he recognizes the mixed moral character of the "children of light" and that they do not yet live beyond the threat of temptation and sin. Paul's use of such "language of distinction" as "children of light" should be understood, then,

---

likely setting for this parable in Jesus' ministry is the threat manifest in the presence of the Roman Empire (the "enemy") as represented by local collaborators such as tax collectors ("tares"). Some in Israel, eager for the revelation of God's righteousness, believed they could anticipate that revelation by executing divine judgment through armed revolt against Rome and attacks on any Roman sympathizers. The parable warns that such efforts would have devastating consequences for "the sons of the kingdom" and that such matters should be left to God's initiative. The Jewish revolt against Rome in CE 66 and the eventual destruction of Jerusalem indicate that Jesus' repeated warnings against such an endeavor went unheeded (cf. Luke 19:41–44). The interpretation of the parable urges, then, a patient refusal to respond in kind to the threat of Rome, counsel Niebuhr would likely never recommend. Thanks to my colleague Warren Johnson, who has helped me gain some clarity about the significance of this parable in its setting.

"as an attempt to reinforce a strong sense of positive group identity, and to strengthen the sense of distinction in terms of a boundary between insiders and outsiders."[76] Paul uses the phrase "children of light" not to convince his readers that they presently possess an absolute goodness, but to encourage ongoing identification with and participation among a distinctive people where such goodness can be pursued.

Niebuhr, however, seems to take pains to avoid any affirmation of the church as a peculiar people integral to how God is at work in the world. His admonition for the "children of light" is that they learn a few things from the "children of darkness," one lesson being that they should not take themselves so seriously, as they are not that different from the children of darkness to begin with. At any rate, Niebuhr's employment of the image has nothing to do with the biblical reference to an *ekklesia* called to embody a distinctive witness in the world to God's goodness and righteousness and truth (Eph 5:9). His appeal to such language, like his use of "image of God" and "wheat and tares," serves a completely separate agenda and entirely fails to engage with the recurring emphasis that appears in these images. If he had tried, he could not have offered a more appropriate set of images to communicate what he seems so eager to deny—that God in Christ is present in this world through a people called to live in anticipation of a final redemption to be embodied now in distinctive practices of reconciliation and peace.

Are Niebuhr's points about the moral ambiguity of Christian witness appropriate? Yes. Does the human drama course down a stream of history in which both sensuality and pride threaten even our best efforts at justice? Paul would likely agree. Are his insights as to the strengths and weaknesses of democratic political theory helpful? Granted. There is so much from Niebuhr that testifies to a power of discernment that we are tempted to accept his assessments as offered, and Niebuhr is not reluctant to describe as "stupid" those positions not in accord with his. As Hauerwas says, "Niebuhr's claim to be a realist functioned rhetorically to give him the high ground not only morally, but also intellectually."[77]

To the extent, however, that Niebuhr ignores the church as basic to how God is at work in the world to address its fractured and fragmented

---

76. Horrell, *Solidarity and Difference*, 133, 138; Wayne Meeks argues that this sort of "language of separation" serves to reinforce the "consciousness of a qualitative difference between outsiders and insiders" in the task of the formation of the *ekklesia*. See his *First Urban Christians*, 95–96.

77. Hauerwas with Broadway, "Irony of Reinhold Niebuhr,'" 49.

condition, he is terribly wrong about what is actually real.[78] The dismissal of the need for concrete embodiment of Christian truth by the church finally, though, reflects a central feature of Niebuhr's "Christian realism." We recall the necessary role "myth" plays for Niebuhr's understanding of Christian truth and responsible moral action. To assign the major "events" of Christian faith to specific points in history is to deny their capacity to communicate the transcendent and to diminish their power to reveal both the depths and limitations of human existence. While Niebuhr would surely frown at the assessment, it is hard to avoid the conclusion voiced by Hauerwas that Niebuhr's "account of Christian convictions . . . renders their historicity virtually irrelevant to the meaning and/or truth of their own existence."[79] Yet Niebuhr's insistence that the love command embodied in the cross cannot actually be expressed within history is either double-talk or it evacuates the cross of Christ from explicit expression in history. "In short," says Hauerwas, "Niebuhr's account of the cross is finally another variation of the Gnostic temptation to turn the cross into a knowledge that is meaningful separate from the actual death of a man called Jesus."[80]

The evacuation of the cross from history is closely tied to the eclipse of ecclesiology in Niebuhr. In his view, for events in history to enjoy ongoing significance they must be remembered by and embodied in the practices of a particular community. Such particularity, though, "can not produce a universe of meaning above the level of the life of the individual

78. Niebuhr displays the eclipse of ecclesiology not simply in his criticisms of the church or in his misuse of the biblical themes discussed here. When Niebuhr recounts the major features of what he calls "the Christian world view," he discusses creation, fall, incarnation, atonement, and last judgment. Notably missing is God's covenant with Israel or the formation of the church (see Niebuhr, "As Deceivers, Yet True," 3–24). When he suggests what significance "the resources of the Christian faith" might have "in a dynamic civilization and expanding society," we are not surprised to hear an emphasis on Christ, who "symbolizes both the indeterminate possibilities of historical achievement and also the divine mercy which understands the tensions and contradiction between all forms of human virtue and achievement and the divine will" (Niebuhr, "Resources of the Christian," 155). Nowhere does Niebuhr suggest, though, that witness to this Christ requires concrete embodiment by a historical community capable of demonstrating that mercy even in the midst of its own tensions and contradictions. The channel through which such resources might be made available to "society" is now, says Moulaison, "the individual theologian, for whom the necessity of the church was no longer apparent" (see Moulaison, "Theology, Church and Political Change," 181).

79. Hauerwas, "History as Fate," 42.

80. Ibid. See also Hays, *Moral Vision of the New Testament*, 218.

or a tribe or nation." For the Christian faith, therefore, to uphold its claim to comprehend "the whole of history, and not only the story of a particular people," it cannot simply be "a faith which gives meaning to history through memory" such as possessed by a particular people (*FH* 21–22). What is required, according to Niebuhr, is not a particular people capable of embodying a remembered past through its worship and practices, but religious symbols that reflect and articulate the universal human condition. "As a result, Niebuhr is simply unable to comprehend the radical [ecclesiological] perspective found in the New Testament."[81]

In his effort to relate the Christian faith to the problems of a fractured and fragmented world, Niebuhr offers a specific understanding of the relationship between the particular and the universal, between the particular claims of the Christian faith and the concern to find universal significance for human history that can give meaning to the struggles and perplexities of evil we both suffer and cause. The particular claims of the Christian faith obtain universal significance as that set of symbols that reveal humanity's paradoxical and tensive condition, the inevitability of the sin that issues from that condition, and the judgment and grace that enable and require ongoing commitment to the approximation of love through justice in particular situations. Christian symbols encourage realistic appraisal of social relationships and the balance of power within those relationships to produce a society in which there will be just enough (and no more) coercion and violence to stave off total chaos. Commitment to those symbols that make democracy possible and necessary creates a situation that in turn requires Christians to domesticate their faith for the sake of the prior claims of a communal harmony that recognizes no greater good than the harmony required to enable the limited pursuit of individual self-interest. The reality of a church defined by some good greater than the empty space provided by liberal democracy is not something Niebuhr acknowledges.

Niebuhr would resist the alternative dialectic between particularity and universality offered by Douglas Harink: "While the God of Israel is intent on saving the peoples of the earth through the power of the gospel, he does so by calling forth a people from among the peoples. The mission is universal, the means is always particular, timely, and local." Niebuhr

---

81. Hauerwas, "History as Fate," 43. I have substituted the word "ecclesiological" for Hauerwas' "eschatological"; while I certainly agree with the original statement, given other sentiments expressed by Hauerwas in his essay, I do not believe he would object to the change in emphasis.

would dismiss as irresponsible Harink's insistence that "the task of this people-among-peoples is not to acquire control of the helm of worldly history, but to enact an alternative history as a witness to the lordship of the crucified Christ among them and to bring praise to the God of Israel among the nations."[82] Harink describes a reality in which God's justice, God's way of setting things right, takes a very different shape from that envisioned by Niebuhr.

Whether Niebuhr's account simply represents the default setting by which many Christians understand how the Christian faith obtains public significance, or whether it is itself the operating program, is hard to say. What is obvious to others is that the ecclesial dimension of the gospel has suffered the eroding effects of a modernity that identifies self-interest as the defining feature of human existence. The demands of participation in a community defined not by self-interest but by a narrative placing the cross of Christ at the center of God's governance can only be perplexing in a setting that expects "religion" to service a society dedicated to the proposition that all are endowed with the inalienable right to live however they please. Niebuhr expresses an outlook concerned to manage the inevitable conflicts created by such an arrangement. What we will find in Ephesians is not an effort to manage such conflicts, but an account of how God calls the church to bear witness to a fundamentally different strategy for addressing the fracture and fragmentation that underlies them.

EPHESIANS AND THE ONE BODY OF CHRIST

We have approached Christian ethics as a task concerned with the question, "What is God doing about evil?" Evil, as Niebuhr recognized, most often has to do with the issues of division, hostility, conflict, and enmity narrated over and again in Scripture and echoed throughout history. The earliest biblical narratives describe sin as rupturing the relationship between God and humans, humans and the rest of creation, and humans from one another. The account of the sin of Adam and Eve in Genesis 3 is followed quickly by an instance of fratricide when Cain slays his brother Abel (Genesis 4). We do not have to read far into the Bible until we reach the sad description of Genesis 6:11—"And the earth was filled with violence." An original peace and blessing are now corrupted by human transgression, with the result a fragmented and fractured humanity.

---

82. Harink, *Paul among the Postliberals*, 243.

One major feature of this tragedy is that God's intent for humans to live in fellowship with one another (see Gen 2:18: "It is not good for the man to be alone") is threatened by the rivalry and conflict that too often dominate our lives.

Christian ethics has as one of its major tasks an account of how God addresses the evils that mark a world of conflict and hostility, enmity and division. What is God doing about bitter strife and contention, the sad ending of relationships in hatred and malice, or nations seemingly locked in unending war and injustice? God's good creation knew from the beginning the provision of fellowship and community that sin threatens and continues to corrupt. What is God doing about this? Niebuhr's response is that humans have access to symbols that inspire the formation of democratic institutions that, at their best, manage the conflict created by anxious and self-interested individuals. Ephesians will offer an alternative response: through God's redemptive work, God is creating *a people*. Since evil has a fundamental social quality to it, so also what God is doing about evil has a fundamental social character. Christian ethics will identify this social character as ecclesial in nature.[83] That is, Christian ethics has to do with God's creation of the church. As far as the Christian faith is concerned, and in spite of Niebuhr's neglect of this dynamic, "ecclesiology *is* ethics, and ethics *is* ecclesiology."[84] The ecclesial quality of Paul's moral vision for humanity is evident in the very character of his moral discourse. As Hays says, "Paul speaks only to the community of faith. He articulates no basis for a general ethics applicable to those outside the church."[85] This ecclesial focus, though, is not because Paul is a modern liberal who retreats from the public realm and limits the significance of the Christian faith to "religious" matters. Paul does not operate with the modernist notion of a public arena secular in character marked off and protected from a private arena of personal faith. What Paul asserts as the inherently social, relational dimension of salvation called "church" serves as public witness to the power of the gospel to reconcile. The split

83. Cavanaugh says, "If sin is scattering into mutual enmity—both between God and humanity and among humans—then redemption will take the form of restoring unity through participation in Christ's body" (*Theopolitical Imagination*, 13). See also his "Pilgrim People," 88–105.

84. Wannenwetsch, "Ecclesiology and Ethics," 59. See also Bonhoeffer (*Ethics*, 97), who even argues, "The starting point of Christian ethics is the body of Christ, the form of Christ in the form of the church."

85. Hays, *Moral Vision of the New Testament*, 33.

between personal faith and secular public is overcome with a faithful public named church.

The communal character of Paul's moral vision is nowhere more evident than in Ephesians. Paul displays this emphasis in many ways throughout the letter.[86] Throughout this variety, however, there is a recurring concern to understand the role of the church in terms of matters we have already met in our exploration of Ephesians.

Specifically, we must understand Paul's focus on the church in Ephesians in light of the twin concerns with which Paul introduces and concludes his letter—God's grace and peace (1:2; 6:23–24). Ephesians celebrates the divine initiative expressed through the redemptive work of Christ to restore a fractured creation and to reconcile humanity to God and to one another. Paul announces in Eph 1:9–10 the mystery of God's will, God's intent to unite all things together in Christ, the things in the heavens and the things upon the earth. That cosmic reconciliation is, according to Paul, "suitable to the fullness of the times" (1:10), and a broken world still waits for that day of healing. Yet God is at work now to demonstrate concretely how it is that the gospel reconciles. The historical, visible, tangible witness to the power of the gospel to reconcile is the church—the one body of Christ. Paul's ecclesial ethic may be explored as we first examine how the church as the body of Christ figures in God's *oikonomia*, God's plan to unite all things in Christ. We will then look at how Paul's parenesis in Ephesians 4–6 serves to affirm and enable the specific role the church plays in what God is doing about evil. In the last portion of this chapter we will examine how the claims of an ecclesial ethic take specific shape in one of the most challenging arenas of life—marriage.

God's *Oikonomia* and the Body of Christ

A fractured world awaits its ultimate reconciliation. Whether we detect that fracture at the intimate level of personal shame, the familial level of strained marriages, the social level of class and economic disparity, the cultural level of racial division, the global level of terrorism and warfare, or the conflict between humanity and the rest of creation, it is obvious that the vision of God's *oikonomia* announced in Eph 1:9–10 remains the

86. For a survey of the images employed in Ephesians to speak of the church, see Lincoln, "Theology of Ephesians," 91–102.

object of hope. Ephesians, however, does not, in the meantime, permit retreat from and/or resignation to a world marked by enmity and conflict. Ephesians proclaims a gospel that expresses both God's initiative of grace and God's agenda of peace on behalf of a conflicted creation. Essential to this gospel is the cross of Christ through which former enemies are made into "one new humanity" (2:15) and hostile parties are reconciled "in one body to God through the cross" (2:16). In this way and through this one body, God is now at work "establishing peace" (2:15). It is the task of this one body—the church—to embody a witness today to God's ultimate intent for all of creation, yet to be realized "in the fullness of time." The significance of this agenda and means of establishing peace is best understood as we examine those instances in Ephesians where Paul speaks of the church as "the body" of Christ.

Christ's Sovereign Power on Behalf of the Church

In Eph 1:15–23 Paul offers thanks on behalf of his readers for two reasons. First, he has heard of their "faith in the Lord Jesus Christ." He has also heard of their "love for all the saints." This pairing of the vertical ("faith in the Lord Jesus Christ") and horizontal ("love for all the saints") dimensions of Christian existence is simply one of the ways in which Paul underscores the significance of the relational aspect of life in Christ. In this prayer Paul also asks for God to open the eyes of his readers' hearts that they "might know what is the hope of [God's] calling." We earlier suggested that this calling has two aspects. First, Paul prays that his readers would realize how blessed they are to be part of God's people (1:18). Second, Paul prays that his readers would understand the magnitude of the power of God at work in their lives, a power measured by the resurrection of Christ from the dead (1:19–20). Paul describes the extent of that power in terms of Christ's triumph over the powers identified in 1:21–22.[87] What is the relationship between these two aspects of God's calling—inclusion in the people of God, the church, and Christ's triumph over the powers?

While Paul eventually unfolds the significance of this triumph over the powers in terms of new life in Christ (2:1–10), he first slips in a brief but noteworthy reference to the church as the body of Christ (1:22–23). Christ's triumph over the powers, established by his having been raised

---

87. The identity and character of these powers will be discussed below.

from the dead, is described by Paul in terms of Christ as "head over all things." Here, Paul speaks of Christ as "head" (*kephalē*) over the powers with respect to his authority over them.[88] His sovereignty over the powers, however, is on behalf of the church, Paul says, inasmuch as God has "put all things in subjection under his feet, and gave him as head over all things to the church, which is his body [*sōma*]" (1:22–23a).

A couple of concerns are critical for us to note here as they will figure significantly in other aspects of Paul's ecclesial ethic. First, the "head"/"body" language used here is of a different sort than what will show up in other places in Ephesians where this relationship is explored. In other locations in Ephesians, Christ is "head" in terms of his relationship to his "body" the church (4:15–16; 5:23). Here in Eph 1:22–23, though, Christ is "head," sovereign over "all things," specifically all the powers listed in 1:21. Christ is then "given as head over all things to the church." That is, Christ's "headship," or "sovereignty," over all the powers that otherwise threaten the purpose of God is a sovereignty that is for the benefit of Christ's body, the church. But here, the church is not related to Christ as its head in terms of the church's subjugation to Christ; it is the powers that are in subjection to Christ, the "head."[89]

Clearly, though, as Christ's body the church enjoys a unique relationship to Christ. The church is described as "the fullness of him who fills all in all" (1:23). The phrase comes with its share of interpretive difficulties,[90] but it seems to assert that while Christ's sovereign presence pervades the cosmos, he is particularly present and his sovereignty specifically on display in and through the church. Lincoln suggests that Paul's readers "are to sense their privileged status. Through its relation to the cosmic

88. Dawes, *Body in Question*, 139. Dawes argues that the allusion to Ps 8:7 in the same verse ("he has placed all things under his feet") makes the emphasis on Christ's authority over the powers clear.

89. "Strictly speaking," says Lincoln (*Ephesians*, 68), "the images of 'head' and 'body' are kept separate here. Christ's headship refers to his relation to the cosmos and then 'body' is brought in as a description of the Church to which Christ is given." See also Williams, *Paul's Metaphors*, 90. Williams cautions that Paul employs two distinct metaphors, the "head"/"body" metaphor and the "body" metaphor, and that "each metaphor stands on its own; each has its own meaning. Paul does not picture the church as a headless body or Christ as a bodiless head." Dawes (*Body in Question*, 248) speaks respectively of the "partitive" ("head"/"body") and "unitive" ("body") metaphors

90. O'Brien (*Ephesians*, 149) describes the phrase as "one of the most complex in Ephesians." Dawes (*Body in Question*, 236–50) commits a lengthy appendix to its investigation.

Christ, the Church, as his fullness, is the present focus for and medium of that presence, which now fills the cosmos in a hidden way but which will [eventually] do so openly and completely."[91] The question arises, though: what purpose does the church, as the present expression and display of Christ's sovereignty over the powers, have as creation awaits "the fullness of times"? That purpose becomes clearer as we examine other instances in Ephesians where Paul speaks of the church as the "body" of Christ.

Christ's Reconciling Work Displayed in the Church

In Eph 2:11–22 Paul describes the horizontal dimensions of God's formation of one new humanity as the formerly hostile parties of Jew and Gentile are reconciled to God through participation in the one body of Christ. To appreciate the significance of what Paul describes here and to underscore the role played by the body of Christ in God's *oikonomia*, a brief comparison with Eph 2:1–10 is important. There is a remarkable correspondence in terms of the shape and structure of Eph 2:11–22 with the earlier paragraph of 2:1–10. We have already seen that Paul's account of salvation in 2:1–10 is much more encompassing and life-affirming than some (e.g., Nietzsche's) understandings of salvation often maintain. When we consider the relationship between 2:1–10 and 2:11–22, we can see that Paul's account of salvation is also much more relational than is sometimes appreciated.

In both passages Paul makes use of the "once-now" pattern, contrasting a past life apart from Christ with a present life "in Christ Jesus."[92] In 2:1–10, Paul contrasts the *former* life of his Gentile readers (2:1–3) with the new life occasioned by God's grace (2:4–7). Those who once walked in their "trespasses and sins" are now "God's workmanship, created in Christ Jesus for good works . . . that we should walk in them" (2:10). In 2:12–22, Paul contrasts the *former* estrangement and alienation of his Gentile readers (2:12) with the inclusion of both Jewish and Gentile believers in the "one new humanity . . . one body to God" (2:13–18). Those who were once "strangers and aliens" are now "fellow-citizens with the saints and are of God's household"; they are "a holy temple in the

---

91. Lincoln, "Theology of Ephesians," 100.

92. Observance of the parallels is standard among commentators. See, for example, O'Brien, *Ephesians*, 183–85; Lincoln, *Ephesians*, 124–26; Gorman, *Apostle of the Crucified Lord*, 511.

Lord . . . a dwelling of God in the Spirit" (2:19–22). If in 2:1–10 God's saving work through Christ creates new life out of death, in 2:11–22 God's
reconciling work overcomes the enmity between formerly hostile parties
and establishes peace in the one body of Christ. As in Paul's thanksgiving in 1:15 and his intercessory prayer of 1:16–23, so also in Ephesians
2 are both the vertical and horizontal dimensions of God's redemptive
work in Christ explored and celebrated. The parallels between 2:1–10 and
2:11–22 indicate that just as new life in Christ is basic to God's work of
salvation, so also is this new life in Christ new life in the one body of
Christ.

The "body" metaphor is one of many Paul employs in 2:11–22 to
speak of the relational/horizontal dimensions of the Christian life. The
images of "citizenship" and "household" (2:19), "building," and "temple"
(2:21) all offer various shades of the significance of the corporate aspects
of new life in Christ. It is the "body" metaphor, though, that underscores
the connection between this passage and what Ephesians announces
earlier about God's *oikonomia*, God's plan to unite all things together in
Christ.

Paul unfolds a number of key emphases in this portion of Ephesians,
but central to the letter's theme as a whole is his assertion in 2:14: "For he
[Christ] himself is our peace, who made both groups into one." For Paul
there is no more glaring expression of a world marked by enmity and
division than the hostility between Jew and Gentile.[93] He insists, though,
that the very purpose of the death of Jesus on the cross was that "he might
make the two into one new humanity, thus establishing peace, and might
reconcile them both in one body to God through the cross, by it having
put to death the enmity" (2:15–16). As Dawes puts it, "This 'one body' is
the locus of Christ's reconciling activity."[94]

The final realization of God's plan to unite all things in Christ awaits
"the fullness of the times" (1:10). Already, though, God has created
through the cross the present expression of that ultimate reconciliation
in a community, the very existence of which is testimony to the power of
the gospel to reconcile. The "one body," Dawes observes, is variously described in this passage. Parallel phrases such as "in his flesh" and "in himself" (2:15) highlight the significance of Paul's language of the church as

93. See Yee, "The Gentiles as the Jews Saw Them," in *Jews, Gentiles and Ethnic Reconciliation*, 72–87. See also Lau, *Politics of Peace*, 82–86.

94. Dawes, *Body in Question*, 159.

the body of Christ.[95] Paul insists that Christ "himself is our peace" (2:14) and that "in himself he might make the two [Jewish and Gentile believers] into one new humanity, establishing peace" (2:15). These parallels suggest that with the phrase "one body" Paul offers the most profound affirmation of the church's identification with Christ as the concrete and tangible expression in this world of the divine agenda for peace. In this context, the church is identified in a way that is almost indistinguishable from Christ. If in 1:23 Paul affirms that Christ's presence dwells in the church in a unique way so as to display his sovereignty over the powers, here in 2:16 Paul affirms that the church is the very presence of Christ in this world so as to display the power of the gospel to reconcile hostile parties.

One further matter deserves attention at this point. Dawes insists, "It is important to note that in Eph 2:16 *sōma* ["body"] stands alone; it is not associated with *kephalē* ('head')."[96] In this way, as was the case in 1:23, identification between Christ and the church is made even stronger as there is no contrast or distinction implied between Christ as "head" and the church as "body." In 1:19–23, Paul announces that the church as the body of Christ enjoys and displays the sovereignty of Christ over the powers. In 2:11–22, Paul reveals that the church as the body of Christ embodies the reconciling work of God in Christ. How these two dimensions of the church as the body of Christ are related to one another, as well as to God's *oikonomia*, becomes apparent in Paul's next use of the "body" metaphor in Eph 3:6.

The Mystery of Christ and the Witness of the Church

New Testament scholars routinely characterize Ephesians 3 in terms that suggest its secondary significance.[97] One even expresses bewilderment at why twelve verses (3:2–13) are devoted "to an exposition of Paul's status."[98] Timothy Gombis, though, insists the passage, in which Paul recounts his role and suffering as an apostle "for the sake of you Gentiles"

95. Ibid. Thus, to use Dawes's language, this passage employs the "unitive" ("body") rather than the "partitive" ("head"/"body") metaphor.

96. Ibid., 160.

97. Jeal (*Integrating Theology and Ethics*, 174), describes the chapter formally as a digression, the thought of which perhaps enhances the themes of Ephesians, even if the material is "not crucial to the logic of the epistle."

98. Kitchen, *Ephesians*, 30.

(3:1), serves the larger argument of Ephesians by detailing how God's triumph in Christ over the powers is displayed through Paul's apostleship.[99] How this is so has much to do with what it means for the church to be the body of Christ.

In an account of his imprisonment by the Roman authorities, Paul draws together several emphases that have already appeared in Ephesians to make it clear that, all appearances to the contrary, his imprisonment "is not a defeat, but rather epitomizes the triumph of God in Christ."[100] Matters of God's mystery, God's plan (*oikonomia*) to unite all things together in Christ, are raised in 1:9–10. Paul announces Christ's triumph over the powers on behalf of the church, the body of Christ, in 1:19–23. Christ's triumph over the powers finds concrete expression, even in the present age, when those who were once dead in their trespasses and sins enjoy new life in Christ (2:1–10), and when those who were once separate from Christ and excluded from the commonwealth of Israel are now reconciled along with believing Jews "in one body to God through the cross" (2:11–22).

In Ephesians 3, however, Paul's apostleship to the Gentiles figures centrally in all these matters. The mystery of God's plan (*oikonomia*; 1:9–10) is now Paul's "stewardship" (*oikonomia*), graciously given by God to Paul as by way of revelation Paul obtains "insight into the mystery of Christ" (3:2–3). The mystery proclaimed by Paul is specifically "that the Gentiles are fellow-heirs [*synklēronoma*] and fellow-members of the body [*sussōma*] and fellow-partakers [*summetoxa*] of the promise in Christ Jesus through the gospel" (3:6).[101] Paul's proclamation of this mystery is precisely the means by which God creates the church, the one body of Christ comprised of the formerly hostile parties of Jews and Gentiles (3:8–9). The mystery of God's will in 1:9–10, however, is the uniting of *all things* in Christ. If the joining together of Jews and Gentiles as fellow members of the body of Christ is the mystery revealed in Ephesians 3, then it is a more narrow expression of the wider mystery of God's will announced in Ephesians 1.[102] In addition, Dawes notes, "Eph 2:11–22

99. Gombis, "Triumph of God in Christ," 86–105.

100. Ibid., 89.

101. The body imagery here is used once again, as in 1:23 and 2:16, without the use of "head" imagery. This "unitive" (Dawes) use of this metaphor will be important to our examination of the "head"/"body" language in 5:22–33.

102. Caragounis (*Ephesian Mysterion*, 118) describes Paul's account of "the mystery" in Ephesians 3 as "a more particular facet of the general, programmatic use of the concept in ch. 1."

makes it quite clear that this process [of joining Jew and Gentile in the body of Christ] has already been completed." Yet, in Eph 1:9–10, the uniting of all things together in Christ is something that awaits "the fullness of the times." It must be the case, then, "that the (already achieved) reconciliation of Jew and Gentile within the one body of Christ is a 'proleptic realization' of 'the mystery of his will' (1:9)," a concrete expression in the present of what God intends to accomplish most fully in the future.[103] As Yoder says, "The church is . . . 'first fruits': it is or is to be in itself the beginning of what is to come."[104]

We see how important this mystery is to the character of the gospel Paul proclaims when we understand what role the church as the body of Christ plays with reference to the powers. What Paul calls "the mystery" in 3:3–4, in 3:10 he calls "the manifold wisdom of God,"[105] and he announces that it is "through the church" that this wisdom is now made known "to the rulers [*tais arxais*] and authorities [*tais exousiais*]." While some have suggested that Paul here indicates the preaching role of the church and a prophetic task with respect to the nations at large,[106] the task of preaching in this passage goes to Paul himself (3:8), and the church is described not as "the subject of the making known but the means through which it takes place." How so, if not through preaching? Paul's argument suggests that it is by the "very existence as a new humanity, in which the major division of the first-century world has been overcome, [that] the Church reveals God's secret in action."[107] It is by the very presence in the world of a community defined not by ethnicity, race, or socioeconomic status, whose unity in Christ overcomes ancient hatreds and conflicts, that God makes known to the rulers and authorities—the powers—God's wisdom, God's mystery, God's *oikonomia*. If it is through the resurrection of Christ that God's triumph over the powers is achieved, it is also through the resurrection of Christ that Gentiles and Jews are given new life in the one body of Christ, the present expression of God's plan to reconcile a fractured cosmos. And it is through the presence in the world of this witness to the capacity of the gospel to reconcile that God's triumph

103. Dawes, *Body in Question*, 188.

104. Yoder, "Why Ecclesiology Is Social Ethics," 125–26.

105. Caragounis (*Ephesians* Mysterion, 108), says Paul's move from the use of "mystery" to "wisdom" reflects "an interblending of conceptual components between these two terms."

106. For example, Wink, *Naming the Powers*, 89–96.

107. Lincoln, *Ephesians*, 186–87.

over the powers is made evident. How the making known of this mystery has any bearing on the task of an ecclesial ethic becomes clearer as we determine more precisely the character of "the rulers and authorities" that are witness to the mystery of the church.[108]

If all we had in Ephesians about the powers was what we read in Eph 1:21, then matters might not be so complicated. Likewise, if all we had in Ephesians about the powers was what we read in Eph 6:10–12, then certain conclusions concerning their identity might be obvious. An initial encounter by a first-century Ephesian audience with a list referring to "all rule [*arxēs*] and authority [*exousias*] and power [*dunameōs*] and dominion [*kuriotētos*]" (1:21) would likely suggest to them the titles of various offices and positions within the administrative system of the Roman Empire. Ephesians 6:10–12, though, names these powers as "the spiritual forces of wickedness in the heavenly places." Paul again speaks of the "rulers" (*arxas*) and the "powers" (*exousias*) here, though, in "what is essentially . . . a heaping up of terms to describe the ineffable, invisible world-enveloping reach of a spiritual network of powers inimical to life."[109]

The apparent contrast between Ephesians 1 and Ephesians 6 on the identity of the powers funds competing theories on the issue. Yoder Neufeld describes a continuum of views concerning the powers in Ephesians. At one end of the spectrum (highlighting the language of Ephesians 1) is the insistence that terms such as "rulers" and "authorities" primarily refer to "impersonal social and cultural forces, structures, and institutions that bring war, violence, and oppression." At the other end (emphasizing features of Ephesians 6) is the view that these terms refer to "personal demonic forces" that confront the church with the challenge of "spiritual warfare."[110] Obviously, as Yoder Neufeld says, "Christians are at quite different points in their view of the powers and in the task that implies for the church."[111] Perhaps Paul's reference to "the rulers and the authorities in the heavenly places" in Eph 3:10 can help clarify matters.

---

108. For a helpful survey of some of the literature on this widely discussed issue, but one whose conclusions are not completely shared here, see Lincoln, "Liberation from the Powers," 335–54.

109. Wink, *Naming the Powers*, 85.

110. Yoder Neufeld, *Ephesians*, 355. Wink (*Naming the Powers*) is generally understood to represent the first of these views. As we shall see, though, his view is actually more nuanced than that. The second view is most ably presented by Arnold, *Ephesians*.

111. Yoder Neufeld, *Ephesians*, 357.

We have already had occasion to note Paul's use of the phrase "heavenly places" in Ephesians. With this phrase, Paul insists that the world in which the church witnesses to the mystery of Christ cannot be reduced to the immediate and the apparent. Yet, the phrase cannot be taken as referring to some sort of transcendent existence or realm that has no bearing on the concrete realities of the world in which we live. While believers, for example, have been "co-raised and co-seated *in the heavenly places* in Christ Jesus" (2:6), that does not mean they have left this world behind or experience some sort of disembodied, ahistorical existence; rather, such a situation—having been "created in Christ Jesus"—makes possible the walk in good works with all its various responsibilities, relationships, and challenges in this world. The same sort of expansive definition of reality needs to be brought to our understanding of the "rulers and authorities" in Eph 3:10.

The rulers and the authorities that are witness to the church's display of God's wisdom must not simply be viewed as mundane and "earthbound" in character. And yet, we cannot dismiss the larger setting in which the church's witness to the powers is discussed. Paul's argument in Ephesians 3 is that his imprisonment and consequent tribulations (3:1, 13), which appear to contradict the triumph of God in Christ over the powers, are "actually an epitome—a concrete manifestation—of that triumph."[112] How so?

Gombis argues that Paul identifies two ways in this passage by which the triumph of God in Christ over the powers is displayed. First, through God's creation of the church, "one unified, multi-racial body consisting of formerly divided groups of people," God makes known God's "multifaceted and many-splendored wisdom."[113] Second, though, Paul stresses that his own situation as imprisoned apostle plays an important role. An important feature of all this is that Paul's circumstances reflect the paradoxical dynamic of the gospel itself. The gospel is preached by "the prisoner of Jesus Christ"—Paul, who calls himself "the least of all the saints" and whose weakness and tribulation come at the hand of the powers. Gombis observes, "Paul is in a position of utter defeat at the hands of the powers, being completely in their grasp. Seen in terms of the present age, he could not be in a weaker, more shameful or more vulnerable position." Even so, "it is by his preaching of the gospel that the creative power of

---

112. Gombis, "Triumph of God in Christ," 100.

113. Ibid., 98.

God is unleashed and engaged, and the church—the arena of the triumph of God—is called into being, thereby displaying the wisdom of God to the powers."[114]

The powers appeared to have the upper hand against Jesus. When Rome kills you, you are supposed to stay dead. Yet God, having raised Christ from the dead, "seated him at the right hand in the heavenly places, far above all rule and authority and power and dominion" (1:20–21). The powers appeared to have the upper hand against Paul, whom they imprisoned. When Rome imprisons you, it is for the purpose of shame and dishonor.[115] And yet, it is through the proclamation of Paul the prisoner that God brings the church into being so that the mystery of the gospel, God's way of reconciling divided humanity, "might now be made known to the rulers and the authorities in the heavenly places" (3:10). Such circumstances are the occasion not for shame but for glory, says Paul (3:11), as they display God's triumph over the powers.

Paul's account in 3:1–13, however, moves from reference to his Roman imprisonment to an insistence that his circumstances figure in the church's witness to "the rulers and authorities in the heavenly places." If in Ephesians 1 the language of the "rulers and authorities" suggests engagement with very real earthly powers, but Ephesians 6 indicates encounter with powerful spiritual beings, what do we have in Ephesians 3?

A growing view in biblical scholarship is that Paul certainly warns believers that our conflict with evil cannot be reduced to mundane and manageable forces of human social and cultural institutions and structures, but that we have to contend with hostile spiritual forces that steadfastly oppose the good God intends for creation. And yet, those forces operate in and through the very concrete and historical social and cultural institutions that are basic to human experience. Wink offers an account that rejects the conventional division between "spiritual" and "material," insisting that the powers of which Paul speaks "are both visible *and* invisible, earthly *and* heavenly, spiritual *and* institutional." The "rulers and authorities" of Eph 3:10, for example, "possess an outer, physical manifestation . . . and an inner, spiritual reality."[116] Paul's account in Ephesians 3 of the church's witness to the powers of the wisdom of God, in spite of Paul's imprisonment and tribulation at the hands of the

---

114. Ibid., 99.

115. On this see Rapske, *Book of Acts in Its First-Century Setting*, 283–312.

116. Wink, *Engaging the Powers*, 3.

Roman Empire, suggests that Paul sees a very close connection between the power of Rome expressed through its administrative structures and institutions and the "spiritual forces of wickedness in the heavenly places" (6:12).[117] In this sense, then, "these rulers and authorities are not simply invisible spiritual realities residing in a distant heaven, but centers of power deeply affecting human life" through the looming presence and power of Rome.[118]

Paul insists in Ephesians 3 that the existence of a community that embodies the gospel's capacity to reconcile serves as witness of God's wisdom to the rulers and authorities embodied in the ways of Rome. What, then, is the significance of the church as the body of Christ in terms of God's triumph over the evil that fractures and fragments humanity? It has everything to do with competing versions of what counts for peace and how peace is achieved and maintained. It has everything to do with what Paul says about the divine initiative and agenda. On the one hand is the offer and demand of *Pax Romana*, Roman peace. On the other hand is the offer and challenge of *Pax Christi*, the peace of Christ. Paul's imprisonment itself expresses the character and tactics of *Pax Romana*. The body of Christ, created by God through Paul's proclamation of the mystery of Christ, testifies to the peace of Christ. It is this counter-testimony by the church as the body of Christ that reveals the character of the ecclesial nature of a Christian ethic.[119]

---

117. Paul is not unique in this assessment as far as the New Testament goes. The temptation accounts in Matthew (4:8–9) and Luke (4:6–7) depict the "kingdoms of the world," which certainly included the Roman Empire, as under the sway of the devil. Mark's account of the Gerasene demoniac (5:1–20) names the demon "Legion" after the basic unit of the Roman military. Of course, the book of Revelation presents the Roman Empire as representative of and authorized by "a great red dragon . . . who is called the devil and Satan" (12:3, 9; 13:4). For discussion of this point, see Carter, *Roman Empire and the New Testament*, 16–18.

118. Yoder Neufeld, *Ephesians*, 145. Elsewhere (*"Put on the Armour of God,"* 123–24), Yoder Neufeld insists, "This characterization of the powers prevents a choice between sociologically and politically identifiable 'powers' and those perceived as 'spiritual' and thus described mythologically. Both are intended. Better yet, the author of Ephesians would not have seen these as alternative categories, but as diverse manifestations of a seamless web of reality hostile to God."

119. Paul's very use of "body" imagery for the church as the arena of God's peace suggests he is making an explicit contrast with the claims of *Pax Romana*. The use of "body" imagery in appeals for unity in the Roman Empire is widely attested; for example, Marcus Aurelius, *Med.* 2.1; 7.13; Epictetus, *Diss.* 2.10-3-4; Seneca, *Ep.* 95.52. See further Lau, *Politics of Peace*, 108–10.

The Rome that crucified Jesus and imprisoned Paul expressed an ideology that combined imperial religion with imperial conquest as the foundation for and justification of its vision of peace. Roman emperors, identified in ancient inscriptions as "savior" and "the son of God," were viewed as the great benefactors of the world, whose victories in battle were announced as "good news" (*euangelion*, "gospel") and whose rule brought peace.[120] Of course, *Pax Romana* was of a particular sort achieved and maintained at a particular price. As Klaus Wengst puts it, "The peace which Rome brings is a victory-peace for the Romans, while for the vanquished it is a peace of subjugation. . . . Peace produced and maintained by military force is accompanied with streams of blood and tears of unimaginable proportions."[121] The Roman historian Tacitus reports the sentiment of the Batavian prince Civilis that the Romans "falsely gave to a wretched slavery the name of peace" (*Histories* 4.17.2). He voices the indictment of the Briton general Calgacus against the Romans: "to plunder, butcher, steal, these things [the Romans] misname empire; they make a desolation and call it peace" (*Agricola* 31.2).

To contrast the vision of peace offered in Ephesians with the brand of peace pursued by the Roman Empire might meet with any number of objections by contemporary Christians, particularly those trained in the ways of Western liberal democratic traditions. We are quick to assign the New Testament language of "peace" to a restricted role, limited to "peace with God" or peaceable relations between individuals. After all, even Christians in America will often affirm a strong affinity for a type of *Pax Americana* when we speak today of "peace through strength" and claim national prerogative to use whatever military means are necessary to preserve America's standing in the world. Paul *must* be talking about some other brand of peace than that which has to do with social groups and political powers in the world!

It has become increasingly apparent in contemporary biblical scholarship, however, that an "apolitical" reading of the New Testament in general, and of Paul in particular, is no longer possible. As N. T. Wright insists, "We must recognize that the modern western separation of theology and society, religion and politics, would have made no sense either to Paul or to his contemporaries, whether Jewish, Greek, or Roman."[122]

120. For examples, see Price, "Rituals and Power," 47–71.

121. Wengst, *Pax Romana and the Peace of Jesus Christ*, 13–14.

122. Wright, *Paul: In Fresh Perspective*, 60. Warren Carter provides a survey of recent scholarship on the issue in "Paul and the Roman Empire," 7–26.

Ephesians, specifically, has become recognized as a document strongly reflecting the general posture of the Apostle Paul and the character of his apostolic endeavors *vis á vis* the Roman Empire. Margaret MacDonald notes, "Ephesians was proclaimed in a society saturated with symbols of imperial power" and its "politically charged language" offers an explicit contrast to the "imperial propaganda for . . . *Pax Romana*."[123] When read without the blinders imposed by a modernist privatization of religion, the message of Ephesians becomes apparent: "Not the emperor, but Christ himself is the true bringer of peace and the reconciler."[124] Specifically, the contrast to the claims of *Pax Romana* is put on display through the church, the body of Christ who "is himself our peace."

Christian ethics asks the question, "What is God doing about evil?" Scripture depicts that evil in terms that are social and communal; also, the regular insistence in Scripture is that what God is doing about evil has to do with the creation of a people called to embody what God has intended for humanity from the beginning.[125] It is crucial to note, however, that Paul asserts in Ephesians that the gospel is the means by which God is at work creating such a people, not in the absence of community and peace, but in contrast to a false vision of community and peace. *Pax Romana* signaled a brand of peace and social order that offered security and benefit to a privileged elite that came at the expense of conquered peoples; its legitimacy was presented and its benefits accessed in the imperial cult where the emperor's obvious power was celebrated and channeled to favored clients of the empire; its ultimate symbol was the cross that served to sustain the order of the empire through intimidation and

123. MacDonald, "Politics of Identity in Ephesians," 425, 438. Similarly, Gosnell L. Yorke insists, "When the early Christians (Jews and Gentiles alike) in Ephesus and elsewhere in Asia Minor . . . heard and saw the letter performed, it is inconceivable that peace (*eirēnē*) would not have generated acoustic resonance with the *Pax Romana*. . . . Rather, the statistics and sound of *eirēnē* in Ephesians strongly suggest that we are dealing here with a veiled but critical engagement with Roman imperial ideology and propaganda." See his "Hearing the Politics of Peace in Ephesians," 120.

124. Schnelle, *Theology of the New Testament*, 562.

125. It should not surprise us that in Eph 2:15 Paul once again employs the language of creation (*ktisē*) to describe God's reconciling work that creates "one new humanity . . . the one body," or that Paul's account in 3:9–10 of the revelation of God's manifold wisdom through the church to the powers is the work of the God "who created all things" (*ta panta ktisanti*). If, as earlier explored, Paul's language of salvation through Christ describes that work in terms of the fulfillment of what God has intended for humanity from the beginning ("created in Christ Jesus," 2:10), then his ecclesial language of reconciliation in 2:11–22 and 3:1–13 strikes the same chord.

threat of violence. It was peace of a sort, but of a sort where the fracture and divisions within humanity were not genuinely resolved in reconciliatio but managed through oppressive presence.

Paul's diagnosis of such a vision is that it represents, in quite concrete and historical fashion, a transcendent form of evil inexplicable simply in terms of immanent and mundane forces of imperial politics and militaristic expansionism. What is God doing about that evil? The divine initiative and agenda proclaim God's redemptive work through Christ, who creates out of formerly hostile parties one new humanity—the body of Christ. Through the very presence in the world of this body, God's *oikonomia*—God's wisdom, God's intent to reconcile fractured humanity—is put on display. In explicit contrast to false visions of peace and community that really only express "the stratagems of the devil" (6:11), the redemptive work of God achieves what God has intended from the beginning. By God's grace, humanity can know God's peace.

Does God intend the church, the body of Christ, the one new humanity made up of reconciled enemies, to bear witness of the divine agenda of peace to the rulers and authorities? Surely the church must restrict itself to properly spiritual matters, and its talk of peace must be of a different sort than public matters of conflict and turmoil among the nations. William S. Campbell insists, however, "To depict the peace that Christ enables merely as a sentimental, internalized emotion experienced only in worship, is to deny the gospel of Christ and its power to transform even the most depraved societies or individuals. 'He is our peace' . . . is a real political and social peace that Christ enables and, moreover, demands of those who truly belong to His kingdom."[126]

Perhaps it is Campbell's reminder that this vision of an ecclesial ethic "demands" certain commitments and practices of those who belong to God's kingdom that drives the concern to accept a brand of faith that frees Christians to employ alternative methods for addressing matters of conflict among the nations. Yoder is explicit in his suspicion that the church has so often accepted such arrangements because of "the natural concern to shun the risk of . . . [an] allegiance bound to the crucified Jesus and the cost of following his way."[127] What God is doing about evil,

126. W. S. Campbell, "Unity and Diversity in the Church," 24–25.

127. Yoder, "Why Ecclesiology Is Social Ethics," 111. Niebuhr interestingly comments (*HN* 147) that the "historic incarnation of a perfect love . . . actually transcends history, and can appear in it only to be crucified." One might ask if Niebuhr's willingness to subordinate Christian identity to democratic institutions is intended to avoid this cost.

though, has everything to do with the formation of a people who will display in this world the pattern of God's *oikonomia*, God's way of reconciling a fractured creation. Of course, God's way of reconciling is the way of the crucified Christ. What demands that implies for the body of Christ are such practices and commitments that reflect and sustain the identity of the church as the one new humanity. The parenesis of Eph 4:1—6:20 indicates something of what those practices and commitments look like, and thus something of how the church presently participates in and demonstrates God's triumph through Christ over the powers.

The Worthy Walk and the Body of Christ

Paul begins his moral exhortation in Ephesians 4–6 by insisting on a close connection with what he has so far had to say in his letter. The "therefore" of 4:1 implies a relationship between the admonitions of 4:1—6:20 and "the earlier chapters' depiction of what God has done in Christ for human well-being."[128] That he encourages his readers to "walk worthy of your calling" echoes his prayer of 1:18–23 that they "may know what is the hope of [God's] calling." That calling is precisely what God has done in Christ for human well-being, and now Paul indicates that there is a fitting response on the part of his readers that finds its measure in that calling.[129]

In Paul's earlier prayer, that calling has two features: the blessing of inclusion in the people of God (the church), and the great power of God displayed through Christ's triumph over the powers (for the sake of the church). We have explored how Paul's account of the church as the "body of Christ" reveals the close relationship between those two dimensions of the one hope of God's calling. It is through the one body of Christ that the power of the gospel to reconcile is revealed to the powers. The Christ who has been given to the church as sovereign over the powers is also the

128. Lincoln, *Ephesians*, 234. Jeal (*Integrating Theology and Ethics*, 177–78) insists that the relationship is strictly rhetorical and not causal and that there are even elements "in Ephesians 1–3 that are in apparent contradiction to the moral exhortations of chapters 4–6." We have already suggested that Jeal (like many interpreters of Ephesians) overestimates the "realized" aspects of the eschatology of Ephesians.

129. The language of "worthy" (4:1) renders Paul's use of *axios* and indicates reference to a standard of measure by which daily life with all its responsibilities, challenges, and temptations must be judged. "Here in Ephesians," says Lincoln (*Ephesians*, 235), "the criterion and the determining factor for believers' living is to be the call itself."

Christ who reconciles formerly hostile parties in one body to God. That work of reconciliation is the divine mystery/wisdom that the church now makes known to "the rulers and authorities in the heavenly places." The very existence of the church testifies to an alternative brand of peace and social order than that offered by *Pax Romana*. The church is called into being in order to participate in and put on display God's triumph over evil. The church does this through a walk worthy of that calling. That is, as Gombis puts it, the parenesis of Ephesians 4–6 articulates "the manner in which the church is to participate in the triumph of God in Christ over the powers and authorities ruling the present evil age."[130]

We will not pursue here a detailed analysis of every aspect of Paul's moral exhortations in Ephesians 4–6. A few general observations concerning the overall thrust of these chapters will make clear, though, that for Paul the moral life that God intends for humanity, as an ecclesial ethic, finds expression in the "one new humanity" (2:15) and is measured by whatever sustains and supports "the unity of the Spirit in the bond of peace" (4:3).

Boundary Issues

One feature that needs mention is that this entire portion of the letter is enclosed within a twofold reference to Paul's current status: he is "the prisoner of the Lord" (4:1) as well as "an ambassador in chains" (6:20). This use of "inclusion" (marking off the boundaries of a passage by paired ideas or themes) suggests that Paul's own imprisonment needs to be kept in mind as a point of reference for understanding the moral exhortation found within these borders. We have already seen how Paul's imprisonment is a paradoxical demonstration of God's triumph over the powers. In Eph 3:1–13 the confident proclamation of Paul the prisoner is the means by which God creates a multicultural church that reveals the power of the gospel to effect true peace in contrast to the false peace of the powers. In 6:19–20 the "ambassador in chains" asks his readers to pray for him that he may confidently make known "the mystery of the gospel," the very message that God employs to create the one body of Christ. The bracketing of Paul's parenesis within this twofold reference to his imprisonment suggests to his readers that "just as Paul's position of shame and humiliation makes manifest the triumph of God in Christ,

130. Gombis, "Triumph of God in Christ," 133.

so too they are to follow his example and see to it that they actualize the triumph of God in Christ in their life together as the community of God's people."[131] We should expect there to be, then, a similarly paradoxical quality to the way in which this triumph will be actualized through Paul's ecclesial ethic.

Another structural feature of these chapters provides an important clue as to the character of the ecclesial ethic offered in Ephesians. While the admonitory character of Ephesians 4–6 is obvious, more subtle analysis of the chapters distinguishes 4:1–16 and 6:10–20 from the more properly parenetic portions extending from 4:17—6:9. These two passages provide the outer framework within which the more explicit parenesis of these chapters is contextualized.

The first section, Eph 4:1–16, while it begins with an admonitory tone (4:1–3), quickly moves to an account of the unity of Christian fellowship in the body of Christ (4:4–6), in which the triumphant Christ is at work to gift his church (4:7–12) with the resources needed for its ongoing growth as the body of Christ toward a maturity measured by Christ himself (4:13–16). The last section, Eph 6:10–20, concludes the parenesis with a challenge for the church to engage in the conflict with evil by putting on the divine armor, that is, by engaging in the conflict in the same manner as does God. These passages provide the setting in which the admonitions of 4:17—6:9 must be evaluated and their function made clear.[132] Paul's moral instructions in Ephesians are not simply about matters of personal moral purity or individual moral achievement.[133] The "worthy walk" encouraged by Paul is a way of life that reflects and sustains the unity, fellowship, and growth toward Christlikeness of the one body of Christ and is itself the means by which the church engages in the

---

131. Ibid., 110. See also Wild, "Warrior and the Prisoner," 284–98.

132. Frank J. Matera notes, "The paraenesis of Ephesians . . . is prefaced by an exhortation to maintain the unity of the church (4:1–16), and it concludes with an exhortation to put on the armor of God, since believers are engaged in a cosmic struggle (6:10–20). Consequently . . . Ephesians views the moral life against the horizon of the church universal, which is engaged in a cosmic struggle." See his *New Testament Ethics*, 220.

133. See Reinhard, "Ephesians 6:10–18," 521–32. Reinhard emphasizes that Paul's admonition to "put on" (*endusasthe*) the divine armor in 6:11 echoes the admonition in 4:24 to "put on [*endusasthai*] the new humanity," which she rightly understands as "putting on Christ" (531). She fails to note, however, that this "new humanity" has also been previously described with the corporate imagery of the "one body" in 2:15–16. See Lau, *Politics of Peace*, 148.

conflict with evil in the same manner as God. In other words, the divine armor described in Eph 6:10–12 is largely a summary of the ecclesial ethic of Eph 4:17—6:9, as well as the indication of its significance.[134] It matters whether or not the church engages in practices that reflect God's truth, justice, and peace—practices that embody the impact of the gospel—for by such practices the church participates in and puts on display what God is doing about evil as it models an alternative mode of society than that embodied by *Pax Romana*. A closer look at Paul's moral instruction in Ephesians 4–6 reveals how this is so.

The Worthy Walk

The parenesis of Ephesians 4–6 manifests several key features as it describes how the one body of Christ provides a concrete witness to the powers of God's *oikonomia*. Paul's ecclesial ethic calls for the formation of a distinctive community that displays a cruciform way of life. We can explore how the parenesis of Ephesians 4–6 serves Paul's ecclesial ethic by examining its focus on a 1) community 2) of contrast that 3) takes the cross of Christ as the pattern for its distinctive form of communal witness.

Certainly Paul begins his parenesis in Ephesians 4–6 with a strong emphasis on the ecclesial context of the worthy walk. The initial section of 4:1–16 clearly stresses participation in the "one body" (4:4), in which each member is graciously gifted by the triumphant Christ (4:7–10) to serve in ways that strengthen and "build up" the "body of Christ" (4:12). Toward this end, Christ the head of the body provides the resources necessary for each member to contribute to the ongoing "growth of the body" toward a maturity measured by the likeness of Christ himself (4:13–16).

The communal emphasis, however, permeates Paul's moral instruction in Ephesians. Paul's insistence, for example, that believers "speak truth, each one of you with your neighbor" reflects his understanding that his readers are "members of one another" (4:25; *allēlōn*, "one another"). He gives repeated attention to this "one another" dimension of the moral life within the church (4:2), encouraging his readers to avoid attitudes and dispositions that threaten relationships (bitterness, anger, wrath, clamor, and malice), calling instead for practices that strengthen the bonds of fellowship: "be kind to one another [*allēlous*], compassionate,

---

134. Yoder Neufeld, *"Put on the Armour of God,"* 110–11.

forgiving each other as God in Christ has forgiven you" (4:31–32). The ecclesial dimension of the life of believers is most obvious when Paul describes the gathered community in worship, thanksgiving, and mutual service ("subjecting yourselves to one another" [*allēlous*], 5:21) as the arena in which the Holy Spirit is at work to grant the guidance needed to "walk not as the unwise, but as the wise" (5:15–21). Paul says much in his parenesis that has been taken simply as general moral admonition to a virtuous way of life that any ancient Hellenistic moralist would recommend. To draw such a conclusion is to miss the running emphasis on practices that highlight "the corporate dimension of believers' existence" as "foundational to their living in the world." For Paul, "Christian ethics is first of all a call to participate in a distinctive community, the Church."[135]

The instruction in 5:15 to "walk not as the unwise, but as the wise," though, illustrates another key feature of Paul's ethical instruction in Ephesians. The "not"/"but" contrast is but one of several ways in Ephesians by which Paul emphasizes what Michael Gorman calls "one of the persistent themes in the entire New Testament . . . the need for believers to be different from their old selves and from their nonbelieving neighbors."[136] Paul's moral vision does not simply emphasize the communal character of the moral life of believers; he also wants to stress the importance of the Christian community as a moral alternative to the mode of community and social relations exhibited in the surrounding culture. While Niebuhr would mock this as pretentious, Paul insists on it as necessary.

Within the boundaries of Paul's emphasis on the unity of the body of Christ (4:1–16) and the call to conflict with the powers (6:10–20), the parenesis proper begins with the challenge for believers to "walk no longer as the Gentiles walk" (4:17). For believers to continue in the way of life that marked previous patterns of thought and conduct would simply be incongruous with the truth that they have believed (cf. 1:13) and affirmed in their turning to Christ (4:20–21). Believers are, as if changing garments, to "put off the old self," that way of life that belongs to and characterizes the present evil age that will not bear the test of time and eternity (4:22). In contrast, they are to "put on the new self," that way of life that reflects and embodies the just and holy existence that God intended for creation from the beginning (4:23–24).

135. Lincoln, *Ephesians*, 269.
136. Gorman, *Apostle of the Crucified Lord*, 519.

The call for a clear contrast between former and present existence is repeated, but with different imagery, in 5:3–14. The change is not from old clothing to new, but from darkness to light (5:8). Paul's view of the Gentile world is strongly negative. In both 4:17–19 and 5:3–5, Paul highlights sins of sexual impurity and greed as characteristic of Gentile conduct. Conduct representative of the old self or of darkness might be understood as a self-centeredness that is ready to use other people in any way necessary or to acquire at any cost resources that enhance one's own pleasure or status at the expense of others.

To what degree the non-Christian neighbors of Paul's initial audience reflected the unflattering assessment given them in Ephesians is a matter of dispute.[137] What cannot be disputed, according to Paul, is that such prohibited behavior should not even be the subject of conversation among believers (5:3–4), does entail exclusion (despite false assurances otherwise) from the kingdom of God and Christ (5:5–6), and requires some measure of disengagement by believers from the larger culture in which they live (5:7–12). That this disengagement does not entail a complete withdrawal from the larger society into some form of Christian ghetto is clear from the hope Paul expresses that the distinctive way of life maintained by the Christian community ("walk as children of light," 5:8) has the capacity both to expose the destructive practices of darkness for what they are (5:13) and to provide a transformative witness that points to Christ as the source of light and life (5:14).[138]

This last point, though, assumes that the distinctiveness to which Paul calls the Christian community is not just any oddness that contrasts Christians with their surrounding culture. Paul certainly intends his readers to embody a way of life that distinguishes them from patterns of life and practices that prevailed in a context dominated by the Roman

137. See Best, "Two Types of Existence," 139–55. Best believes the author of Ephesians deliberately draws absolute distinctions between Christian and non-Christian existence as a rhetorical device employed in order to strengthen internal bonds within the Christian community. See also Horrell, *Solidarity and Difference*, 133–40; Meeks, *First Urban Christians*, 84–107; Punt, "'Unethical' Language in the Pauline Letters?" 212–31.

138. Eph 5:11–14 (especially v. 14) carries with it many interpretive challenges (see Holloway, *Peripateō*, 212–16). Heil (*Ephesians*, 227) suggests the quotation cited in v. 14 by Paul (from where?) "alerts the audience to the potential that their lifestyle of 'walking in love' and as children of 'light' (5:8) . . . has for converting unbelievers from the unfruitful and shameful works of the darkness done in secret (5:11–12), so that they may be transformed into 'light' (5:14a) by the Christ shining on them."

Empire. No more blatant contrast to the established values and norms of this context could be found than in the way of Christ that has shown itself triumphant over the powers. Paul intends his readers to embody a cruciform pattern of life whereby the self-giving of Christ on the cross is the standard by which relations within the church are measured. Paul does not, though, call for a cruciform pattern of life just so the church can appear as a contrast to prevailing expressions of social order.[139] The way of Christ is the way by which God has triumphed over the powers, and by embodying that way the church participates in what God is doing about evil.

Attentive readers of Ephesians 1–3 might object that the focus of the relationship between believers and Christ, particularly in 2:1–10, is hardly on the cross of Christ as the dominant reality shaping Christian existence. The focus is rather on the significance of the resurrection of Christ from the dead as the means by which believers know liberation from forces that held them in bondage (2:1–3) and share in new life (2:4–6). Ephesians 3 concludes with a doxology that reveals an exalted status of the church such as is offered nowhere else in the New Testament (3:20–21). How do we go from the church as participating in Christ's triumph over the powers and sharing in God's eternal glory to an emphasis on life measured by the humility and sacrifice of the cross?[140] How could such a move reflect the church's status as "the place in which the reign of the Risen and exalted Christ over all creation is made actual and manifest"?[141]

To appreciate what is going on here in Ephesians, we need to underscore that Paul urges on the church a way of life that takes the cross of Christ as the pattern for its distinctive form of communal witness. Three passages within the last three chapters of Ephesians serve to illustrate this

139. Martin Hengel has marshaled extensive evidence to the effect that "for the men of the ancient world, Greeks, Romans, barbarians, and Jews, the cross was not just a matter of indifference, just any kind of death. It was an utterly offensive affair, 'obscene' in the original sense of the word." See his *Cross of the Son of God*, 114. Hengel cites (134), for example, Cicero's insistence that "the very word 'cross' should be far removed not only from the person of a Roman citizen, but from his thoughts, his eyes and his ears."

140. Of course, Jeal (*Integrating Theology and Ethics*, 179) says the move is not a logical one, since the parenesis of Ephesians 4–6 "is not directly supported by chapters 1–3."

141. Daniel J. Harrington's assessment of the status of the church as described in Ephesians. See his *Church According to the New Testament*, 87.

emphasis. The walk worthy of God's calling is first of all one measured by *tapeinophrosunē*, "humility of mind" (4:1–2). Commentators frequently note that this quality was held in low esteem in the Greco-Roman world, and its inclusion here (as well as it place of priority) "would have probably surprised Gentile readers when as Christians they first encountered it." [142] The near contemporary of Paul, the Stoic philosopher Epictetus, also places it at the head of a list, but of qualities that are not to be commended (*Diss.* 3.24.54–56)![143]

Why would humility take first place among the features of the worthy walk? At one level it only makes sense in the context of Paul's concern to build and strengthen the sense of community and unity among the believers he addresses. There is no quicker path toward fracture and division within a community than for pride and arrogance to disrupt and set one party against the other. Certainly the display of *tapeinophrosunē* supports a communal ethic of distinction given the broader cultural environment of Paul's day.[144] Paul, however, does not simply urge an ethic for a distinctive community. He calls for a communal ethic shaped by the cross of Christ, and for Paul the cross of Christ drastically revaluates the quality of humility from the disposition of contemptible servility to the attitude displayed by Christ in his self-giving on the cross (cf. Phil 2:1–11). For Paul, says O'Brien, "Christ's action in humbling himself is the pattern for believers."[145] The admonition to humility expresses Paul's concern to foster the cruciform ethic that must characterize the distinctive witness of the church to the powers.

A second passage makes a more overt appeal to the cross of Christ as the pattern for a distinctive communal ethic: 4:25—5:2. The entire paragraph expresses concerns for both the communal dimension of Paul's moral vision (note the "members" reference in 4:25 and the "one another" language of 4:32) as well as the concern for a distinctive way of life (the "not"/"but" contrast is used repeatedly). But Paul is not concerned simply to create distinctive communities that enjoy camaraderie and some cultural distance from a larger host society. Paul's appeal, "walk

142. Best, *Ephesians*, 362.

143. MacIntyre (*After Virtue*, 182–83) notes the difference between New Testament accounts of virtue from the wider Hellenistic environment, but also from more contemporary accounts such as represented by Ben Franklin.

144. See Yoder Neufeld, *Ephesians*, 172: "Paul understood it to be the necessary glue to hold the body of Christ together."

145. O'Brien, *Ephesians*, 277.

in love" (5:2), certainly sums up the concerns of 4:25—5:2 for believers to exhibit behavior and dispositions toward one another that support life together and serve to strengthen group identity over against the unbelieving world.[146] But the measure of that love is the sacrificial self-giving of Christ on the cross: "walk in love, just as Christ also loved you, and gave himself up for us, an offering and a sacrifice." Truth-telling, practices of reconciliation, the meeting of physical needs, and encouraging speech are all concrete means by which relationships in the body of Christ are supported and maintained. Expressions of kindness, compassion, and forgiveness all serve to strengthen the sense of identity of a minority element within a much larger, potentially threatening culture. According to Paul, however, all these practices are primarily ways in which the cruciform pattern of life finds specific demonstration in the distinctive communal witness of the church.

One other passage highlights the cruciform pattern to the ecclesial ethic of Ephesians. In Eph 5:19–21, Paul describes the setting in which the Spirit of God is at work to provide guidance so that believers can walk not as the unwise but as the wise (5:15–18). The setting is that of the community of faith gathered in praise and gratitude (5:19–20), but also in mutual submission or service to "one another" (5:21).[147] Believers are to "submit yourselves one to another in the fear of Christ." The communal emphasis of the passage is apparent ("one another"), as is the concern for the distinctiveness of the community ("not"/"but" in 5:15, 17, and 18). But the call for mutual submission is another expression of the constant emphasis in Pauline writings "on a disposition of putting others first, or of seeking their welfare above one's own."[148]

We best observe the specifically cruciform character of this disposition when we understand 5:21, not only in relation to what Paul has said in the entire paragraph of 5:15–21, but also in relation to what Paul will say in the next paragraph of 5:22–33.[149] Ephesians 5:21 is widely understood to serve as the heading for the "household code" of 5:22—6:9, in which Paul applies his ecclesial ethic for God's household (cf. 2:19) to

---

146. Holloway, *Peripateō*, 208–10.

147. This understanding insists that when Paul says "one another" (*allēlois*) he has in mind a mutual obligation held by all believers to all other believers. We will see below that this interpretation is contested.

148. Yoder Neufeld, *Ephesians*, 244.

149. The grammatical basis for this understanding will be explored in the next section that treats Paul's admonitions to wives and husbands in 5:22–33.

the smaller unit of the domestic household. We shall see that the call for mutual submission in 5:21 qualifies all of what Paul has to say to the various "component parts" of the Greco-Roman household: wives/husbands, children/parents, slaves/masters. In a sense, though, what Paul will have to say to these different members of the household also qualifies something of what is meant by "submit yourselves to one another." Paul will admonish husbands to "love your wives just as Christ also loved the church and gave himself up for her" (5:25). The practice of submission within the household takes the self-giving Christ of the cross as its pattern. The general call of believers to mutual submission offers one more instance of what Hays describes as "the paradigmatic significance of Jesus' death."[150] Ben Witherington puts it simply: "The cross is at the heart of what undergirds and shapes Paul's ethics."[151]

What accounts, then, for the move from Paul's exalted view of the church—as the body of the Christ who reigns supreme over the powers (1:22-23), as the embodiment of a radically new humanity (2:15), as the entity that educates the powers as to God's wisdom (3:10) and shares in God's eternal glory along with Christ (3:21)—to a way of life measured by what the Greco-Roman world viewed with disdain and contempt and what the Roman Empire employed as one of its most brutal tools of intimidation?[152] How does a church that takes the cross of Christ as the pattern for its distinctive form of communal witness display God's triumph over the powers?

Here is where it is important to remember the twofold reference to Paul's imprisonment at the boundaries of the parenesis (4:1; 6:20) and the account of his imprisonment as a paradoxical display of God's triumph through Christ over the powers. Gombis has argued, we remember, that Ephesians 3 is not an inexplicable digression but "integrally relates to the argument of the epistle, being driven by the concern to help Paul's readers understand how his imprisonment is consistent with God's triumph in Christ."[153] Gombis' argument might be extended to suggest that Ephesians 3 also provides Paul's readers the interpretive perspective by which to understand properly the relationship between the grand accounts of

150. Hays, *Moral Vision of the New Testament*, 28. Gorman (*Cruciformity*, 263) argues that the "equation of the terms 'love' and 'being subject' is confirmed by their use in 5:21-33."

151. Witherington, *Indelible Image*, 613.

152. See Hengel, *Cross of the Son of God*, 114-24, 138-42.

153. Gombis, "Triumph of God in Christ," 106.

the body of Christ in the first half of the letter and the call to distinctive communal practices measured by the cross in the second half. If death and resurrection are truly the means by which God triumphs over the powers, and if Paul, "the very least of all saints," can insist his tribulations really count as glory, then conventional accounts of power, glory, triumph, and exaltation—conventional in terms established by Rome—are all destabilized and subverted.[154]

It is not the case, then, that Ephesians, on the one hand, describes the exalted status of the church and then, on the other hand, promotes a distinctive form of communal witness that departs from or conflicts with that status. The triumphant Christ, head over all things, is the Christ of the cross. The apostle who bestows "glory" on his readers is the "prisoner of Christ" (3:1, 13). The body of Christ, the church, shares and exhibits the glory of Christ (3:21) when believers walk worthy of their calling "with all humility" (4:1–2), when they "walk in love as Christ loved" (5:2), and when they subject themselves to one another (5:21). These affirmations are not irreconcilable tensions representing Pauline incoherency. Rather, they are the gospel that exposes the pretensions of the powers for what they are and creates a people who exhibit God's triumph over them by embodying the way of Christ in the world.

Christian ethics has as one of its major tasks an account of how God addresses the evils that mark a world of conflict and hostility, enmity and division. What is God doing about such a world? Through God's redemptive work, God is creating a people, the one body of Christ that bears witness to the rulers and authorities of the power of the gospel to reconcile. This witness finds expression as the church models an alternative mode of society than that embodied by *Pax Romana*—an alternative mode of society that takes the cross of Christ as the pattern for its distinctive form of communal witness. How this witness takes concrete shape can be further explored as we examine Paul's admonitions in Ephesians concerning marriage relations.

---

154. Joerg Rieger (*Christ & Empire*, 52) concludes his treatment of Paul's anti-imperial gospel in a way that resonates with our analysis: "The deeper theological issues should now be clear: God in Christ is a different kind of lord who is not in solidarity with the powerful but in solidarity with the lowly. To be more precise, Christ's way of being in solidarity with the powerful is by being in solidarity with the lowly; the powerful are not outside of the reach of Christ's lordship, but their notions of what it means to be lord are radically reversed. This position—at the heart of the new world proclaimed by Paul—directly contradicts the logic of the Roman Empire."

A CHRISTIAN ETHIC OF RECONCILIATION:
CHRISTIAN ETHICS IN THE HOME

Ephesians 5:22—6:9 addresses relationships within the household as understood in the Greco-Roman world of Paul's day and as part of his challenge for the church to present a witness to the powers of how the gospel reconciles. Both parts of the previous sentence merit comment. In contrast to how some interpret Ephesians as decidedly anti-world and as advocating complete withdrawal from society (in light of passages like 5:3–14), when he addresses household relationships Paul does not at all suggest the abandonment of a basic social institution of his day. On the other hand, what he has to say about those relationships does not exactly reflect the standard account of household relations intended to replicate the interests and character of the imperial household. In other words, what Paul has to say to wives and husbands is a basic feature of a theological politics of resistance to the claims of the powers to be the means by which peace and order are secured. The significance of what Paul is doing might be better seen when contrasted with the way Niebuhr sought to give public significance to the Christian faith.

Niebuhr sought to translate the particular history narrated in Scripture into universal symbols so that Christian claims about love and justice could be approximated in the larger arenas of national and international relations. Paul insists on the particular significance for household relationships of the cosmic sovereignty of Christ that finds expression in loving service. Niebuhr argues that for Christians to be of any use to the larger arena of democratic society they must subordinate any particular features of their faith to the fragile harmony of liberal democracy. Paul offers in Ephesians a witness to the powers that requires believers to subordinate themselves to one another within the Christian fellowship and to allow that practice to shape relationships within the household. What Paul has to say in Ephesians 5 concerning wife/husband relationships needs to be seen as part of his challenge for believers to "walk as children of light" and thus witness to the transformative power of Christ.

We better understand what Paul has to say in Ephesians about wife/ husband relationships if we place his admonitions to wives and husbands not only in the broader context of Paul's Letter to the Ephesians as a whole, but also in the sociocultural context of household relations in the first-century Mediterranean world. This passage has often been used to support agendas for which Paul had no concern whatsoever. When we treat this passage as something other than a resource for slogans taken out of sociocultural and literary contexts, we gain an appreciation for an issue at the heart of Ephesians: Christian marriage is not an end in and of itself, but can serve as witness to God's triumph over evil.

Household Management in the Greco-Roman World

Christians are not the only ones who get married, and Christians like Paul are not the only ones who have had something to say about wife/husband relations. What Paul says in Ephesians 5 cannot be considered as if it were produced in a social vacuum devoid of conventional understandings and expectations concerning household roles and relationships. The topic of household management (*oikonomia*) was taken up as far back as Plato and Aristotle (fifth and fourth centuries BCE) and was routinely considered by moralists of both Hellenistic and Jewish backgrounds. There are some common threads running through various writers that reflect what were likely widely held assumptions concerning household matters. Aristotle offers analysis of household relations in both his *Nicomachean Ethics* and his *Politics* that is later echoed by other writers, so we might take what he has to say as somewhat representative of the broad consensus that would hold on such matters in Paul's day.[155]

It is notable that Aristotle discusses household relations in his work *Politics*, and in doing so offers what is for many a sociological truism—that there is some sort of relationship between the welfare of a society at large and what takes place in the more immediate environment of the family. For Aristotle, "The state is by nature clearly prior to the family . . . since the whole is of necessity prior to the part."[156] The state, though, "is made up of households," so Aristotle first gives extended treatment to what he calls "household management" (*oikonomia*) before he discusses the state. We hear from Aristotle that the household, at minimum, is made up of three sets of relations: "master and slave, husband and wife, father and children." Aristotle then notes what becomes a matter of significant discussion for the next several sections of *Politics*, that a "principle part" of

155. David L. Balch indicates that, even in spite of the diminished influence of Aristotle in the centuries after his death, "the continuity of the Aristotelian topos" on household management is evident in a wide variety of writers even in the New Testament period. See his *Let Wives Be Submissive*, 45.

156. *Politics*, 1235a19. Subsequent references to this work will be indicated within the text by section number.

household management is "the art of getting wealth." By this he indicates a feature of household relations that has been true for most of human history up to the industrial age—that the household has generally served as the basic arena for economic production.[157]

Aristotle views the three sets of relations in the household in terms of the relationship between the ruler and ruled, a natural order of things known by reason and by fact, "for that some should rule and others be ruled is a thing not only necessary, but expedient; from the hour of their birth, some are marked out for subjection, others for rule" (1254a20–23). It is due to "the very constitution of the soul," says Aristotle, that one "naturally rules, and the other is subject." What Aristotle means by this is that those who rule enjoy their position by virtue of their capacity for rational deliberation, while those who are subject are naturally so because they lack that capacity: "For the slave has no deliberative faculty at all; the woman has, but it is without authority, and the child has, but it is immature" (1260a5–14).

It should be clear that in any particular household, the ruler is the same person—the master, the husband, the father—while the ruled— slave, wives, and children—naturally find themselves in a subordinate status due to their relative lack of the "deliberative faculty," the capacity to make responsible moral decisions for themselves.[158] Lacking this capacity, it is only fitting and just that slaves, children, and wives submit themselves to the rule of master, father, and husband.

This set of relationships served a certain set of functions in the Greco-Roman world, functions that appear strange and distant from a culture such as ours that highly prizes individualism, autonomy, and romantic attraction. Marriage was viewed quite differently in the world of Paul than it is in the context of contemporary American evangelical Christianity. Paul would not find himself addressing newlyweds in a young couples

---

157. We need to keep this is mind when we consider the inclusion of slaves in the household context and when we ask about the significance of the Ephesians household code for an environment such as ours where the economic considerations are very different.

158. This Aristotelian outlook would find echo in later voices such as Areius Dydimus, a Stoic philosopher of the secnd century BCE. In his *Epitome* (sec. 149, 5–7), Areius closely parallels Aristotle: "The man has the rule of this house by nature. For the deliberative faculty in a woman is inferior, in children it does not exist, and it is completely foreign to slaves." Text in Balch, *Let Wives Be Submissive*, 42. On the importance and character of "the deliberative faculty" in Aristotle, see Wiggins, "Deliberation and Practical Reason," 221–40.

Sunday school class who had met at church (or on the campus of a Christian university), fallen in love, and determined that it was God's will for their lives that they marry. Osiek and Balch give a brief summary of the function of marriage that prevailed in Paul's day: traditional marriage in the Mediterranean world of the first century was "a legal and social contract between two families for the promotion of the status of each, the production of legitimate offspring, and the appropriate preservation and transferal of property to the next generation."[159] Marriages were arranged by families seeking appropriate mates for their children and to position families within the patron-client system of Mediterranean society. Females were usually in their early teen years when married, and males were usually in their late twenties. The distance between how many contemporary Christians might want to talk about marriage and the general outlook concerning marriage in Paul's day might best be revealed in the words of in the fourth-century BCE Athenian orator Apollodorus: "We have courtesans for pleasure, concubines for day-to-day care of the body, and wives to bear legitimate children and to maintain faithful guardianship of household affairs."[160] With this understanding of marriage in the Greco-Roman context in mind, one cannot help thinking of the pop hit from the 1990s that asked, "What's love got to do with it?"[161]

In Paul's day, marriage was a relationship arranged by parents for purposes of attaining or maintaining a certain social status (in the patron-client system), and it functioned to serve the economic interests of those involved. This included, as indicated by Apollodorus, demands on the wife's fidelity so as to insure that the husband's property would be transmitted only to his offspring. The husband's fidelity was a different

159. Osiek and Balch, *Families in the New Testament World*, 42.

160. Cited by Ferguson, *Backgrounds of Early Christianity*, 58. Of course, Apollodorus is probably simply revealing standard practices of his day. A Stoic moralist such as Musonius Rufus (first century CE), though, could both note what was likely widespread behavior and condemn it. See his "On Sexual Indulgence," cited in Malherbe, *Moral Exhortation*, 153.

161. To be fair, there is evidence that some measure of marital affection could develop between husband and wife (see Osiek and Balch, *Families in the New Testament World*, 61), and Aristotle does indicate that a type of friendship might "naturally" develop between husband and wife, "as they help each other by throwing their peculiar gifts into the common stock" (*Nicomachean Ethics*, 1162a15–25). Aristotle, however, will insist that this is a friendship not between equals, but "between dissimilars" and resembles more the type of friendship seen between a king and his subjects, as the king "confers benefits on his subjects if being a good man he cares for them with a view to their well-being" (*Nicomachean Ethics*, 1161a10–25).

matter altogether. Generally speaking, men did not commit adultery—against their own wives, that is. One man might commit adultery against another man if he infringed on the other's marriage. But sexual relations with prostitutes ("courtesans"), slave girls, or concubines were not seen as a violation of the relationship with a wife.[162] In fact, in his "Advice to Bride and Groom," the first-century CE Greek essayist Plutarch urges, "If therefore a man in private life, who is incontinent and dissolute in regard to his pleasures, commit some peccadillo with a paramour or a maidservant, his wedded wife ought not to be indignant or angry, but she should reason that it is respect for her which leads him to share his debauchery, licentiousness, and wantonness with another woman."[163] Raging sexual lust was "properly" expressed with someone other than the wife; the wife's role was to support the economic interests of the husband by producing legitimate heirs.

Still, some level of affection and friendship might be expected in the marriage relationship, and its absence could occasion divorce. Issues of adultery and infertility (both the fault of the wife!) were, however, the leading causes of divorce in the Greco-Roman world. Divorce, commonly practiced in ancient Mediterranean societies, was generally initiated by the husband. Just as marriages were arranged by families securing appropriate mates for their children, so divorces were generally approved with mutual consent by the wider families involved.[164]

We might fill out the account of marriage in the Greco-Roman context given above by Osiek and Balch by adding that marriage in that setting was a hierarchal, patriarchal relationship within the broader context of a set of relationships between the ruler (in this instance, the husband) and the ruled (the wife) reflecting the still broader context of the patron-client system of the Roman Empire. Marriage in this environment served the function of attaining or changing social status, was more concerned with matters of social status than issues of affection, intimacy, and fidelity, and was subject to a high degree of impermanence. It will be important for us to ask to what degree Paul affirms or challenges the understanding of and practices related to marriage that prevailed in his day. Before we examine the details of his address to wives and husbands,

162. See Pomeroy, *Goddesses, Whores, Wives, and Slaves,* 86–92.

163. Cited in Osiek and Balch, *Families in the New Testament World,* 112.

164. Ibid., 62. See also Bradley, *Discovering the Roman Family,* 56–60, for how the frequent dissolution of families in this setting placed children in situations of instability and uncertainty.

though, we must also place the household code in the wider setting of Ephesians as a whole.

The Literary Setting of the Ephesian Household Code

New Testament scholar Francis Watson insists, "Where it is forgotten that [Eph 5:22–33] is an integral part of the text known as 'the Epistle of Paul to the Ephesians,' its interpretation will be seriously impaired." Sadly, this is precisely how the passage is often treated. The only way to undo the damage done by such treatment, Watson insists, is "by restoring the exhortation to wives and husbands to its immediate context, but above all by allowing the richness and complexity of the letter as a whole to inform our reading of this part of it."[165] What bearing will such an emphasis on the broader context of Ephesians have on our understanding of what Paul has to say to wives and husbands in Eph 5:22–33?

The Household and God's Oikonomia

Ephesians 1–3 announces God's *oikonomia*, God's intent to unite all things together in Christ. God's agenda is to achieve God's peace. What will take place in the "fullness" of time, however, has already been anticipated in the redemptive work of Christ that grants new life in the one body of Christ. God calls us to participate in a life that enjoys Christ's triumph over the powers as displayed through the formation of a people whose very existence is testimony to the capacity of the gospel to reconcile. Paul's challenge in Ephesians 4–6 is for believers to walk worthy of their calling—to demonstrate in the everyday practices of life this triumph over the powers, powers concretely exemplified in the false form of social relations seen in *Pax Romana*. This worthy walk has an explicitly ecclesial character, as Paul encourages practices that take the cross of Christ as the pattern for a distinctive form of communal witness that embodies a different manner of achieving and sustaining peace in the world as witness to God's intent to unite all things in Christ. *Pax Romana* displayed in the world a corrupt form of peace through a violence

---

165. Watson, *Agape, Eros, Gender*, 223–24. Dawes (*Body in Question*, 10) observes, "Given the number of studies . . . devoted to the New Testament 'household codes' . . . it is surprising how few of the existing studies have attempted to read the passage within the context of the letter as a whole."

that sustained a distorted mode of human relationships in a stratified, hierarchal, pyramidal form of society where patrons provided benefits to clients and clients served the interests of patrons. Proper observance of respective roles afforded honor to each one involved and meant stability both for the household and the empire. The macrocosm of the state was to be mirrored in the microcosm of the household in which the ruler (husband, father, master) was patron to his clients (wife, children, and slaves).

A fundamental question for any interpretation of the Ephesian household code is whether Paul simply "baptizes" the pattern of house-hold relations that prevailed in the Greco-Roman world for Christian use. Major streams of New Testament interpretation have asserted precisely that. Earlier voices in New Testament critical scholarship argued that by the time Ephesians was written, hope for the quick return of Christ had dimmed. In place of the spontaneous and vital spirit that had at first energized a radical obedience among believers, there grew the need to construct ecclesial institutions and provide instructions for orderly living so that Christians might be seen as responsible, contributing members of the wider society. The household code of Ephesians, it is said, represents a clear reliance on widely held understandings of household relations that were simply adopted into Christian usage by second-generation Chris-tians who replaced eschatological hope with ecclesiastical control.[166]

Interestingly enough, more current advocates of the "adoption" model for interpreting the Ephesian household code provide an almost opposite justification. Instead of the loss of eschatological enthusiasm as the cause behind such an adoption, it is precisely due to apocalyptic fervor that such an adoption was necessary. According to this view, as the first century progressed leaders in the early church became concerned that wider society had begun to look with suspicion on Christians and pros-pects for persecution of Christians seemed to be on the rise. The concern was that Christians, with their distinctive way of life pointing to the age to come, were perceived by many as antagonistic toward mainstream cul-ture. Church leaders could lessen the sharp edge between the church and the wider world, and thus underscore that the church was no real threat to the stability of society at large, by pointing to approved practices for

---

166. A once standard work by Jack T. Sanders, *Ethics in the New Testament*, repre-sents this interpretive approach; see 1–29, 73–76. See also Cannon, *Use of Traditional Materials in Colossians*, 124–25. For discussion of this approach to Pauline ethics in general, see Horrell, *Solidarity and Difference*, 19–24.

household relations on display among members of the Christian community. So, while someone like Paul might call for a radically distinct way of life from believers in most areas of life, with respect to household relations the standards and norms that served *Pax Romana* were taken as sufficient to display *Pax Christi* as well.[167]

This sort of apologetic interpretation of the household code of Ephesians also seems present in the Southern Baptist Convention's *Baptist Faith & Message*, which begins its article on the family by describing the family as the foundation of society as a whole. There is good reason to question, though, whether Paul is simply "a Christian theologian writing generally about marriage in order to shore up Greco-Roman society or American urban society."[168] Particularly is there reason to question this when Paul strongly insists that his readers "walk no longer as the Gentiles walk" (4:17), that believers are to "put off the old self" and "put on the new" (4:22–24), and that while his readers were "once darkness," now they are "children of light" and must "walk as children of light" (5:8), refusing to "participate in the unfruitful deeds of darkness" (5:11).[169]

The most immediate context for the household code of Ephesians is the paragraph of 5:15–21. Paul's concern to draw a sharp line of distinction between the behavior of believers and what he considers typical features of the Gentile world continues in the repeated "not"/"but" contrasts of 5:15–18. In a world where the unwise, foolish, debauched behavior of the surrounding culture presents a persistent temptation, believers are to walk as the wise, understand the will of the Lord, and be filled with the Spirit. Given what will be seen as the close grammatical relationship between this paragraph and the household code of 5:22–33, any interpretation of the household code that suggests Paul has all of a sudden reversed course on his call for the Christian community to present a witness of distinctive contrast to the prevailing patterns of life in the

167. James D. G. Dunn says the New Testament household codes, which he insists offer nothing distinctively Christian in substance, "indicate a growing awareness that Christians had to counter suspicion that they were socially disruptive. . . . In such a situation the apologetic requirement could very well become irresistible." See his "Household Rules in the New Testament," 54–55; Lincoln (*Ephesians*, 360) also holds this perspective.

168. Osiek and Balch, *Families in the New Testament World*, 104.

169. With respect to the household code in Colossians (Col 3:18—4:1), N. T. Wright says similarly, "It is, in fact, extremely unlikely that Paul, having warned the young Christians against conforming their lives to the present world, would now require just that of them after all." See his *Colossians and Philemon*, 147.

broader culture carries a heavy burden of proof.[170] *Pax Christi* is not the same as *Pax Romana*.

Further, while ancient writers like Aristotle were explicit in asserting the link between the household and the state, Paul is at pains to emphasize the contrast between the Christian community and broader society. He comments not at all about any relationship between the household and the state. There is an important relationship between the household and a wider communal context, but that context is the community of faith gathered for worship, not the empire.[171] It is that relationship that provides the most important clue from the literary context of Ephesians as to how we must approach Paul's admonitions to wives and husbands. This leads to one of the most important issues regarding proper interpretation of the household code of Ephesians: where does it actually begin?

The Call to Mutual Submission

Many translations of Ephesians indicate a strong break between Paul's admonition to wives in 5:22—"Wives, subject yourselves to your own husbands, as to the Lord"—and the prior paragraph of 5:15–21, which concludes with an account of the proper relationship among all believers—"being subject to one another in the fear of Christ" (v. 21). The New American Standard translation, for example, places an editorial heading between v. 21 and v. 22—"Marriage Like Christ and the Church"—and indicates that v. 22 is the start of a new paragraph. The New Revised Standard Version, on the other hand, places a heading between v. 20 and v. 21—"The Christian Household"—and more directly relates v. 21 to v. 22.

What does any of this matter? The different editorial presentations of this passage indicate different ways of observing (or ignoring) an important grammatical feature of the household code of Ephesians. In the Greek text of Eph 5:22 there is no verb translated "submit." Why then do

170. Daniel K. Darko insists "there is a lack of consistency" in any social strategy "that encourages a withdrawal or introversionist stance on one hand, and seeks to integrate its readers to that very society on the other hand." See his *No Longer Living as the Gentiles*, 12. While it is debated to what degree Ephesians actually advocates a "withdrawal stance," Darko's point is well taken.

171. Darko challenges the "apologetic" thesis for explaining the Ephesians household code, insisting (after a wide survey of the data) "that a household code that is designed to integrate the church into the wider society or curb accusations against a breakdown of civic order would have customarily addressed or made the issue a central piece of the instruction." See his *No Longer Living as the Gentiles*, 81.

translators render v. 22 "Wives, *submit* yourselves to your own husbands" when there is no verb for "submit" in Paul's Greek? They are not taking liberties when they do this, and decisions of this sort are made all the time in any work of translating a document from one language to another. Translators look for a verb in order to render v. 22 in a clear, sensible way and they find one in v. 21, where Paul has earlier described how believers are called to relate to one another in terms of mutual subjection. In need of a verb to render v. 22 a complete sentence, translators appropriately appeal to Paul's use of *hypotassomenoi* ("being subject") in v. 21 to supply what is missing in v. 22.

That there is in the Greek text of Eph 5:22 no verb translated "submit" is clear; the significance of a reliance on v. 21 for the supply of that verb, though, has been variously understood. One matter affecting any interpretation of the relationship between v. 21 and what follows is how the "one another" language of v. 21 is construed. What can "being subject to one another" mean when it is then followed by an apparently unilateral admonition for wives to subject themselves to their own husbands? One interpretation allows what follows in 5:22—6:9 to determine the interpretation of 5:21. Given the apparent hierarchal pattern of household relationships between the ruler and the ruled in 5:22—6:9, the "one another" of 5:21 must be interpreted in some way other than as a call for mutual subjection among all believers. Peter O'Brien argues that there are occasions in Greek literature in general and the New Testament in particular where *allēlous* ("one another") does not imply mutual obligation, but indicates the relationship of members of one category to members of another category. In this way, 5:21 can be understood as a general introduction to the household code of 5:22—6:9 in which members of one category, the ruled (wives, children, slaves), are instructed to submit themselves to members of another category, the ruler (husband, father, master). "The particular ways in which Christians are to submit themselves to others," says O'Brien, "are . . . specified in the household table for wives, children, and servants." O'Brien is specific regarding 5:21: "It is not mutual submission that is in view . . . but submission to appropriate authorities."[172]

---

172. O'Brien, *Ephesians*, 401. The only example O'Brien gives for this use of *allēlous* in Paul (Gal 6:2), though, is not a very convincing one and few commentators on Galatians follow him on this (see Horrell, *Solidarity and Difference*, 224). Further, the use of *allēlous* we have seen elsewhere in Ephesians can in no way be understood as anything but a call for certain obligations and commitments to be expressed by all

An alternative reading allows 5:21 to influence the interpretation of what follows in 5:22—6:9 and consequently challenges conventional renderings of Ephesians as simply an attempt to "Christianize" familiar standards of conduct. To hear Paul's call for believers to mutual submission in 5:21 as the background for what Paul then says to wives and husbands is to place his admonitions to wives and husbands in a context with significant ramifications for how 5:22-33 must be understood. For example, the grammatical link between 5:22 and what precedes makes it clear that we cannot abstract what Paul has to say to wives and husbands in particular from what Paul has already said in general about new life in the one body of Christ. Specifically, not only does the lack of a verb in v. 22 require a link back to v. 21, but v. 21 is itself a dependent clause linked back, with all of vv. 19-21, to the command of 5:18—"Be filled with the Spirit"—and a paragraph that highlights the context in which the Spirit of God is active to enable lives that reflect the will of God—a context of worship, gratitude, and mutual service (5:15-21). Within that paragraph, Watson insists, "The exhortations to thankfulness and to mutual subjection are addressed to all, irrespective of gender, age or socio-economic status. It is irrelevant to the exhortation, 'being subject to one another . . .', that one is a male householder or a female slave, a female householder or a male slave."[173]

It is not just the immediately preceding paragraph, however, that must shape our understanding of what Paul says to wives and husbands. It is the entire letter with its grand concerns for the creation of a people whose practices embody a witness to God's plan for the reconciliation of the cosmos. We cannot dismiss the importance for the household of what Paul says about such qualities as humility, gentleness, patience, and forbearing love. Certainly these qualities are vital for a fellowship charged with the task of demonstrating to a fractured world the power of the gospel to create communities of reconciliation and peace (4:1-3). Since Paul's grammar does not allow his admonitions to wives and husbands to be abstracted from the wider concerns of Ephesians, though, we should be

---

believers in relationship to all other believers (see 4:2, 25, 32). Not only does O'Brien's rendering of 5:22—6:9 require a reversal of course from the persistent theme of a distinctively cruciform community toward accommodation to the norms of the Greco-Roman household, but it requires a sudden shift away from the repeated emphasis on mutual obligations to be upheld by all believers that is stressed throughout the rest of Ephesians 4–6.

173. Watson, *Agape, Eros, Gender*, 224.

ready to find the significance for marriage relationships in such qualities and practices as he outlines in 4:1–3. This is important not just for 4:1–3, however, but for the entire parenesis of 4:1—5:21. Consider 4:15 ("speaking the truth in love"), 4:25 ("speak truth each one with his neighbor, because we are members of one another"), 4:29 ("let no unwholesome word proceed out of your mouth, but only such as is good for edification"), and 4:31—5:2 ("let all bitterness and wrath and anger and outcry and slander be put away from you with all malice. Be kind to one another . . . and walk in love as Christ loved you and gave himself up for you"). The entire set of practices and skills that Paul highlights as essential to a Christian fellowship is also significant for what Paul has to say to the household. While Aristotle's vision of the household was concerned to see the structure of the state duplicated on the smaller scale of the household, Paul wants to see the qualities and practices that mark the distinctive character of the church on display in the wife/husband relationship. Anyone who has been married beyond the so-called honeymoon stage can likely testify to how vital qualities such as those mentioned in 4:1–3 or 4:32—5:2 might be in a marriage relationship. For Paul, however, they serve not only as key practices to sustain a marriage, but as part of the church's witness to the world of God's *oikonomia*.

Paul's Admonitions to Wives and Husbands

What we have examined so far indicates that any attempt to read Eph 5:22–33 as simply Paul's attempt to "baptize" Aristotle or the standard account of the Greco-Roman household of the first century is suspect. There have been many attempts to read this passage this way, and if we were to ignore the broader literary context of Ephesians in comparison with the broader sociocultural context of the Greco-Roman world, perhaps no questions would arise. Perhaps, but not necessarily, for when details of the passage are themselves examined more closely—and such details matter—a reading of Paul's admonitions as a unilateral call for wifely submission to a male "headship" representing divine rule comes under question. The details of the passage must surely figure in our assessment of the whole and our assessment of the significance of the whole passage for the character of Christian marriage.

Paul's Admonition to Wives

However Paul's admonition to wives is interpreted, that Paul even addresses wives is somewhat out of the ordinary. Clearly he addresses wives as responsible moral agents and in so doing distinguishes his outlook from the conventional view that justified the relationship between ruler (husband) and ruled (wife) as natural, since the ruled do not sufficiently possess "the deliberative capacity." At the same time, it is entirely appropriate that the verb from 5:21, *hypotassomenoi*, serve to indicate something of the proper relationship between wife and husband; it is just that the traditional reading of this passage that describes "being subject" as a one-sided obligation on the part of wives needs to be reevaluated. A slightly different translation of 5:21–22 might indicate something of the significance of the grammatical link: "Being subject to one another out of reverence for Christ—wives, *for example*, to your own husbands as to the Lord."[174] This translation carries through to v. 22 the emphasis of the challenge Paul has presented to all believers in v. 21, but it also serves to remind that the admonition to wives in v. 22 is a specific example of what Paul calls for in general on the part of all believers. In other words, Paul does call upon wives to subject themselves to their own husbands; he does so, though, not in order to sanction the hierarchical structure of the Greco-Roman household, but as an insistence that what is true of relationships among believers in general must find expression in the more intimate arena of the family as well.

This understanding, that the admonition to the wives is a specific example of what Paul has said to believers in general, helps make sense of what Paul means when he says that the wife's submission to her own husband is done "as to the Lord." While various interpretations have been offered for this phrase,[175] Lynn Cohick reminds us that "a close reading of Paul's injunctions suggests that he shapes the common understanding so that believers comprehend their actions as unto Christ." Cohick appropriately invokes the repeated account in Ephesians of new life as new life "in Christ," and "if the believer's life is hid in Christ, if the believer died in Christ and is raised to new life, then submitting to another believer is merely submitting to Christ himself."[176] That is, the wife's submission has nothing to do with some natural order of things reflected in her lack of

---

174. Similarly, see Gorman, *Cruciformity*, 265.

175. See Lincoln, *Ephesians*, 368; O'Brien, *Ephesians*, 412.

176. Cohick, *Ephesians*, 135–36.

"the deliberative capacity," but has everything to do with giving concrete expression to what it means to be a follower of Christ as a member of the body of Christ.

Paul does, however, offer a different rationale at this point for the wife's willing submission to her own husband.[177] The wife's submission to her husband is seen as analogous to the church's submission to Christ: "For the husband is the head [*kephalē*] of the wife as [*hos*] also Christ is head [*kephalē*] of the church, he himself being savior of the body [*sōmatos*]." It is no exaggeration to say that this is one of the most controversial statements in all the New Testament, with much of the controversy focused on the significance of Paul's metaphorical use of *kephalē*. Usually debate centers on whether *kephalē* is to be understood as indicating "authority," or "source," with various ancient resources (e.g., the LXX) scoured for evidence.[178] While such discussions can sometimes be illuminating, as Dawes notes, "The particular nuances which a living metaphor conveys will emerge only from a study of the word in its context. A study of previous uses of the word . . . will be of limited value."[179] The important reminder from Dawes is that a word *means* how it is *used*. How does Paul use *kephalē* in Ephesians 5:23?

Earlier, in Eph 1:22–23, Paul had employed the "head" metaphor in association with the language of "subjection" to speak of Christ's sovereignty over the powers on behalf of his body, the church. Clearly, though, in this passage Christ's "headship" pertains to his sovereignty over the powers, as their subjection "under his feet" makes clear. Christ is not described as *kephalē* in relationship to his body, the church, in terms of "head" = "sovereign" over "his body" = "the church." Rather, Christ is "head" = "sovereign" over the powers and as such is given by God to the church for the benefit of the church's existence in the world. In addition,

---

177. Two important exegetical observations need to be made at this point. First, subjection is to a wife's own husband (*tois idiois andrasin*, 5:22) does not in any way sanction a wider demand for the submission of women to men in general, except as believers are called to submit to one another in general; see Hoehner, *Ephesians*, 732. Second, the language drawn from 5:21 suggests a voluntary act on the part of one who willingly defers to the best interests of the other. In no way can 5:22 be used to impose what is properly a personal commitment to follow the leadership of the Holy Spirit; see Cohick, *Ephesians*, 137.

178. For "authority" see, for example, Grudem, "Does *kephalē* ('Head') Mean 'Source,'" 38–59; for "source" see, for example, Mickelsen, "What Does *kephalē* Mean in the New Testament?" 97–110.

179. Dawes, *Body in Question*, 133.

as we have already seen, the "body" language of 1:23 is an instance of what Dawes has called the "unitive" use of the "body" metaphor, where there is no real distinction between Christ and "his body," so that the church itself represents the presence of Christ in the world, the Christ who is sovereign over the powers.[180] Be that as it may, the use of "head" in 1:22–23 still clearly indicates Paul's use of *kephalē* as a metaphor for authority.

On the other hand, in 4:15–16 it seems Paul has *kephalē* as "source" in mind when he speaks of Christ who, as the head of the body, provides the resources needed for every individual member of the body of Christ to participate in the "growth of the body for the building up of itself in love." The metaphors of "head" and "body" are not related here as "sovereign" to "subordinate," but as "source of life" to "organic whole." Dawes concludes, "These metaphors therefore emphasize the dependence of the Church on Christ. 'Beheaded,' the Church would die, for he is the source of its life and growth."[181]

So, Paul can use *kephalē* elsewhere in Ephesians as a metaphor for either "authority" (1:22) or "source" (4:15–16). How are we to understand Paul use of *kephalē* in 5:23–24?

That Paul draws on the analogy of Christ as head of a subordinate church to explain the wife's submission to her husband makes it apparent that he is using *kephalē* as a metaphor for "authority" in 5:23–24. Such "surface features of the text" are not sufficient, however, to give a full account of Paul's intent and the "complexities, tensions, and ambiguities" found in the text.[182] We have already encountered one contribution to ambiguity in the relationship between Paul's general call for mutual submission between believers in 5:21 and his specific admonition to wives in 5:22. There are other features of this text, though, that complicate any reading of this passage as simply a "Christianized" rendering of Aristotle's *oikonomia*.

One such feature is Paul's indication that he wants to limit the point of the analogy between Christ as head of the church and the husband as head of the wife. Wherever analogy operates it is important to ask what correspondence there is between the two distinct referents an analogy brings into comparison. Comparisons are normally restricted to a

---

180. Ibid., 141–42, 157.

181. Ibid., 164.

182. Ibid., 231.

limited range of possibilities that are generally indicated by context. Paul makes it clear that just as much as he wants to draw an analogy between Christ as head of the church and the husband as the head of the wife, so he wants to limit the analogy.[183] He does this by interrupting the flow of his argument with an important qualification concerning the relationship between Christ and the church.

In vv. 22–23a Paul calls for the wife's submission to her own husband, "because the husband is the head of the wife as also Christ is head of the church." In v. 24, Paul reasserts the analogy: "But as the church submits to Christ, so also should the wives [submit] to their husbands in all things." The word "but" (*alla*) that introduces v. 24 offers a tone of contrast to what precedes; and what immediately precedes is itself a point of contrast that Paul offers in order to limit the analogy between Christ as head of the church and the husband as head of the wife. In v. 23b Paul introduces the important qualification that Christ "himself is the savior of the body." While some interpreters have wanted to broaden (or downplay) the role of "savior" to include such matters as "protector" or "provider,"[184] the emphatic "himself" of v. 23b and the strong "but" of v. 24 suggest that Paul wants to place limits on the analogy between Christ and the husband. As Watson insists concerning the husband, "He is the head of the wife *as* and *only as* Christ is head of the church. It is not said that his role is the same as Christ's, only that it is like Christ's (and being 'like' rather than 'the same,' also unlike Christ's)." What are the limits to the analogy? "The husband is not 'head of the church,' he is not 'saviour of the body,' he is not saviour of his wife, he is not the object of her thanksgiving and song (cf. 5:18–19)."[185]

If Paul wants to limit the scope of the analogy between Christ as head of the church and the husband as head of the wife, what then is the point of the comparison? Oddly enough, Paul does not make this clear in his use of *kephalē* in vv. 23–24. Paul will continue using the analogy between Christ and husbands in his admonition to them in vv. 25–33, but by that time he drops use of the *kephalē* metaphor completely. That shift represents another one of the features of this passage that creates

183. See Caird, *Language and Imagery of the Bible*, 145, where he warns concerning mistakes at this point, "There is an intended point of comparison on which we are being asked to concentrate to the exclusion of all irrelevant fact; and communication breaks down, with ludicrous and even disastrous effect, if we wrongly identify it."

184. For discussion on this point, see Lincoln, *Ephesians*, 370.

185. Watson, *Agape, Eros, Gender*, 232.

tension and heightens the ambiguity, for Paul does not explicitly address husbands as "head" of their wives. Paul makes use of that metaphor within the context of his admonition to wives, but he does not employ the metaphor in a direct way when addressing husbands. He will continue to employ a Christ/husband analogy and will make use of "body" language in his instruction to husbands. As we shall see, however, the way he makes use of these images effects such a contrast with the picture of the wife/husband relationship of vv. 22–24 that either Paul has simply become incoherent,[186] or he is deliberately effecting tensions within the passage in order to continue the task of destabilizing the "ruler"/"ruled" pattern of the Greco-Roman household he began when he called for mutual submission between all believers, including mutual submission between wives and husbands.

Before we examine Paul's admonitions to husbands, it will be helpful to summarize what we have found with respect to Paul's admonitions to wives. Paul's instruction for wives to submit to their own husbands 1) presupposes that wives have the capacity to operate as responsible moral agents, 2) is a specific application for the household of how believers are to relate to one another in general, 3) is a means by which wives display their service within the body of Christ, 4) is sanctioned by appeal to an analogy between Christ/church and husband/wife, an analogy upon which Paul places specific limits, and 5) is an analogy that implies a certain type of authority enjoyed by the husband as head of the wife, a type of authority that Paul has yet to explain.

Paul's Admonitions to Husbands

An important feature of the life and ministry of Jesus is that whenever he points to his own authority over his disciples as providing any pattern for their relationships with one another, it is an expression of authority in strong contrast to how authority was conceived in the broader culture of his day. In contrast to the view of authority among the Gentiles, among Jesus' disciples the first must be last, and the greatest become a servant, "For the son of man did not come to be served, but to serve and to give his life a ransom for many" (Mark 10:42–45). "You call me teacher and lord, and you are right, for so I am," says Jesus to his disciples. "If I then, the lord and teacher, washed your feet, you also ought to wash one

---

186. Some have suggested precisely this; see Mitton, *Ephesians*, 210.

another's feet. For I gave you an example that you also should do as I did to you" (John 13:13–14). That Jesus took the towel and the basin of water to wash the feet of his disciples is the clearest indication—apart from the cross—that Jesus' sense of authority is not constrained or defined by conventional accounts or the need to protect status within any structure of rank and honor. While many Christians heartily endorse this "great reversal" concerning matters of status and rank in theory, it seems that such an inversion of values often has no bearing on their understanding of wife/husband relationships. Instead, the drastic redefinition of leadership and authority embodied in and demanded by Jesus is resisted when appeal is made to Ephesians 5 in order to assert the notion of the husband as ruler of the household in terms of "unitary executive power." Does Paul sanction such a practice?

We have already noted that Paul drops the "head" metaphor when he specifically addresses husbands in 5:25–33. That does not mean that he moves away from the analogy between Christ/church and husband/wife, however. He will continue to employ "body" language as well, but in a way that differs from his use of it in his admonition to wives. How, then, are husbands to be likened to Christ? And how does Paul understand the wife as the husband's "body" when the husband is no longer viewed as "head"?

Paul invokes the language of analogy again in v. 25 and draws another comparison between Christ/church and husband/wife. In this instance he makes the point of the analogy as clear as possible: "Husbands, love your wives, just as Christ also loved the church and gave himself up for her." What is the point of comparison between Christ and husbands? Watson writes, "Husbands are to love their wives as Christ loved the Church . . . and here the point of similarity is confined to the term 'love.'"[187] What instruction does Paul offer husbands that gives specific content to the Christ/church = husband/wife relationship? Nothing is said about matters of authority in decision-making; nothing is said about specific roles in terms of household duties; nothing is said about matters of structure. Rather, Paul employs an analogy that circumvents, indeed, subverts all such concerns for rank, status, and conventional understandings of authority.

When Paul appeals to the cross as the measure of Christ's love for the church ("he loved her and gave himself up for her"), which in turn

187. Watson, *Agape, Eros, Gender*, 248.

serves as the measure of the husband's love for his wife, he invokes a symbol that, as we have already seen, played an important role in maintaining the structure and order of *Pax Romana*. In that setting, however, the cross served as a symbol of threat and intimidation. An imposed order of subjugation was maintained by threat of crucifixion, an intentionally brutal and shameful mode of public execution intended to humiliate and terrorize. For Christians who regularly sing hymns and choruses highlighting the cross as the expression of God's love and mercy, it is difficult for us to remember that the cross was "to the Jews a stumbling block, and to the Gentiles foolishness" (1 Cor 1:23). For Paul to invoke the cross of Christ as the singular pattern for measuring the husband's love for his wife certainly "precludes any interpretation of the text that would grant the husband some sort of power over his wife that contradicts that self-giving, altruistic love of Christ."[188] The association also attaches to the husband a marker of status "at the lowest end of the spectrum" in the surrounding culture, one that places him at odds with conventional expectations for what counts as honorable and appropriate.[189] When the cross of Christ is the pattern by which the husband's love for the wife is measured, it is impossible to understand Paul as simply giving sanction to the "ruler"/"ruled" relationship of the Greco-Roman household. Were Aristotle to have read Eph 5:25, he would have been absolutely perplexed.

Paul's use of "body" imagery in 5:28–30 also challenges conventional understandings of wife/husband relationships and creates a tension with his use of the "head"/"body" metaphor of 5:22–24. In the earlier portion of this passage, Paul employed what Dawes has called the "partitive" use of the "body" metaphor. There "head" and "body" are distinct and identified one (Christ/husband) over against the other (church/wife). In 5:28–30, by which time Paul has dropped the use of *kephalē*, he employs what Dawes calls the "unitive" use of *sōma* to emphasize not distinction of one over against the other, but unity.[190] In this sense, husband and wife are not viewed as competing forces locked in a battle for control, so that one must attain mastery over the other. Rather, husband and wife are joined in a union comparable only to the union between Christ and the church, which is his body.

---

188. Gorman, *Cruciformity*, 265.

189. deSilva, *Honor, Patronage, Kinship & Purity*, 51.

190. Dawes, *Body in Question*, 202–3.

Paul's use of the "unitive" sense of "body" language is one way he gives content and justification to his admonition that husbands are to love their wives as Christ also loved the church. Thus, in v. 28 Paul argues that "husbands ought to love their own wives as their own *bodies*," explaining that "he who loves his own wife loves *himself*; for no one ever hated his own *flesh*, but nourishes and cherishes it, just as Christ also does the church." The "unitive" use of *sōma* becomes obvious when we see that in vv. 28–29 "the wife is actually identified with the husband's 'self' and is described as his very 'flesh.'"[191] This association of "body," "himself," and "flesh" is an echo of the appearance of these terms in Eph 2:14–16 where Paul's use of "himself," "flesh," and "body" underscores the unity between Christ and the church, so much so that they are in that passage indistinguishable. As in Eph 2:14–16, so in 5:28–29 the "body" metaphor is used without reference to "head" to emphasize the radical oneness both of Christ and his church and husband and wife. This "unitive" use of "body" language stands in (deliberate) tension with the "partitive" use of the "head"/"body" metaphor of vv. 22–24 and qualifies (as does the grammatical link between 5:21 and 5:22) the picture of unilateral submission we might otherwise take from 5:22 if we read that verse in isolation from its context. A hierarchical reading of this passage, one that sanctions a ruler/ruled relationship between husband and wife, presupposes not unity but competing agendas. In a ruler/ruled relationship one agenda must be subordinated to the other. With his use of the "unitive" image in which husband and wife are "one body," Paul presupposes not competition between husband and wife, but partnership.

The next use of "body" language, however, introduces a new element into Paul's argument and offers yet another insight into the intended relationship between husband and wife. If in 5:22–23 the "partitive" use of the "head"/"body" metaphor distinguishes husband from wife, and in 5:28 the "unitive" use of "body" language identifies them in the most intimate manner, in 5:30 Paul's use of "body" emphasizes the unity of husband and wife once again (but in a different way) and furthers the argument for husbands to love their wives as Christ loves the church.

The focus of Paul's argument shifts slightly from what it was in 5:28–29. In 5:28–29 Paul offers support for his assertion in 5:25 that husbands should love their wives as Christ also loved the church. Why should they do this? At this point Paul offers a parallel between husband/

191. Ibid., 98.

wife and Christ/church. Since the church is the body of Christ and is loved by Christ as "himself" and as "his flesh," so a husband should love his wife as "himself" and as "his flesh."[192] In v. 30, though, Paul presents a slightly different reason for why husbands ought to love their wives as Christ loved the church: not because husband and wife are united *as* one body, but because husband and wife are united *in* one body—"because we are members of his body." Husbands are to love their wives because with their wives they are fellow members of the body of Christ and that is how believers are supposed to act toward one another.[193] Indeed, Paul has already made it explicit that believers are to love one another with a love measured by the sacrificial self-giving of Christ (5:1–2). When Paul admonishes husbands to love their wives with the cross of Christ as the measure of that love, he is making specific application to the husband/wife relationship what was to be practiced among believers in general.

If it is the case, however, that Paul's admonition to husbands in 5:25–30 is a specific expression of what is a general Christian responsibility, we have in Paul's admonition to husbands something of an echo of his admonition to wives. Just as the admonition to wives to "submit yourselves" to their own husbands (5:22) is a particular expression of what is to be a general practice among all believers (5:21), so also is the admonition for husbands to love their wives as Christ also loved the church and gave himself up for her (5:25) a specific example of a general obligation on the part of all Christians (5:1–2). In other words, with his admonitions to wives and husbands, Paul seems to be concerned to apply what are general features of his ecclesial ethic to married couples, "the implication being that marriage is one of the areas of life in which these commands must be lived out."[194]

192. Two observations can be made at this point. First, in 5:28 Paul is likely echoing the commandment concerning neighbor love found in Lev 19:18. Second, Paul nowhere argues *for* his analogy between Christ/church and husband/wife; he simply argues *from* the analogy.

193. 5:30 is more immediately related to the last clause of 5:29—"just as Christ also does the church"—and serves to explain Christ's love for the church. That does not lessen the significance, though, of Paul's insistence that all believers, regardless of gender, are members of the body of Christ.

194. Dawes, *Body in Question*, 224. And so it seems logical to assume that, while he does not state it explicitly, Paul would clearly support the notion that wives are also to love their husbands as Christ loved the church. So ibid., 231; Watson, *Agape, Eros, Gender*, 244–45; Cohick, *Ephesians*, 140.

While our modern, romanticized images of marriage might want more of an emphasis by Paul on the singular significance of the marriage relationship, highlighting its exclusive nature over all other relationships, that is not the concern in Ephesians. Paul writes to a situation in which there were clearly defined roles and expectations assigned to those whose marriages had been arranged for them, primarily for the sake of social and economic status in the patron-client system of the Greco-Roman world. His concern to see the practices of Christian faith expressed in household relations marks a radical departure from many of the basic assumptions and practices of wife/husband relations in that context. Aristotle could only imagine husband and wife as friends to the degree that a king condescends to provide material benefits for his subjects. Paul's emphasis on mutual submission and sacrificial love in Ephesians offers a different prospect for those devoted to giving expression to Christian commitment in their homes.

Before we conclude this exploration of what Paul has to say to wives and husbands in Eph 5:21–33, it will be helpful to summarize the main features of his admonitions to husbands. Paul's instruction for husbands concerning the relationship to their wives 1) does not include any direct reference to the husband as the "head" of the wife, but 2) does emphasize the analogy between Christ/church and husband/wife, an analogy 3) limited in terms of Christ's self-giving sacrificial love for the church and 4) defined by an image, the cross, that subverts conventional accounts of status and authority and 5) emphasizes the unity of the relationship between husband and wife.

Happily Ever After?

Paul nowhere provides a comprehensive, all-encompassing discussion of every aspect of family life or the marriage relationship. His counsel to wives and husbands in Eph 5:22–33 does not pretend to address many of the questions and issues that might come up in a marriage relationship. What Paul does is call for the expression of basic and necessary practices of Christian disposition and demeanor within what for many is the most challenging and demanding of all day-to-day relationships—the family. Whether the demand is for humble submission or sacrificial love, the reference point is the same—Christ's model of self-giving service to the point of death on a cross (cf. Phil 2:1–8). Paul makes no comment about who oversees family finances, who does the dishes or mows the lawn, or who decides whether stray dogs are taken in. He offers no license for unilateral expressions of power one way or the other. What he does do is call upon believers to act like Christians in their homes. The worthy walk must find a pathway even into the domestic arena.

That Paul does not get overly specific in his instructions concerning family relationships might be one reason he has been read as sanctioning a view of marriage that calls for the singular submission of the wife to a husband who serves as the channel of God's will and direction. Family life can get messy, and one of the easiest ways of avoiding problems is to establish a bureaucratic structure where the lines of authority are clear and everybody knows his or her place and who calls the shots. Many have read Paul's instructions in Eph 5:22—6:9 as addressing this problem by sanctioning a specific structure for household relations—the relationship between the ruler and the ruled. If Paul's concern is with structure, though, an important issue then arises. As Watson puts it, "The text takes it for granted . . . that the household will include not only parents and children but also slaves. The crucial question is whether, in the end, the text merely provides a new religious legitimation for the existing form [of the household] or whether, taking the existing form as its starting point, it nevertheless transforms it."[195]

Watson's question requires the contemporary reader of Ephesians to consider whether, if Paul is concerned to sanction a particular household structure, he then provides divine sanction for slavery. Just as there were appeals to Eph 6:5 in the nineteenth century to give legitimacy for slavery ("Slaves, obey your masters"), so appeals to Eph 5:22 continue to serve arguments that would maintain a ruler-ruled relationship between husband and wife.[196] If Paul is concerned to give eternal sanction to structure in 5:22–33, the same holds for 6:5–9. Ephesians cannot be selectively quoted whenever certain of its elements seem handy to support culturally inspired tendencies toward domination of whatever sort.

The argument here is that Paul has not been concerned with structure, that Paul does take a particular structure for granted, but that he is concerned to explore how it is that Christian witness can find transformative expression in that context. The (deliberate) tensions evoked

195. Watson, *Agape, Eros, Gender*, 228–29.

196. Wayne Meeks suggests biblically based arguments for the subordination of women "are often strikingly analogous" to those used by the pro-slavery apologists of the nineteenth century. See his "'Haustafeln' and American Slavery," 251.

by Paul when he links the wife's submission to her own husband to the obligation of mutual submission among all believers, when he defines the likeness between Christ and husbands strictly in terms of the cross of Christ, and when he argues for the husband's love for his wife on the basis of their mutual membership in the body of Christ all indicate that while "the form of 'patriarchal marriage' is maintained . . . its substance has been subverted and transformed."[197]

Still, family life can be messy. The constant temptation of modernity is to manage conflict by establishing structures that bypass the demands of genuine reconciliation through the imposition of procedural systems that displace the need for virtue.[198] Ours is "a nation of laws, not of men," as John Adams put it, illustrating the point. If appeal can be made to a particular bureaucratic structure that promises order over chaos, then the difficult work of building relationships on the basis of virtues like humility, gentleness, patience, and forbearing love, and through the expression of such practices as forgiveness and self-denial, is not necessary.

Watson asks, though, "If Jesus 'is our peace, who has made us both one' (2:14), is this a peace that affirms existing social structures by denying the legitimacy of conflict, or does it overcome a conflict endemic to the structures themselves?"[199] To put it another way, is the Christian form of marriage one that mirrors the order of *Pax Romana*, which manages conflict by imposing a structure protected by the threat of crucifixion? Or is the Christian form of marriage one that embodies *Pax Christi*, which effects genuine reconciliation through lives of mutual service and sacrificial love supremely displayed in the cross of Christ?

Does the cheerful reading of Eph 5:21–33 given here, though, simply ignore the inevitable conflicts and differences that arise in any marriage? Does the focus on mutuality and unity by Paul not take seriously the reality of competing agendas and the fact that someone, finally, has to be in charge? It would surprise Paul to hear the suggestion that he does not take the realities of conflict and hostility in the world seriously. That the

---

197. Watson, *Agape, Eros, Gender*, 234. Hays similarly says that in the Ephesians household code, "The conventional authority structures of the ancient household are thereby subverted even while they are left in place." See his *Moral Vision of the New Testament*, 64.

198. Thus, MacIntyre's *After Virtue* insists that the bureaucratic manager is the dominant character of our emotivist age embodying "the claim to possess systematic effectiveness in controlling certain aspects of social reality" (74).

199. Watson, *Agape, Eros, Gender*, 229.

explicit parenesis of his ecclesial ethic begins with the call to exhibit such qualities as humility of mind, gentleness, patience, and forbearing love suggests that Paul "has no rosey-eyed picture" of the Christian community "as composed only of perfect Christians."[200] Patience and forbearing love are generally not needed in situations where the sailing is perpetually smooth. The question, however, is by what means are God's people "to maintain the unity of the Spirit in the bond of peace" (4:3)?

Of course, another way of putting the question is, "What is God doing about evil?" In Ephesians, Paul offers that God, through God's redemptive work, is creating a people whose lives, sustained in worship, bear witness to God's purpose for creation. This chapter has focused on the formation of a people, the *ecclesia*, whose very existence in the world is testimony to the power of the gospel to reconcile. Paul's ecclesial ethic offers a vision of how the divine initiative of grace achieves the divine agenda of peace. Paul's vision is of the creation of the body of Christ, the one new humanity formed by the reconciliation of previously hostile parties through the cross of Christ. A community so established, however, will only be sustained in ways that reflect its origins. So, Paul's ecclesial ethic emphasizes the cross of Christ as the pattern for its distinctive form of communal witness. The parenesis of Eph 4:1—5:20 highlights qualities and practices that are themselves the means by which God's people "maintain the unity of the Spirit in the bond of peace." As God's people walk worthy of their calling "with all humility" (4:2), as they "walk in love, just as Christ also loved you and gave himself up for us" (5:2), and as they join together as a worshiping community of mutual submission (5:19–20), they embody a set of practices that takes the cross of Christ as the pattern for their witness to God's grace and peace. This is what God is doing about a fractured world and how it is that God's people bear witness to God's purpose for creation.

It should be clear by now that in his admonitions to wives and husbands Paul is concerned to highlight the marriage relationship as one important arena in which what is the case with God's household (*oikos*; see 2:19) as a whole must find expression in the more intimate relationship between husband and wife. Our examination of the details of Paul's instruction in 5:21–30 has shown that Paul emphasizes this in many ways. Still, family life can be messy. What does Paul offer for marriage partners who still live this side of the final day of redemption (4:30)?

200. Mitton, *Ephesians*, 138–39.

Nowhere else in Ephesians does Paul suggest that the conventional methods of managing conflict, expressed in *Pax Romana*, provide the model for God's household. Rather, God's household is to offer the world an alternative vision and is explicitly challenged to "walk no longer as the Gentiles walk" (4:17). For Paul, the microcosm of the household is to reflect not the macrocosm of the state (as in Aristotle), but the community of faith gathered for worship. Any effort to read Paul as offering uncritical endorsement of the structure of the Greco-Roman household must be seen as a betrayal of the church's identity as a distinctive people.

Paul makes no concession to the difficult demands of achieving genuine reconciliation in the home through the practices of an ecclesial ethic. He will not be satisfied with structural strategies that manage conflict rather than break through to peace. His vision will not permit us to accommodate to conventional interpretations of the real. Instead, he prays that the eyes of our hearts might be enlightened to recognize new possibilities for life as God intended from the beginning. Thus, we should not be surprised when in Eph 5:31 Paul cites Gen 2:24 in support of his argument that husband and wife must see themselves not as competitors in conflict, but in a relationship as intimate as that between Christ and his church: "For this cause a man shall leave his father and mother, and shall cleave to his wife; and the two shall become *one flesh*."

When Paul enlists Gen 2:24, however, the impact is not simply to underscore the unity of the one flesh relationship between husband and wife. The citation also "speaks of marriage—not in the distorted forms it takes after the fall (Gen 3.16) but in the original, created form that still subsists beneath the distortions and that becomes visible again when the existing institution of marriage is exposed to the light of Christ."[201] In other words, the vision for marriage Paul offers in Ephesians is one more expression of how God's redemptive work through Christ brings to realization God's intent for creation. What is that intent and how does the Christian form of marriage offered in Eph 5:21–33 express it?

Paul has already announced "the mystery of [God's] will" in 1:9–10 as "the gathering together of all things in Christ, things in the heavens and things upon the earth." In Eph 3:1–13 "the mystery of Christ" is the inclusion of Jew and Gentile in the one body of Christ, the church, whose existence bears witness to the rulers and authorities of the power of the gospel to reconcile. In Eph 5:31 Paul cites Gen 2:24 to emphasize that the

---

201. Watson, *Agape, Eros, Gender*, 256.

unity of husband and wife is like that enjoyed by Christ and his body, the church. "This mystery is great," proclaims Paul in 5:32. What mystery is that? "I am speaking with reference to Christ and the church," he says.

We can be excused for thinking that Paul has been speaking with reference to wife/husband relations (because he has), but Paul's concern is once again to hold Christ/church and wife/husband in close connection.[202] The existence and task of the church is as witness to God's ultimate intent for all of creation to be achieved in the "fullness of time." The divine initiative of grace pursues the divine agenda of peace by reconciling formerly hostile parties and creating through the cross one body to God (2:13–16). Paul's ecclesial ethic in Ephesians 4–6 calls for a way of life that puts that work of reconciliation on display through the qualities of humility and gentleness and through the practices of forgiveness and love. Marriage partners that recognize their responsibility to bring the fundamental practices and commitments of Christian community into their relationship know that God's work of redemption finds its expression in the formation of a people whose lives demonstrate to the world the capacity of the gospel to reconcile.

Family life can be messy. The temptation to invoke a structure of ruler to the ruled departs from the trajectory found in Ephesians. That trajectory emphasizes God's intent to unite all things in Christ, God's present work of reconciliation in the body of Christ, the call for practices and commitments that reflect the cross as the means of upholding the unity of the body of Christ, and the arena of marriage as one in which those practices and commitments find explicit and concrete application. What will this look like? "Being subject to one another in reverence of Christ—wives, for example, to your own husbands. . . . Husbands, love your wives as Christ loved the church and gave himself up for her." What answer might husband and wife give to the question of why the ecclesial ethic of Ephesians—practices and commitments shaped by the cross of Christ—must find expression in the home? "Because we are members of his body" (5:30).

---

202. See Moritz, *Profound Mystery*, 145–46, where he says, "A good case can be made for regarding Eph 5:32 as an application of the gospel mystery to marriage, just as the same mystery has elsewhere been applied to the inclusion of the gentiles into God's new society. . . . The readers are urged that awareness of being 'members of his body' (v. 30) has ramifications in all areas of life, even the intimacy of marriage."

What Ephesians offers for how these practices and commitments might be so formed in our lives and how such witness makes a difference in the world is the concern of the second volume of this work.

Bibliography

Adorno, T. W. *Minima Moralia*. Translated by E. F. N. Jephcott. London: Verso, 1987.

Allison, David B. *Reading the New Nietzsche*. Lanham, MD: Rowman & Littlefield, 2001.

Ansell-Pearson, Keith. *How to Read Nietzsche*. New York: Norton, 2005.

Aristotle. *Politics*. In *The Works of Aristotle*, vol. 2. Translated by Benjamin Jowett. Chicago: William Benton, 1952.

Arnold, Clinton E. *Ephesians: Power and Magic, The Concept of Power in Ephesians in Light of Its Historical Setting*. SNTSMS 63. Cambridge: Cambridge University Press, 1989.

Avram, Wes, editor. *Anxious About Empire: Theological Essays on the New Global Realities*. Grand Rapids: Brazos, 2004.

Aydin, Ciang, and Herman Siemens. Review of *Writings from the Late Notebooks*, edited by Rüdiger Bittner. *Journal of Nietzsche Studies* 33 (2007) 94–104.

Ayers, Robert H. "Methodological, Epistemological, and Ontological Motifs in the Thought of Reinhold Niebuhr." *Modern Theology* 7.2 (1991) 153–74.

———. "'Myth' in Theological Discourse: A Profusion of Confusion." *Anglican Theological Review* 48.2 (1966) 200–217.

Bacevich, Andrew J. *The Limits of Power: The End of American Exceptionalism*. New York: Metropolitan, 2008.

———. "Prophets and Poseurs: Niebuhr and Our Times." *World Affairs* 170.3 (2008) 24–37.

Badiou, Alain. *Ethics: An Essay on the Understanding of Evil*. Translated by Peter Hallward. New York: Verso, 2001.

Balch, David L. *Let Wives Be Submissive: The Domestic Code in 1 Peter*. SBLMS 26. Chico, CA: Scholars, 1981.

Banner, Michael. *Christian Ethics: A Brief History*. Malden, MA: Wiley-Blackwell, 2009.

Barth, Karl. *Church Dogmatics* III/3. *The Doctrine of Creation*. Translated by G. W. Bromiley and R. J. Ehrlich. Edinburgh: T. & T. Clark, 1960.

Bartholomew, Craig G., and Michael W. Goheen. *The Drama of Scripture: Finding Our Place in the Story of the Bible*. Grand Rapids: Baker Academic, 2004.

Bauckham, Richard. "Reading Scripture as a Coherent Story." In *The Art of Reading Scripture*, edited by Ellen F. Davis and Richard B. Hays, 38–53. Grand Rapids: Eerdmans, 2003.

Bayer, Oswald. *Freedom in Response: Lutheran Ethics: Sources and Controversies*. Translated by Jeffrey F. Cayzer. Oxford Studies in Theological Ethics. Oxford: Oxford University Press, 2007.

Bibliography

Beach-Verhey, Tim. Review of *American Providence: A Nation with a Mission*, by Stephen H. Webb. *Political Theology* 10.2 (2009) 376–78.

Beale, G. K. *The Book of Revelation*. NIGTC. Grand Rapids: Eerdmans, 1999.

Beinhart, Peter. "A Fighting Faith: An Argument for a New Liberalism." *The New Republic* 231.24 (2004) 17–29.

Bell, Daniel M. Review of *American Providence: A Nation with a Mission*, by Stephen H. Webb. *Journal of Church and State* 48.1 (2006) 228–30.

Benson, Bruce Ellis. *Pious Nietzsche: Decadence and Dionysian Faith*. Bloomington: Indiana University Press, 2008.

Benson, Bruce Ellis, and Peter Goodwin Heltzel, editors. *Evangelicals and Empire: Christian Alternatives to the Political Status Quo*. Grand Rapids: Brazos, 2008.

Berger, Peter. *The Sacred Canopy: Elements of a Sociological Theory of Religion*. Garden City, NY: Anchor, 1969.

Best, Ernest. *A Critical and Exegetical Commentary on Ephesians*. International Critical Commentary. Edinburgh: T. & T. Clark, 1998.

———. "Ephesians 4.28: Thieves in the Church." In *Essays on Ephesians*, 189–203. Edinburgh: T. & T. Clark, 1997.

———. "Two Types of Existence." In *Essays on Ephesians*, 139–55. Edinburgh: T. & T. Clark, 1997.

Betsworth, Roger G. *Social Ethics: An Examination of American Moral Traditions*. Louisville: Westminster John Knox, 1990.

Bettenson, Henry, editor. *Documents of the Christian Church*. 2nd ed. London: Oxford University Press, 1963.

Betz, Hans Dieter. *Galatians*. Hermeneia. Philadelphia: Fortress, 1979.

Bloom, Harold. *American Religion: The Emergence of the Post-Christian Nation*. New York: Simon & Schuster, 1992.

Bonhoeffer, Dietrich. *Ethics*. Translated by Richard Krauss, Charles C. West, and Douglas W. Stott. Dietrich Bonhoeffer Works 6. Minneapolis: Fortress, 2005.

Bradley, Keith. *Discovering the Roman Family: Studies in Roman Social History*. Oxford: Oxford University Press, 1991.

Briggs, Richard S. "Speech-Act Theory." In *Words & The Word: Explorations in Interpretation & Literary Theory*, edited by David G. Firth and Jamie A. Grant, 75–110. Downers Grove: InterVarsity, 2008.

Brooks, David. "Obama, Gospel and Verse." *New York Times*, April 26, 2007. Online: http://select.nytimes.com/2007/04/26/opinion/26brooks.html?_r=1&ref=reinhold_niebuhr.

Brown, Charles C. *Niebuhr and His Age: Reinhold Niebuhr's Prophetic Role and Legacy*. Harrisburg, PA: Trinity, 2002.

Brown, Joanne Carlson, and Rebecca Parker. "For God So Loved the World?" In *Christianity, Patriarchy, and Abuse: A Feminist Critique*, edited by Joanne Carlson Brown and Carole R. Bohn, 1–30. New York: Pilgrim, 1989.

Brueggemann, Walter. *Theology of the Old Testament: Testimony, Dispute, Advocacy*. Minneapolis: Fortress, 1997.

Buckley, Michael J. *At the Origins of Modern Atheism*. New Haven: Yale University Press, 1987.

Burridge, Richard. *Imitating Jesus: An Inclusive Approach to New Testament Ethics*. Grand Rapids: Eerdmans, 2007.

Caird, G. B. *The Language and Imagery of the Bible*. Philadelphia: Westminster, 1980.

Calkins, Raymond. *The Modern Message of the Minor Prophets*. New York: Harper & Row, 1947.

Calvin, John. *Institutes of the Christian Religion*. Translated by Ford Lewis Battles. Edited by John T. McNeil. Philadelphia: Westminster, 1960.

Campbell, Douglas A. *The Deliverance of God: An Apocalyptic Rereading of Justification in Paul*. Grand Rapids: Eerdmans, 2009.

———. *The Quest for Paul's Gospel: A Suggested Strategy*. London: T. & T. Clark, 2005.

Campbell, William S. "Unity and Diversity in the Church: Transformed Identities and the Peace of Christ in Ephesians." *Transformation* 24.1 (2008) 15–31.

Cannon, George E. *The Use of Traditional Materials in Colossians*. Macon, GA: Mercer University Press, 1983.

Caragounis, Chrys C. *The Ephesian* Mysterion: *Meaning and Context*. Lund: Gleerup, 1977.

Carson, D. A. "Maintaining Scientific and Christian Truths in a Postmodern World." *Science & Christian Belief* 14.2 (2002) 107–22.

Carter, Warren. "Paul and the Roman Empire: Recent Perspectives." In *Paul Unbound: Other Perspectives on the Apostle*, edited by Mark Given. Peabody, MA: Hendrickson, 2010.

———. *The Roman Empire and the New Testament: An Essential Guide*. Nashville: Abingdon, 2006.

Cartwright, Michael G. *Practices, Politics, and Performances: Toward a Communal Hermeneutic for Christian Ethics*. Princeton Theological Monograph Series. Eugene, OR: Pickwick, 2006.

Cate, Curtis. *Friedrich Nietzsche*. Woodstock: Overlook, 2005.

Cavanaugh, William T. "'A Fire Strong Enough to Consume the House': The Wars of Religion and the Rise of the State." *Modern Theology* 11.4 (1995) 397–420.

———. *The Myth of Religious Violence: Secular Ideology and the Roots of Modern Conflict*. Oxford: Oxford University Press, 2009.

———. "Pilgrim People." In *Gathered for the Journey: Moral Theology in a Catholic Perspective*, edited by David Matzko McCarthy and M. Therese Lysaught, 88–105. Grand Rapids: Eerdmans, 2007.

———. *Theopolitical Imagination: Discovering the Liturgy as a Political Act in an Age of Global Consumerism*. London: T. & T. Clark, 2002.

Chapman, Audrey R. "Genetic Engineering and Theology: Exploring the Connections." *Theology Today* 59.1 (2002) 78.

Childs, Brevard S. *Old Testament Theology in a Canonical Context*. Philadelphia: Fortress, 1986.

Clapp, Rodney. "God Is Not 'A Stranger on the Bus.'" In *God Is Not . . . Religious, Nice, "One of Us," An American, A Capitalist*, edited by D. Brent Laytham, 23–38. Grand Rapids: Brazos, 2004.

Clark, Maudemarie. "Nietzsche's Doctrines of the Will to Power." In *Nietzsche*, edited by John Richardson and Brian Leiter, 139–49. Oxford: Oxford University Press, 2001.

Cohick, Lynn H. *Ephesians*. New Covenant Commentary Series. Eugene, OR: Cascade Books, 2010.

Cook, Stephen L. *The Apocalyptic Literature*. Nashville: Abingdon, 2003.

Crenshaw, James. *Defending God: Biblical Responses to the Problem of Evil*. New York: Oxford University Press, 2005.

———. "Theodicy and Prophetic Literature." In *Theodicy in the World of the Bible*, edited by Antti Laato and Johannes C. de Moor, 236–55. Leiden: Brill, 2003.

Crouter, Richard. *Reinhold Niebuhr: On Politics, Religion, and Christian Faith*. Oxford: Oxford University Press, 2010.

Dackson, Wendy. "Reinhold Niebuhr's 'Outsider Ecclesiology.'" In *Reinhold Niebuhr & Contemporary Politics: God & Power*, edited by Richard Harries and Stephen Platten, 87–101. Oxford: Oxford University Press, 2010.

Darko, Daniel K. *No Longer Living as the Gentiles: Differentiation and Shared Ethical Values in Ephesians 4:17—6:9*. Library of New Testament Studies 375. London: T. & T. Clark, 2008.

Davies, Margaret. "Work and Slavery in the New Testament: Impoverishments of Traditions." In *The Bible in Ethics: The Second Sheffield Colloquium*, edited by John W. Rogerson, Margaret Davies, and M. Daniel Carroll R., 315–47. Sheffield: Sheffield Academic, 1995.

Dawes, Gregory W. *The Body in Question: Metaphor & Meaning in the Interpretation of Ephesians 5:21–33*. Leiden: Brill, 1998.

Dawkins, Richard. *The God Delusion*. Boston: Houghton Mifflin, 2006.

De Boer, M. C. "Paul and Apocalyptic Eschatology." In *The Encyclopedia of Apocalypticism: Volume 1, The Origins of Apocalypticism in Judaism and Christianity*, edited by John J. Collins, 345–83. New York: Continuum, 2006.

———. "Paul, Theologian of God's Apocalypse." *Interpretation* 56.1 (2002) 21–33.

Dell'Oro, Roberto. "Theological Anthropology and Bioethics." In *Health and Human Flourishing: Religion, Medicine, and Moral Anthropology*, edited by Carol R. Taylor and Roberto Dell'Oro, 13–32. Washington, DC: Georgetown University Press, 2006.

DeSilva, David A. *Honor, Patronage, Kinship & Purity: Unlocking New Testament Culture*. Downers Grove: InterVarsity, 2000.

Dictionary for Theological Interpretation of the Bible. Edited by Kevin J. Vanhoozer et al. Grand Rapids: Baker Academic, 2005.

Dorrien, Gary. *Imperial Designs: Neoconservativism and the New Pax Americana*. New York: Routledge, 2004.

Dostoevsky, Fyodor Mikhailovich. *The Brothers Karamazov*. Translated by Constance Garnett. Chicago: William Benton, 1952.

Dunn, James D. G. "The Household Rules in the New Testament." In *The Family in Theological Perspective*, edited by Stephen C. Barton, 43–63. Edinburgh: T. & T. Clark, 1996.

———. *The Theology of Paul the Apostle*. Grand Rapids: Eerdmans, 1997.

Durst, Dennis L. "Evangelical Engagement with Eugenics, 1900–1940." *Ethics & Medicine* 18.2 (2002) 45–53.

Elie, Paul. "A Man for All Reasons." *Atlantic Monthly* 300.4 (November 2007) 82–96.

Elliott, Neil. *The Arrogance of Nations: Reading Romans in the Shadow of Empire*. Minneapolis: Fortress, 2008.

Elshtain, Jean Bethke. "The Body and the Quest for Control." In *Is Human Nature Obsolete? Genetics, Bioengineering, and the Future of the Human Condition*, edited by Harold W. Baillie and Timothy K. Casey, 155–75. Cambridge: MIT Press, 2005.

———. *Just War against Terror: The Burden of American Power in a Violent World*. New York: Basic Books, 2004.

Fackre, Gabriel. "Was Reinhold Niebuhr a Christian?" *First Things* 126 (October 2002) 25–27.

Fee, Gordon. "Paul and the Metaphors for Salvation." In *The Redemption: An Interdisciplinary Symposium on Christ as Redeemer*, edited by Stephen T. Davis, Daniel Kendall, Gerald O'Collins, 43–67. Oxford: Oxford University Press, 2004.

Ferguson, Everett. *Backgrounds of Early Christianity*. Grand Rapids: Eerdmans, 1987.

Finstuen, Andrew. "This American Mess: Where Is Reinhold Niebuhr When We Need Him?" *Christian Century* 126.24 (December 1, 2009) 11–12.

Fitch, David E. *The End of Evangelicalism? Discerning a New Faithfulness for Mission: Towards an Evangelical Political Theology*. Theopolitical Visions 9. Eugene, OR: Cascade Books, 2011.

Fletcher, Joseph. *Morals and Medicine*. Princeton: Princeton University Press, 1954.

Ford, David F. *Self and Salvation: Being Transformed*. Cambridge: Cambridge University Press, 1999.

Fox, Richard. *Reinhold Niebuhr: A Biography*. San Francisco: Harper & Row, 1986.

Fowl, Stephen E. "Making Stealing Possible: Criminal Thoughts on Building an Ecclesial Common Life." In *Engaging Scripture*, 161–77. Oxford: Blackwell, 1998.

Fraser, Giles. *Redeeming Nietzsche: On the Piety of Unbelief*. London: Routledge, 2002.

French, David. "Evangelicals' Collapsing Cultural Influence." Online: http://www.nationalreview.com/corner/293457/evangelicals-collapsing-cultural-influence-david-french.

Fretheim, Terence E. *God and World in the Old Testament: A Relational Theology of Creation*. Nashville: Abingdon, 2005.

———. *Jeremiah*. Macon, GA: Smyth & Helwys, 2002.

Furnish, Victor Paul. *Theology and Ethics in Paul*. 1968. Reprint, Louisville: Westminster John Knox, 2009.

Gilkey, Langdon. *On Niebuhr: A Theological Study*. Chicago: University of Chicago Press, 2001.

Gillespie, Michael Allen. *Nihilism Before Nietzsche*. Chicago: University of Chicago Press, 1995.

Goheen, Michael W. "The Urgency of Reading the Bible as One Story." *Theology Today* 64 (2008) 469–83.

Gombis, Timothy G. "The Triumph of God in Christ: Divine Warfare in the Argument of Ephesians." PhD diss., University of St. Andrews, 2005.

Gorman, Michael J. *Apostle of the Crucified Lord: A Theological Introduction to Paul & His Letters*. Grand Rapids: Eerdmans, 2004.

———. *Cruciformity: Paul's Narrative Spirituality of the Cross*. Grand Rapids: Eerdmans, 2001.

———. *Inhabiting the Cruciform God: Kenosis, Justification, and Theosis in Paul's Narrative Soteriology*. Grand Rapids: Eerdmans, 2009.

Gorringe, Timothy. *God's Just Vengeance: Crime, Violence and the Rhetoric of Salvation*. Cambridge: Cambridge University Press, 1996.

Gowan, Donald E. *Theology of the Prophetic Books: The Death and Resurrection of Israel*. Louisville: Westminster John Knox, 1998.

Gräbe, Petrus J. "Salvation in Colossians and Ephesians." In *Salvation in the New Testament: Perspectives on Soteriology*, edited by Jan G. van der Watt, 287–304. Leiden: Brill, 2005.

Graham, Gordon. *Evil and Christian Ethics*. Cambridge: Cambridge University Press, 2001.

Green, Garrett. *Theology, Hermeneutics, and Imagination: The Crisis of Interpretation at the End of Modernity.* Cambridge: Cambridge University Press, 2000.

Green, Joel B., and Mark D. Baker. *Recovering the Scandal of the Cross: Atonement in New Testament & Contemporary Contexts.* Downers Grove: InterVarsity, 2000.

Grudem, Wayne. "Does *kephalē* ('Head') Mean 'Source' or 'Authority Over' in Greek Literature? A Survey of 2336 Examples." *Trinity Journal* 6, n.s. (1985) 38–59.

Gustafson, James M. *Ethics from a Theocentric Perspective.* 2 vols. Chicago: University of Chicago Press, 1981–84.

———. "Theology in the Service of Ethics: An Interpretation of Reinhold Niebuhr's Theological Ethics." In *Reinhold Niebuhr and the Issues of Our Time*, edited by Richard Harries, 24–45. Grand Rapids: Eerdmans, 1986.

Hall, Amy Laura. "To Form a More Perfect Union: Mainline Protestantism and the Popularization of Eugenics." In *Theology, Disability and the New Genetics: Why Science Needs the Church*, edited by John Swinton and Brian Brock, 75–95. London: T. & T. Clark, 2007.

Halliwell, Martin. *The Constant Dialogue: Reinhold Niebuhr & American Intellectual Culture.* Lanham, MD: Rowman & Littlefield, 2005.

Hampson, Daphne. "Reinhold Niebuhr on Sin: A Critique." In *Reinhold Niebuhr and the Issues of Our Time*, edited by Richard Harries, 46–60. Grand Rapids: Eerdmans, 1986.

Hardy, Lee. *The Fabric of This World: Inquiries into Calling, Career Choice, and the Design of Human Work.* Grand Rapids: Eerdmans, 1990.

Harink, Douglas. *Paul among the Postliberals: Pauline Theology beyond Christendom and Modernity.* Grand Rapids: Brazos, 2003.

Harries, Richard, editor. *Reinhold Niebuhr and the Issues of Our Time.* Grand Rapids: Eerdmans, 1986.

Harries, Richard, and Stephen Platten, editors. *Reinhold Niebuhr & Contemporary Politics: God & Power.* Oxford: Oxford University Press, 2010.

Harrington, Daniel J. *The Church According to the New Testament: What the Wisdom and Witness of Early Christianity Teach Us Today.* Lanham, MD: Sheed & Ward, 2001.

Hart, David Bentley. *The Beauty of the Infinite: The Aesthetics of Christian Truth.* Grand Rapids: Eerdmans, 2003.

Hauerwas, Stanley. "Communitarians and Medical Ethicists or 'Why I Am None of the Above.'" In *Dispatches from the Front: Theological Engagements with the Secular*, 156–63. Durham: Duke University Press, 1994.

———. "Creation as Apocalyptic: A Tribute to William Stringfellow." In *Dispatches from the Front: Theological Engagements with the Secular*, 107–15. Durham: Duke University Press, 1994.

———. "The Democratic Policing of Christianity." In *Dispatches from the Front: Theological Engagements with the Secular*, 91–106. Durham: Duke University Press, 1994.

———. "God the Measurer." Review of *Ethics from a Theocentric Perspective: Volume 1, Theology and Ethics*, by James M. Gustafson. *Journal of Religion* 62.4 (1982) 402–11.

———. "History as Fate: How Justification by Faith Became Anthropology (and History) in America." In *Wilderness Wanderings: Probing Twentieth-Century Theology and Philosophy*, 32–47. Boulder, CO: Westview, 1997.

———. *Naming the Silences: God, Medicine, and the Problem of Suffering.* Grand Rapids: Eerdmans, 1990.

———. *The Peaceable Kingdom: A Primer in Christian Ethics.* Notre Dame: University of Notre Dame Press, 1983.

———. *Sanctify Them in the Truth: Holiness Exemplified.* Nashville: Abingdon, 1998.

———. *Vision and Virtue: Essays in Christian Ethical Reflection.* Notre Dame: University of Notre Dame Press, 1974.

———. *With the Grain of the Universe: The Church's Witness and Natural Theology.* Grand Rapids: Brazos, 2001.

———. "Work as Co-Creation: A Critique of a Remarkably Bad Idea." In *In Good Company: The Church as Polis*, 109–24. Notre Dame: University of Notre Dame Press, 1995.

Hauerwas, Stanley, with Michael Broadway. "The Irony of Reinhold Niebuhr: The Ideological Character of 'Christian Realism.'" In *Wilderness Wanderings: Probing Twentieth-Century Theology and Philosophy*, by Stanley M. Hauerwas, 48–61. Boulder, CO: Westview, 1997.

Hauerwas, Stanley, and Samuel Wells. "The Gift of the Church and the Gifts God Gives It." In *The Blackwell Companion to Christian Ethics*, 2nd ed., edited by Stanley Hauerwas and Samuel Wells, 13–27. Oxford: Blackwell, 2011.

Hays, Richard B. "Crucified with Christ: A Synthesis of the Theology of 1 and 2 Thessalonians, Philemon, Philippians, and Galatians." In *Pauline Theology, Volume 1: Thessalonians, Philippians, Galatians, Philemon*, edited by Jouette M. Bassler, 227–43. Minneapolis: Fortress, 1991.

———. *Echoes of Scripture in the Letters of Paul.* New Haven: Yale University Press, 1989.

———. *The Faith of Jesus Christ: The Narrative Substructure of Galatians 3:1—4:11.* 2nd edition. Grand Rapids: Eerdmans, 2002.

Heil, John P. *Ephesians: Empowerment to Walk in Love for the Unity of All in Christ.* Studies in Biblical Literature. Atlanta: Society of Biblical Literature, 2007.

Hengel, Martin. *The Cross of the Son of God.* Translated by John Bowden. London: SCM, 1986.

Hick, John. *Evil and the God of Love.* Rev. ed. San Francisco: Harper & Row, 1977.

Hiebert, Theodore. "The Book of Habakkuk: Introduction, Commentary, and Reflections." In *The New Interpreter's Bible*, 7:621–55. Nashville: Abingdon, 1996.

Hoehner, Harold W. *Ephesians: An Exegetical Commentary.* Grand Rapids: Baker Academic, 2002.

Holloway, Joseph. *Peripateō as a Thematic Marker for Pauline Ethics.* Lewiston, NY: Mellen Research University Press, 1992.

Hook, C. Christopher. "Genetic Testing and Confidentiality." In *Genetic Ethics: Do the Ends Justify the Genes?*, edited by John F. Kilner, Rebecca D. Pentz, and Frank E. Young, 124–35. Grand Rapids: Eerdmans, 1997.

Horrell, David G. *Solidarity and Difference: A Contemporary Reading of Paul's Ethics.* Edinburgh: T. & T. Clark, 2005.

Horsley, Richard A. "General Introduction." In *Paul and Empire: Religion and Power in Roman Imperial Society*, edited by Richard A. Horsley, 1–8. Harrisburg, PA: Trinity, 1997.

———, editor. *Paul and Politics: Ekklesia, Israel, Imperium, Interpretation.* Harrisburg, PA: Trinity, 2000.

Bibliography

————, editor. *Paul and the Roman Imperial Order*. Harrisburg, PA: Trinity, 2004.

Hovey, Craig. *Nietzsche and Theology*. London: T. & T. Clark, 2008.

Hubben, William. *Dostoevsky, Kierkegaard, Nietzsche, & Kafka*. New York: Touchstone, 1992.

Huebner, Harry J. *An Introduction to Christian Ethics: History, Movements, People*. Waco: Baylor University Press, 2012.

Hughes, John. *The End of Work: Theological Critiques of Capitalism*. Malden, MA: Blackwell, 2007.

Hughes, Richard T. *Christian America and the Kingdom of God*. Urbana: University of Illinois Press, 2009.

————. *Myths America Lives By*. Urbana: University of Illinois Press, 2003.

Irwin, Neil, and Amit R. Paley. "Greenspan Says He Was Wrong on Regulation." *Washington Post*, October 24, 2008. Online: http://www.washingtonpost.com/wp-dyn/content/article/2008/10/23/AR2008102300193.html?hpid=topnews.

Jacoby, Jeff. "Choosing to Eliminate Unwanted Daughters." *Boston Globe*, April 6, 2006. Online: http://www.boston.com/bostonglobe/editorial_opinion/oped/articles/2008/04/06/choosing_to_eliminate_unwanted_daughters/.

Jeal, Roy R. *Integrating Theology and Ethics in Ephesians*. Lewiston, NY: Edwin Mellen, 2000.

Jensen, David H. *Responsive Labor: A Theology of Work*. Louisville: Westminster John Knox, 2006.

Johanson, Maryann. Review of *The Truman Show*. Online: http://www.flickfilosopher.com/blog/1998/06/the_truman_show_review.html.

Johnson, Chalmers. *Nemesis: The Last Days of the American Republic*. New York: Metropolitan, 2007.

Jones, Joe. *A Grammar of Christian Faith: Systematic Explorations in Christian Life and Doctrine*. Lanham, MD: Rowman & Littlefield, 2002.

Kain, Philip J. "Nietzsche, Eternal Recurrence, and the Horror of Existence." *Journal of Nietzsche Studies* 33 (2007) 49–63.

Kant, Immanuel. *The Critique of Practical Reason*. Translated by T. K. Abbott. Chicago: William Benton, 1952.

————. *The Critique of Pure Reason*. Translated by J. M. D. Meiklejohn. Chicago: William Benton, 1952.

————. "Foundations of the Metaphysics of Morals." In *Foundations of the Metaphysics of Morals and What Is Enlightenment?*, translated by Lewis White Black, 3–83. Indianapolis: Bobbs-Merrill, 1959.

————. "What Is Enlightenment?" In *Foundations of the Metaphysics of Morals and What Is Enlightenment?*, translated by Lewis White Black, 85–92. Indianapolis: Bobbs-Merrill, 1959.

Katongole, Emmanuel. *Beyond Universal Reason: The Relation between Religion and Ethics in the Work of Stanley Hauerwas*. Notre Dame: University of Notre Dame Press, 2000.

Kaufman, Gordon D. "How Is God to Be Understood in a Theocentric Ethic?" In *James M. Gustafson's Theocentric Ethics: Interpretations and Assessments*, edited by Harlan R. Beckley and Charles M. Swezey, 13–37. Macon, GA: Mercer University Press, 1988.

Kaufmann, Walter. *Nietzsche: Philosopher, Psychologist, Antichrist*. 4th ed. Princeton: Princeton University Press, 1974.

Kegley, Charles W., editor. *Reinhold Niebuhr: His Religious, Social, and Political Thought.* New York: Pilgrim, 1984.

Kelsey, David. *Eccentric Existence: A Theological Anthropology.* Vol. 2. Louisville: Westminster John Knox, 2009.

Kenny, Anthony. *A New History of Philosophy.* Vol. 4, *Philosophy in the Modern World.* Oxford: Oxford University Press, 2007.

Kierkegaard, Søren. *Attack upon Christendom.* Translated by Walter Lowrie. Princeton: Princeton University Press, 1968.

Kitchen, Martin. *Ephesians.* London: Routledge, 1994.

Klein, Ralph W. *Israel in Exile: A Theological Interpretation.* Philadelphia: Fortress, 1979.

Laato, Antti, and Johannes C. de Moor, editors. *Theodicy in the World of the Bible.* Leiden: Brill, 2003.

Lampe, Peter. "Paul, Patrons, and Clients." In *Paul in the Greco-Roman World: A Handbook,* edited by J. Paul Sampley, 488–523. Harrisburg, PA: Trinity, 2003.

Lau, Te-Li. *The Politics of Peace: Ephesians, Dio Chrysostom, and the Confucian Four Books.* STNT 133. Leiden: Brill, 2010.

Lawrence, Matt. *Like a Splinter in Your Mind: The Philosophy Behind the Matrix Trilogy.* Malden, MA: Blackwell, 2004.

Laytham, D. Brent, editor. *God Is Not . . . Religious, Nice, "One of Us," An American, A Capitalist.* Grand Rapids: Brazos, 2004.

Lincoln, Andrew T. *Ephesians.* Word Biblical Commentary 42. Dallas: Word, 1990.

———. "Liberation from the Powers: Supernatural Spirits or Societal Structures?" In *The Bible in Human Society: Essays in Honour of John Rogerson,* edited by M. Daniel Carroll R., David J. A. Clines, and Philip R. Davies, 335–54. JSOTSS 200. Sheffield: Sheffield Academic, 1995.

———. *Paradise Now and Not Yet: Studies in the Role of the Heavenly Dimension in Paul's Thought with Special Reference to His Eschatology.* SNTSMS 43. Cambridge: Cambridge University Press, 1981.

———. "The Theology of Ephesians." In *The Theology of the Later Paulines,* by Andrew T. Lincoln and A. J. M. Wedderburn, 75–166. Cambridge: Cambridge University Press, 1993.

Lindberg, Carter. *The European Reformations.* Cambridge, MA: Blackwell, 1996.

Logan, James. *Good Punishment: Christian Moral Practice and U.S. Imprisonment.* Grand Rapids: Eerdmans, 2008.

Long, D. Stephen. *The Goodness of God: Theology, Church, and the Social Order.* Grand Rapids: Brazos, 2001.

Long, D. Stephen, and Nancy Ruth Fox with Tripp York. *Calculated Futures: Theology, Ethics, and Economics.* Waco: Baylor University Press, 2007.

Long, Fredrick J. "Paul's Political Theology in Ephesians." Paper presented at the annual meeting of the Evangelical Theological Society, San Diego, CA, November 14–16, 2007.

Longenecker, Bruce W., editor. *Narrative Dynamics in Paul: A Critical Assessment.* Louisville: Westminster John Knox, 2002.

Lovatt, Mark F. W. *Confronting the Will-to-Power: A Reconsideration of the Theology of Reinhold Niebuhr.* Paternoster Biblical and Theological Monographs. Carlisle: Paternoster, 2001.

Lovin, Robin W. *Reinhold Niebuhr.* Nashville: Abingdon, 2007.

Bibliography

———. *Reinhold Niebuhr and Christian Realism*. Cambridge: Cambridge University Press, 1995.

———. "Reinhold Niebuhr in Contemporary Scholarship." *Journal of Religious Ethics* 31.3 (2003) 489–505.

———. "Reinhold Niebuhr's 'The Nature and Destiny of Man.'" In *The Oxford Handbook of Theological Ethics*, edited by Gilbert Meilaender and William Werpehowski, 487–502. Oxford: Oxford University Press, 2005.

Löwith, Karl. *From Hegel to Nietzsche: The Revolution in Nineteenth-Century Thought*. New York: Columbia University Press, 1964.

Luther, Martin. *Notes on Ecclesiastes*. In vol. 15 of *Luther's Works*, edited and translated by Jaroslav Pelikan, 3–193. St. Louis: Concordia, 1972.

MacDonald, Margaret Y. *Colossians and Ephesians*. Collegeville, MN: Liturgical, 2008.

———. "The Politics of Identity in Ephesians." *JSNT* 26.4 (2004) 425–38.

MacIntyre, Alasdair. *After Virtue: A Study in Moral Theory*. 2nd ed. Notre Dame: University of Notre Dame Press, 1984.

———. "I'm Not a Communitarian, But . . ." *The Responsive Community* 1 (1991) 91–92.

Macpherson, C. B. *The Political Theory of Possessive Individualism: Hobbes to Locke*. Oxford: Oxford University Press, 1962.

Maguire, Daniel C. Review of *Ethics from a Theocentric Perspective: Volume I, Theology and Ethics*, by James M. Gustafson. *Union Seminary Quarterly Review* 37.3 (1982) 256–59.

Malherbe, Abraham. *Moral Exhortation: A Greco-Roman Sourcebook*. Philadelphia: Westminster, 1986.

Martin, Raymond, and John Barresi. *The Rise and Fall of Soul and Self: An Intellectual History of Personal Identity*. New York: Columbia University Press, 2006.

Martinez, Florentino García. "Apocalypticism in the Dead Sea Scrolls." In *The Encyclopedia of Apocalypticism*, vol. 1, *The Origins of Apocalypticism in Judaism and Christianity*, edited by John J. Collins, 162–92. New York: Continuum, 2006.

Martyn, J. Louis. *Galatians: A New Translation with Introduction and Commentary*. Anchor Bible 33A. New York: Doubleday, 1997.

Matera, Frank J. *New Testament Ethics: The Legacies of Jesus and Paul*. Louisville: Westminster John Knox, 1996.

Mathewes, Charles T. *Evil and the Augustinian Tradition*. Cambridge: Cambridge University Press, 2001.

Matlock, R. Barry. *Unveiling the Apocalyptic Paul: Paul's Interpreters and the Rhetoric of Criticism*. JSNTSS 127. Sheffield: Sheffield Academic, 1996.

McCann, Dennis P. "Hermeneutics and Ethics: The Example of Reinhold Niebuhr." *The Journal of Religious Ethics* 8.1 (1980) 27–53.

McClay, Wilfred M. "The Continuing Irony of American History." *First Things* 120 (2002) 20–25.

———. "Reinhold Niebuhr and the Problem of Religious Pluralism." In *Reinhold Niebuhr & Contemporary Politics: God & Power*, edited by Richard Harries and Stephen Platten, 218–33. Oxford: Oxford University Press, 2010.

McCorkle, Mac. "On Recent Political Uses of Reinhold Niebuhr: Toward a New Appreciation of His Legacy." In *Reinhold Niebuhr & Contemporary Politics: God & Power*, edited by Richard Harries and Stephen Platten, 18–41. Oxford: Oxford University Press, 2010.

McCormick, Richard. "Gustafson's God: Who? What? Where? (Etc.)." *Journal of Religious Ethics* 13.1 (1985) 53–70.

McKenny, Gerald P. *To Relieve the Human Condition: Bioethics, Technology, and the Body.* Albany: State University of New York Press, 1997.

Meadors, Edward P. "'It Never Entered My Mind': The Problematic Theodicy of Theistic Determinism." *Bulletin for Biblical Research* 19.2 (2009) 185–214.

Meeks, M. Douglas. *God the Economist: The Doctrine of God and Political Economy.* Minneapolis: Fortress, 1989.

Meeks, Wayne. *The First Urban Christians: The Social World of the Apostle Paul.* New Haven: Yale University Press, 1983.

———. "The 'Haustafeln' and American Slavery: A Hermeneutical Challenge." In *Theology and Ethics in Paul and His Interpreters: Essays in Honor of Victor Paul Furnish*, edited by Eugene H. Lovering, Jr. and Jerry L. Sumney, 232–53. Nashville: Abingdon, 1996.

Meilaender, Gilbert. *Bioethics: A Primer for Christians.* 2nd ed. Grand Rapids: Eerdmans, 2004.

Mickelsen, Berkely, and Alvera Mickelsen. "What Does *kephalē* Mean in the New Testament?" In *Woman, Authority and the Bible*, edited by Alvera Mickelsen, 97–110. Downers Grove: InterVarsity, 1986.

Middleton, J. Richard. "A New Heaven and a New Earth: The Case for a Holistic Reading of the Biblical Story of Redemption." *Journal for Christian Theological Research* 11 (2006) 73–97.

Miller, David W. *God at Work: The History and Promise of the Faith at Work Movement.* New York: Oxford University Press, 2007.

Miller, Walter M., Jr. *A Canticle for Leibowitz.* New York: J. P. Lippencott, 1959.

Mitton, C. Leslie. *Ephesians.* New Century Bible. Grand Rapids: Eerdmans, 1982.

Moberly, R. W. L. *Prophecy and Discernment.* Cambridge: Cambridge University Press, 2006.

Moltmann, Jürgen. *Hope and Planning.* Translated by Margaret Clarkson. New York: Harper & Row, 1971.

Moritz, Thorsten. *A Profound Mystery: The Use of the Old Testament in Ephesians.* SNT 85. Leiden: Brill, 1996.

Moulaison, Jane Barter. "Theology, Church and Political Change: Engaging Reinhold Niebuhr's Ecclesiology." *Didaskalia* (2008) 179–90.

Murphy, Tim. *Nietzsche, Metaphor, Religion.* Albany: State University of New York Press, 2001.

Nehamas, Alexander. "The Eternal Recurrence." In *Nietzsche*, edited by John Richardson and Brian Leiter, 118–38. Oxford: Oxford University Press, 2001.

Neiman, Susan. *Evil in Modern Thought: An Alternative History of Philosophy.* Princeton: Princeton University Press, 2003.

Newman, Carey C. "Election and Predestination in Ephesians 1:4–6a: An Exegetical-Theological Study of the Historical, Christological Realization of God's Purpose." *Review & Expositor* 93.2 (1996) 237–47.

Niebuhr, Reinhold. "As Deceivers, Yet True." In *Beyond Tragedy: Essays on the Christian Interpretation of History*, 1–24. New York: Scribners, 1938.

———. *The Children of Light and the Children of Darkness: A Vindication of Democracy and a Critique of Its Traditional Defenders.* London: Nisbet, 1945.

Bibliography

————. "Christian Faith and Social Action." In *Christian Faith and Social Action: A Symposium*, edited by John A. Hutchison, 225–42. New York: Scribner, 1953.

————. *The Essential Reinhold Niebuhr: Selected Essays and Addresses*, edited by Robert McAfee Brown. New Haven: Yale University Press, 1986.

————. *Faith and History: A Comparison of Christian and Modern Views of History*. New York: Scribner, 1949.

————. "How Philanthropic Is Henry Ford?" In *Love & Justice: Selections from the Shorter Writings of Reinhold Niebuhr*, edited by D. B. Robertson, 98–103. Gloucester, MA: Peter Smith, 1976.

————. "The Idolatry of America." In *Love & Justice: Selections from the Shorter Writings of Reinhold Niebuhr*, edited by D. B. Robertson, 94–97. Gloucester, MA: Peter Smith, 1976.

————. *An Interpretation of Christian Ethics*. 1935. Reprint, New York: Seabury, 1979.

————. *Justice & Mercy*. 1974. Reprint, Louisville: Westminster John Knox, 1991.

————. "Liberty and Equality." In *Faith and Politics: A Commentary on Religious, Social and Political Thought in a Technological Age*, edited by Ronald H. Stone, 185–98. New York: George Braziller, 1968.

————. *Man's Nature and His Communities*. New York: Scribner, 1965.

————. *Moral Man and Immoral Society: A Study in Ethics and Politics*. New York: Scribner's, 1932.

————. "Mystery and Meaning." In *The Essential Reinhold Niebuhr: Selected Essays and Addresses*, edited by Robert McAfee Brown, 237–49. New Haven: Yale University Press, 1986.

————. *The Nature and Destiny of Man*. 2 vols. New York: Scribner, 1941–43.

————. "Optimism, Pessimism, and Religious Faith." In *The Essential Reinhold Niebuhr: Selected Essays and Addresses*, edited by Robert McAfee Brown, 3–17. New Haven: Yale University Press, 1986.

————. "Reply to Interpretation and Criticism." In *Reinhold Niebuhr: His Religious, Social and Political Thought*, edited by Charles W. Kegley, 505–27. New York: Pilgrim, 1984.

————. "The Resources of the Christian Faith in a Dynamic Civilization and an Expanding Society." In *The Self and the Dramas of History*, 147–62. New York: Scribner, 1955.

————. "To Prevent the Triumph of an Intolerable Tyranny." In *Love & Justice: Selections from the Shorter Writings of Reinhold Niebuhr*, edited by D. B. Robertson, 272–78. Gloucester, MA: Peter Smith, 1976.

————. "The Truth in Myths." In *Faith and Politics: A Commentary on Religious, Social and Political Thought in a Technological Age*, edited by Ronald H. Stone, 15–31. New York: George Braziller, 1968.

————. "A View of Life from the Sidelines." In *The Essential Reinhold Niebuhr: Selected Essays and Addresses*, edited by Robert McAfee Brown, 250–57. New Haven: Yale University Press, 1986.

Niebuhr, Ursula M. "Introduction." In *Justice & Mercy*, edited by Ursula M. Niebuhr, 1–9. 1974. Reprint, Louisville: Westminster John Knox, 1991.

Nietzsche, Friedrich. "The Antichrist." In *The Anti-Christ, Ecce Homo, Twilight of the Idols and Other Writings*, edited by Aaron Ridley and Judith Norman, 1–67. Cambridge: Cambridge University Press, 2005.

———. *Beyond Good and Evil: Prelude to a Philosophy of the Future*. Translated by R. J. Hollingdale. London: Penguin, 1973.

———. *The Birth of Tragedy and Other Writings*. Translated by Ronald Speirs. Edited by Raymond Guess and Ronald Speirs. Cambridge: Cambridge University Press, 1999.

———. *Daybreak: Thoughts on the Prejudices of Morality*. Translated by R. J. Hollingdale. Edited by Maudemarie Clark and Brian Leiter. Cambridge: Cambridge University Press, 1997.

———. *The Gay Science*. Translated by Josefine Nauckhoff. Edited by Bernard Williams. Cambridge: Cambridge University Press, 2001.

———. *Human, All Too Human: A Book for Free Spirits*. Translated by R. J. Hollingdale. Cambridge: Cambridge University Press, 1986.

———. "Letter to His Sister." In *The Portable Nietzsche*, translated and edited by Walter Kaufmann, 29–30. New York: Penguin, 1954.

———. *On the Genealogy of Morality*. Rev. ed. Translated by Carol Diethe. Edited by Keith Ansell-Pearson. Cambridge: Cambridge University Press, 1997.

———. *Thus Spoke Zarathustra*. Translated by Adrian Del Caro. Edited by Adrian Del Caro and Robert Pippin. Cambridge: Cambridge University Press, 2006.

———. *Twilight of the Idols or How to Philosophize with a Hammer*. In *The Anti-Christ, Ecce Homo, Twilight of the Idols and Other Writings*, edited by Aaron Ridley and Judith Norman, 153–229. Cambridge: Cambridge University Press, 2005.

———. "Why I Am So Clever." In *The Anti-Christ, Ecce Homo, Twilight of the Idols and Other Writings*, edited by Aaron Ridley and Judith Norman, 85–99. Cambridge: Cambridge University Press, 2005.

———. *The Will to Power*. Translated by Walter Kaufmann and R. J. Hollingdale. Edited by Walter Kaufmann. New York: Vintage, 1968.

———. *Writings from the Late Notebooks*. Translated by Kate Sturge. Edited by Rüdiger Bittner. Cambridge: Cambridge University Press, 2003.

Noble, David F. *The Religion of Technology: The Divinity of Man and the Spirit of Invention*. New York: Knopf, 1997.

Northcott, Michael S. *An Angel Directs the Storm: Apocalyptic Religion and American Empire*. London: SCM, 2007.

O'Brien, Peter T. *The Letter to the Ephesians*. Pillar New Testament Commentary. Grand Rapids: Eerdmans, 1999.

Och, Bernard. "Creation and Redemption: Towards a Theology of Creation." *Judaism* 44.2 (2005) 226–43.

O'Donovan, Oliver. *The Desire of the Nations: Rediscovering the Roots of Political Theology*. Cambridge: Cambridge University Press, 1996.

———. *Resurrection and Moral Order: An Outline for Evangelical Ethics*. 2nd ed. Grand Rapids: Eerdmans, 1994.

Osiek, Carolyn, and David L. Balch. *Families in the New Testament World: Households and House Churches*. Family, Religion, and Culture. Louisville: Westminster John Knox, 1997.

Overholt, Thomas. *The Threat of Falsehood: A Study in the Theology of the Book of Jeremiah*. London: SCM, 1970.

Peters, Ted. "Six Ways of Salvation: How Does Jesus Save?" *Dialog* 45.3 (Fall 2006) 223–35.

Petersen, David L. *Haggai and Zechariah 1–8*. Philadelphia: Westminster, 1984.

Bibliography

Placher, William C. *The Domestication of Transcendence: How Modern Thinking about God Went Wrong*. Louisville: Westminster John Knox, 1996.

Plato. *The Gorgias*. In *The Dialogues of Plato*, translated by Benjamin Jowett. Chicago: William Benton, 1952.

———. *The Republic*. In *The Dialogues of Plato*, translated by Benjamin Jowett. Chicago: William Benton, 1952.

Pomeroy, Sarah B. *Goddesses, Whores, Wives, and Slaves: Women in Classical Antiquity*. New York: Schocken, 1975.

The President's Council on Bioethics. *Beyond Therapy: Biotechnology and the Pursuit of Happiness*. Washington, DC: GPO, 2003.

Price, S. R. F. "Rituals and Power." In *Paul and Empire: Religion and Power in Roman Imperial Society*, edited by Richard A. Horsley, 47–71. Harrisburg, PA: Trinity, 1997.

Pritchard, James B., editor. *The Ancient Near East: An Anthology of Texts and Pictures*. Princeton: Princeton University Press, 1958.

Punt, Jeremy. "'Unethical' Language in the Pauline Letters? Stereotyping, Vilification and Identity Matters." In *Moral Language in the New Testament*, edited by Ruben Zimmermann and Jan G. van der Watt, 212–31. WUNT 2. Reihe 296. Tübingen: Mohr Siebeck, 2010.

Rapske, Brian. *The Book of Acts in Its First-Century Setting*. Vol. 3, *Paul in Roman Custody*. Grand Rapids: Eerdmans, 1994.

Reginster, Bernard. *The Affirmation of Life: Nietzsche on Overcoming Nihilism*. Cambridge: Harvard University Press, 2006.

Reinders, Hans. "Life's Goodness: On Disability, Genetics, and 'Choice.'" In *Theology, Disability and the New Genetics: Why Science Needs the Church*, edited by John Swinton and Brian Brock, 163–80. London: T. & T. Clark, 2007.

Reinhard, Donna R. "Ephesians 6:10–18: A Call to Personal Piety or Another Way of Describing Union with Christ?" *JETS* 48.3 (2005) 521–32.

Reinhartz, Adele. *Scripture on the Silver Screen*. Louisville: Westminster John Knox, 2003.

Reno, Russell R. "Redemption and Ethics." In *The Oxford Handbook of Theological Ethics*, edited by Gilbert Meilaender and William Werpehowski, 25–40. Oxford: Oxford University Press, 2005.

Reuschling, Wyndy Corbin. *Reviving Evangelical Ethics: The Promises and Pitfalls of Classic Models of Morality*. Grand Rapids: Brazos, 2008.

Rice, Daniel F. "Niebuhr's Critique of Religion in America." In *Reinhold Niebuhr Revisited: Engagements with an American Original*, edited by Daniel F. Rice, 317–37. Grand Rapids: Eerdmans, 2009.

———, editor. *Reinhold Niebuhr Revisited: Engagements with an American Original*. Grand Rapids: Eerdmans, 2009.

Richardson, John. *Nietzsche's System*. Oxford: Oxford University Press, 1996.

Rieger, Joerg. *Christ & Empire: From Paul to Postcolonial Times*. Minneapolis: Fortress, 2007.

Robertson, D. B. *Reinhold Niebuhr's Works: A Bibliography*. Lanham, MD: University Press of America, 1983.

Robinson, Carin, and Clyde Wilcox. "The Faith of George W. Bush: The Personal, Practical, and Political." In *Religion and the American Presidency*, edited by Mark J. Rozell and Gleaves Witney, 215–38. New York: Palgrave Macmillan, 2007.

Rosner, Brian S. *Greed as Idolatry: The Origin and Meaning of a Pauline Metaphor.* Grand Rapids: Eerdmans, 2007.

Sanders, Jack T. *Ethics in the New Testament: Change and Development.* London: SCM, 1975.

Sarot, M."Theodicy and Modernity: An Inquiry into the Historicity of Modernity." In *Theodicy in the World of the Bible,* edited by Antti Laato and Johannes C. de Moor, 1–26. Leiden: Brill, 2003.

Schneewind, J. B. *The Invention of Autonomy: A History of Modern Moral Philosophy.* Cambridge: Cambridge University Press, 1997.

Schnelle, Udo. *Theology of the New Testament.* Translated by M. Eugene Boring. Grand Rapids: Baker Academic, 2009.

Schrag, Calvin O. *The Self after Postmodernity.* New Haven: Yale University Press, 1997.

Shuman, Joel. *The Body of Compassion: Ethics, Medicine, and the Church.* Boulder, CO: Westview, 1999.

Sifton, Elisabeth. *The Serenity Prayer: Faith and Politics in Times of Peace and War.* New York: Norton, 2003.

Siker, Jeffrey S. "Reinhold Niebuhr: Scripture as Symbol." In *Scripture and Ethics: Twentieth-Century Portraits,* 8–24. Oxford: Oxford University Press, 1997.

Smith, Adam. *An Inquiry into the Nature and Causes of the Wealth of Nations.* Chicago: William Benton, 1952.

Snodgrass, Klyne. *Ephesians.* NIV Application Commentary. Grand Rapids: Zondervan, 1996.

———. *Stories with Intent: A Comprehensive Guide to the Parables of Jesus.* Grand Rapids: Eerdmans, 2008.

Solomon, Robert C. *Living with Nietzsche: What the Great 'Immoralist' Has to Teach Us.* Oxford: Oxford University Press, 2003.

———. "One Hundred Years of *Ressentiment*: Nietzsche's *Genealogy of Morals.*" In *Nietzsche, Genealogy, Morality: Essays on Nietzsche's* The Genealogy of Morals, edited by Richard Schacht, 95–126. Berkeley: University of California Press, 1994.

Soloveitchik, Joseph. *Halakhic Man.* New York: Jewish Publication Society, 1983.

Song, Robert. *Human Genetics: Fabricating the Future.* Cleveland: Pilgrim, 2002.

———. "The Human Genome Project as Soteriological Project." In *Brave New World: Theology, Ethics and the Human Genome,* edited by Celia Deane-Drummond, 164–84. London: T. & T. Clark, 2003.

Soulen, R. Kendall. "Cruising toward Bethlehem: Human Dignity and the New Eugenics." In *God and Human Dignity,* edited by R. Kendall Soulen and Linda Woodhead, 104–20. Grand Rapids: Eerdmans, 2006.

Steffen, Lloyd. Review of *American Providence: A Nation with a Mission,* by Stephen H. Webb. *Christian Century* 122.7 (2005) 33–38.

Stoeber, Michael. "Dostoevsky's Devil: The Will to Power." *Journal of Religion* 74.1 (1994) 26–44.

Stone, Ronald H. *Professor Reinhold Niebuhr: A Mentor to the Twentieth Century.* Louisville: Westminster John Knox, 1992.

Stout, Jeffrey. *Ethics after Babel: The Languages of Morals and Their Discontents.* Boston: Beacon, 1988.

———. *The Flight from Authority: Religion, Morality, and the Quest for Autonomy.* Notre Dame: University of Notre Dame Press, 1981.

Surin, Kenneth. *Theology and the Problem of Evil.* Oxford: Blackwell, 1986.

Bibliography

Swartley, Willard M. *Slavery, Sabbath, War, and Women: Case Issues in Biblical Interpretation.* Scottdale, PA: Herald, 1983.

Tachau, Peter. *"Einst" und "Jetz" im Neuen Testament: Beobachtungen zu einem urchristlichen Predigtschema in der neutestamentliche Briefliterature und zu seiner Vorgeschichte.* Göttingen: Vandenhoeck & Ruprecht, 1972.

Tannehill, Robert C. "Participation in Christ: A Central Theme in Pauline Soteriology." In *The Shape of the Gospel: New Testament Essays,* 223–37. Eugene, OR: Cascade Books, 2007.

Taylor, Charles. *Sources of the Self: The Making of the Modern Identity.* Cambridge: Harvard University Press, 1989.

Taylor, Mark Lewis. *Religion, Politics, and the Christian Right: Post-9/11 Powers and American Empire.* Minneapolis: Fortress, 2005.

Thielicke, Helmut. *The Evangelical Faith.* 3 vols. Translated and edited by Geoffrey W. Bromiley. Edinburgh: T. & T. Clark, 1974.

Thiselton, Anthony. *The Hermeneutics of Doctrine.* Grand Rapids: Eerdmans, 2007.

Tilley, Terrence W. *The Evils of Theodicy.* Washington, DC: Georgetown University Press, 1991.

Tuveson, Ernest Lee. *Redeemer Nation: The Idea of America's Millennial Role.* Chicago: University of Chicago Press, 1968.

Verhey, Alan. *Reading the Bible in the Strange World of Medicine.* Grand Rapids: Eerdmans, 2003.

———. *Remembering Jesus: Christian Community, Scripture, and the Moral Life.* Grand Rapids: Eerdmans, 2002.

Volf, Miroslav. *Work in the Spirit: Toward a Theology of Work.* 1991. Reprint, Eugene, OR: Wipf & Stock, 2001.

Wadell, Paul J. *Happiness and the Christian Moral Life: An Introduction to Christian Ethics.* 2nd ed. Lanham, MD: Rowman & Littlefield, 2012.

Wallis, Jim. "Dangerous Religion: George W. Bush's Theology of Empire." In *Evangelicals and Empire: Christian Alternatives to the Political Status Quo,* edited by Bruce Ellis Benson and Peter Goodwin Heltzel, 25–32. Grand Rapids: Brazos, 2008.

Walsh, Brian J., and Sylvia C. Keesmaat. *Colossians Remixed: Subverting the Empire.* Downers Grove: InterVarsity, 2004.

Walters, LeRoy. "Human Genetic Intervention: Past, Present, and Future." In *Is Human Nature Obsolete? Genetics, Bioengineering, and the Future of the Human Condition,* edited by Harold W. Baillie and Timothy K. Casey, 367–84. Cambridge: MIT Press, 2005.

Wannenwetsch, Bernd. "Ecclesiology and Ethics." In *The Oxford Handbook of Theological Ethics,* edited by Gilbert Meilaender and William Werpehowski, 57–73. Oxford: Oxford University Press, 2005.

———. *Political Worship: Ethics for Christian Citizens.* Oxford Studies in Theological Ethics. Oxford: Oxford University Press, 2004.

Watson, Francis. *Agape, Eros, Gender: Towards a Pauline Sexual Ethic.* Cambridge: Cambridge University Press, 2000.

———. *Paul, Judaism, and the Gentiles: Beyond the New Perspective.* Rev. ed. Grand Rapids: Eerdmans, 2007.

Weaver, J. Denny. "Narrative *Christus Victor*: The Answer to Anselmian Atonement Violence." In *Atonement and Violence: A Theological Conversation,* edited by John Sanders, 1–29. Nashville: Abingdon, 2006.

————. *The Nonviolent Atonement.* Grand Rapids: Eerdmans, 2001.

Webb, Stephen A. *American Providence: A Nation with a Mission.* New York: Continuum, 2004.

————. "From Prudentius to President Bush: Providence, Empire and Paranoia." In *The Providence of God,* edited by Francesca Aran Murphy and Philip G. Ziegler, 231–54. London: T. & T. Clark, 2009.

Weber, Max. *The Protestant Ethic and the Spirit of Capitalism.* Translated by Talcot Parsons. New York: Scribner's, 1930.

Wells, Samuel. *God's Companions: Reimagining Christian Ethics.* Oxford: Blackwell, 2006.

————. *Improvisation: The Drama of Christian Ethics.* Grand Rapids: Brazos, 2004.

Welshon, Rex. *The Philosophy of Nietzsche.* Montreal: McGill-Queen's University Press, 2004.

Wengst, Klaus. *Pax Romana and the Peace of Jesus Christ.* Translated by John Bowden. Philadelphia: Fortress, 1987.

Wenham, David. *Paul: Follower of Jesus or Founder of Christianity?* Grand Rapids: Eerdmans, 1995.

Westerholm, Stephen. *Perspectives Old and New on Paul: The "Lutheran" Paul and His Critics.* Grand Rapids: Eerdmans, 2004.

Whyte, Max. "The Uses and Abuses of Nietzsche in the Third Reich: Alfred Bauemler's 'Heroic Realism.'" *Journal of Contemporary History* 43.2 (2008) 171–94.

Wiggins, David. "Deliberation and Practical Reason." In *Essays on Aristotle's Ethics,* edited by Amélie Oksenberg Rorty, 221–40. Berkeley: University of California Press, 1980.

Wild, Robert A. "The Warrior and the Prisoner: Some Reflections on Ephesians 6:10–20." *Catholic Biblical Quarterly* 46 (1984) 284–98.

Williams, David J. *Paul's Metaphors: The Context and Character.* Peabody, MA: Hendrickson, 1999.

Williams, Stephen N. "Dionysius against the Crucified: Nietzsche Contra Christianity, Part I." *Tyndale Bulletin* 48:2 (1997) 219–43.

————. "Dionysus against the Crucified: Nietzsche Contra Christianity, Part II." *Tyndale Bulletin* 49:1 (1998) 132–50.

————. *The Shadow of the Anti-Christ: Nietzsche's Critique of Christianity.* Grand Rapids: Baker Academic, 2006.

Wink, Walter. *Engaging the Powers: Discernment and Resistance in a World of Domination.* Minneapolis: Fortress, 1992.

————. *Naming the Powers: The Language of Power in the New Testament.* The Powers 1. Philadelphia: Fortress, 1984.

Witherington, Ben. *The Indelible Image: The Theological and Ethical Thought World of the New Testament.* Vol. 2, *The Collective Witness.* Downers Grove: InterVarsity, 2010.

Wolf, William John. "Reinhold Niebuhr's Doctrine of Man." In *Reinhold Niebuhr: His Religious, Social, and Political Thought,* edited by Charles W. Kegley, 305–25. New York: Pilgrim, 1984.

Wood, Charles M. *The Question of Providence.* Louisville: Westminster John Knox, 2008.

Wright, N. T. *The Climax of the Covenant: Christ and the Law in Pauline Thought.* Minneapolis: Fortress, 1993.

———. *Colossians and Philemon*. TNTC. Grand Rapids: Eerdmans, 1986.

———. *The New Testament and the People of God*. Minneapolis: Fortress, 1992.

———. *Paul: In Fresh Perspective*. Minneapolis: Fortress, 2005.

———. "Redemption from the New Perspective? Toward a Multi-Layered Pauline Theology of the Cross." In *The Redemption: An Interdisciplinary Symposium on Christ as Redeemer*, edited by Stephen T. Davis, Daniel Kendall, and Gerald O'Collins, 69–100. Oxford: Oxford University Press, 2004.

———. *The Resurrection of the Son of God*. Minneapolis: Fortress, 2003.

Wuthnow, Robert. *God and Mammon in America*. New York: Free Press, 1994.

Yee, Tet-Lim N. *Jews, Gentiles and Ethnic Reconciliation: Paul's Jewish Identity and Ephesians*. SNTSMS 130. Cambridge: Cambridge University Press, 2005.

Yoder, John Howard. "Reinhold Niebuhr's 'Realist' Critique." In *Christian Attitudes to War, Peace, and Revolution*, edited by Theodore J. Koontz and Andy Alexis-Baker, 285–98. Grand Rapids: Brazos, 2009.

———. "Why Ecclesiology Is Social Ethics: Gospel Ethics versus the Wider Wisdom." In *The Royal Priesthood: Essays Ecclesiological and Ecumenical*, edited by Michael G. Cartwright, 102–26. Grand Rapids: Eerdmans, 1994.

Yoder Neufeld, Thomas R. *Ephesians*. Scottdale, PA: Herald, 2002.

———. *"Put on the Armour of God": The Divine Warrior from Isaiah to Ephesians*. JSNTSS 140. Sheffield: Sheffield Academic, 1977.

Yorke, Gosnell L. "Hearing the Politics of Peace in Ephesians: A Proposal from an African Postcolonial Perspective." *JSNT* 30.1 (2007) 120.

Young, Julian. *Nietzsche's Philosophy of Religion*. Cambridge: Cambridge University Press, 2006.

Author Index

Adorno, T. W., 99
Allison, David B., 119n49
Ansell-Pearson, Keith, 123n55
Aquinas, 76n130
Aristotle, xi, 75, 179n20, 239–41,
  246, 249, 252, 256, 259, 263
Arnold, Clinton E., 222
Augustine, Saint, 2–5, 11, 207
Avram, Wes, 23n56, 25n70
Aydin, Ciang, 110n28
Ayers, Robert H., 178n19, 189n37

Bacevich, Andrew J., 25n71,
  199n50
Badiou, Alain, 5, 12
Baker, Mark D., 131n76
Balch, David L., 239n155, 240n158,
  241, 242, 245n168
Banner, Michael, 79n138
Barresi, John, 160n154, 160n155,
  162
Barth, Karl, 26
Bartholomew, Craig G., 9–11
Bauckham, Richard, 9, 22–23
Bayer, Oswald, 31n1, 32, 47, 48
Beach-Verhey, Tim, 25n69
Beale, G. K., 133n83
Beinhart, Peter, 199n49
Bell, Daniel M., 25n69
Benson, Bruce Ellis, 25n70,
  103n11, 104n14, 121, 125,
  130n74
Berger, Peter, 2

Best, Ernest, 71n115, 102n7,
  144n112, 232n137, 234n142
Betsworth, Roger G., 87n164
Bettenson, Henry, 79n137
Betz, Hans Dieter, 50–51
Bittner, Rüdiger, 110n28
Bloom, Harold, 34n10
Bohn, Carole R., 133
Bonhoeffer, Dietrich, 6–7, 164,
  211n84
Bradley, Keith, 242
Briggs, Richard S., 54n66
Broadway, Michael, 207n77
Brooks, David, 175n11
Brown, Charles C., 177n10, 178n12
Brown, Joanne Carlson, 131
Brueggemann, Walter, 18, 22n53,
  203
Buckley, Michael J., 48n49
Burridge, Richard, 49n54, 50,
  102n9

Caird, G. B., 253n183
Calkins, Raymond, 21n50
Calvin, John, 27n75, 65, 81–83,
  87, 131
Campbell, Douglas A., 50n57,
  131n79, 137n94
Campbell, William S., 226
Cannon, George E., 244n166
Caragounis, Chrys C., 59–60,
  218n102, 219n105
Carson, D. A., 8